The Architect's Dream

The Architect's Dream

Form and Philosophy in Architectural Imagination

Sean Pickersgill

Bristol, UK / Chicago, USA

First published in the UK in 2023 by Intellect, The Mill, Parnall Road, Fishponds, Bristol, BS16 3JG, UK

First published in the USA in 2023 by Intellect, The University of Chicago Press, 1427 E. 60th Street, Chicago, IL 60637, USA

Copyright © 2023 Intellect Ltd

All rights reserved. No part of this publication may be reproduced, stored in a retrieval system, or transmitted, in any form or by any means, electronic, mechanical, photocopying, recording, or otherwise, without written permission.

A catalogue record for this book is available from the British Library.

Copy editor: MPS Limited
Cover designer: Tanya Montefusco
Cover image: Sam Jolly and Damian Heffernan, City of Nickel, Kambalda
Production manager: Debora Nicosia
Typesetter: MPS Limited

Hardback ISBN 978-1-78938-740-7
Paperback ISBN 978-1-78938-872-5
ePDF ISBN 978-1-78938-741-4
ePUB ISBN 978-1-78938-742-1

To find out about all our publications, please visit our website.
There you can subscribe to our e-newsletter, browse or download our current catalogue and buy any titles that are in print.

www.intellectbooks.com

This is a peer-reviewed publication.

For JH, AHP & JHP

The Architect's Dream

Contents

The Architect's Dream		2
Introduction: Architects Must Dream		2
1: The Mutability of Objects		10
Proposition 1:	*The Large Glass*	13
Proposition 2:	Inside the Box	18
Proposition 3:	Life's Harvest	23
Proposition 4:	Site Cycle	28
2: Memory		31
Proposition 5:	Calvino's City of Memory	34
Proposition 6:	The Machine of History	39
Proposition 7:	Redemptive Objects	43
Proposition 8:	Borges's Library	47
3: Reflective/Reflexive		50
Proposition 9:	Glass and *Glas*	53
Proposition 10:	*No* City	58
Proposition 11:	*No* Interior	62
Proposition 12:	*No* Form	66
4: War		71
Proposition 13:	Conflict	74
Proposition 14:	Healing	80
Proposition 15:	Hygiene	84
5: Language		87
Proposition 16:	Language	90
Proposition 17:	Ecological Symbiosis	96
Proposition 18:	Flat Out	101

6: Destruction		104
Proposition 19:	Fire	107
Proposition 20:	Plato's Cave	113
Proposition 21:	Earth	118
Proposition 22:	Clouds	122
Proposition 23:	Perversions	127
7: Measure		131
Proposition 24:	Money	134
Proposition 25:	Wittgenstein	141
Proposition 26:	Contractual Obligation	147
Proposition 27:	Life	153
8: Site		158
Proposition 28:	Site Affectivity/Transgressions	161
Proposition 29:	Highway	165
Proposition 30:	High Way	170
Proposition 31:	Manufactured	175
Proposition 32:	Other Ecologies	181
9: Fidelity		184
Proposition 33:	Synaesthetic	187
Proposition 34:	Fidelity	193
Proposition 35:	Non-Euclidean	198
10: Melancholy		202
Proposition 36:	Soap	205
Proposition 37:	Shopping	210

Proposition 38:	Working Models	214
Proposition 39:	Odysseus	218
11: Metamorphosis		**223**
Proposition 40:	Metamorphosis	226
Proposition 41:	Bestiary	233
Proposition 42:	Kennels	239
Proposition 43:	Mechanization Takes Command	244
12: Fiction		**248**
Proposition 44:	Future Archaeology	251
Proposition 45:	Dreams	256
Proposition 46:	Doppelgänger	260
Proposition 47:	Cinema	265
Proposition 48:	The puzzle	271
13: Crime		**275**
Proposition 49:	Forgeries	278
Proposition 50:	Detectives	285
Proposition 51:	TV Eye	290
Proposition 52:	Punishment	296
Proposition 53:	Cannibalism	302
14: Surface		**306**
Proposition 54:	Knots	309
Proposition 55:	Collage	315
Proposition 56:	Discotheque	321
Proposition 57:	*Sfumato*	325

15: Hope		328
Proposition 58: Hope		331
Proposition 59: *Tractatus*		336
Proposition 60: Trust		340
Afterword		344
Constant Gardening		344
Bibliography		347
Index		367

34 F Fi	49 C Fo	22 D Cl	11 Rr Ni	36 Me So	39 Me Od	24 M Mo	1 Mo Lg
21 D Ea	10 Rr Nc	35 F Ne	50 C De	23 D Pe	12 Rr Nf	37 Me Sh	40 Mt Me
48 Fi Tp	33 F Sy	62 	57 Su Sf	38 Me Wm	25 D Wi	2 Mo Ib	13 W Cn
9 Rr Gg	20 D Pc	51 C Tv	54 Su Kn	63 	60 H Ts	41 Mt Be	26 M CO
32 Si Oe	47 Fi Ci	58 H Ho	61 	56 Su Di	53 C Ca	14 W He	3 Mo Lh
19 D Fi	8 Me Bl	55 Su Co	52 C Pu	59 H Tr	64 	27 M Li	42 Mt Ke
46 Fi Do	31 Si Ma	6 Me Mh	17 L Es	44 Fi Fa	29 Si Hw	4 Mo Sc	15 W Hy
7 Me Ro	18 L FO	45 Fi Dr	30 Si HW	5 Me Ccm	16 L La	43 Mt Mtc	28 M Sa/t

The Architect's Dream – Knight's Tale Rebus

The Architect's Dream

Introduction: Architects Must Dream

The Architect's Dream
The Thomas Cole painting, *The Architect's Dream* (1840), shares its title with this book. It should be said, at the outset, that the painting, whatever its merits, is not the inspiration for the following propositions in the 60 chapters that follow since this is achieved most eloquently by Edward Hollis's *The Secret Lives of Buildings* (2009). Nevertheless, we see that the painting depicts a gargantuan perspective of Greek, Roman and Egyptian forms stretching into a misty vanishing point consistent with recorded western history and preoccupations in the early nineteenth century. In the foreground, a Gothic church is nestled amongst a verdant landscape and, most oddly, the 'architect' is depicted reclining on an enormous capital, like a miniaturized character from Lilliput. What to make of this? Notoriously, the painting was rejected by the man who commissioned it, the architect Ithiel Town, on the grounds that it was excessively architectural. Whatever we can make of this circumstance, the book you are reading *is* also excessively architectural. Though it does not share Cole's preoccupation with a conventional historical timeline, it shares the strange dislocation of time and scale that the painting creates. A similarly intoxicating painting by Cole and one that is probably more attuned to the contents of this book is *The Titan's Goblet* (1833) in which a surreal goblet of enormous scale is incorporated into an idyllic landscape. Is it a natural phenomenon, the lost evidence of a time when gods roamed the earth, a case of imaginative longing for the sublime? The dissonance between the power of desire and the evidence of reality that *The Titan's Goblet* presents is the space within which this book operates. But this is a book about architecture, and more particularly the process of thinking about *how* to address the world through architecture, so it is a book about dreams, critically conceived and researched architectural dreams.

The Knight's Tour
Architecture, or more specifically, the process of thinking about, conceiving, defining, designing, analyzing and explaining architecture, is a complicated process. Further, the vast culture of architecture as a historical, professional and theoretical discipline makes most attempts to give a comprehensive overview of it an impossible task. A few moments of considering what might be included in this type of overview, as anyone who has to construct an academic course will attest, bring the uncomfortable question of what worthy, nuanced and exquisite work to leave out. Like any exercise in selecting 'greatest hits' or 'most valuable players', unless the terms of selection are tightly defined, the list of candidate material quickly becomes overwhelming.

This is not a book about making definitive boundaries, but it is about the purpose of boundary conditions and the complex definitional attitude necessary to understand architecture and to see the value of boundaries as guides for future action. It is also, quite explicitly, a book about ideas relevant to architecture and to those aspects of critical reflection that swirl around the designing of architecture. Just as architecture is, most often, a highly technical and instrumental discipline that engages with our material circumstances, it is also representative of the deeply semantic relationship between textual 'constructions' and the assessment of their effects.

General structure
In terms of methodology, then, this book is constructed using a spatial device borrowed from the game of chess, or more correctly, from one of the structural conditions of chess: the knight's tour. Chess has a topological structure and a set of defined moves that govern all aspects of the game-play, from opening gambit to end game. The various properties of the pieces and the defined field within which their operations occur constitute the universe of possible permutations which, of course, in the hands of great players allows them to strategically combat an opponent and gain sufficient territorial advantages to impose defeat. The knight, as a particular type of piece, has the unique property of being able to travel two spaces in one direction and one in another. As such, it will always start on one colour of the board and land on another. The knight's tour, as a mathematical exercise unconnected to game-play, is a simple programmatic challenge to see how a piece might be able to traverse the 64 (8 × 8) squares of the board, landing on every square without repeating a location. While the exercise is simple enough, the knight's tour serves as an analogy, in this book, for the process of defining a position, and then moving to successive other locations without the redundancy of repetition.

The second spatial and territorial analogy employed is with the Periodic Table of elements that is foundational to the study of chemistry. The currently agreed model, devised by Dmitri Mendeleev (1869), organizes the fundamental elements according to atomic weight, state and valencies. Of course, the table itself is a function of the need for representational clarity of chemical properties and can only capture so much information. Yet it is clearly a powerful tool in bridging the gap between the complexities of our material world and the abstract knowledge base of chemistry as a scientific discipline. Importantly, it sets out adjacencies between elements that define shared or similar characteristics through their position within the representational axes, while distinguishing and acknowledging their specific uniqueness. Importantly also, as a mode of definition and representation, it was also able to predict the discovery of certain elements. So the table is both definitive and predictive, asserting certain proximities and speculating on the type and operations of others. Historically, as chemistry evolved from the nineteenth century, the table proved robust enough to correctly accommodate elements such as Gallium (1875) and Germanium (1886) that were discovered subsequent to Mendeleev's table.

Two sequences
Taking both the tactical operations and defined movements of the knight's tour, and the representational properties of the Periodic Table, I have organized the categories for discussion in two sequences. The first is the simple numeric sequence from 1 to 60 that has evolved from a process of identifying some key, but non-standard, features in architectural theory. One of the core challenges in architectural design is to convincingly demonstrate a material, formal relationship between architecture as a 'constructed' reality and the complex Venn diagram of ideas that impinge upon both the creation and the reception of the work. The most familiar expression of this state is the triadic relationship between 'firmness, commodity and delight', which is popular for its simplicity, but largely ineffective as a constant measure of the value of a project. Without necessarily rejecting this interpretive lens, I think it is worthwhile, and a more realistic description of the complex co-dependency on ideas and interpretation, to set out a series of analogous propositions directly addressing the transformation of ideas into form.

The second sequence is the knight's tour itself that is set out in the *Knight's Tale Rebus* table and is diagrammed in the small 4 or 5 square fragments (called a rebus) on the page prior to a proposition. As the piece lands, metaphorically, on an idea it is already bordered by a set of cognate ideas and there is the expectation that the adjacent propositions may (or may not) exert some influence on the subject proposition. All propositions, thus, are territorially located and acknowledge the adjacencies of other ideas and behaviours. Hopefully, as a reader and someone engaged with the substance of the book overall, you will see opportunities for considering the mutuality of influences and interests in this process. Importantly, and this cannot be stressed enough, this spatial and formal conceit is not a Universal Grand Theory of architectural ideas. It is principally a consistent methodology for asserting that no proposition exists in a vacuum.

Rebus
The territory of propositions set out on the 64 square board has been called a rebus, just as the 60 smaller diagrams are similarly termed. It is worth making a few

comments on this choice of name. A rebus is, essentially, a visual puzzle in which a word or phrase is illustrated by images that are homophones of the components of the solution or are diagrams of certain relationships between the parts of the image and the phrase to be deciphered. In essence, the purpose in using the term and alluding to the process has been to initiate a process of decipherment of the individual fragments. In some respect, it is a reinforcement of the positional intelligence that is part of chess, the awareness that any location of a piece must always be assessed in relation to the threats of the opponents' pieces and the potential for further advantageous movement. The 60 rebus fragments set out a field. They are not components of a greater theory, as I indicated above, but there is a value in examining them for possible rhetorical opportunities.

For example, 'Proposition 14 – Healing' is surrounded by 'Proposition 3 – Life's Harvest', 'Proposition 27 – Life', 'Proposition 53 – Cannibalism' and 'Proposition 41 – Bestiary'. While there are complexities within these categories that the text explores and which is internal to the consideration of the particular topics, there is also the outwards-facing opportunity to consider the contexts of 'Life's Harvest', 'Life', 'Cannibalism' and 'Bestiary' as complementary, or complexifying, issues that have relevance to the central subject, 'Healing'. Whether this process is coherent is dependent on the result of critically considering the semantic opportunities inherent in the material, but principally it requires a specifically *architectural* engagement to discover what might be possible. Along with the, hopefully, challenging and interesting content of the individual propositions, they are part of a larger scheme that might be equally engaging.

Since a rebus is essentially a puzzle in which the solution is both the unpacking of a evidential incongruities and the visceral satisfaction of completing the task, the overall structure of the 60 propositions provides the opportunity for further interrogation. I've created this for the specific purpose of suggesting that while critical architectural analysis is puzzle-like, it is also non-trivial.

Architecture, and the consequences of considering the evidence of the world and our behaviours within it, is a transitive and mutable process. Discerning a solution, proposing a formal and material outcome, is a temporary estoppal of the fundamentally entropic nature of the world, like any constructivist model. While there has not been space to speak to the particular use of representations that architecture employs in this book, the idea that architecture employs representations rhetorically as intuition prompts is fundamental.

Rhetoric
Considering the propositions singularly, many of them are essentially rhetorical challenges to the reader to consider the process of thinking through semantic associations, what does a term such as 'crime' or 'hope' mean for architecture. Not all architecture is home-like or prison-like, yet they share certain properties for which it makes sense to characterize them as such. If an architect is looking to speak to certain values that they cannot simply show through (usually) visual means, it makes sense to have recourse to language instead (and as well). While generally I subscribe to the meaning-as-use aspects of language, in which the 'meaning' of a term or proposition is coeval with its intensional role in a communicative act, it is also the case that the semantically ambiguous aspects of language are of equal and alternate value. Say what you mean but also understand that a gap in interpretation is useful for thinking about shared, inter-subjective associations. For all the reasons that have been alluded to by architectural commentators regarding the broad field of influence that the discipline describes, it makes sense to think of architecture as being grounded in the transformations of language as much as the transformations of environments.

In this respect, the text has fifteen general categories that organize the propositions thematically. These are: The Mutability of Objects; Memory; Reflective/reflexive; War; Language; Destruction; Measure; Site; Fidelity; Melancholy; Metamorphosis; Fiction; Crime; Surface; and Hope. These categories are not, as before, intended to provide a summation of all things architectural, but they do attempt to capture some core aspects of how architecture and ideas intersect. If we think of them more as suburbs of a city, their territorial interdependence, as with the Knights Tour, also becomes clear. The names of the suburbs, as with any city, are the consequence of a naming process that is descriptive, historical and imaginative.

I have no doubt that there are additional categories, propositions, graphical representations and finely grained interpretations that have been missed in this book. That is fine, in my view, as the general methodological principle in defining characteristics has been their place within a larger and more complex 'city' of possibilities. Just as a city, as Edward Glaeser has noted, is one of the great laboratories for understanding the complexities of human relations, I subscribe to the general analogy that the process of thinking about architecture requires the same sensitivity to complex interdependence. For this reason, just as cities are always works in evolution, so too a book about architectural theory and the process of coming to design is only ever a 'blueprint' for further action.

Text vs. image
Of course, as an architectural book, one of the core challenges in writing about the evolution and applicability of ideas is the intensely visual nature of the profession and the reliance on images to communicate the substance of design solutions. Like all architects, I understand the relationship between ideas and design proposals is usually, and ultimately, tested by the creation of representations. Whether the representation is of an overall immersive environment, or of a process of construction and detailing, we are trained to see the coherence of imagery as a primal mode of seeing and believing. So is an architectural book without images missing the final proof of its credibility? No, it is not.

The process of design always commences with some form of blank space, or void, into which the evidence of the project is aggregated, and from which the 'design' is made coherent and presented. The gap between the blank space and the emergence of potential visual representations, architecture, that form a visual proposition is a space of rhetorical possibilities. What form should emerge? Should it be familiar or novel? Is it simple or complex? Is it a holistic view or fragmentary? Most perplexingly, should the idea be prior to the form or is it the other way around?

Form is not meaning
Ultimately, this book takes the view that architectural form does not have any intrinsic meaning any more than any other mode of material production and is not prior to any mode of semantic definition. Trivially, of course all material form has finite definitions expressed in the languages of mathematics, chemistry and physics but for a profession that works with a broad palette of significatory systems the general view taken is that meaning has to be critically constructed alongside whatever conscious or unconscious formal expressions take place. Neither form nor meaning are prior to each other and for this reason they should be considered as mutually reinforcing, or not, depending on the force of the critical and rhetorical argument.

This book is not intended, as will become obvious when reviewing the number of rhetorical propositions it contains, to provide solutions. It is intended to challenge the reader to employ their own skills to engage with the subject matter and find those indexical and specific solutions that will suit their needs. This is the responsibility that all architects carry, to find a way to organise information into an outcome that reconfigures the world in a sensate, mostly coherent, sometimes complex, occasionally confrontational fashion. Part of this process is the use of text-based references as a form of *Grundfragen*, or fundamental questioning, of architectural propinquities – of what architecture might become.

Non-fiction texts that explicitly discuss architecture and its acculturated meanings and those that position it within larger cultural movements are important parts of establishing this context, but there is room also for fiction. Many of the propositions in the book commence from fictional work, either as literature or film, and rely on the complex world-making that is a part of the specific modality of fictional environments. While obviously there are fundamental technical differences in forms of suspension-of-disbelief in film and literature, their capacity to present a world that is naratologically coherent has an important influence on how we imagine architecture might be. The allusions to this work forms an important part of the development of ideas and arguments within this book and they are referenced both in the text and in the subsequent bibliography for each chapter. Much in the same fashion that Jonathan Hill looks beyond conventional frames of reference in his excellent *Immaterial Architecture* (2006), I have also sought to construct arguments for the plurality of optoins available in architectural theory.

Perec and OuLiPo
As may be obvious to many, the use of the knight's tour as a methodological instrument in this book has been borrowed from a well known and highly regarded book by the French author, Georges Perec. *Life: A User's Manual* (1979, 1987) employs the knight's tour as a method for moving around different spaces of a Parisian apartment building, bringing together the complex cast of characters, objects and actions the narrative describes. Perec, as a foundational member of the OuLiPo (*Ouvroir de littérature potentielle*) group, obsessively employed structural organization as a method of presenting a multitude of narratives in search of an elusive resolution to a text. The mechanical possibilities of this process were intentionally both a perverse hindrance to the narrative(s) and an acknowledgment of the inherently structuralist characteristics of narratives as a whole. In this book, *The Architect's Dream*, the topological shifts and the associated adjacencies employ a similar method, though without pretending to the deep complexity of Perec's work. But just as Perec created a text fascinated with jigsaws and the relationship between the shape and the size of pieces searching for their complementary outline, it is hoped that the same sense of confronting a puzzle is within this text.

Finally, and making a further reference to Perec and the OuLiPo group, the animating agency in reviewing the 60 chapters to follow is the practice of architecture as a method of thinking and representing the world. For Perec and his associates, the term 'clinamen' was used to denote the irruptions of order that animate change. For this book, it is the actions of considering architecture as a mutable instrument. Architecture is, at its most basic, a fundamental re-structuring of the world, like a tool. But as with a tool, it is always the process that defines architectural thinking, not simply the outcomes.

1: The Mutability of Objects

This first section of the book is concerned with our relationship to objects in the world and how we approach the radius of the effect of objects on a process of thinking. The chapters in this section introduce the methodology of defining, consecutively, how objects of study are always inherently complex irrespective of their empirical or material simplicity, how we contain objects, how we then catalogue objects and represent their relative propinquities and how the boundary and context conditions of this process, the parergon, is in itself an active theoretical element. The four chapters summatively ask the question: if we are to look at any object, and in the case of the first chapter, an art object, the process of thinking is necessarily and equally exploratory as it may be explanatory.

Following the complex example of an art object as an 'object', the second chapter considers what might be thought to be the simplest act of enframement, the box, as both a container of objects and as a thing in itself. Whereas in set theory, it is the contents of the set that is important, and the characteristics of the parentheses symbols trivial, it can be argued that the box (as a form of three-dimensional parentheses) has both an identity and a role in organizing the objects of the world – much like architecture. Further, if access to the 'box' is mediated by a series of constructed impediments that manage our engagement with its contents, then a box is inherently also a form of a puzzle.

The third chapter is concerned with the question of cataloguing and how catalogues construct the 'life' of their contents. To be catalogued is to have the members of its set placed in active relations with each other, and to imply that inclusion in this set is non-trivial and rhetorically engaged. A catalogue is more than a loosely organized collection of discrete items, and it can also be considered an organizational system that expresses both its overt and latent values, even when those latent values seem incongruous and conflict with the original organizational premise. In parallel, a catalogue brings forth a cast of characters whose interactions constitute the world of the system. Of course, the more hermetic and apparently incongruous the conditions of a system, the greater the challenge in determining whether its complexity is profound or merely confused.

And finally, the fourth chapter addresses the idea of context, likening it to the architectural understanding of 'site'. Where a site is a ground condition, a situation where fundamental questions (*Grundfragen*) appear, we can speculate that architecture is similarly driven by self-conscious definitions of what constitutes its plane of appearance.

Objects, containers, catalogues and sites in the argument of the following chapters are all mutable characteristics. While architecture is not usually considered an 'object' as such, more generally an environment, if we begin a process of rethinking how architecture might be approached theoretically, then the most fundamental relationship is between an individual and the objects of the world. It is always tempting to consider that some aspects of architecture are constant so that those aspects of its effects can be recognized as they transform from one state to another; however, what if everything was mutable?

Consider this analogy: if you are on a fair-ground ride and the world is moving around you at a dizzying and frenetic pace (the point of the ride), what if the geometry of the ride itself was also changing? And what if the consequences of that change of geometry were to make the world appear stable, much like two cars travelling adjacent to each other may appear stable? Loosely speaking, the four chapters open up the question of how we might continue to change the geometry and 'ground' condition of architectural thinking. Architecture can start as an object, an entity with boundary conditions, and can then be explored as a site for supporting the complexities of the human condition, while also creating material governances of that condition. Whether it is stable or not remains to be seen.

24 M	1 Mo
Mo	**Lg**
37 Me	40 Mt
Sh	**Me**

Rebus 1

The Mutability of Objects

Proposition 1: *The Large Glass*

Marcel Duchamp's *The Bride Stripped Bare by Her Bachelors, Even* (*The Large Glass*) (1923) is a complex work that is famous, among several other qualities, for its representation of analogical relationships between technology and desire. As an 'art object', it provides a useful example of the power of objects to act as conceptual models of alternate states of affairs. Employing it as a catalyst for architectural thinking, it can be approached in several ways, as a trope of visual representation, as a meditation on desire and as a form of engagement with technology.

For an architect, the work is of interest because it has clear diagrammatic functions, though they appear hermetically sealed, and a narrative of contact and exchange that appears to match some form of programmatic functioning. The work has two zones, two topological spaces that define the binary relationship of marriage and consummation of the actors (The Bachelors and The Bride) but might also speak to architectural interest in the definition of thresholds of actions between different spatial moments. This relationship, divided by the physical frame of the work, captures a moment of potential completion.

Similarly, it is a 'looking glass' that changes the solidity of traditional forms of representation. *The Large Glass* is simultaneously a window, a painting, a map or plan and ultimately a herald of the surreal imagination. Its architectonic invites formal analysis, a rehearsal of the moment of perspective, of Brunelleschi and Dürer. And it is iconographic. A strange cousin of the Renaissance cosmology of Aby Warburg, the glass introduces a series of characters, or characteristics, who occupy functional relationships in a cosmology more astrological than scientific. These relationships mimic the functional constellation of *existenzminimum*, of the positive organization of material relations within the interior. The iconic figures within the two panels, the malic moulds, or 'empty livery', of the bachelors are metaphorical components of a technical representation of the consummation of a marriage. As Ramirez (1998) notes, the mechanisms are simultaneously solipsistic and conjunctive since Duchamp himself was more interested in the depiction of a transformative geometry that alluded to a regime of proof than the actuality of creating an accurate diagrammatic model. For this reason, the allusion to frustrated sexuality in the work rests on the counter-intuitive premise that eroticism can be depicted mechanically.

How are *The Large Glass* thematics to be organized?

If considered as a model for an architectural project, *The Large Glass* is both plan, threshold, exterior and interior. It materially locates the exchange of human relations in the frustrated machinery of preformed Bride and produced Bachelors. It is the transformation of raw material into objects of consumption; the social relation of making, selling and buying, and the mercurial, transformative properties of taste, all are held as a potential in the erotic relation of bride to suitors. While some of the 'actions' proposed in the work are self-referential and solipsistic, the proposition of the work is that the mechanism is always seeking completion and consummation – much like an architectural drawing. Where does the energy come from, and how is it dissipated or transformed into motion? How does gas (invisible) create and define shape (through a mould) and transmit energy (aerodynamics)? For architecture, it points to the transformation of an environment that is inherently entropic into a fixed instrument for the direction of the flow of material accretion and dissipation, heat and light. It is also an instrument for recognizing and directing the movement of desire lines.

While *The Large Glass* can be read as a shallow perspectival rendering of a process in that it has a duality recognizable in architectural strategies, the presence of accompanying drawings in the Green Box material, subsequently released by Duchamp, paradoxically complicates the inductive relationship between drawings and form. The plan and elevation of the Bachelor Machine serve to mystify the transformation rather than describe a process of construction and completion. So it is all about machinery and machinic processes, whether frustrated or consummated. This relationship is at the core of both the work and commentary.

By opening the oppositions of up/down, inside/outside, private/public, nature/culture, design/realization, etc., we come to the most immediately recognizable architectural form of criticism that is relevant to Duchamp's work. In architecture, these are the terms that spring instinctively to mind, irrespective of the project under consideration, since the language of architecture is often a rehearsal of these oppositions. In fact, architectural theory is deviled by these couplets. Leftover, but hardly understood, from the nineteenth-century preoccupation with German Romantic philosophy, architecture seems incurably Manichean, switching between alternate states as analysis requires it. *The Large Glass*, to its credit, is disjunctive. There is no obvious symmetry between the panels although trivially they are of the same size. Further, for the purposes of considering, it to be a catalyst of architectural thinking and designing, *The Large Glass* is necessarily complex for it is prearchitectural. It is the brief of architecture *before* production, *before* transformation and hence *before* history.

But some binary arrangement is occurring. It is an Annunciation, a moment when transcendence is made magically real and tangible. It is a threshold, a window (a more complex *Fresh Widow*), acting as a filter, that re-presents the transcendent in the everyday. What, after all, does one see when one looks through the glass?

How is this architectural?
So specifically, *The Large Glass* can be employed in architectural thinking to illustrate thematics consistent with the dualities outlined above, while not being a slave to them. It can do this by employing the following:

> 1. The process of dividing an architectural project into two conjoined conditions illustrates the value in binary couplets relevant to architectural strategies.
> 2. Specific references to gender and sexuality in the rituals of courtship and marriage can be mapped onto ideas of autonomy and personal identity as generators of architectural boundary conditions.
> 3. The allusions to technology and the 'functioning' of relationships in *The Large Glass* mirror the instrumentality of architectural design and its insistence on spatializing functional relations.
> 4. Provocatively, it also allows for the frustration and failure of the designed approach.
> 5. Its status as an 'art object' encourages homological comparison with other 'seeing machines', including Alberti's *Window*.
> 6. The work introduces a series of transformational mechanisms that are considered to be architectural: water wheel, gears, grinder, rotating mechanisms, capillary tubes, scissors, filters, pipework, churn and suction pump.

What are the diagrammatic outcomes?
The process of initially diagramming, then designing, through *The Large Glass* can initiate several key diagramming relationships:

> 1. Illustrate a series of threshold conditions within an architectural programme and consider the degree to which the transition to one or the other is seamless, mediated or impeded.

2. Superimpose different desire-threshold conditions onto architectural plans and sections, asking:
   a. How does a desire-threshold change the nature of transition between parts of a programme?
   b. What is the programmatic outcome of determining personal and private thresholds?
   c. What occurs when desire-threshold strategies are superimposed? Do they double or multiply the degree of connection or frustration?
   d. How do the mechanistic aspects of *The Large Glass* translate into the environmental systems of a building, and what is it to elaborate and enhance their presence in the building?

Proposition: Checkpoint Marcel
One of the most fraught political spaces in current times is the infrastructure that exists at borders between countries. While the fences and barriers are obvious manifestations of inherent hostilities between states, the break in these lines of exclusion occurs at border stations. It is here that the opposing forces of human need and governmental control stand in mediated opposition. While the obvious thematic lens to view a project such as this is through competing politics and issues of economic opportunity and human rights, an alternate view might see aspects of desire and frustration. Both the applicants for passage and those tasked with moderating entry are in a complex ethical marriage in which frustration and consummation are key goals.

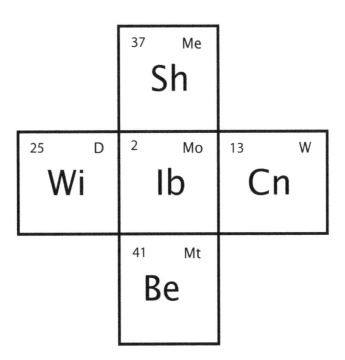

Rebus 2

The Mutability of Objects

Proposition 2: Inside the Box

One of the simplest associations in architecture is the comparison of a building with a box. A box is a container, a limit, and emulates the same basic function of architecture of course. But of course, there is a great deal more to say in terms of the comparisons. Pandora's box, for example, was essentially an ethical structure for concealing the need for individual morality. It was enclosed, it functioned as a surprise, perhaps a present, and a warning. In some instances, a box contains instructions, parts, perhaps a completed item, perhaps a puzzle to be completed. Joseph Cornell's boxes contain tableaux of possible surreal worlds making them both an enclosed and hermetic world, and also a catalyst into an other, counter-factual, state of affairs. Further, like a jigsaw puzzle that contains a future waiting to be enacted, a box is the ideal device for containing a future fulfilment, since what box contains an incomplete puzzle? A puzzle implies functional instructions and a process of enactment. From this, we can ask the question: What sort of puzzle is 'constructed' in the sense that architecture is constructed, as an outcome of the solution and as the box itself?

Why are puzzles always formed by expectations of success? How do they promise the expectation of transformation through process? If we are asked how to represent the world as a transformative experience, then the process of change leaves its temporal residue in the forms of the world. This is represented historically (and cosmologically) in the 'argument by design', but now finds a hermetic application in the assumption that the evidence of the world, the stuff in the box, may indeed affect some redemptive plan.

The plan
Are all expectations of functional utility in architecture shadowed by the puzzle of material culture and the expectation of solutions? In architecture, we need to only see the function to which the evidence is put to see the plan as a 'plan' (for something) and as a solution. We can consider an architectural plan as a puzzle, and that the most banal of plans is a rebus that hides its dissimulating function in plain sight. Think of the plan of the Barcelona Pavilion (1929). As a plan, is it also an (almost) empty box? Further, do the contents of the plan-as-box contain the evidence or tools to understand its purpose or solution? Complexity in planning can indicate an over-abundance of relationships between material form and use patterns, some of which are clear in how they are intended to affect experience, but we must recognize

that in reviewing a plan we are looking at more than an instruction to construct. The complexity always exceeds the fact of its making. So a simple plan may be graphically clearer and project the belief that it is materially (not just constructionally) simple, but does it contain enough clues to its unpacking?

Marcel Duchamp's *Boîte-en-valise* (*Box in a Suitcase*) (1935–41) is a collection of reproductions and objects relevant to Duchamp's artistic career. Unusually as an 'artwork', but usual for Duchamp, the collection simultaneously memorializes Duchamp while compromising claims to originality (he made ten versions of the work; they contain reproductions). So, as a box, it reveals an identity when opened, but also makes the viewer wonder whether it is a full description, literally: are all the pieces there? If we remember the most basic of diagrammatic propositions regarding a plan, that it is meant to illustrate clarity of purpose, then why would it be possible to consider plans as problematic, a puzzle?

The approach might come from the proposition that a box, as a container, might be considered the standard of philosophical containment and revelation. Schrödinger's cat may have lived and may have died, within its box as a thought experiment, but most importantly it is considered, from the view of quantum mechanics, to be simultaneously both alive and dead since the quantum superposition (the paradox) persists until it is observed.

Mystery box
To look at an architectural work, we can superimpose, but not in the quantum sense, the conditions of both Schrödinger's and Duchamp's boxes and ask a couple of questions regarding architectural boxes generally:

> 1. If architecture is a box, does its role as a container mean anything, if its contents are mutable and transient?
> 2. If the contents are not subject to observation, what state are they in?
> 3. At what point are the contents of the box indistinguishable from the container?
> 4. What if the box and the contents are sentient?
> 5. If the process of observation emulates the determination of reality, what of the puzzle-like nature of the evidence? Are they clues or tools?
> 6. Is a proof of reality the elimination of the original purpose of the box?

Schrödinger's experiment is also a search for reality as a condition of macroscopic observation. If nothing else, the cat observes its demise, and it understands the nature of a tomb, sadly. For no other reason than it would seem decent to respect the cat's experience in this exercise, we can address the questions from the perspective of architecture and help us find consolation for the animal.

>1. The box matters when the passage to its interior (the cat's reality) is instrumentally governed by the material conditions of the box, the architecture. The transparency of that process, including the literal transparency or porosity of the box which provides evidence for an effect, governs the perceptual path to reality.
>2. Bishop Berkeley famously suggested that *esse ist percipi* (to be is to be perceived). In one sense, the state of the box's contents is non-existent until they are observed, and their material reality becomes co-extensive with the observer. If they are not observed, arguably, the puzzle persists until they are placed within a reality. In architecture, this means that the uncovering of the contents is the uncovering of their potential reality. This point is potentially trivial, does it matter if an object persists or not when we are well accustomed to the expectation of object persistence?
>3. The entanglement of the box and contents, the point when they are indistinguishable, importantly transforms the question of revelation and entry to reality. Architecture and its contents become part of a process of solving the puzzle and the purpose of reality. Arguably, and speculatively, the purpose of architecture, beyond basic utility, is to construct a living experience in which the *solving* of the puzzle is the experience.
>4. In this instance, architecture is both the scene of the puzzle, the place in which it is organized, and the components of the puzzle. Architectural plans, architectural drawings generally, are the setting of a puzzle for the uncovering of the reality of the contents, including the reality of built content.
>5. Importantly, and ultimately, the box that contains the puzzle becomes purposeless in both the Duchamp and Schrödinger examples. However for architecture, once the establishment of reality is completed and the puzzle is solved, the role of iteratively recreating box and contents continues.

For example, when we think of the big box projects of SITE in the 1970s, we can see that some of the motivations of both the Best Company and James Wines coincide. The company wants to entice shoppers into the structure, and SITE wanted the skin of the building to complicate the process of transition to the point where the objects themselves became fused with the building envelope. The big box store is successful once the box is opened and the contents are emptied. Similarly, the Parisian hôtel in Georges Perec's *Life: A User's Manual* (1978) is a building-as-box containing an infinite regress of further boxes of puzzles.

Proposition: Edith in a bottle
Initially, the tendency when working through these ideas would be to design and construct a puzzle, perhaps a maze, in which the permanent boundaries of the work limit variability of movement, a puzzle-on-rails so to speak. But the project might become more interesting when the relationship between visibility and reality is interrogated. If the Farnsworth house, for example, is a box in which revelation is immediate and apparent, how might it be configured to be a closed system that requires unpacking, unpuzzling and re-puzzling? Or what if the Glass House became an Escape Room?

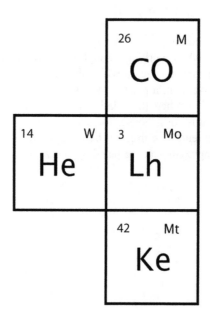

Rebus 3

The Mutability of Objects

Proposition 3: Life's Harvest

James George Frazer's *The Golden Bough* (1890) is a famous study on the presence of ritualized behaviours across an array of different societies with different forms of social organization. One of anthropology's most famous and embarrassing texts has been influential principally for the reason that the level of speculation he brought to the subject matter flamboyantly exceeded the intimate structural knowledge of the material being described. Frazer's technique was essentially combinatory and comparative, seeing consistency in ritualized behaviour and certain cyclical narratives across many cultures, including (scandalously in the nineteenth century) Christianity. Rituals of regicide, for example, were considered to be a function of all patriarchal societies irrespective of other governing systems. What it did bring to attention however was a process of cross-thematic speculation that has its basis in iconography, particularly in the visual arts. And while Frazer's work has been criticized for its insistence on a single developmental model for social formations, from magic to science, he nonetheless brought into the light the possibility of thinking that reason and magic may well coexist and exert structural influence upon each other.

In contrast, Bronislaw Malinowski's *Argonauts of the Western Pacific* (1922) contains a far more methodologically consistent engagement with its subject matter, attempting to communicate the reality of lived experiences from the perspective of the subjects, rather than that of an academic western observer. In fact, Frazer's work is so methodologically incommensurate with the modern anthropological assumptions regarding observer interference in a cultural study that the value of his work is closer to that of surreal fictional imaginings of locations. The counter-factual conditions of imaginary worlds are described in Raymond Roussel's *Impressions of Africa* (1909), or Franz Kafka's *Amerika* (1929), both of which describe journeys to locations of which neither author had any first-hand experience.

A discourse of difference

So how does this affect architecture? William Taylor's *The Vital Landscape* (2004) provides a clear analysis and description of the emergence of techniques of life cultivation in the design of nineteenth-century glasshouses and conservatories. Taylor, looking at the work of Charles Loudon and Charles Perrault, sees a parallel between the cultivation of botanical exotica and the development of more bespoke social engineering solutions within architecture, such as the panopticon by Jeremy Bentham. The degree of coercive control these examples demonstrated corresponded with the desire to manage the full life cycle of the inhabitants. So, of course, the identification of certain types of normative social behaviours became the subject of architectural theorists who inferred a relationship between environment and social formations. Social Darwinism of this type is a core aspect of the development of modern theories of programme and functionality, either as a response to existing social formations or for ambitions to create new behavioural instrumentalities.

In terms of speculative architectural design, a conundrum emerges: Is it better to design in an environment in which the designer accepts conventional social formations and focusses on novel tectonics, or is it better to disregard the aesthetics of visual innovation and address social and ethical values? It is the classic problem of cultural Marxism of the twentieth century, and in all probability cannot be meaningfully addressed at a macro-social level.

History itself shows us that the incremental approaches of particular examples: Pugin and the neo-Gothic, Wright and the American Arts and Crafts movement, Aalto and Finnish modernism, Gehry and the culture of the multinational arts industry, all demonstrate inflections of the question in some part without demonstrating any consistent or meaningful solution. Analysis of these architectural approaches, critical historiography, tends to promote the more-or-less suppressed premise that the work intentionally embodies a series of meta-cultural thematics regarding social identity. But so what? Does it actually matter in a meaningful way when the question of 'how' to design emerges?

Perhaps a more asymptotic approach to the question of social formations and architectural outcomes may well come from a creative approach to models such as the example of Frazer's *The Golden Bough*. If we consider the text to be a work of speculative fiction, and not modern anthropology in its strictest sense, the work's subject matter aligns it with other forms of taxonomical thinking such as Georges Bataille's *Critical Dictionary* (1930) published in his surrealist magazine *Documents*, or Aby Warburg's *Mnemosyne Atlas*. Bataille's work, whose method of categorizing and discussing has been clearly emulated in this book, is both a compendium of observations on a diverse number of subjects and a general approach to *la vie Surrealiste*. Bataille, briefly and unremarkably, summarizes architecture as a constraint on the human condition but sees the overcoming of architecture as a necessary 'bestial monstrosity' that escapes the 'architectural straightjacket'. Unusually the person suited for this task is the painter.

Mnemosyne
Of considerably, and arguably, much greater intellectual depth is the *Mnemosyne Atlas* of Aby Warburg, director of the Warburg Institute in London. The Institute, and ultimately the gnostic contents of the *Atlas*, was centred around his private library located within the Courtauld Institute. The *Atlas* was an attempt to trace persistent iconographic representations of western visual thematics, those that expressed the intersection between representation and critical thinking – but are cloaked in the experience of aesthesis. So an image of a melancholic angel in Dürer's *Melencolia I* (1514), for example, is not just a simple task of image making, it is a cartographic study in thematic visual adjacency. Warburg's *Atlas* was a project on an even larger scale, involving the thematic adjacency of hundreds of images of considerable art-historical complexity over 63 door-sized panels. As Warburg died before the project was 'finished', if that had been possible, it has been left to scholars to trace the didactic intentions of the work. Like Bataille, Warburg sought to make the incongruity of adjacency the source of intellectual work. Unlike Bataille, the *Atlas* was an attempt at a *Gesamtkunstwerk*, in which the ambition for completeness was paramount.

How is this architectural?
The lesson for architecture is methodological and relates to the earlier observations on the intimate relationship between anthropology and the definition of ritualized social practices. What is architecture's role, assuming it is monolithic for a moment, in creating and confirming objective categories of subjects?

> 1. Can architecture escape the transcendental/empirical couplet of simultaneously wishing to adhere to conventionalized subject types, while encouraging the nuanced exploration of aberrant behaviour (Bataille)?
> 2. What is the proposed life cycle of effects of an architecture that is intentionally piecemeal or absurdist?
> 3. Is there a lexicon of thema that make sense to a project that is also sufficiently absurdist to provoke a sense of intellectual adjacency, a puzzle, while also remaining sufficiently realistic to command attention and ward off complaints of solipsism and self-referencing (Warburg)?
> 4. Are there counter-factual definitions of what constitutes the domain of architecture that allow it to be something other than a representation of the real (Roussel, Kafka, literature generally)?

Proposition: Earwitness
Elias Canetti's *Earwitness* (1979) is a study of character types with extravagant and monomaniacal interests. Each of the 50 figures is succinctly described in terms of their obsessions, manners and (in)ability to exist within society. What could a village, an apartment building, a workplace or some other collective of these people be? Reviewing each of the heteronymic figures would allow architecture to create a *tableau vivant* of subjects, inherently mutable.

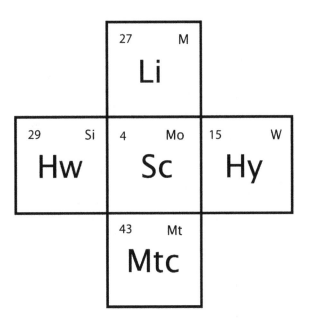

Rebus 4

The Mutability of Objects

Proposition 4: Site Cycle

The final exploration of the mutability of objects will commence from Duchamp again. *Étant donnés* (1946–66), his installation in the Philadelphia Museum of Art, is a complicated and challenging construction. It deliberately entangles issues of painterly composition, sexuality, vision and the constant question: Why do we make purposeless things? While this is clearly a fundamental question for the art world, given the long and fraught relationship between intention, value, purpose and the market, it is a question for architecture as well. While verbal description cannot do the work justice, it is sufficient for us to know that it involves a diorama of an anonymous naked female torso reclining in a landscape with one hand raised holding a lantern. In the context of Duchamp's complex body of work, the final piece was left as a riddle. Deliberately suppressed until after he died, it is a kind of *memento mori*, or perhaps a warning, regarding the transactional and complicit relationship between subject and object.

What makes the work disturbing, apart from the highly orchestrated manner in which the viewer singularly approaches the installation and peeps through the eyeholes, is the immediate engagement with the naked figure. Naked, not nude, the figure has the appearance of a revivified corpse. Like much later confrontational installation and performance art, the viewer is more than an audience, they are a co-participant. The environment that is created, which resembles a kind of allegorical murder scene, entangles us in a claustrophobic landscape that we have stumbled upon by chance. Perversely, the explosion of psychological dramas centred on serial killing that has grown as a genre in popular culture in the early twenty-first century finds its precedent in Duchamp's work. While Duchamp may himself have been familiar with a certain form of behavioural extremism in literature, including the Marquis de Sade and Georges Bataille's *Story of the Eye* (1928), it is extraordinary that this work seems to make clear the role of the constructed place in giving context to a proposition. And again, it is a box.

Site analysis
While an allegorical landscape is not a new concept in aesthetic history, or in many forms of story-telling, it would be fair to say that the emphasis, in architectural modernity, on the constructing of architectural models of reality does not give much space to the purpose of landscape. While environmental concerns are now common, it is through a lens of scientific conservation that the context of architecture is usually

considered. In *Étant donnés* the landscape is the scene of the crime; it has the role of providing the forensics of the event that must be reverse-engineered. In order to find the purposiveness of the tableau, the landscape must reveal its evidence.

Site is generally a fundamental driver of architectural design responses, whether it is within some form of 'natural' landscape, or degrees of mediated and constructed locations. It is not within the scope of this book to cover all of the idiosyncrasies of different site types, but it is worthwhile at this juncture to discuss the general disposition towards what a 'speaking' landscape for architecture might mean. This is the value of *Étant donnés*. The work distils the different components to present only as much information as is necessary to create the propositional effect of the piece.

One of the most convincing historical surveys of how the mythologization of landscape, how it is made to 'speak' and has been incorporated into aspects of the western tradition is in Simon Schama's *Landscape and Memory* (1995). Schama's work captures the deep thematic engagement with landscape at the heart of many nationalist myths, but it is his general proposition that mediations of a 'natural' world prefigure those of a more reflexive direction, which is most important.

How is this architectural?
How can we consider this as a fundamental question of an architectural project? The first question, before we ask what are the site characteristics of a location, is how does the concept of context work? It is the *parergon*, the work outside of the work that constitutes this context. For *Étant donnés* that is the approach to the work through the blank gallery, the relocated vernacular barn doors, and then the scene within which the figure is positioned. By the time the viewer is in the intellectual space of the work they are already engaged with the figure/context relationship that has been determined by Duchamp.

While it is obvious that no site is neutral in its effect, it is not always clear how the perlocutionary effect of the site is to be considered. To recognize this, the architectural project must have a strategy for recognizing and interpreting the voice of the landscape. Schama's work shows that these contexts run parallel to most intellectual endeavours as a minor thematic whose effect is felt but not always acknowledged. An architectural project must, as a component of its configuration, also have a strategy for listening, interpreting and speaking to the site. The challenge for an architectural project is to find, like the River Liffey in Joyce's *Finnegan's Wake* (1939), voices that are not simply those of geography, botany and geology.

Proposition: The speaking site
An architectural project that worked from the building back to the location, as a form of inverted site engineering could engage with the proposition here. Ultimately, and interestingly, the work would require you to remove the built component, the architecture, and leave only the site as a frame. The residue of the process, the thematic and physical frame, would leave the space for other architectures to emerge.

2: Memory

The question of memory, as opposed to history, is an important aspect of architectural theory. The challenges of architectural history, like most questions concerned with historiographic method, turn on issues themselves derived from the philosophy of history and technical questions of how history is recorded, written and read. What constitutes historical evidence, how do we interpret the behaviours of historical figures and what the material means for us in the present day continue to govern conventional history and are intrinsic to the level of authenticity the discipline requires for credibility.

Architectural history, like the history of many disciplines, has technical standards of evidence that strive for objectivity, or at least acknowledge the need for some form of objectivity – even in idiosyncratic and contested accounts. Memory however is a different thing, even though it is essentially based in some sense on a temporal moment that has passed. Memory in architecture, moreover, is generally discussed as a deeply personal version of the transitive nature of individual existence, and in particular the memory of encounters with, and in, architecture. The four chapters that follow describe different approaches to the employment of memory within architectural design. These approaches, however, are not conventional in the sense that they do not reflect personal memories. Instead, they describe and develop particular ideas on how 'memory' as an illusive and indeterminant aspect of personal experience might be transformed into techniques of design methodology.

The first chapter covers the popular use of the work of the Italian author, Italo Calvino, rehearsing the use of *Invisible Cities* and *The Castle of Crossed Destinies* as narratological contexts for design studios. Memory, in these instances, is present as the principal driver of the plot and includes descriptive passages of personal experience. What they share is a clear strategy to conflate memory, narrative and (within the texts) structuralist organization. This organization proposes architecture that is not only deeply personal but also objectively present and represented. In the next chapter, memory is discussed as a mechanical device, or rather memory is presented as the mechanistic outcome of a series of mechanical permutations. Daniel Libeskind's *Three Lessons in Architecture* provocatively creates a predigital, and indeed premodern, challenge to the idea that memory is purely personal. His machines create mechanical constellations of ideas which encourage us to consider a mutable and constructivist approach to thinking about architectural theory.

The third chapter looks at the physical dividend of memory, the vast array of commodified objects that we surround ourselves with, and for which we create architecture to meaningfully house. Commodity fetishism, it is argued, has created a glut of objects that exercise a deep fascination for us. How we recognize ourselves in these objects and how we choreograph their place in the world fundamentally asks questions regarding the role of architecture as a plane of appearances, a stage set.

The fourth chapter, referencing Jorge Luis Borges's *Library of Babel*, continues to look at the deep structure of possibilities for creating an architecture that strategically houses and positions the evidence we gather to make sense of the world. Where individual architectural projects limit themselves to specific domains of functionality and object sets, Borges's library presents the idea of the *ur*-library, encompassing both public history (the texts in the library) and private memories (the acts of searching for these texts). So memory, for architecture, is a process of structuring evidential narratives that, as a consequence of the dispositional presence of mnemonic objects and effects, provide architecture with its primary historical role.

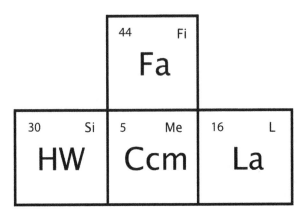

Rebus 5

Memory

Proposition 5: Calvino's City of Memory

The Italian author Italo Calvino's *Invisible Cities* (1978) is one of the most recognizable literary sources employed in architecture schools. It combines a density of mythical imagination with the romance of travel: travel for the characters within the tales, most notably Marco Polo, but also for Design Studio participants for whom the text is a challenge to broaden 'horizons' historically and spatially. As a pseudo-historical account, the travel within *Invisible Cities* purportedly describes exotic locations visited by Polo, conveying the unique characteristics they display. By employing the structural thematics consistent with the OuLiPo group of authors, particularly the architectural organization of Georges Perec's *Life: A User's Manual* (1978), *Invisible Cities* provides a descriptive brief of imaginary locations organized as a structured table of attributes. Compliance with a formalist device for composing narratological sequences of events meant, for OuLiPo members, that the act of creation (writing and narrative in their case) was to be found 'within and through' the bounds of the architectonic structure. The structure was both the organizational context of the story/stories, within the OuLiPo method, and the demonstration of their inherent connectedness.

In the context of studio, *Invisible Cities* provides a model for 55 different variants of city form and/or 'poetics' that students can illustrate depending on their imaginative engagement and communicative skill. Studio staff can direct students to undertake individual and cooperative explorations of the various aspects of the novel, confident that the unity of the text will bring together the studio solutions as a pedagogically consistent exercise. *Invisible Cities* introduces the student to the epicurean absolutes of texture, history and the experience of fragmentary and unified narratives. In particular, it mythologized the city of Venice as a palimpsest of attributes and attributed to them a gendered identity. While there is more of David Lean's *Summertime* (1955) in this project than Nicolas Roeg's *Don't Look Now* (1973), the imaginary Venice of *Invisible Cities* is a thematic landscape that has echoes in many similar narrative cityscapes, in particular Sophie Calle's *Suite Vénitienne* (1983, 2014), with the accompanying text, *Please follow me*, by Jean Baudrillard. Yet even in these narratives, the motivations are similar: the imaginary city is the foil of an 'other', real city in all its complexity.

The diversity of cities in *Invisible Cities* allows for choice. His descriptions are tantalizingly moderate which permits engagement and interpretation on the architect's behalf, and the cities have characteristics that are sufficiently simple enough to permit a fairly free re-presentation of their virtues. Elemental attributes may be alluded to even within the constrained decorative palette of contemporary design. It is not necessary to repeat the lustrous complexity of a Titian, Canaletto or Tiepolo, the mere presence of a single feature or colour can stand in for the city.

While *Invisible Cities* clearly functions well as a studio thematic for some of the reasons outlined earlier, arguably a better model is another novella of Calvino's, *The Castle of Crossed Destinies* (1974). In this work, combinatory formalism is matched to a scholastic world-view (with echoes of Umberto Eco's work on significatory systems) in which all signs constitute part of a greater lexicon of meaning. The genius of Calvino is the complexity of architectonic imagery it conjures up. It gives to the imaginative student the possibility of creating spatial algorithms of various narrative elements that animate the voices of the author, the character and the reader. Within the text, magically dumb-struck travellers must recreate their personal stories through the use of Tarot cards, each tale setting out a sequence of events.

Arcana
The cumulative array of cards becomes a collective diagram of their stories and acts as a spatialized narrative chart that diagrams the key thematic moments of the tale. The cards themselves, of course, are rich with associations to a medieval world-view governed by an imminent and interventionist God, or a pagan Fortuna, directing the affairs of mortals. Taken together, *Invisible Cities* and *The Castle of Crossed Destinies* provide a model for illustrating a singular location as well as narrating a sequence of events that are relevant to that location. In normal architectural practice, this might be the beginnings of a data visualization or programming map – which would then be shaped into the narrative coherency of an architectural brief. Because the placing of the Tarot cards is spatialized relative to each other, and to the meta-purpose of describing an individual's overall fortune, the movement between states emulates the construction of a narrative, as the Celtic Cross layout demonstrates.

Irrespective of the truthfulness of the process, the practice of diagramming chance relationships between characters/characteristics is a powerful analogy to the emplacement of programme characteristics within an architectural diagram. Similarly, it has a variability of scale that can be applied from the single chamber containing mnemonic objects to, potentially, an urban layout. When we overlay the poetic and impressionistic qualia of Calvino's textual work through the filter of structuralism, the diagramming of a narrative also encodes the lived aspects of a city.

Calvino's final, unwritten, *tertium quid* or 'unknown third' to the story of *The Castle of Crossed Destinies* is the 'Motel of Crossed Destinies', in which post-apocalyptic survivors attempt to communicate with each other via the medium of graphic novels. Here is a further engagement between the text and the idea of an architectural proposition. The question is: how is this contemporary dystopic city to be survived experienced and completed? What are the fragmentary tales of a city that may be woven together to form a composite new urban portrait *pace* Calvino?

Here the author changes the content of the cards, presumably the Major Arcana, from a historical tradition to a contemporary graphic format that demonstrates iconographic consistency with the traditional Tarot set. The architectural project that emerges from this version of structural narrative making is directed to a future form that is yet to be known, perhaps post-apocalyptic, that requires communication and shared values to be recognized. In studio, it becomes a project directed at questions of critical circumstances engaging values of preservation, survival and sustainability.

How is this architectural?
Taken together Calvino's two novellas provide a method for exploring architectural narrative. From the relatively simple process of illustrating individual cities, as described, and thus transforming text into image, to the more complex process of creating sequential narratives that match the narrative sequences of *The Castle of Crossed Destinies*. Students can identify city/urban qualities that form a composite of a single class project, then narrate the experience of travelling through the city, its neighbourhoods and boroughs, as a visual and spatial journey. The building becomes the city, and Esmeralda becomes Everytown.

A final supplement to employing Calvino would include a discussion of Aldo Rossi's Analogical City, addressed in his *Architecture of the City* (1982), in which architecture becomes an object with a compelling sense of temporality – one that has endured as an archetypal and autonomous form. Within the studio, the challenge is to produce a series of objects that appear immutable and inevitable. Similarly, their relationship with each other will demonstrate potential attractions and repulsions. Collectively they are like assembled actors on the stage set of the city, or like chess pieces in the middle of a game.

What are the diagrammatic outcomes?
As an architectural proposition, this can be replicated by considering buildings (and building types) as characters. From this, questions emerge:

1. How do we determine the 'character of the building/piece within a game space'?
2. What is the hierarchy of movement permitted to the character pieces?
3. How long does the movement pattern play out, a moment, an event, a cycle?
4. So if it is a topological game, such as the board games *Carcassonne* or *Settlers of Catan*, the goal is the recognition that the architectural urban form is a greater dividend than the economic advantage.

Proposition: Lover's hotel
A potential sample expression of this project will involve any form of spatialized encounter in which desire/movement are core attributes of recursive behaviour. Desire can be characterized from the filial to the sexual and can be located within any architectural programme that entails a degree of personal and private space. An individual house based on some form of human partnership, or the extrapolation of this condition into a public building, a hotel, could be employed.

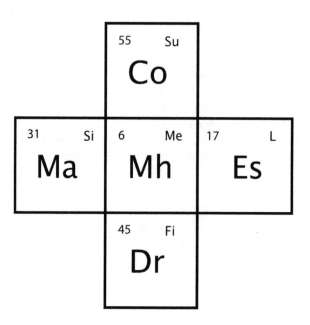

Rebus 6

Memory

Proposition 6: The Machine of History

One of the most influential of abstract architectural projects, perhaps because of its hermetic and inexplicable content, perhaps because of the subsequent fame of Daniel Libeskind and perhaps because of the extraordinary intensity of its vision was *Three Lessons in Architecture* (1985) completed for the 1985 Venice Biennale. Libeskind's projects, completed with students at the Cranbrook Academy of Art, are extraordinary items of contemplation which stood out, perhaps with the exception of Venturi and Scott Brown's L'Accademia Bridge project, from all the other submitted works predominantly on paper. The structures, by their physical presence, dominated the gallery space in the Arsenale Building. But their most significant characteristic is that they were so clearly *machines*. It seemed counter-intuitive that within an exhibition that was specifically dedicated to an investigation and renovation of the anti-modern aspects of Venice and the Veneto region, three inscrutable timber machines would appear: Reading Architecture, Remembering Architecture and Writing Architecture.

Libeskind's project, amongst a number of its trajectories, illuminated the interesting conjunction of machinery and memory. In her book, *The Art of Memory* (1966), Frances Yates details the evolution of mnemonic practice in the Renaissance, culminating in the memory theatre of Giordano Bruno and the memory machine of Giulio Camillo. Part of the development is the study of the *ars rhetorica*, the art of rhetoric. As an aid to remembering long tracts of argument, students of rhetoric devised schema for calling up specific passages or ideas from which they could either recite predetermined phrases or upon which they could comfortably extemporize. These schemas had specific representational and architectural characteristics. One, in particular, called for the student to divide the speech to be learnt into a specific house, containing a number of rooms. These rooms represented specific chapters or distinct ideas within the speech. Within the rooms themselves, objects were nominated as representing specific items to be remembered. So sequentially, by moving from room to room and observing the objects therein, a sequence of loci was established, each with an associated mnemonic characteristic. The architectonic possibilities of this are considerable. Consider the idea that the process of memory of the Renaissance rhetorician is similar to that of the urban inhabitant. The same forms of rhetorical devices, sculpture, landscape, capriccii and architecture could be similarly called on to 'map' the locutionary meaning of an urban experience. This potential recognized the correspondence between function and meaning yet again.

In addition, Camillo's Memory Theatre represented a fusion between the cultivation of mnemonic loci and the creation, from first principles, of a dedicated architectural structure that would positively reinforce the sequential and hierarchical purpose of memory. Conceived as a series of concentric semi-circular rings, similar to the seating of an amphitheatre the structure was organized radially, and along the arcs, to contain the sum of all possible quanta of memory. These themes included aspects of astrology, myth, the elements, aspects of the quadrivium and trivium, and gnosticism. Most importantly, the selection of material presumed a classificatory consistency between the levels, indicating that knowledge appeared in a variety of consistent but materially different forms of appearance. Hence, a material such as mercury would have the properties of a metal and a liquid, whilst also being associated with the personality trait of being mercurial and an association with the Roman god Mercury. Further, as with Ovid's *Metamorphoses*, the premise of the theatre suggested that these states were constantly transitive, or demonstrating temporal instability.

The theatre then was the attempt to put a solid configuration onto the substance of knowledge while acknowledging that every experience of knowledge was partial. Even though the central point of the concentric structure was a singular location, a locus in which the King was intended to sit to receive the output of the machine, that experience, as far as Yates could tell, was essentially a process of browsing. Was it Google *avant la lettre*? Did it contain a preference engine that would predict the operation of the machine? This is unknown, but it is interesting to speculate. At face value, it would seem that the theatre/machine was intended to be summative insofar as there was no intended omission of knowledge, yet the operation involved partial sequencing of revelation.

The Remembering Machine of Libeskind's *Three Lessons* speculatively recreated a fragment of the device, demonstrating a Rube Goldberg or Heath Robinson array of weights, pulleys, spindles, levers, cards, etc. that may or may not have worked. Where the Reading and Writing machines contained gears and cogs that functioned as a closed system, the Remembering machine as constructed was only partial. What to make of this? I don't think this relates to any specific ideas on the partiality of memory in comparison with reading and writing, but it does indicate that the project was not clearly scaleable in the way of the other two – though the scaling of the writing machine is exponential. A larger, more complex reading and writing machine can be imagined – but how does remembering increase? Paradoxically, we can still only read or write one text at a time, irrespective of its size – but we can remember quite complex arrays of experiences during the practice of reading and writing.

Moreover, why machines? These projects were not an attempt to propose some originary medieval intercession with our encounter with technology, despite Libeskind asserting that medievalism is the ultimate source of the computer and the automatic weapon. The externalization of human functions onto a series of mechanical processes succeeds because the process of emulation is successful, but the suppressed premise is always that the qualia of human experience are more diverse and more complex.

In many respects, the machines more fully demonstrate, deliberately because of the obsolescence of the technology, a fundamental anxiety towards the *outcome* of reading, remembering and writing. Why devise a machine if not for the anxiety that it will function consistently and effectively every time its services are needed? Architects don't read, they don't remember and they don't write (draw/design), so a machine that will perform these functions fulfils the obligation for authenticity that architects (and architecture) may lack at the moment.

It is also worth discussing because there is none in the literature, the use of certain terms in the books for the Reading machine. *Geist*, will-to-power, *Dasein*, to name three of the terms printed over and over in the hand-made books on the machine, form part of the specific lexicon of German philosophical idealism of the nineteenth and the twentieth century. As the future architect of the Extension to the Berlin Museum (the Jewish Museum), these terms are sequentially associated with Hegel, Nietzsche and Heidegger, all of whom had complex ideas regarding the trajectory of history and the role of the (German) State. On the significance of this, we can only speculate.

But the question is, what to make of the employment of a historical artefact, a recent project and the general question of how does architecture engage with technology and history? How does architecture function as a mnemonic machine itself? Do the fragments of historical experience add up to some form of eschatology? Libeskind's project answers some of these questions by creating material objects that function, despite their intrinsic obsolescence, and that it is clearly a model that will work.

Proposition: Three lessons in Libeskind
Three machines for reproducing the complex associations of Libeskind's project(s). Employing the premise and methodology of his work, but casting the process wider to engage with other machines and other histories, a goal emerges. Free from the need to produce a project that summarizes its conceptual drivers completely, the exploration between machine and artefact can be explored to find an architecture machine.

46 Fi	31 Si
Do	**Ma**
7 Me	18 L
Ro	**FO**

Rebus 7

Memory

Proposition 7: Redemptive Objects

Coupled with memory systems (Proposition 5) and the erasure of the interior (Proposition 11), the redemptive interior looks at the role of objects in determining a constellation of mnemonic consciousness. Objects are both the authentic dividend of other experiences (if they are not functional) and the demonstration of the continuity of the past into the present. Their purpose is to re-affirm that continuity. They also demonstrate an iconographic group identity (such as Aby Warburg's *Mnemosyne Atlas* we saw earlier) insofar as they have a topological relationship with each other. But if we are thinking about the interior, and the objects that populate them, we should consider also the question of taste and of commodity fetishism.

'Commodity fetishism' as a term comes from Marx's analysis of the difference between purpose and value in objects. In *Capital* (1867, 1991), Marx describes the obvious transformation that a product undergoes once its exchange value exceeds its purpose value, its utility. Inasmuch as the industrialized marketplace creates objects that are speculatively produced for sale, there exists a gap between the production of the object and the talismanic value it might attain once the desire for the product is tested in the market. Scarcity plays a clear role in this process, as well as levels of associative value that are idiosyncratic to a buyer. The general term for the desire for 'things', for Marx, is commodity fetishism.

Marx was not the first to understand, and indeed marvel, at the obsessional hold that 'things' had for people. Indeed the accumulation of objects of value has been consistent with all forms of monetary economies which employ forms of coinage to represent exchange value. For people not only buy bread and oxen with money but also jewels and works of religious value, to name two. For Marx, one of the key philosophical aspects of modern society was the volume and ubiquitousness of objects that come into being in the wake of industrialization. As Terry Eagleton notes in *The Ideology of the Aesthetic* (1988), the concept of taste evolves from the parlours of dissolute libertines within the *Ancien Regime*, to become the obsessional crucible of value in the vast modern marketplace of nineteenth-century metropolises such as London, Paris and New York. But what distinguishes the idea of commodity fetishism is the psychological commitment to objects as mirrors of the self.

In this world, the objects we desire exercise this power because of their ability to represent evidence of existence, and of a life that has been meaningfully experienced.

That a complex apparatus, the marketplace, exists to capture this interest is nothing new, but it is rarely acknowledged in architecture that the fundamental encounter we have in our private worlds is with these material talismans. Loos, of course, spoke of these objects and Morris and Ruskin before, but the question of obsessional behaviour and the erasure of objects have their clearest modernist description in the Bauhaus objection to bourgeois taste and the bourgeois interior, building on the general premise of the Deutsche Werkbund and the establishment of commercialized industrial design. Similarly, Le Corbusier's *objet-types* fulfil the function of providing a concession to the need for consumer items that are functional and demonstrate evidence of a design sensibility that rejects allusions to a conventional hegemony of taste.

However, if we avoid dragging the fetishism of things, commodities, labour and class consciousness into an exclusively political framework, we are still left with the issue of obsessional mirroring. In the absence of a life in which all material objects, all demonstrations of sentimentality, are banished, then the question of how to meaningfully organize the taxonomy of possessions in our lives remains. Outside of architectural theory and the visual economy of architectural publications, the world continues to be fascinated with things and their ontological value.

How is this architectural?
So the question is to what degree are objects aggregated together indiscriminately, or are they topologized by architecture? The proposition is that there are ways in which the typologies of furniture, for example, blend the specificity of the identity of the object with the strategic opportunities of the designed interior. Is the interior a historical museum which emulates the historical indexicality of the objects; or a white museum? Is it a stage set, a gallery? Is it *Heimlich*? *Hygge*? Cosy?

Of course, at one end of the spectrum of obsessional relationships with objects is hoarding which, while a recognized psycho-social disorder, is fascinatingly architectural since the goal of the hoarder, among other things, is to expunge all habitable space from their interior. As Sylia Lavin (2011) asks, were John Soane or Rae Eames hoarders? On the other, there is the ethical issue of (over)consumption and the decision process of selecting only those things that are genuinely meaningful.

In many respects, modernity has prepared persons within design culture to engage with the issue of moderated consumption, but not with the danger of exaggerated acquisition and existence. Is commodity fetishism after modernity, with its deliberate engagement with the object, a redemptive project? It is also the most ubiquitous material engagement with indvidual memory, centred on the self and the reflexive process of self-situating external representations of our thoughts, it is that area of subjectivity that modernity forgot.

Proposition: Hoarders hotel
The architectural project will interrogate the complicit relationship between things and architecture. Considering the relationship between objects, existence and occupation, the life of hoarding is usually centred on a stable site, the home. What is it to create a hotel for hoarders in which the tension between transience and permanence of objects is contested? Alternatively, what is it to develop an architecture from a single, or multiple, fetishized commodity. How does a suburban or urban form emerge from those behaviours in which the fetish transcends and distorts all other use values?

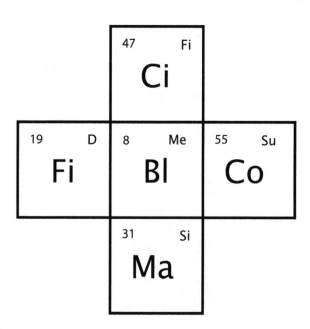

Rebus 8

Memory

Proposition 8: Borges's Library

Within the class of projects that investigate the organization and interrogation of the stuff of memory, the programme of the library occupies a special position in architectural thinking. Etienne Louis Boullée's *Interior of a Library* (1785) famously shows the single-point perspective view of a cavernous, barrel-vaulted library. The composition of the space is modelled on Raphael's *School of Athens* (1509–11), substituting an anonymous darkened doorway for the figures of Plato and Aristotle. Developing the discussion of redemptive objects, the library has traditionally represented a form of collective memory, and in particular an organizational system that can either be methodically explored or permit the random, deep engagement of arbitrary selection. If you think about the degree of deep intentionality in a library's organizational system vs. the chaotic possibility that there is no inter-textual meaning, this implies that every problem of association, the kindred cataloguing of thema, teeters between profound organization and meaninglessness. The contents of the library, and latterly the museum, are intended to describe a potential universe that, effectively, always exceeds comprehension.

Jorge Luis Borges's short story, *The Library of Babel* (1941), describes the geometry and organization of a, seemingly, infinite library. It famously describes the structure, order, behaviour and frustrations that the library, its contents and its librarians enjoy and endure. Importantly, and this point is I think missed quite often, the library exists as an ongoing and unfathomably complex reality in the lives of the librarians and their greater society. News of finds within the library is communicated to outside persons, the generational experiences of previous librarians are told and re-told, and specific accounts of book destruction are all relayed by the narrator. While it is relatively simple to assume that the library is a metaphor for the world, or more specifically the world of knowledge, it is far more interesting to contemplate the effects of the analogy on some alternate scenarios. What if the library was an infinite forest or landscape? What if it was a description of an infinite exploration of space beyond earth?

A brilliant examination of Borges's library by William Goldbloom Bloch (2008) takes seriously the descriptive passages of the text and sets out to calculate the scale of the building, the books, their layout and the possible paths that might exist within the edifice. Borges describes a hexagonal assortment of rooms that have two openings per hexagon, a circular stair, a sleeping chamber and toilet/bath for the librarians and a single circular and cavernous air shaft that the librarians are constantly in danger of falling into. While Bloch, a mathematician, gives a lively and elegant description of the process of calculation that infinitely large numbers associated with the claims of the library's scale, we understandably hear little of the purpose of the narrative. He does, however, in discussing the optimized packing of hexagonal chambers to create sequential pathways, speculate on an event that may have taken place: a murder. In this scenario, librarians hear evidence of a violent exchange and the imminent threat of violence. In order to get to the scene of the conflict, they have to find the optimum path towards it. Despite the fact that the rescuers are certain the sounds came from an adjacent hexagon, they search through the potential pathways only to find no access. Bloch calculates the permutations of pathways and library organization that would support this scenario in order to confirm whether the library is organized on a single or multiple planes.

While Bloch's insertion of this scenario serves as an intuition pump for calculating the pattern-based geometry of nesting and path formation within geometry, it also echoes the concluding events of Umberto Eco's novel of historical fiction, *The Name of the Rose* (1980). The novel is too marvellous to give away the ending here, suffice to say that it makes use of an event, a fire, to constrain the locus of attention to a boundary of experience, the library. Bloch and Eco introduce into the infinite regress of Borges's library, the phenomena of the event which is structurally governed by the organization of the library's principal function, the cataloguing of information. In Eco's book in particular, the search for a missing text constitutes one of the potential pathways that will uncover evidence of malfeasance. When we reflect back on these developed scenarios from Borges's text we find that beyond the sublime contemplation of infinite (or impossibly large) variations, it is the situational encounter with this state-of-affairs that provides the fundamental experience. And this experience is episodic, result-based and meaningful within the boundaries of the text's purpose. The narrative, it can be argued, is the purpose of the text. It is a confessional summary of the limits with which we engage with the order of the world.

So for Bloch, murder is a temporally urgent event (like the fire in *The Name of the Rose*) that ensures there is a finitude that needs to be addressed and a completed calculation made of the optimum path to its completion. Bloch's description of the locked-room scenario is essentially a function, like any architectural function, that requires spatialization and enactment.

How is this architectural?

Apart from the obvious exercise of constructing a version of Borges's library that adheres to the text, how are we to explore this architecturally? There are a number of governing issues available:

> 1. The structure must, as a general principle, be organized around a classificatory system that explores similarity and differentiation.
> 2. The structure must demonstrate a capacity to house its contents, without simply displaying them. Borges's library assumes that within each text are further depths that are not apparent on the plane of the librarian. The plane of the scholar surveys the structure of the individual text and sees, in microcosm, a further organizational world.
> 3. The structure must be within a context, a domain, a city or a world that is separate from the library. Entry to the library is required from this domain, though it is not clear if the exterior of the library is visible, or whether it has an outside.
> 4. The structure must be the scene of an event.
> 5. The logic of behaviour within the event must, in part, be governed by the structure.
> 6. Resolution may or may not be possible.

The nature of an infinite regress is that it telescopes in both directions, the infinitely large and the infinitely small. While this is mathematically compelling to Bloch, he also acknowledges the structural limits created by the story, and by Borges's sense of the humanity of the struggle, that defines conditions that, if consistent, create a comprehensible boundary to the experience of (in)finitude.

Proposition: Unpack your library

Gather a collection of books, things, situations and events and catalogue them. Place them in proximity to each other and move on to the next. What must be adhered to is the volume of parts; there must be many constituent components and many variables that need ordering. From this process, it is clear that there already exists an architecture of ordering, of presenting the most compelling aspects of the material as a table of fabula. Most importantly, you are the librarian.

3: Reflective/Reflexive

The questions, and propositions, contained in this section commence from the specific consideration of the visually reflective and philosophically reflexive condition of glass. Glass, it is argued, is a particularly modern material as it demonstrates the simultaneous property of being present and absent. On the surface, this is an unremarkable observation, but if we make the effort to imagine the uniqueness of glass as a material for the early twentieth-century avant-garde, the importance becomes clearer. In an era defined by the iconoclastic process of rejecting all previous formal and material solutions, glass architecture inevitably represented a profound break from historical traditions. At a more theoretically developed level, a material that seems to represent a concordance with Hegelian ideas of transcendence-through-absence is an ideal place to start a discussion of the absence of theoretical certainty and the mutability of outcomes.

The question of absence is non-trivial in contemporary architectural discussion because of the tension between solutions that exceed some material budget of expression, the Baroque generally, and those that optimize their use of form. Mies is the great proponent of this approach, to efficiently produce the 'almost nothing' version of design. In the first chapter, we look at some philosophical questions that attach themselves to the use of glass, and in the homonymic text that matches it, Jacques Derrida's *Glas*. Following Derrida, we consider that reflectivity, of course, differs according to the material surface light encounters, much like the variability of texts that appear to contain the same premise but take different paths. In this vein, the following chapter '*No* City', City, asks whether the context for the appearance of a design, its location/site/situation, must always be real.

Considering the counter-factual possibilities of fictional locations, the question of how a design project could meaningfully 'reflect' that location is discussed. The *No* City, it is proposed, obeys the same narratological requirements that a real city, or context, might but it varies in its ability to support the surreality of fiction. Similarly, the *No* Interior extends the discussion of object-existence and asks what the role of everyday objects might be if they are considered 'magical' in some sense. Magic, in this sense, is used anthropologically to describe systems of fetishization that are characterized as ontologically consistent with everyday life. In terms of reflexivity, the argument is that totemic objects abound within the aestheticized experience of the modern interior. Moreover, this slippage between functionality and fetishization allows us to imagine the interior, much as the design company Alessi or the stories of John Cowper-Powys do, as a tableau of sentient objects that populate and share our lives. While Alessi considers this a *jeu d'esprit*, a game of the imagination to promote the zoomorphic nature of their products, they also point to the uncanny (and largely invisible) obsession that contemporary culture has with the objects of taste. In this sense, the reflexivity of the discussion is pointed at recognizing the surreal in the everyday.

The final chapter of this section, '*No* Form', Form, builds on this discussion and looks at the idea of *Stilfragen* through the work of Alois Riegl. What is a 'question of style'? And why should style matter other than as some form of historical indexing? Of course, as Riegl notes, the question of style and its expression as a form is fundamental to the idea of *Kunstwollen*, the 'will-to-art', that continues to matter to everyone within the design economy. While I do not have the answer to what is, definitively, the style of our time (and what is 'our' time?), it seems clear that the contest of the question is as important as the answers that emerge from it.

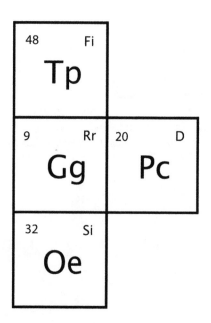

Rebus 9

Reflective/Reflexive

Proposition 9: Glass and *Glas*

Arguably, the most evocative and possibly definitive of modern materials is glass. As an architectural substance, it occupies a special place in the discussion of the psychology of materials and also in approaches to architectural judgement given the ubiquitous presence of modernism. In Hegelian terms, it is able to fulfil the idea of *Aufhebung*, to cancel and to preserve, to simultaneously appear and also transcend its appearance. Glass is always *there*, but when it functions normally it is ostensibly not present as well since we ignore its role as a mediating filter for vision: its materiality is always/never present. Glass architecture, from the Arcades of nineteenth-century Paris to Mies's Friedrichstrasse projects (1917), the Tauts, the Glass Architecture of Pierre Missac (1996), to Philip Johnson's Crystal Cathedral (1980) all participate in this condition.

The first and most obvious speculation we can make regarding glass as a material is the physics of reflection and transparency. Tellingly, these two properties, to reflect and to be transparent, also figure in practices of thinking associated with personal awareness and behaviour. For philosophy, the originary questions of who we are and how are we self-aware are foundational. Metaphorically, the quality of transparency signals an openness to observation and a lack of guile in presenting oneself to the world. Reflectivity also describes a similar level of awareness and a re-presentation of the self in the world. Similarly in architecture, there is speculation that transparency and reflectivity are core characteristics of modernity as a social condition and modernism as a material expression. Transparency relates to the enhanced use of glass as a surface medium in architecture which inherently, and obviously, permits mutuality of observation from inside and outside a building.

Reflectivity in architecture has a somewhat more problematic status insofar as it implies that the process of vision, the ocular-centric relationship between the seer and the seen, creates a mutuality between the two participants; either the viewing subject sees themselves reflected within architecture, or they are the observational subject comprehending (or spatially apprehending) the complex geometry of reflection within a multi-surfaced interior. Two forms of subjectivity are implied here: self-recognition through mirroring and a destabilizing sense of spatial presence because of false, arguably virtual, forms of depth perception. Jonathan Crary's (1988) definitive study of vision in the nineteenth century presents the strong argument that the emergence of technical apparatus for enhancing and recording vision changed the way in which subjectivity (or the self-awareness of the observer) has been mediated by technological devices. In architecture, the ability to see oneself presented by the reflective surfaces of modernity has surprisingly not produced generations of narcissists but has made us uncomfortably aware of our presence within a modern domain.

So transparency and reflectivity in architecture have mutually similar conditions, without necessarily the same outcome. A transparent pane of glass can be reflective at certain angles and in certain lighting conditions, while many polished materials can be reflective though rarely with the effectiveness of glass: indeed glass is often simultaneously transparent and reflective of course.

But what are the implications of this? Other than reflecting (pun intended) on the employment of metaphors of visuality in critical thinking, including psychoanalysis, how do we activate these qualities as an expression of architectural thinking and practice? Beyond the obvious qualities of creating glazed structures that dissimulate themselves entirely, the questions of reflection and transparency can apply in more subtle and developed forms. Similar to discussions of literal and phenomenal transparency, there are developed ideas regarding reflectivity that identify the ontological status of the observer as well as gradations of how reflectivity is a consequence of a material reality. For example, while the Barcelona Pavilion is interesting for its transparency, it is arguably more phenomenologically complex because of its management of reflectivity.

Interestingly, it was the visuality of mechanical reproduction, photography and film, that discovered this as a core aspect of modernity before modern architectural theory shifted to the Corbusian emphasis on 'openness' as a moral quality as well as the obsessive celebration of light as a phenomenal constituent of architecture. Many of the classic 'architectural' films understood and employed the complexity of viewpoint and gaze inherent in modern interiors before they became specific drivers of architectural thinking. When Kenneth Frampton identified qualities of *sfumato* in the late-modern work of Japanese architects, a sheen on surfaces that seemed entirely at odds with an engagement with the organic world, he was doing more than trying to explain the aestheticization of industrialism. The indeterminate boundaries of *sfumato* in painting are emulated by the arbitrary and inconstant reflectivity of processed materials. So reflectivity generally requires more development as a critical design practice.

Some architectural questions:

>1. What is the design difference between transparency and reflectivity?
>2. How do you effectively harness reflectivity as a visual quality while also creating a proposition about the observer?
>3. Is the reflection that of a phenomenal moment, or a constant mutable state?
>4. Is reflection an expression of spatial complexities, real and virtual?
>5. Is there literal and phenomenal depth in reflectivity?
>6. Who or what is being reflected and is recognized (or re-thought) through the apperception of reflection?

Further, if we also consider the homological qualities of Jacques Derrida's text on G. W. F. Hegel and Jean Genet, *Glas* (1986), we have another possible mode of 'reflectivity'. In *Glas*, Derrida investigates the already given within Hegelian thinking and the stain of identity and signature that writing carries. Be it in the social configurations of Marxist social analysis, the definitions of opposites of western thought or the kinship of idea, agency and form, the urge to consider the mimetic relationship between idea and experience remains. The inconstancy of reflection in glass-like materials, including metals, is matched in the interpretive gulf between world-views in *Glas*. Materials reflect in an infinitely complex variety of modes, making the term almost too general to be applicable as a design parti. So we are left with the 'objecthood' of location and agency, who is reflected and how do they recognize themselves and others? For architecture, or for someone thinking about architecture, reflectivity is a space between texts in which, unusually a third form emerges.

So it is important to consider how effective ideas of transparency and reflectiveness can actually be in an architectural project. The fact that Derrida employs it in an analogous fashion for his meditation on the relationship between Hegel and Genet and that the famous interchange, summarized by Vidler (2005), between Derrida, Eisenman and others on *khora* (place) produced considerable complexity without obvious outcomes, should tell us that reflectivity is more useful when it is considered the active intention of the architect rather than an immediate outcome. Architects 'reflect' themselves to a more or less distorted degree depending on how they manage the surface disturbances of their thinking and the question of how and what form may merge from this process. The *sfumato* mentioned previously, the smokiness or smoothness of thinking, becomes part of the process of reconciling different agencies to appear as coherent parts of the whole.

In summary, glass is the syllogistic consequence of the evolution of modern architectural thinking. It redefines, amongst almost everything else, the interior/exterior relationship of thought to the world. Its presence is always known only through its irruptions or its imperfections, the complexities of its reflectivity. The breath on the glass; the frost of an early morning; the refractive spectrum of the glass pane turned on end; the broken glass of the window or door; the destruction of viewpoints and the spatial complexity of halls of mirrors, all constitute different modalities of how reflective architecture might be thought.

Proposition: Drunken architect, the Alembic Brewery
In proto-modern science, the alembic vessel was used to isolate and transform the chemical properties of materials, essentially acting as a still for the creation of alcoholic spirits. Because the process is mutable, but irreversible, it is also like the act of creating architecture. Once the process of thinking about the combination of different elements is under way, the inevitability of architecture is present. So too for this project in which the challenge is to distil an enhanced sense of objective presence of the architect-as-alchemist or architect as drunken master.

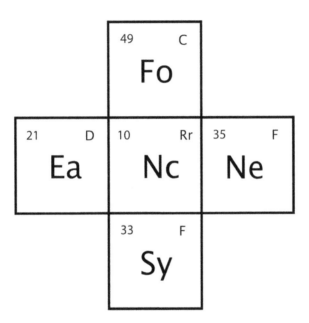

Rebus 10

Reflective/Reflexive

Proposition 10: *No* City

Continuing the thematic of reflection and reflexivity, it is worth thinking about the ground on which these forms of reflectivity are situated, or more accurately the collective urban consequences of architectural thinking when we start to challenge orthodox design methods. In general, of course, common-sense applications of urban planning analysis and design give the most unproblematic approach to any contextual analysis. We define a site, assess its dimensions, review relevant codes and speculate on common-sense and (reasonably) viable potential developments. The consequences of this decision-making process become the ground of the project and the de facto definition of its urban identity. However, if we problematize the definition of urban and of the factors that contribute to the urban identity, we can, and should, introduce any number of aberrant criteria that narrate the story of an urbanity.

How urban formations have developed and the myriad of agencies that have brought about the form and functions of urbanity is a continuous process of understanding, but at the level of the single architectural project, it is also important to be able to reverse engineer the urban consequences of design approaches within a context. How does the architectural work recalibrate the identity of its context? When Karl Scheffler and August Endell (Eisenschmidt 2014) speculate on the inherent beauty of the metropolis of late nineteenth-century Berlin, it is not just for reasons of political positioning within a quarrel between ancient and modern forms of urban consciousness. Inheriting the idea that a city is a 'creative outcome' of aestheticized principles (Collins 2006), Scheffler and Endell undertake a kind of urban taxonomy, seeing beauty in the tumult of industrialization and development of urban Berlin. An approach that, a century later, theorists such as Geoff Murnaugh (2009) continue to mine as a method of the critical reappraisal of urban experience. What is clear from both approaches, the top-down imposition of a series of general principles of urban design designed for consistency of application vs. the city as laboratory is that the presence of new architectural propositions continues to nuance the nature of the urban environment. The challenge is to be clearer in understanding the effects of the architectural stranger, and the reflective consequences this create.

For the purposes of the argument being developed in this, and subsequent chapters, and to give a clearer idea of the distinctiveness of this approach, we will call this the *No* City. While the *No* City can be recognized, and created, in existing locations, it is worth thinking first about the role of 'iconic' forms of architecture that may demonstrate the type of situational influence that percolates through this approach. Simone Brott discusses Gehry's Guggenheim Museum in Bilbao (1997) and critically appraises the degree to which the complexity of form and expression exists prior to its realization as a material reality. For Brott (2012), discussing Adorno, this constitutes an irruption of the Real, where the fantasies of media culture surprisingly and unnervingly become present in the world. Bilbao the city, as a consequence of their Faustian pact with the Guggenheim Foundation, must deal with the presence of this architectural object and the associated warping of reality that it imposes on its context. The *No* City is, like Bilbao, fundamentally affected by the critical 'weight' of the incident project, and its rippling effects create revaluation of many of the normative considerations of urban analysis and identity.

If the challenge of the Glass/*Glas* analogy was to develop self-awareness, to put it simply, of the situated thinking of the architect, the *No* City is the consequence of that reflexivity. A loose analogy might follow the lines that the city, as currently systematized and ordered, is the expression of certain Hegelian historical rationalities and the incursions of material event environments (including not only architecture but also performances, demonstrations, weather events, etc.) are like the organic phenomena of desire identified by Genet. So how are *No* Cities imagined? For this, we can turn to the literary genre of Magic realism for some information.

We mentioned the ethnographic text *The Golden Bough* in Chapter 3, to explain the drive towards creating a taxonomy of ethnographic observances. If Fraser's analysis of how certain religious practices are meant to be pan-cultural was rendered suspect with further empirical study, it is also true that the concept of magical thinking generally has nevertheless persisted, though named and discussed differently. Claude Levi-Strauss (1942), famously, pulled apart certain aspects of 'magical' thinking to situate it within premodern societies in which scepticism towards magical outcomes existed as the petri dish within which strains of magic experience grew. Levi-Strauss, despite his interest in Surrealism, sought to explain the epistemological contract and suspension of belief that 'magic' entailed when considered in various societal forms irrespective of their 'advanced' nature.

Magic realism, in creative fields and particularly in narratology-based expression, does not seemingly carry the same requirements of legitimacy that anthropological study seeks, but no small amount of evidence exists to demonstrate that interpretive drift occurs in the encounter with architecture.

Magic realism has both coherent and incoherent explanatory systems for context disruption, sometimes we see unusual consequences caused by characters, and sometimes things happen inexplicably or follow rules that are not coherently understood. Usually, and there are many caveats here, one of the defining features of magic realism in literature is that the fictional world bears considerable cosmetic similarities to the real world and that it is only when certain illogicalities emerge that the reader is aware that a significant irruption of the logic of events and behaviour have been sanctioned to occur. The thrill of the narrative is in exploring how these illogicalities are encountered and conquered. In some sense, this was the intention of Fredrick Kiesler writing on magic architecture (Sabatino 2010) or the Group 6 portion of the 1956 *This is Tomorrow* exhibition put on by Alison and Peter Smithson, Nigel Henderson and Eduardo Paolozzi at the Whitechapel Gallery in London. Both of these, specifically architectural examples, looked to find a kind of magic 'aura' in the ruins of contemporary society, drawing clear parallels between the detritus of the everyday world and their fetishized role as talismans of progress and primitivism.

Proposition: Magic city
The *No* City is the consequence of the explosion in communication that has typified the late twentieth century. It is also, typically, a place of bewildering complexity. So many connectivities can be made that the prospect of a network disappears. We have no city. In its stead is the ongoing wager as to whether the machinery will work or not, for how long, and with what inconsistencies. Travelling in and through the *No* City is an act of suppressed bravery for we are constantly presented with the prospect of calamity. Violent accidents occur, or violent disruptions, when the limits of technology are found. Danger, as Ernst Junger pointed out, is a continuous presence that the modern city delivers. Interestingly, this is always presented as a breach of moral values, or etiquette. So technology and ethics combine to preserve the autonomy of connections. The Machine Age is not about machines, but about this collusion.

Create a *No* City constituted by more than the architectonic of communication. Make it about the space between the circuits on the circuit board, the volume that surrounds the inner workings of machines. Make it the magical 'ground' of the positive and predictable communications of technology and the place where the 'curiosity' of Being exists (Heidegger, *Being and Time*: 172–73).

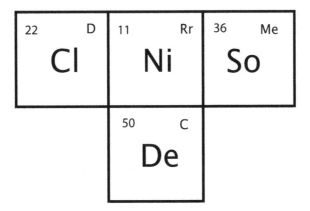

Rebus 11

Reflective/Reflexive

Proposition 11: *No* Interior

Shadowing the cult of cleanliness and the erasure of decorative embellishment in modernity, nostalgia has been one of the sustaining dreams of domesticity in the late twentieth century. While the issues of cleanliness and the matching of clinical standards with residential experience is a subject in itself, the parallel condition of the over-full and obsessively contrived interior illuminates a collective identity of modern individuals who may feel, consciously or otherwise, un-housed and un-homed. By this I mean the strata of society for whom housing is not a desperate and immediate need, but a luxury that has aspirationally or already been attained. The material of domestic nostalgia: character homes, furnishings and tasteful objects occupy a highly developed ontological space as demonstrations of the *personal* expression of the continuity of history. Even the contested relationship between kitsch and taste sits within this space since they are both expressions, simplistically, of attitudes to historicized social value.

As described in Proposition 7 earlier, regarding redemptive objects, objects themselves are part of the economics of commodity fetishism, which when developed to excess result in the indiscriminate acquisition of the flotsam and jetsam of modern life. The outcome of that chapter was the proposition that we explore the consequences of this behaviour as a form of extreme acquisition, hoarding. What needs to be further addressed is the consequences for those systems of acquisition and display that step back from excessive behaviour and allow for a considered response between object(s) and architecture, or between transitive and intransitive states of affairs.

As noted before, it is a characteristic quality of modern architecture that, in its infancy, there was considerable antipathy to the accumulated decorative items of bourgeois existence. Despite Gropius's (and others') design relationship with German industry and Le Corbusier's celebration of the *objet-type*, these were the compromise solutions to the reality that modern homes still seemed to accumulate, amongst many other things, inherited cupboards, bread bins, vases, antique figurines and coat racks that mark the persistent presence and domesticity of those who see their homes as an extension of their selves for pragmatic as much as psychological reasons. The question regarding how this form of cultural object-permanence demonstrates its own form of engagement with modernity and how it implies a form of architectural practice needs further interrogation. Clearly, there are myriad variations on the patterns and density of how these objects are arranged, and how we might construe the museological organization of personal possessions, but to get there we should consider the relationship to objects themselves within architectural discourse.

The considerable media attention, outside of professional architectural discourse, given to the discovery, fetishization and ownership of nostalgic objects now drives the complex interactions between taste, class and social identifiers in many western societies. Coupled with the economic driver of property ownership and the leveraging of household wealth relative to other political concerns, the management of nostalgic taste, as Terry Eagleton incisively identified in his *Ideology of the Aesthetic* (1988), is intimately connected to political stability and the preservation of status quo within the bourgeoisie.

However, nostalgia also suppresses curiosity by allowing ambivalence to be elevated to a level of philosophical enquiry and novelty to the level of revelation. Nostalgia is, by this measure, the folk expression of a historic consciousness which stands in for a more critical and developed engagement with historic materialism and the revelatory role of objects as mnemonic devices. While Eagleton is concerned predominantly with the evolution of aesthetic experience in philosophical discourse, his intention was to also demonstrate the degree to which academic discussions regarding the aesthetic attitude were deeply rooted in the social space of an emergent class of home-occupiers who were fully committed to the mechanics of commodity fetishism. The ongoing machinery of novelty revelation reveals the technology of curiosity. It becomes a cyclic imperative in which the wonder of new objects either fades from attention or embeds itself into the interior landscape and merges with the general category of 'homely'.

How is this architectural?
There is a tension between the modern interior in which all objects, including built-in furniture, are thoughtfully placed according to the scenographic decisions of the decorator, and the persistent need to house the spoils of commodity consumption when that point is reached when the volume of objects acquired exceeds the decorator's brief. Concomitantly, the often-limited capacity of architectural spaces to absorb excess consumption tests the limit of its capacity to also serve the longevity of the inhabitant's life. Put simply, once you have settled into the Farnsworth House, where do you put the flat screen television, grandmother's crockery and the holiday souvenirs?

The placement of objects, whether in bespoke cabinetwork, on shelves and bookcase surfaces, or on walls and tables, entails the thoughtful presentation of them in relation to the space they occupy and the other objects proximate to them. Every home is a museum of the self, even in the most careless and happenstance of emplacement. Similarly, there are temporal movements of objects, either fixed in place in order to be a-temporal or subject to change as an expression of the subtleties of mood and effect that a moment requires.

Around all this is the question of the form, and the materiality, of the interior. The indexical relations made between the stage set of the spaces and the object-actors arranged therein are intrinsically tied to each other. The question is whether the building form is deliberately shaped to include particular objects because of their size, number or distribution, or whether the design is deliberately indifferent, even hostile, to this accommodation.

No Interior

The *No* Interior is the consequence of this tension as it activates both the drive towards meaningful acquisition of objects, the curation of their interdependence and the concomitant drive to sublate and remove the objects once their purpose has been absorbed into a subsequent narrative. It is clear, in the imagining of Baudelaire, Freud and subsequent others, that the object-rich interior is a representation of a subject's psychological obsessions. The fetishization of objects, and their subsequent placement, movement and, at times, removal, create narratives that have clear mnemonic capacities. Considering the manner in which the objects of an interior may be accommodated, and imagining how the form may be created to address these works, the immediate thought may be to shape the form in the same manner that packaging is shaped to the geometry of the object it is protecting.

Proposition: An interior monologue

Construct a sequence of interiors that transform the domestic space into that of a theatre. Employ objects as props for the description of a person, perhaps yourself, that create a narrative of engagement, entailment, obsession and rejection of objects as mnemonic devices.

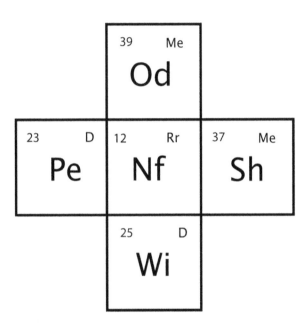

Rebus 12

Reflective/Reflexive

Proposition 12: *No* Form

Completing the discussion of form and formlessness in the consideration of reflectivity, urban influence and the interior, it is worth considering the perpetual question of what constitutes appropriate form in architecture. In many respects, this is often *the* question since the discussion on the importance of architecture turns often on the relationship between its material reality and the consequences of its effects. If we consider some of the major architectural texts of the twentieth century, including *Vers Une Architecture* (1923), *Complexity and Contradiction in Architecture* (1966), *SMLXL* (1995) and *Animate Form* (1999), appropriate and meaningful form is a core question along with the questions regarding how that form is arrived at. Arguably, behind these approaches is the analysis of form and expression outlined by Alois Riegl in his studies of *Kunstwollen* most popularly expressed in his *Stilfragen* (1893).

For Riegl, and importantly for studies into the evolution of meaningful design approaches in architecture, the intellectual analysis of the competing factors that influence 'stylistic' developments in form reward approaches characterized by deep and specific attention to detail. Riegl was interested in the way in which 'transitional' or historically under-represented works demonstrate individual internal coherency rather than minor departures from dominant periods. *Kunstwollen*, or a 'will-to-art', was his term for the drive towards the creation of indexically meaningful forms by an artist (or architect) for their audience. For Riegl, this was also an extension of his greater programme to determine *Stilfragen* (questions of style) regarding the purpose of changes in expression. In architecture, and for the greater architectural project of attempting to understand the purpose of certain design decisions, the process of *Kunstwollen* commences in the empirical understanding of how certain geometries are made, the purposes to which they are employed, the consistency with which these decisions are made across a number of material practices (from art to industrialization) and the greater question that the formal strategies (arguably) demonstrate.

Is this just an unfocused version of the *Zeitgeist* argument, that everything is a demonstration of a world-view that is unambiguous and can be understood unproblematically once placed within an explanatory schema? While the term is, of course, useful, it also carries the danger of being too general and indeterminate to be meaningful. Similarly, there is a danger in seeing Riegl's method as a simple form of grand-historical narrative, unmoored to the reality of the many disparate components of formal expression. However, the integrity with which the empirical evidence of the analysis is presented in effect makes meta-theories a necessary development for the scrutiny of any work. If it does not mean something as evidence of a larger scheme, then it means nothing and that is clearly not the case. Similar to the examples earlier of the *No* City, it is the departures from categorical indicators that indicate the potentially dissonant elements of the work-at-hand.

So the collagist interests of Venturi and Scott Brown, the analogue organicism of Ushida Findlay, the non-standard geometries that have been borrowed from the animation industry of Lynn, or the restless constructivism of Eric Owen Moss all indicate a larger question regarding the empirical capacity and purpose of certain design decisions.

But with the example of Lynn's approach, there is the opportunity to think about the sheer indeterminacy of the outcome. As Lynn is proposing a formal strategy that has no single preferred empirical outcome, either the process is flawed through imprecision – or it is necessary to think about a design environment in which multiple formal outcomes are possible and valid. There are a number of different ways to think about this, either we accept the indeterminant and arbitrary as a compromise approach to making significant form, or we look at the significance itself of indeterminacy, or both? *No* Form is the consequence of current design methodologies in which the execution of certain topological transformations of formal systems is undertaken independently of a critical judgement that prefers 'this' to 'that'. Similarly, the incremental play of determinacy and indeterminacy in Moss's Los Angeles works interrogates the principles of construction while undermining the meta-organizational principle that design solutions must demonstrate a scalable coherence across all instances of design and construction. Principally, work like this confronts and challenges the organizational 'enterprise architecture' of the design and construction industry that constantly demands vertical integration of compliance and consistency. The seemingly 'ad hoc' nature of contemporary architectural projects tests the robustness of the project management process to see if the dominant organizational paradigm can still hold – happily it usually does, unhappily usually via a 'value management' process.

Professionally, this indeterminacy is challenging as it undermines the normal contractual relationship between programme, form and outcome that underpins the basis of client/architect relationships in the professional world. However, in the domains of speculation that academic and avant-garde work occupies, the opportunity for indeterminacy carries the weight of appearing sufficiently abstract and sufficiently opaque to interpretation to satisfy the tribal interests of architecture theorists. This inherent multiplicity is the first outcome of the *No* form process. But more seriously, the indeterminacy and a de-coupling of form from intention seem a more sober response to questions of meaningfulness in architecture in the early twenty-first century. The much-discussed post-theory era of architectural production was a complex intersection of global capital interests, evolving technological tools for design and commuication, enhanced recognition of the immanence of global environmental issues and a de-politicization of architecture as a tool of social behaviourism. While it is not true to say that architecture in this period no longer addressed *Stilfragen*, even at regional and co-cultural levels, the ambitions for meaning diverted to more fragmented and idiosyncratic interests.

Ultimately, this is probably a more mature and coherent method of addressing questions of international architectural culture, recognizing that difference at a general level is more a function of (architectural) brand management than problem responsiveness. However, the lurking fear remains that form is meaningless as far as architects' intentions are concerned. This explains, in part, the emergence of improbably florid formal expression in the projects of BIG, MAD Architects, Zaha Hadid, etc. in which there appears to be a vigorous indifference, if that is possible, to the question of whether formal languages and strategies are comprehensively managed to ensure consistency of metaphorical application, or design strategy, across all aspects of a project. When Koolhaas wrote the confessional essay on Bigness (*SMLXL* 1995), acknowledging the impossibility of architectural effect on all stages of a design process, he was signalling an emerging reality that there was both an appetite for grand-scale architectural projects and the elevation of architects to visionary status, which were simultaneously impossible to control in terms of traditional architect-as-author intentionality. So *No* Form becomes the default position of contemporary architecture, the flirtation with complete meaninglessness in pursuit of 'enough' meaningfulness.

So how is this (not) architectural?
Considering these questions, it is important to remember that the *Stilfragen* text is actually dedicated to the study of ornament and decoration, not of more seemingly fundamental questions regarding significant form. Riegl was reviewing the transformation of effects independently of more structural differences and grand historical narratives, such was his historiographic method, but the question of *what* change meant always arose. *Kunstwollen* was the term he divined in order to address

these issues and to characterize broader stylistic tendencies and the individual's limited role in participating in their cultural milieu.

In terms we might borrow from Riegl, the *Kunstwollen*, of the type of architectural practice of the so-called 'post-critical' and 'post-theoretical' periods we occupy, reveals the tension of intentionality and, arguably the re-focussing of the architectural project towards ideas of style and decorative surfaces to the point where the building is *all* decoration. Because decoration is, generally and chauvanistically, considered a minor form of expression, it has become an acceptable field that architecture can occupy vis-à-vis the self-serving organization of capital. The perverse victories of those architects who manage to procure and deliver seemingly meaningful projects of complex and thematic geometries are buttressed by the apparent philosophical (or perhaps political) emptiness of the objects overall. Like floats in a Christmas or Thanksgiving Pageant, the work occupies a disproportionate volume of attention while armies of attendants march alongside to ensure the continuation of the spectacle.

A second outcome, also considered by Riegl, is the role of the spectator/beholder in determining the coherence of the artwork encountered. Here the question of meaningful form is more complex since the responsibility for coherent expression is not that of the architect, but of the critical observer. Curiously the analogy of the Parade float can continue to be employed. The wonder experienced by the audience, whether a child or otherwise, constitutes a genuine effect of the event structure. Inherently, this 'wonder' can stand in for the transcendental idea that 'art' exists as an aspiration of aesthetic consciousness, just like the expectation that the parade audience will be thrilled. That the degree to which the aesthetic spectacle is governed by the scale of the floats and their identity within a theogony of cartoon characters further reinforces the simplicity, and effectiveness, of the aesthetic effect. For Riegl, his assumption in the *Kunstwollen* proposition is that we exist within the same thematic milieu and that what works at a general level is not the abrogation or diminution of effect, just a more or less complex expression of what everyone experiences.

So, while the debate over the significance of Form, the agency of the creator and the role of the audience is well known, a few more questions persist. Where does one step into the engagement with form vs. decoration? Where is the point where the form is already determined, and at what point do you mark the presence of another agency? Is creativity the moment when form is made monstrous, or unnamed, such that the references of form to other morphologies become the most pressing question of intensionality vs. intention?

Proposition: Sound and fury signifying something
Design a parade of architectural forms, a procession of *Stilfragen* works in the manner described in the *Hypnerotomachia Polyphili* (Colonna 1499) but relevant to a contemporary audience – which is you.

4: War

The three chapters in this section are, at the time of writing, unfortunately timely for a discussion of the relationship between architecture and construction. The consequences of war, conflict and destruction at a number of different scales are one of the most recognized, but under-discussed aspects of architecture as a constructive process. Obviously, at a kind of fundamental level, the prospect of building meaningfully usually commences with the transformation (perhaps destruction) of an existing environment, whether it is an ecological system into which a bespoke cabin is constructed or an insertion into a historic urban fabric. There is always the melancholy recognition that perhaps it might have been better to do nothing. But if we can accept that the constructivist tendencies of architecture, its tendency to see a meaningful building as a positive outcome, can generally be supported, then it makes sense to think about the triadic relationship of destruction, reconstruction and preservation.

The three chapters in this section look at this process commencing with the most violently prosecuted form of destruction, war. In warfare, the strategic annihilation of buildings generally and architecture, in particular, expresses an extreme chauvinism towards the damaged opponent. Because a work of architecture, should it be valued by a society, is so disproportionately costly to replace when damaged, the fear is always that destruction of the fabric of a location will prevent it from a future existence and from playing a part in the identity of a society. Conflict that specifically targets architecture, interestingly, is indifferent to the technical complexity of its original construction and concentrates on destroying the very idea of 'architecture', and its mnemonic value within the subject community. The question that then emerges from this consideration is how do you symmetrically create an architecture that deliberately attempts to reconstruct that mnemonic value?

The question of memory is then linked to the process of reconstruction, creating a material construct that supervenes the circumstances of its creation. The second chapter concentrates on Lebbeus Woods's methodology for proposing reconstructions of damaged sites, and of locations that suffer because of the continued immanence of violence present. Woods's proposals are serious in their focus on real sites of human anguish that could, arguably, benefit from the optimism of constructive interventions, but they are also playful because they propose forms that evolve from speculative wondering. The seriousness of Woods's imagination allows us to see the purpose of monuments, and the investment in remembering they entail.

The final chapter asks whether conflict can be purposefully beneficial, and in particular looks at the construction of resistant 'cities' that challenge the status quo. Like many temporary occupations of sites, such as the original barricades of Paris (1830, 1848 and 1968), to the Aboriginal Tent Embassy in Canberra, Australia (from the 1970s until the current day), the challenge of how to resist dominant values through construction persists. Inevitably solutions that emerged ad hoc from the need to be present at a location were piecemeal in their evolution and were not designed as a conscious philosophical provocation. Despite this evolutionary process though, there are clear messages for anyone thinking of meaningful forms of architectural political resistance. The third chapter looks at the phenomenon of the Occupy movement between 2011 and 2012 and reflects on the deliberately architectural questions that emerge from the original site on Wall Street, New York. As an asymptotic gesture of resistance towards the vast hegemony of international capitalism, the chapter asks whether this phenomenon, like other forms of built resistance, could be considered anything other than architectural.

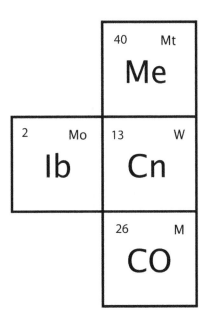

Rebus 13

War

Proposition 13: Conflict

Thinking of architecture and war, it is, of course, almost painfully obvious to point to the degree of destruction caused by armed conflict within urban locations. Quite apart from issues associated with the damage to architectural works, ruined cities are the constant visual evidence of the parallel destruction of lives, social systems and the tenuous grasp of civilized behaviour and mutual trust necessary for a functioning society. Perversely, with all the personal tragedies associated with conflict, it often seems to be the vehemence with which architecture is destroyed that communicates a collective wounding of a city or culture's sense of self. When the Reichstag was stormed by Russian troops in Berlin in 1945, or the US Embassy in Saigon in 1975, or the Twin Towers in New York in 2001, or the Great Mosque of Aleppo in Syria in 2013, the symbolic value of the destruction almost supervenes the event itself. The impossibility of returning the architecture to a state prior to its damage meant that the massive cultural investment these works represented was forever lost.

Significantly, the representative value of these buildings emerges from different value systems. Where the Reichstag was (and is again) the seat of the German government, its destruction in 1945 was the logical outcome of the ethos of the 'Total War' of the Nazi state; the evacuation and storming of the American embassy in Saigon was similarly the repudiation of US foreign policy objectives that drove the conflict in Vietnam and border states and, arguably, an assertion of autonomous identity by the PAVN and Viet Cong. The destruction of the Twin Towers and the damage to the Pentagon, in 2001, are agreed to be the result of significant cultural hostility towards American engagement in Middle East conflicts, yet the buildings are nowhere near the site of these conflicts and the suffering that was occurring in the region.

Whatever the justification, the spatial abstraction of a 'conflict' conducted remotely emphasizes the perceived necessity for a very real material outcome of this antagonism. Bringing a conflict 'home', arguably, demonstrated perfectly the value and the vulnerability of architecture in modern warfare.

Finally, the destruction of the Great Mosque in Aleppo was ultimately an expression of the internecine outcomes of civil war. Competing groups within Syria, including the government forces loyal to Bashr Al-Assad, fought over the city generally and the Mosque was collateral damage in the urban fighting. Thematically then, if we are considering conflict and architecture, or more specifically the consequences of conflict for architecture, the vulnerabilities of works stem from their status as expressions of the following:

> 1. They are the representative forms of a defeated opponent at the site of the opponent's social locus (Reichstag).
> 2. They are the representative forms of an external aggressor that are symbolically expunged as a demonstration of victory and autonomy at the site of the victor's social locus (Saigon).
> 3. They are the representative forms of an antagonist, separate from the purported theatre of war, demonstrating a strategic reframing of the sites of conflict to include the social loci of both parties (New York).
> 4. They are the representative forms of both sides of an antagonism that are nihilistically destroyed as an expression of contested dominance through self-harm (Aleppo).

In all these examples, the relationship between architecture and concepts of territory and symbolic value is present, yet there is relatively little focused attention on the question of critical aesthetic value, and whether that actually constitutes a loss of any significance. For example, Yamasaki's towers in New York were considerably criticized for their banality and for the destruction of parts of the New York Radio Row of commercial businesses to facilitate the original construction in the 1970s. Whether the subsequent destruction of the Towers and the adjoining precinct, besides being a human tragedy, was similarly a tragedy for the urban character and architectural expression of the World Trade Center environs is a contested question. Is the symbolic value of these works significantly more valuable than the contestable aesthetic reputation they enjoyed? This seems to be clearly the case with the US Embassy in Saigon, and is arguable for the other examples, though the Aleppo Mosque is certainly an exception for its historic value.

Andrew Herscher (2008) in an article considering the rhetorical contest surrounding the Omarska Memorial 'constructed' in London at the time of the Olympics in 2012 opens the question of material meaning and relevance. The structure was originally a sponsored gesture by a multinational iron and steel company, ArcelorMittal, to advertise the company and procure favourable reviews for patronage of the designers, including the English sculptor Anish Kapoor. The discovery that the material used would have contained ore mined from an area in Bosnia, Omarska, noted for war crimes inspired human-rights groups to declare the structure a memorial to the victims of the Bosnian genocide of the 1990s.

He describes the questions regarding antagonism towards architecture as a peculiar concern of architectural historians, or those invested in the memorialization of architecture as a demonstration of enhanced cultural and political value. Destroying architectural works, as opposed to commercial, industrial or vernacular examples, is deemed to be more effective as a form of enhanced antagonism towards enemies. Though it is not clear at all that 'architecture' should be limited to examples of historical provenance, as opposed to those considered modern, Herscher's point is that these forms of attack are directed at whatever conception of collective memory might unite a community. Destroying significant forms within a built environment destroys the memory of that place for those who have an emotional attachment, which begs the question – What is more important, the building or the memory? This entails a further category, building on the previous. Theoretically, the targets of war/conflict and the demonstrations of resistance might suggest:

> 5. They are the representative forms of a constructed memory of violence that exists independent of any specific forms but require some chain of embodiment in order to validate their importance (Omarska).

Ultimately, for Herscher, the alternate approach is to create counter-memorials, even if just by reappropriation, for those groups without the access to the resources and signifying practices of dominant cultures, such as the Omarska example. Inherently, though, Herscher is agreeing with the general priority of memory as the principle effect of the consequences of war, rather than questioning whether conflict and antagonism is specifically the preserve of architecture, and is intractably embodied in those structures. So we have a further proposition to consider:

> 6. There are potential forms that represent alternate, non-dominant memories that have no recourse to a dominant narrative yet strive to exist. Potentially these forms have been destroyed but are valid loci of resistance. Inherently, there is no specific architectural characteristic that can define them (every non-architectural destruction).

Considering this, we can see that the issue of how war/conflict targets architecture can be even more removed from the architectural qualities of the contested work. Where the previous examples constituted targets because of their authentic identity, the opportunity exists for both resistance (memorializing) and destruction (de-memorializing) even if the process of resistance is applied after the fact, as with the Omarska example. Yet there remains the issue that, clearly, significant architecture represents the most effective target since it represents a value system to be confronted and destroyed, or preserved.

Contrastingly, in Robert Bevan's *The Destruction of Memory: Architecture at War* (2016), the intention is to speak broadly on the issue of architectural destruction as a consequence of conflict, though Bevan also draws heavily on his knowledge of the Balkan conflict(s) of the 1990s. Like Herscher, the significance of the presence and absence of architectural works as signifiers of conflict is paramount. Unlike Herscher, Bevan concentrates on the value of reconstruction efforts in which architectural works deemed culturally and politically significant are re-built in order to provide redress to the damaged community. Inevitably, whatever the opinion may be on the authenticity of these reconstructions, the core question turns on the fact that architecture is constantly engaged with the memory of violence. This creates a different type of agency for violence and the targets created in order to harm an opponent, whether through nation states against each other, civil conflicts that are intra-state or through terrorist acts, either as ad hoc groups or as covert expressions of international hostilities.

Looking at the effect on architecture, and comparing the difference between nation state conflicts and those enacted by terrorist groups or individuals, the imbalance in power and the consequences of action are clearly different. Where nation state conflict is, perversely, part of a larger geopolitical plan to constructively alter the ideological and economic behaviour of the antagonists, the consequences of the gestural effects of ad hoc terrorism are largely unmanaged (by the terrorists). Neither the Al-Quaeda operatives attacking New York and Washington, nor even Timothy McVeigh in Oklahoma, or the rioters in Washington on 6 January 2021 had any effective plan for what a future architectural consequence of their actions might be.

So, to summarize, reviewing the purpose of architecture in the cultural economies of conflict reveals the symbolic importance of iconic architectural works, but also sometimes the indifference to the architectural qualities of the targets. In responding to attacks on architecture, the potential for cultural trauma in the selective targeting of works concentrates on the mnemonic value of the built form and the lost investment of cultural sophistication required to produce the work in the first instance. Efforts to redress this loss can vary from reconstruction, retention as a ruin or indifference to the event and an effort to erase the conflict's visual legacy. Depending on the larger agenda, or lack thereof, of the combatants, efforts are made to consider the question of where memory is actually located. Finally, as a kind of minor memorialization, like a minor literature, groups without the resources to finance large-scale reconstruction or remembrance projects retain the ability to selectively designate sites for memorialization, just as ad hoc terrorist individuals and groups select sites for antagonistic gestures.

How is this architectural?
Is the consequence of war the need to rebuild, and to do so in as faithful a recreation of collective memory as possible, or to allow the ruins to persist as monuments to an indexical period in which the reality of conflict and the deliberate targeting of buildings has occurred, or is it a third form, drawing on both the persistence and destruction of elements?

The obvious initial response to the intersection of architecture and militarized conflict is the project for reconstruction, rebuilding what was lost. Similarly, the memorialization of the event(s) through the preservation of ruins constitutes a form of constructive (in)action, such as the preservation of the Kaiser Wilhelm Church in Berlin. A more contested response may be the creation of building forms that attempt to represent and memorialize the event through a new-build project such as Kenzo Tange's Hiroshima National Peace Memorial Hall (1955) and indeed the large array of memorials within the Hiroshima Peace Park itself.

More provocatively, if we are considering how individual architectural responses might occur, there is scope for considering, and mirroring, the strategic impulses of ad hoc destruction convolved with terrorism. The inverse of this would be the construction of memorializing projects that were strategic, de-institutionalized and of a limited half-life – but always architectural. Like the impromptu grass-roots memorials of road-crash victims or of tragic events, the impromptu memorial can arise as a response to personal and collective loss, and the need to create a material form that endures for the life of memory. What is different in the trajectory of architectural thinking and meaning-making is the need to interpose an architectural form at these sites, particularly those that are different in origin to accidental death, but require the full capacity of architecture to create something tangible.

Proposition: Everywhere monuments
If architecture is the vehicle for collective memory, either as a cenotaph that contains no evidence of the originary transgression, or a tomb that encapsulates the material remains of the subject of memory, what if we were to memorialize everything? If every significant conflict scenario generated a memorial of some sort, what is the consequence?

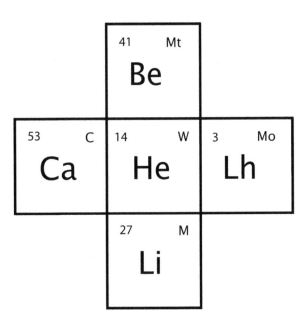

Rebus 14

War

Proposition 14: Healing

> The new spaces of habitation constructed on the existential remnants of war and natural disaster do not celebrate the destruction of an established order, nor do they symbolize or commemorate it. Rather they accept with a certain pride what has been suffered and lost, but also what has been gained.
> (Lebbeus Woods, *Radical Reconstruction*, 1997: 15)

Radical Reconstruction (1997), by Lebbeus Woods, is a significant text for the last 30 years of architectural theory. While there have been many specifically architectural books and articles that have looked at the consequences of military destruction, analyses of the logistical and human toll of conflict, it is rare to find an architectural text that addresses the issue of how to design in the post-conflict scenario. Woods had previously addressed the issue of violence generally in his work on the North and South Korea Demilitarized Zone in his project *Terra Nova DMZ* (1990), reconfiguring the highly dangerous and contested area as a continual architectural structure that would provide a form of physical détente between the opposing combatants. The drawings he created, in keeping with his style of highly evocative renderings for fictional scenarios, visualized a liminal zone in which the agency of architecture would find a way to redefine the opposing forces as co-inhabitants of a complex and spatially rich structure. This form of architecture-as-interregnum provided (literal) shelter to the idea that the permanent balance of hostilities might express itself differently. Rather than be aligned as a direct force–counterforce balance, Woods designed a place in which the vectors of their mutual aim would now be offset and ricochet off the shield-like roofs and thus disperse and be rendered harmless.

First proposed by Woods as a thematic methodology intended to investigate the potential for conflict environments to change and develop *Radical Reconstruction* documents a curious form of state reconstruction, in which the resources of an enlightened state are directed at the creation of architectural projects that address and heal certain consequences of the extreme violence of war or natural disaster. It interposes itself, fantastically, into a recuperation project that demonstrates hope while allowing the trauma to persist. As such, it is an opposite of Mies's (and Hegel's) sublation and *Aufhebung* since there is only a minimal material effort to 'clean up' the disaster of war, or more particularly the technology of entropy that war promotes.

Materially, war is the final entropic purpose for architecture of certain oppositional ideologies: ethnic group vs. ethnic group, technology vs. nature, and continuity vs. catastrophic change. The question is: Is war a form of accelerated ruination, or a staging post in the overcoming of certain morphologies that have been exhausted? Woods's drawings take the real-world conflict of Sarajevo, and the 'natural' disasters both real (Havana) and imagined (San Francisco), and find ways to propose a form that is entirely untethered to instrumental limits. As the drawings are so intensely complex, and the forms so fantastically unprogrammed, the viewer is left to imagine how they might be inhabited. Interestingly also, considering the complexity of the images, the challenge exists to reconstruct the drawing process itself and identify the moments at which Woods departs from conventional draughtsmanship and allows the mark of the pencil to break from the original grid, only then to be re-organized according to a growth pattern that is entirely self-referential. For Woods, this is the architectural moment of healing, as the scar tissue of broken structures close over to create forms that hybridize conflict and order.

For Woods, the process of reconstruction after conflict or disaster does not require the establishment of a *terra nullius*, or a process of cleansing and suppression, it requires the re-tracing of the effects and the hyper-stimulation of its wounds. Destruction, for Woods, is the precursor to creative re-alignment of both the forces of ideological ambition and of the encounter with the chaotic effects of nature. Where the former is partisan and selective in its choice of vulnerabilities, the latter (storms in Havana, earthquakes in San Francisco) entails the balancing of the natural environment with the complex chain of resistances that cities create to remain stable. In particular, when considering the process of destruction, the consequences of military conflict are intended to be instantaneous, optimized and accretional. Once a target is selected, there is an optimized point at which further destruction is logistically pointless and the targeting process moves on.

It is this distinction in Woods's subject matter, the difference between human conflict that is selective and the abstract volume of forces applied by nature that tells us the most about the critical management of post-conflict reconstruction. Woods (almost) avoids the naturalistic fallacy of attributing to environmental conditions the qualities of an abstract and impartial force outside of moral boundaries in contrast to the mapping of ballistic vectors that constitute the moments of destruction via human conflict.

How is this architectural?
The mapping of destruction and the reverse engineering of the logistics of aggression and defence in conflict can allow us to see more clearly the effects on the original

state of a location. In understanding the vectors of sight lines, ballistic trajectories, explosive effects and material resistance, a clearer understanding can be made of the 'fog' of a violent event. The work of Forensic Architecture, a UK-based research group headed by Eyal Weizman, has subsequently developed this capacity as an instrument of social justice and accountability in conflicts (usually) between state actors and populations. While the work of Forensic Architecture does not stray into speculation regarding the appropriate reconstruction of these sites, post event, they provide clear and unambiguous data supporting an objective definition of the circumstances. In effect, their work creates a site for both the administration of justice and the redemption of the event(s).

So while Woods has already charted out a considerable body of formal experimentation based on the political decision to locate his speculative work in contested and 'damaged' locations, the opportunity exists to build on the increasingly precise reconstruction of sites based on Forensic Architecture's work.

Proposition: Oh what a(n) (un)lovely war
Take an analysis of a site of conflict and reconstruct it architecturally. Ask if the war, and the exhaustion of the material, serves a purpose other than the memory of loss. Ask if the design of a remediated site even *should* be (re)constructed. Ask whether justice can be served through architecture?

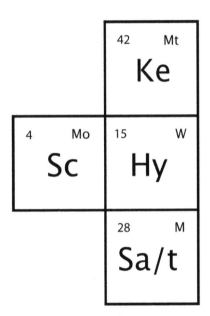

Rebus 15

War

Proposition 15: Hygiene

What is the constructive relationship, if it can be said to exist, between architecture and conflict? Should there be any sort of relationship, or should there be a clear and distinct distance between the general category of conflict and the process of architectural design? The reality of safety concerns within contested urban environments means that security remains a core issue, not simply as a precaution against theft or unlawful trespass, but in the event of organized events that occupy parts of a city, or building, to promote and publicize an ideological point of view. The Occupy movement of 2011 set out to emulate examples of civilian protest that had been occurring in other parts of the world, notably the political unrest associated with the Arab Spring of the early 2010s.

However, instead of defining a specific change in political representation and governance, the Occupy movement generally was concerned with the evidence of income disparity between developed and developing nations and, importantly, inequities that existed within nation states. Wall Street, the iconic centre of the New York financial district was chosen as the symbolic location for a protest regarding ownership of wealth, wealth redistribution and the rights to voice opinions on how government should serve the greater populace and not corporate interests. The Occupy Wall Street (OWS) movement spawned a legion of similar protests across most of the developed world and, for a period, drew attention to the need for more equitable governance of financial entities. Coming a few years after the catastrophic economic events of the 2008 Financial Crisis, the sense that the agents of that series of events and its consequences had not been fully brought to account was palpable. The Wall Street version of the movement lasted some months before it was finally moved on in November 2011 after complaints by neighbouring residents and the park owners regarding sanitation and the behaviour of protesters. However by then, the effect of the protest had been made and, arguably, the limit of public consciousness of the protestor's arguments had been saturated.

Importantly, for the OWS, a space within the financial district and close to Wall Street was crucial for the purposes of media visibility. A local park, Zuccotti Park, which had been established as a POPS (Privately Owned Public Space), is a legacy of concessions regarding building heights and developmental envelopes in New York city planning. The park is owned and maintained by a private entity on the condition that it remains open to the public; however, the design of the park and the degree to which 'openness' is allowed were contested by the OWS movement. Bolton et al. (2013) speak of the transformation of common ground to enclosures that historically allowed the public spaces of New York to be privatized, narrating their first experience of seeing the OWS encampment grow over the months of its existence. As many commentators have suggested, including Louise Rice, these were essentially transgressive acts that tested the resolve of conventional procedures for maintaining and perpetuating ownership relationships of public space within the city.

One of the most important subtleties of this movement is that the goals were generally similar in terms of a radical acknowledgement of citizen rights to express political opinion; however, the management of the different locations was tied to complex, individual local practices of land tenure, civil disobedience law and general social tolerance of disruptive behaviour. The Occupy Movement encountered different managerial challenges and public tolerance for the presence in New York than it did in Madrid or Sydney or London. The consequences of these events were particularly felt within architectural communities since, for some, it demonstrated an active and vibrant ad hoc attitude to constructing a free, living community in the heart of major urban centres where this type of behaviour was discouraged. Architects looked at the instant community structures and realized that they had both nothing to offer in the immediate logistics of mobilizing a protest, and everything to offer in terms of reading the importance of allowing transgressive events to be part of a healthy and functioning democracy.

The conflict contained within this example is not simply one of land ownership or social barriers to movement, it is the necessity of taking the smooth spaces of urban capital and allowing for saturnalian behaviour. It was, once again, a reminder of the value of public space as the window onto the political concerns of a populace and the significant symbolic value of acting within public space.

Similarly, but with a somewhat more disruptive and threatening outcome, the events of 6 January 2021 in Washington in which the supporters of Donald Trump broke into and briefly occupied the Capitol Building in Washington show that the actions of public transgression can be expressed across the political spectrum, and with far less emancipatory aims than the Occupy movement.

How is this architectural?
If we are to consider the opportunity of engaging with these ideas in terms of architectural design, the question arises as to what purpose could the expensive and

complicated process of making architecture with conventional, durable outcomes lend to movements that are essentially transitory? Bernard Tschumi famously considered these questions when he wrote *Architecture and Transgression* in 1976 (Tschumi 1994). For him, the core issue with transgression was its relationship towards a recognition of how architecture creates a level of instrumentalized eroticism. The emergence of sensuality and decay in the consideration of the architectural, everything that undoes the organizational rigour of a project, is subject to the potential for the aesthetic experience – from delight to disgust. What Tschumi considered elsewhere in *Architecture and Disjunction* (1994), but not in his discussion of transgression, was the constant politicization of space. Bringing these together, we can set out some key questions:

> 1. What is the nature of transgression in architecture? If it is determined largely by rule-based design behaviour how can the various instruments be meaningfully transgressed?
> 2. Is design transgression concerned with taste, client identity, stakeholder interests, longevity, meaning?
> 3. Focusing on the issues of the Occupy movement and transgressive political behaviour in public space, do architects attempt to 'design' these *ad hoc* spaces or create forms of social visibility for these events?
> 4. Can architecture create a situation in which social conflict is mediated and, potentially, violence is avoided?

Proposition: Preserving the impermanent
What is the architecture of occupation? Should it be permanent? At what point does it transform from a politics of liberation to one of dominance? Can, and should, you engineer sufficient *ad hoc* transformations for the architecture to be aestheticized? What are the rules?

5: Language

This section covers some preliminary questions regarding the role of language, and linguistic conventions, in understanding architecture. The section is intended to introduce a number of distinctions in how language functions as both the medium for understanding architecture, as well as being a complex set of tools for proposing forms of architectural design methodology. It is simple enough to understand how language sets the limits of interpretation of architecture – you can only say what your language is grammatically capable of expressing. This, of course, allows for a vast and finely grained set of propositions about architecture but it is important to recognize at the outset that the boundaries between sense and nonsense must be acknowledged. We will be discussing the question of language-as-a-limit later in the chapters on Wittgenstein and the *Tractatus* but for now it is enough to introduce the idea that language (and speech) has technical and performative dimensions that help architecture speak of itself.

The first chapter examines the general proposition that architecture is configured in a similar matter to grammar. The idea rests on the proposition that the complex, interleaved formal design decisions in architecture obey a situational role in much the same way that sequences of words do within a grammatically sensible sentence. This type of formalist grammar in architecture has a long history and emerges from the initial encounters between architecture as a practice and the development of texts on architecture that attempt to document and explain its value. From Alberti's *De re aedificatoria*, to Serlio's *Sette Libri d'Architettura* through to Peter Eisenman and Greg Lynn's formalist propositions, there have been numerous versions of architectural theories that catalogue, apply hierarchies and enunciate potential forms of architecture on a linguistic model. Ultimately by distinguishing between locutionary, illocutionary and perlocutionary speech acts, there is the opportunity for some clarity in examining the architecture/language nexus.

In the second chapter, the contemporary phenomenon of object-oriented ontology (OOO) examines a consequence of linguistic theories of form, in particular those that privilege the interests of the speaking and enunciating subject. The chapter argues that, if language is the universal medium of analysis, who is speaking and how they are expressing a privileged interest become important. OOO argues the counter-intuitive position that we share the capacity for being with all other entities in the world. While there are a number of technical questions within philosophy that might challenge this position, it is its application to architecture that interests us. A major proponent of OOO is Graham Harman and, as part of his explanation of its value, he employs the terms *undermining, overmining* and *duomining*. These terms refer to species of attention to an aesthetic experience and, if nothing else, encourage us to continually consider an architectural aesthetic experience as a flat form of engagement. 'Flatness' in this sense means an aesthetic experience that does not consider hierarchies of importance, which is in complete contradiction to the architectural texts mentioned earlier.

Finally, the third chapter explores the homonymic function of language that the previous chapter explores. 'Flat out' for example is a phrase that comes from vernacular language, but also has the capacity to describe an aesthetic experience of architecture that tests our capacity for describing what we experience. This is where the limits of language begin to occur, or at the very least, where we begin to think more creatively about how the mutuality of language and expression feed each other.

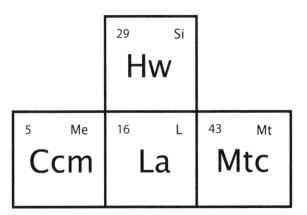

Rebus 16

Language

Proposition 16: Language

Speaking of the work of Carlo Scarpa, Marco Frascari says the following:

> In his architectural objects the *techné* of the *logos*, the construing, becomes the manner of production of signs that are details. The *logos* of the *techné*, the constructing, which results from the expression of Veneto craftsmanship, becomes the dialectical counterpart in the generation of the details as signs.
> (Frascari 1983: n.pag.)

Frascari's general intention in this famous essay is to demonstrate the relationship between the process of drawing, and the determining of details within architectural design and construction, specifically in the work of Carlo Scarpa. He conflates, deliberately, constructing and construing as cognate gestures within the design process to argue that there is an architecture *parlante*, a speaking architecture that communicates whatever it is that architecture can communicate.

The relationship between architecture and language is complex and there are a number of different theoretical iterations, based on an isomorphic similarity, between the complex employment of iterative components in architecture, its 'grammar' and the conventional understanding of the syntax and grammar of written and spoken language as it is organically employed. So, if written and spoken speech acts are the standard form of communicative behaviour, how is architecture some form of second-order discourse that shares aspects of communication – particularly with reference to semantic issues of buildings as a whole and with their component parts? That is, what does a building 'mean' or communicate overall, and in what ways do the component parts of a building, columns, panels and details also communicate a form of 'meaning'?

However, before discussing the potential relationships, it is worth clarifying a few core structural aspects of language in the first place before we consider architectural questions. Grammar, and the organizational conventions within it (syntax), is different from semantics, the imputed 'meaning' of locutionary acts (speech and writing). The former describes the structure while the latter debates the complex outcomes, the reception and effects, of the original communicative act.

The proposition that architecture shares a form of structural similarity with language was articulated clearly by Peter Eisenman in his reading of Noam Chomsky's academic work on deep structure (Patin 1993). The notion that there was a medium of communication, language, that was effective in communicating something without necessarily requiring it to have a 'meaning' appealed to Eisenman as an acknowledgement that the complex formal aspects of architecture, its repetition of elements, rhythms of solid and void and tectonic complexity were organically similar to the relationship between sounds, words, grammar and performance in language.

Allied to this ambition was that the work was inherently 'logical' in its employment of patterns of solid, void and three-dimensionality but with the difference that there was no necessary meaning inherent in an architectural 'locution'. Employing a series of analogies to Chomsky's work, *Syntactic Structures* (1957), Eisenman employed a strictly structuralist and formalist view that argued that there are component elements of architectural understanding that exist prior to their employment in historical and cultural settings. In many respects, Eisenman's position was an extension of the general modernist tendency towards abstraction and the elimination of any idiosyncratic cultural details.

Most particularly, for Eisenman, it was an attempt to create an architecture that was both autonomous in its conception and development and divorced from any expectations of semantic legibility. It was, as Thomas Patin noted, deliberately opaque to interpretation since *that* form of analysis insisted on an idea of representational transparency. Put simply, the early House projects of Eisenman were in no way representations of a 'house'.

Further, Eisenman has a coincident interest in issues of sense and reference, or more specifically the argument that attributable meaning is disengaged from both the intentions of the author/architect (intentionality) and from the material form of the work (essentiality). If we interrogate the relationship towards language further, the connection to Chomsky was of limited use inasmuch as Eisenman ultimately referred to Chomsky's description of 'deep structure' in the phonetic construction of sounds, or more simply, words (and language) are the way they are because of inherent physiological characteristics of our mouths and sound-making capabilities. For Eisenman he realized that this allusion to Chomsky became, unavoidably, a kind of anthropological effect of his idea of the term 'deep structure'.

A more effective method of looking at the issues that Eisenman raises, without committing to the bias that his architecture was intended to be an 'expression' of his intentions, or of an intentionally managed meaningful encounter for clients and users, is to consider the language analysis of J. L. Austin. Austin distinguishes between locutionary, illocutionary and perlocutionary acts, in which he describes the purpose and effect of speech acts (language). The test of this comparison will be the degree to which we can continue to assert a structural and analogous comparison between language and architecture.

As Austin points out (Austin 1962, 1975), language has a sophistication in its application which allows us to create quite complex assertions regarding not only the facts of the world but also questions, requests, oaths, pronouncements, etc. that refer not only to the present tense but also the subtle transformations of tense that (some) languages permit. It would be distracting in the context of this chapter to discuss the purpose of tense-based architectural propositions, but it suffices to say that there remains work to be done in considering the relationship between time-based (tense) propositions in architecture that employ temporality to situate themselves in discourse.

For our purposes, we can define the difference between Austin's speech acts as follows: locutionary acts are the actual utterance, illocutionary acts are the effect of the original utterance and perlocutionary acts are the (expected) consequences of the original utterance. For the locutionary utterance 'Perforate this', the expectation (illocutionary effect) is that the thing will be perforated, and the subsequent perforation is the intended (perlocutionary) outcome. So, in this instance, design commands are potentially isomorphically organized according to the linguistic paradigm that Austin describes.

How is this architectural?
Given Eisenman's interest in this subject matter, the most obvious method for investigating the potential for considering architecture linguistically could stem from an examination of his projects, particularly the eleven houses (House I–House XI) that Eisenman designed and, in some cases, built. These works set a standard for following the formalist investigations of pattern making in design, divorced from questions of programmatic use, or even naming conventions. Eisenman is not the sole individual to be interested in the separation of design intent from the outcome, Christopher Alexander et al.'s *A Pattern Language* (1977) and subsequent attempts to formalize the employment of parametric

design commands equally stress an architectural formalism that seeks to be autonomous and self-referential.

Self-referentiality and an obsession with formalist transformations is one avenue for considering the proposition that architecture is linguistically formed and that the patterns of formal transformations it employs constitute communicative 'acts'. A locutionary act in architecture, then, is the presentation of formal complexity that may be interrogated for meaning – much as we might hear and comprehend the auditory sounds of speech, or the graphic signs of writing, it is the 'scene' of design in which intention is set in motion and some consequence takes place. It is possible to think of this state as similar to the infinitive in language, 'to design', or 'to design that' is the core locutionary disposition.

The illocutionary consequence is the material presentation of the locutionary acts as material effects, either as drawings, models, built structures, etc. Finally, the perlocutionary effect of these, which are not necessarily causally related, is the expectation that a formal, architectural structure can be 'read' or 'understood' to entail some enhanced meaning other than its simple presence. So, we ask ourselves, what does a work of architecture communicate other than itself? Do differing syntactic variations in architectural form constitute different locutionary acts? To complete this short summary and proceed to a proposition about how this might be activated architecturally, we need to refer to the distinction between sense and reference.

The classic modernist dilemma, a consequence of the abstraction and elimination of historical referents, is the question of what contemporary architecture refers to, if it refers or 'means' anything at all other than its indexical, historical reality. If we assume that forms of architectural expression have some type of referential notoriety, we recognize a column *as* a column, then there is some form of identification between the sense of the visual experience and what it might plausibly refer to. This relationship has been analyzed at some length by discussions related to the semiotics of architecture, but we can see that if something *appears* to have meaning, what that meaning *is* are not ineluctably tied together.

So for our discussion of language, and in response to Frascari's inversion of *techné* and *logos*, we can see that the *techné* he refers to involves the triad of locutionary act (the intention to communicate architecturally), the illocutionary act (the sketches of Scarpa) which have 'sense' and the perlocutionary effect which is the divination that the drawings refer to potential actions, if only to further interrogate the array of illocutionary images on the sheet. Holistically, Frascari is suggesting that the drawing is a propositional act that behaves in the same manner as a language (*logos*).

Proposition
The Architect's Tombstone
What are the last words of the architect? What do they wish to communicate to some other party that may wish to hear and see their final intentions? Are they drawings, words, models or structures? What do they command?

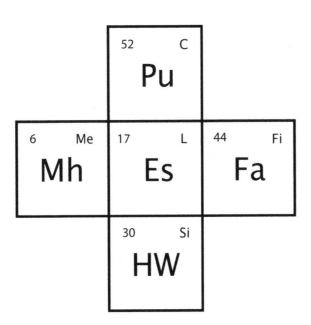

Rebus 17

Language

Proposition 17: Ecological Symbiosis

One of the consistent methods that architectural culture has employed to find relevance within changing domains of critical knowledge has centred on the rubrics of content and methodology, what do we know and how do we know it. It shares this structural form with knowledge domains that define aspects of human experience and construct models of organization and behaviour that are coherent within that domain. Architecture is similar to, for example, anthropology in the way it deals with social structures that have consistent and defined forms, assumes that people act rationally and with both self-interested and altruistic goals, etc. The question is then, for architecture, how can it better undertake its role of environment-shaping with the benefit of the knowledge acquired from parallel disciplines? Similar approaches could be pursued for many different domains, including political science, sociology, philosophical aesthetics, psychology, etc. all of which have sufficient family resemblances to the architectural project to be relevant members of the complex Venn diagram of shared interests.

Generally, the significant similarities between architectural theory and other methodologies for defining and acting upon the world have followed the route of reviewing how architectural theoretical praxis understands the defining characteristics of the discipline, and then looks to alternate domains of investigation to see if there are correspondences in terms of subject matter (what is being looked at) and methodology (how is the process of scrutiny defined, and what counts as evidence) are fulfilled. And while some of these relationships have been foundational in the emergence of architecture as a critical discipline, questions of engineering, construction, theology, and representation are a few, and there are novel areas that have structural complexities that add to the traditional categories. The most important of these areas, in recent decades, has concerned the practice and consequences of digital modelling of architecture and the symbiotic relationship between the technical apparatus of digital modelling and documentation, and through this the process of creating an appropriate and coherent architectural design.

There is a current school of thought in architectural discourse that currently thrives within the major 'thought-leading' schools of architecture within the United States, the United Kingdom and the European Union and other satellites, a conversation focused on a close coherence between current synthetic digital capacities and a form of philosophy called object-orientated ontology (OOO). Further, as a form of engagement with this field, persons such as Mark Foster Gage (2015) have developed a reputation for their 'return' to aesthetics as a relevant area of interest for architectural theory. OOO, to summarize, expresses the idea that the objects of the world have a reality that exists independently of human perception, the Kantian noumena/phenomena relationship; however, it differs from Kant in that it (OOO) insists that there is a vast, but finite, number of realities that human experience cannot perceive. If we insist on the intuitive reality that human perception is more interesting than that of a road sign, there is, it is suggested, an anthropomorphic bias that disallows us to glimpse the complexities of inter-object relations. While there is considerable commentary that can be made regarding the legitimacy of this approach, when we consider its employment in architecture certain comments can be made.

The principle coherence, for architecture, is the proposition that all objects in the world act in a tool-like manner towards each other, enacting relationships that are specific to their capacities and situation (the locutionary and illocutionary acts of the previous chapter). Thus, all the minutiae of componentry that architecture employs (or is constructed from) have a palpable and interrelated reality because of their complex agency between each other. For a discipline such as architecture, but we can include others such as musical performance, it is the combined effect of all of the parts that can be mindfully considered even though we are not privy to all of these relations given the limits of human perception. The componentry of musical instruments, the biology of performers and audience, and the environmental effects of locations similarly constitute an immensely complex construction of effects that we call a musical performance. Moreover, here architecture is a little different; the musical performance has an indexical life limited to, but not solely defined by, the performance.

For OOO, and for its principal proponent Graham Harman (Harman 2020), the tool-like characteristics of objects should not be limited just to entities that have a material reality such as architecture, and clarinets, but also to the processes of an organization that helps position the componentry of reality. So digital software that can be employed to design a building, or illustrate a cartoon character, is equally part of the ecology of interdependence between tool-effects. The ambivalence with which current proponents of parametric and non-standard architecture determine appropriate form speaks to the reality that this ecology could equally give life to a variety of equally viable alternate outcomes, dependent on agencies within the tool-environment of form-making.

This is an important point, and one that has generally had little scrutiny perhaps for fear of being considered reactionary. Stating that the parametric variations have equal and indistinct variability, apart from some cosmetic variations, does not merely acknowledge the arbitrariness of the design process but also asserts that the infinite array of formal alternatives generated by iterative formal algorithms has equal and indistinguishable claims to scrutiny. This is flexibility in design approach at best and cynical indifference at worst. It is also the point at which the attractiveness of OOO begins to make sense. Harman's insistence on a 'flat' ontology that seeks to remove the role of human-centred attention in determining the ontic qualities of the world as being 'for us' coheres with the architectural interest in system-based generative approaches. For Gage, and others in this conversation, these are 'design' methodologies that emulate the complexity of the world, without requiring the speculative activities and selective decision matrix of the designer. In the discussion regarding form vs. matter in architecture, and the revival of Aristotle's idea of hylomorphism by Manual DeLanda, generative systems express the inherent tendencies within complex systems to attain form, much as a soap bubble expresses the interaction of surface viscosity and tension, air pressure and the chemical make-up of soap.

Gage, in developing a version of OOO that suits his own role as an academic and practitioner, has given particular emphasis on the experience of the 'aesthetic' as a way of giving substance to the collision between the objects of the world and our need to organize them in some explanatory schema. For Gage, the enactment of this process is through understanding the experience of the aesthetic which, for him, is the commonplace observation that all phenomenal encounters with the world entail some type of complex synaesthetic experience. Arguably his position is little different to Kant's 'Analytic of the Beautiful' in *The Critique of Judgement* (1790), in particular the argument regarding purposiveness, but for Gage and the proponents of OOO, there is something particularly compelling in rediscovering the aesthetic attitude. Borrowing terms from Harman, he calls the experience of the world overmining, undermining and duomining, three terms original to OOO which help them to establish the uniqueness of their approach.

Overmining is the term for considering objects to be merely representatives of other, more complex systems of organization that the object expresses through its existence, for example, a tree is the product of an interlocked set of environmental and biological systems that express themselves through the object that is 'the tree'. Undermining is the converse opinion that objects are fundamentally just collections of discrete components that constitute the 'essential' aspects of the object, the tree is the collection of all the biological components, the object *qualia* such as branches, leaves, trunk, and bark that go to make up the collective entity that is a tree. Duomining, much like Goldilocks's 'just right' porridge, is the median position that, using Harman's Heideggerian phraseology, indicates how the complex componentry of things make themselves known, or remain hidden, because of the species of our attention. The point, for Gage, is to recognize this complexity and resist hasty essentialist, or simple linguistic/semantic definitions.

How is this architectural?
Apart from the use of OOO by Gage, the general interest in the ontology of objects potentially asks architects to consider the balance of discrete forms within the complex array of objects that is architecture, including the choreography of objects that constitute the furnishings, instruments, collections, etc. that architecture provides a location. Considering the employment of 'decorative' elements within the fabric of a building asks us to consider them as things-in-themselves (Kant's *ding-an-sich*), as it did for Riegl previously. For example, one of the challenges of reading the work of Shin Takamatsu, to date, has been the question of how and why the metal-fetishist elements of his work could be attributed to some general theory of architecture. Arguably this is where the effect of considering these parts as indivisible aspects of the 'architecture' means that they occupy a 'not-yet' status in terms of analysis and semiotic explanation, and perhaps a 'not ever' status. OOO has brought attention to the complexity of aesthetic experience and challenged the undermining aspects of system theory in architecture, whether it has escaped Fredric Jameson's 'prison house' of language is another matter.

Proposition: Harman's garage
A garage is a facility that contains a manifold array of tools for the purpose of, historically, fixing and servicing motor vehicles. It also has a virtual relationship to the further manifold of vehicles and other objects for which the tools have a potential engagement. What if these tools are the client(s)?

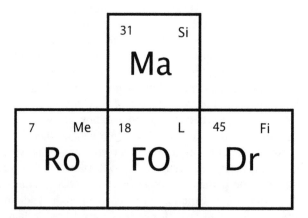

Rebus 18

Language

Proposition 18: Flat Out

The use of language to drive ideas in architectural thinking can sometimes turn on various homonymic coincidences: site/sight, interior/interiority and the expanded and multiple meanings of terms such as sense/reference. An analysis of idiomatic terms, when employed in architecture, indicates that they come to signify certain complexities in intention and effect, such as Fin d'Ou T Hou S (1983) by Eisenman, Villa Malcontenta (1558–60) by Palladio, Soft and Hairy House (1992–94) by Ushida Findlay and The Killing Moon (1988) by Shin Takamatsu. The difference between a descriptive name and the employment of a language form that is performatively ambiguous is that the idiomatic expression is intended to describe a greater boundary of possible meanings and motivations than simple descriptive terms might allow.

Further, there is considerable opportunity for this wordplay to return to the enunciating subject and make them question what it is they are saying. Idiomatic speech generally employs these types of terms in order to allow the speaker to cognitively describe certain circumstances without the need for complex and specific descriptive passages, permitting the speaker to remain on the track of their original narrative without requiring extended qualifications, at least in the first instance before responsion. What appears in the mouth, the *amuse bouche* in French cuisine, (more interesting than the English term, appetiser), carries with it the *Not I* (1973) of Samuel Beckett. Beckett's play is a highly focused enactment of the speaking subject wrestling with the limits of language to convey a sense of urgency and discomfort that the playwright saw within the character.

As with all of Beckett's work, it is incredibly specific in what it wants to convey but very much abstract in the economy with which this is achieved. The result is that speech becomes an incredibly plastic form of communication, shifting from unadorned description to idiomatic phrases that betray the class, gender and worldview of the speaking subject. In *Not I*, this is an old woman narrating fragments of, possibly, her own memories but also describing a deep and indescribable *horror vacui* that the centre of human experience is empty. When performed, the mouth of the female actor is isolated within a black costume, lit by a single spotlight, and the words are rapidly expressed to avoid them being 'acted' in any sense. Language and the muscularity of the speaking individual carry the play in its entirety as there are no stage directions to speak of and no other characters than a shadowy figure that silently stands to one side.

It is a play at the limits of narrative language, presenting the curiosity of an actor who shares the same space as the audience, but who is communicating (if it is communicating) an inner monologue that is more akin to the scramble of obsessive private thoughts than a critical discussion. And yet it works. It shows us that language, and in particular idiomatic language, allows us to conjure up the most absurd coincidences of sound and image and yet still be able to find sense within it.

In Australia, the term 'flat out', for example, refers to the use of maximum speed and effort to accomplish something, or to travel at a maximum speed. So, in some small part in the Australian vernacular unconscious, the idea of working at a maximum is also associated with motor racing, or at a pinch for horse racing. But why 'flat', and why 'out'? It is not clear why this conjunction has come together to illustrate the unambiguous idea of maximal effort. It is similar to the expression 'flat chat' which means the same thing, is specifically Australian but is not, to my knowledge, shared in other English language cultures. So, while the idiomatic term 'Flat Out' can refer to speed, it also alludes to extreme compression, to the extremity of effort in achieving a goal and the limit of a capacity being reached. To be 'flat' is to have no, or negligible, value in the third dimension and for this to be reached as a limit of potential. 'Flat out' is thus the expression of the velocity with which this state is reached.

How is this architectural?
There are both simple and complex pathways towards how we can approach the ambiguities of idiomatic expressions within architecture. The simple path is to merely illustrate the referential components of the phrase and point to their existence within the project description. Libeskind's 'Between the Lines' descriptor for the original project of the Extension to the Berlin Museum (Libeskind 1990), literally referred to a design strategy that sought to find content in the space between the processes of mapping and the cognate ideas of intellectual influences he was interested in pursuing. While the pattern of thinking that is described and discussed in texts on this project, in particular David Krell's analysis, is certainly not simple, the relationship between descriptor and project aims at clarifying, not complexifying, that relationship. Where the title seems to allude to a goal that is beyond everyday observation, it is in fact the simplest way of pointing to other intellectual depths that, ultimately, are more interesting than the project title.

In contrast, a complex path for engaging with idiomatic expression might, at first thought, deal with the relationship between idiomatic expression and self-conscious attempts to critically re-present aspects of architecture through popular culture. Just as idiomatic language is, generally, accessible to most members of a language group, so too are the iconic and ubiquitous forms of everyday architecture. Venturi, Scott Brown and Izenour's *Learning From Las Vegas* (1972) quite literally reproduces the flotsam and jetsam of commercial design while framing the process as a self-conscious interrogation of the vitality of everyday form-making, or at least that relevant to Las Vegas and the culture of commercial strip urbanity. The idiomatic expressions, for Venturi and Scott Brown, are the physical examples they distort and reproduce, requiring the viewer to simultaneously recognize both the original and the 'architectural' expression. As a practice, it suggests the constant formal quotation of the built environment is a kind of visual word-play.

Another path to the use of idiomatic language, more akin to the examples at the beginning of this chapter, lies in the granular investigation of the relationship between naming and seeing that descriptive language creates. More specifically, the exploration of the homonymic opportunities that these terms to create and describe certain design thema. In this respect, a project on the idea of Flat Out can be not only about the limits of form and space outlined above but also about minimum forms of accommodation and the flat-packing of space. As an attempt to emulate the concision and intensity of the Beckett process, the search for the discomfiting and idiosyncratic consequences of idiomatic language (is it really raining cats and dogs) can be both humorous and surreally terrifying.

Proposition: Kowalski's Flat Out Motel
The Kowalski's Flat Out Motel is an accommodation that exists towards a vanishing point. It is subject to the compressive forces of perspective and the need to approach it at maximum speed. It is, like Duchamp's *Bôite-en-valise*, a structure that is built for travel and, temporarily, as a standard stoppage.

6: Destruction

The chapters in this section deal with the idea of destructive forces within the process of thinking about architecture. In part, it is concerned with the material threat to architecture, its vulnerability to environmental threats, but the principal areas of concern are with those forms of thinking that threaten its stability as a body of knowledge. Because architecture is almost always a constructive process that creates material changes in the world, the converse position, an architecture that teeters towards destruction, could be thought of as an equal and inverse proposition.

In the first chapter, we deal with the idea of fire as an elemental aspect of architecture. It could have been some other alchemical state, but fire serves the purpose of bridging between the manufacturing process of steel and masonry and the subsequent resistance these materials offer to destruction through combustion. In a book on architectural theory, or at least the disposition to think about architecture, sections covering the elements, fire, air, earth and water, would make popular sense. However, the phenomenology of these states has been covered by many others so it serves no purpose to rehearse them here. Instead, the threat of destruction as an entropic state is examined to see how architecture might be engaged with its transformative properties.

The contrast to other conditions commences with an examination of the allegory of the cave in Plato. The philosophical purpose of the narrative turns on the problem of phenomenal experiences of reality. The chained children in the story represent certain types of encumbered thinking that can only be escaped once the prisoner understands the nature of their constraints. It is more, though, than a simple discussion of relative apperception when we consider the structure of the narrative itself. Clearly the cave and the geometry of its organization as a defined space, its architecture, govern the functionality of the allegory. By destroying this architecture, or thinking of its destruction, the problem of perception disappears.

The third and fourth chapters look further at the role of language, but this time reflect on the role of 'naming' as a gesture towards the stability of reality. To name something is to position it within the grammar of sense and more effectively allow it to become part of an explanatory or exploratory narrative. Using the examples of Don DeLillo's *The Names* (1982) and Luke Howard's *On the Modification of Clouds* (1832), we see how the fundamentally transitive and mutable aspects of our relationship to phenomena constantly destabilize our attempts to ground them in certainty. This is also a method for, after the fact, addressing elemental properties without wishing to cement them as archetypes. Ultimately the purpose of this discussion is that narratives of destruction, decay and transformation are as deeply architectural as those of constructive and accretional methodologies.

The final chapter rounds out the thema of destruction by taking another look at the transgressive works of Jean Jacques Lequeu. Lequeu's unclassifiable catalogue of images toy with the boundaries between taste and disgust, asking the viewer to wonder whether architecture can be independent of desire. In the context of this section, the final chapter asks whether transgressive desire can focus on those fetishized representations of the self that exists in the long and grotesque taxonomy of architectural details.

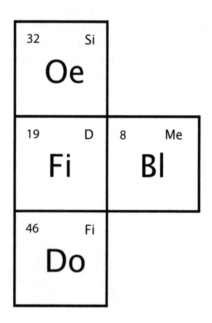

Rebus 19

Destruction

Proposition 19: Fire

One of the clear consequences of changes in the global climate has been the increased incidence of extreme weather events. Whether from anecdotal memory or from statistical certainty, the experience of changed weather patterns is currently a leitmotif of our news cycle. One of the most cataclysmic examples of this is the experience of large-scale forest and bush fires that occur regularly in the United States, Australia, South East Asia and Mediterranean countries as well as the Amazon Basin. The coincidence between wild landscapes and occupation that promises a form of symbiotic existence also comes with the constant existential threat that a major event may destroy the entirety of this cultural and physical ecosystem.

While the consequences of these events are clear in terms of land management, a parallel question can turn on how architecture might respond to these types of events. The most prudent methods revolve around prevention and survival strategies for people, animals and property. Combustion, as a form of accelerated chemical reaction, can occur in small (a match) or large (bushfire) configurations. It differs only in scale and the level of external control exercised upon it. It is also a form of entropic dispersion of energy that fundamentally changes the physical form of the material that fuels the process. So, architecture is both a subject of combustion and a form of resistance to its processes, either as a material that burns or one that contains, prevents and directs the process.

Serious management of the danger of fire should responsibly be a priority, but we can still speculate on the thematic richness of fire as a driver of architectural speculation. How can architecture work with the limits of this danger and profit from that proximity? We can consider it in four ways: fire as a purgative process in which extreme temperature tempers and forges a material experience; fire as a process and an event of disappearance and extinction; fire as a destructive agent to materials that are carriers of knowledge (a book, a building, a person), and; fire as a constant, indexical threat – a latency of the three above. In some senses, this engages with Immanuel Kant's four moments of the beautiful, where aesthetic judgement, in Kant's formulation, involves judgements of quality, quantity, relation and modality (Kant 1790, 1987).

While Kant is quite specific regarding the distinction between different modalities of judgment, the comparison to forms of engagement with fire can follow an instructive parallel path. The translation is not simple but is worth analyzing with some depth in order to see the opportunity for departing from normative solutions. Kant first distinguishes between aesthetic experiences that are sensorially pleasant or are valued because they demonstrate a recognizable purpose. This represents any form of aesthetic production that has an inherent thematic or use, including architecture, though we will see that this is not as simple a process as first appears. Since most architecture involves some form of directed purpose, we might think that it is that particular purpose that is the defining characteristic.

Philosophical aesthetics, and in particular Kant's discussion of it, is methodologically interested in our experience of how we judge our perceptions of the environment we inhabit, including both natural and created experiences. Washing your hands or observing a sunset is as much an aesthetic experience as looking at a sculpture or listening to music. What interests Kant is how we engage with experiences that we feel to be, disinterestedly, of significance. By this, Kant means something quite specific where we see purposiveness, or evidence of some structuring purpose, without recognizing the end point of that purpose or its use value.

In the examples of fire-based experience, we see quite idiosyncratic examples of Kant's general theory, particularly since fire itself is inherently an entropic and destructive process with which we have a syncretic but ambivalent relationship. Looking first at the example of fire as a formative and purgative process, we can think of fire as a substance that is intrinsic to the forming and forging of architectural materials, such as masonry and cast metals. The firing of clay into bricks or porcelain. A design studio that centres on these materials and attributes would concentrate on the physical and material properties of the media, and perhaps the history of their use in pre-modern and modern society. These types of approaches are unremarkable, though certainly demonstrated beautifully through work published by students and practitioners. So, the first aspect of the fire/architecture quadrivium is the least problematic – that our practice utilizes the transformative properties of fire in manufacturing to create its constructive units.

More challenging is the concept of fire as a destructive process that is seemingly purposeless. What is it to create a studio premised on the destructive and irreparable aspects of fire that negate the conventionally constructive and resistant aspects of architecture? While the pathways of immolation are clearly purposive in the logic of fire, and the final state the consequence of the climatic environment, as architects it is interesting to think of fire and destruction *as* the project. When the Glass Tower burns in *The Towering Inferno* (1974), the dramaturgy is directed at the hubris of architects and developers creating a structure that is inherently unsafe, a lesson sadly demonstrated in recent memory in the fire in London's Grenfell Tower in 2017. However, when Andrei Tarkovsky burns the idyllic home in *The Sacrifice* (1986), or Anselm Kiefer includes scorched elements in the surface of his paintings, clearly the purpose is for the residue to persevere and for its purposelessness to be registered.

The third aspect of fire/architecture is the splendour and terror of the moment. Fire as an event, from the *auto de fé* of the Spanish Inquisition, to the Ghats in Varanasi to the book-burning of the National Socialists in Germany in the 1930s. The fire-event is a singular, designed experience which actively disintegrates material as a ritual of extinction and removal. Architecturally the design of the fire-event is a condition in which its synchronic qualities, the heat, noise and smoke, overwhelm the senses and exceed attempts at control and extension. For something so specifically empirical and inviting of *a posteriori* analysis, it is important to recognize that its singularity is consistent with Kant's ideas on the singularity, the second moment of the aesthetic, and hermetic, individuality of every fire event. Coop Himmelb(l)au's *Blazing Wing* project from Graz in 1980 clearly points at this condition. Beautiful, terrible, dangerous and unrepeatable, the project summarized the question of how does an event that is complex and singular form a practice that is repeatable?

The final aspect of the architecture/fire nexus is the persistent latency of the question itself. Fire is one of the more extreme examples of an 'anarchitecture' (1974), Gordon Matta-Clark's contraction of 'anarchy' and 'architecture', that poses the challenge to find a practice that addresses the fundamentally entropic aspects of the material world to which architecture's constructive ethic seems to be opposed. It should be more than a perverse and symbolic gesture (symbolic of what) to create an architecture that destroys itself or is simply the outcome of a catastrophic event, but how do we think about this?

In Kant's fourth formulation of aesthetic judgement, he presents the issue of the 'necessity' of judgement. If you are certain that there is authenticity in your engagement with an aesthetic event, one concerning fire in our current discussion, then it is not enough to consider it a solipsistic experience that you own yourself and to which others are indifferent. In seeing that there is a purposiveness present in either constructive or destructive conditions necessarily makes the consideration of that purpose inherent in the event a core aspect of our cognitive facilities, and of others.

How is this architectural?
To clarify the relationship between Kant's moments of the beautiful and the practice of architectural design, it is important to be very clear regarding the distinction between a design 'intent' that wishes the project to create feelings of general phenomenological engagement such as comfort and shelter; a design intent that represents a value system that reflects an ethical relationship to the myriad social economies and ecologies that a design may involve, intentional or otherwise, and; a design intent that is significantly, and merely, attempting to isolate a sense of purposiveness without purpose. While it is usually counterintuitive for an architectural design to parse this distinction in the normal course of practice, by doing so we can see the distinct intellectual components that make up the complex and syncretic process of design.

For the discussion above, the principle thematics that the relationship to fire and architecture bring up can be summarized as follows:

>1. How does the process of heating, forming and firing affect and determine the fundamental components of architectural construction and design (bricks, tiles, ceramics), and how does their material reality infer a tectonic consciousness in the designer?
>2. To what degree does the systematized nature of these constructive units reflect complex pattern-making strategies that confirm, enhance or resist the meta-logic of a unitized system? To what degree, does it simultaneously recognize its destruction?
>3. How do we regard the purposiveness of these systems? Do they merely represent the metrification of a unit's extensionality or do they fulfil some symbolic role consistent to the uniquely architectural idea of 'Order'? Further, does this metrification constitute a form of grammar of purposiveness? Does the metrification of destruction constitute a grammar of purposelessness?
>4. Do these metrifications, as with Kant's 2nd Moment, infer a universal expression of value, or at least the proposition that universality can be considered? Is there a general theory of fire?

Considering, for a moment, the idea that we retain a quasi-mystical relationship to elemental experiences such as fire, there is a vast trove of deliberations on the purpose, value and meaning in fire. Before modern texts such as Gaston Bachelard's *The Psychoanalysis of Fire* (1938), the tradition of considering fire as a key component in material transformations drove the complex and allusive texts in the alchemical tradition.

That architecture both profits from the experience and products of fire and, is simultaneously susceptible to its destructive capacity, places our practice in a balance. So while we can construct theories of architecture based on purposiveness and resistance to destruction, it carries with it the alchemical 'marriage' of destruction, nothingness and, in the alchemical mindset, the potential for rebirth.

Proposition: Burning man, burning woman
The binary of the conventional man/woman gender divide, while different from current understandings of intersectionality, was a leitmotif of writing in the tradition of alchemy. Generally it referred to the combination of materials in order to produce a third state, for example mercury (female) and sulphur (male) combine to produce Sal (salt), the secret salt of nature. Fire was the energy that contributed to this process. What would be the elemental and constructional outcome of the 'marriage' of burning man and burning woman?

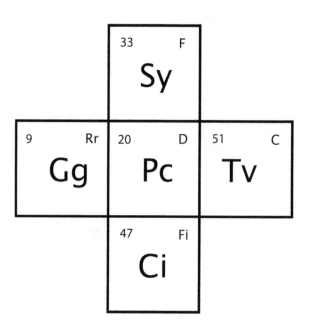

Rebus 20

Destruction

Proposition 20: Plato's Cave

> JUDY: Where's my baby?
> PUNCH: I don't, know.
> JUDY: Where is he? (They look about stage)
> PUNCH: He's not there. (still looking) He's not there! He's not there! He's not there!
> JUDY: Where is he? What have you done with him?
> PUNCH: I threw him out of the window.
>
> (B. F. Tickner, *The Drama of Punch and Judy*, 1937)

> SOCRATES: And if they can get hold of this person who takes it in hand to free them from their chains and to lead them up, and if they could kill him, will they not actually kill him?
> GLAUCON: They certainly will.
>
> (Plato, *Republic*, VII, 375 BCE)

Plato's famous Allegory (analogy) of the Cave describes, through Socrates, the phenomena of the appearance of reality. The elaborate thought experiment Socrates asks his amanuensis, Glaucon, to imagine involves the imprisonment of children in a cave whose only view of reality is the performance of a shadow theatre of objects, illuminated by fire, on the wall of the cave. The presence of the puppeteers and captors is not discussed, nor any elaboration on the moment of self-realization when a freed prisoner is able to turn and see the fire that has been the source of the shadows. The analogy continues when Socrates asks Glaucon to imagine the freed prisoner leaving the cave and seeing the sun and three-dimensional objects that lie outside, before returning to relay this news to the still-imprisoned prisoners who reject it and ridicule the freed prisoner. The story serves a number of purposes in Plato's telling: to illuminate the power of spectacle for uneducated persons; to describe the path to knowledge and the difficulty of communicating this to others; and to emphasize the difference between general categories (Forms) and specific instances of knowledge.

Plato is very specific in describing the conditions of the cell and the limited view the prisoners possess of themselves and of each other. While he imagines that all the auditory noises the puppeteer-captors make can be attributed to the shadows on the wall, he has nothing to say regarding the sounds the prisoners make or of their sense of their own bodies. Since it would not serve the purpose of the analogy, he concentrates on the path to enlightenment rather than the mechanics of the imprisonment.

Paradoxically, Plato creates a scene in which the most brutal of carceral environments is normalized for the benefit of vividly describing a philosophical question regarding perception and reality. For Plato, and for idealism generally, the distinction between appearances and reality was a core question of authentic understanding. In a culture in which childhood was not fetishized as a distinct aspect of human development or one that allowed for diminished capability and responsibility, Plato's 'children' are just examples of the continuity of life and the expectation that we exist within a continuous ontological environment. But what Plato abruptly has us imagine is the idea that life itself is a form of bondage and clearly a fundamentally disempowering and unhappy experience.

The manipulation of reality through the actions of the puppeteers, and indeed the whole apparatus for creating this cruel theatre, reminds us that while Plato's obvert interest is in questions of epistemology and perception, it requires an architecture that materially chains the protagonists to this performance. Moreover, Plato's allegory, because it requires such a pronounced suspension of disbelief, makes us consider the idea that thinking and architecture have an indissoluble relationship in order for the praxis of thinking to be performed. It challenges the idea that thinking is a disembodied practice independent of the apparatus for seeing what might be the case or that it is simply the empirical basis of thought.

But what does this destroy? There are a number of things to consider. The episode itself, as described by Plato, implies the destruction of a certain social order through the violence of imprisonment, implying a relationship between the structure (architecture) and the denial of freedom. It also illustrates, and hence compromises, the relationship between appearance and reality which is the core epistemological question. And beyond this nexus, it also destroys the model of cooperative behaviour that society generally expects in favour of a theatre-life of extreme experiences between the puppeteers and the enslaved audience. It is questionable whether you could say that Plato invented theatre and the cinema here, but there is some argument for him defining the core philosophical questions these media function within.

There are a number of architectural analogies to be drawn from this. First, the cave as a form of architectural construction begs the question whether it could or should be realized in some format. Second, the fixed placement of the prisoner's vision emulates a form of scopic focus on external objectivities vs. self-awareness. Third, the cave itself represents a form of experience in which the theatricality of the shadows is a mode of lived reality.

If we think about the construction of the theatrical space of a shadow theatre, or of a puppet stage, the gap between recognizing the world reality of the characters and that of the puppeteers is shaped architecturally. Like a conventional theatre, the proscenium shields the mechanics of the event and focuses on the effects of the narrative played on the space of the stage. The more developed and technologically capable the theatre is in re-presenting the world, the more it is defined as an architectural problem and/or opportunity.

How is this architectural?
While there are obvious analogies to be made between the Allegory of the Cave and the mechanics of theatre construction, there is the capacity to consider examples of where architectural form directly instrumentalizes a suspension of disbelief. While this could be easily illustrated by looking at the urban transformation of Rome under Julius II and later, including the Villa Giulia, or the baroque transformations of Urban VIII in the seventeenth century, there is a more contemporary example that captures this relationship.

Ashton Raggett McDougall's Storey Hall (1996) renovation in Melbourne, Australia, is a clear evocation of Plato's cave analogy and a particularly focused example of the issues at hand. Located in the central business district of Melbourne, it is a projection of the 'staged' into the space of the real, so clearly distinct from its context and any sense of design continuity with the existing city that it seemed to have emerged, *sui generis*, as a complete proposition in itself. A rich exercise in over-determining the scope of an architectural brief, Storey Hall functions in two principal locations, the space of the street and the volume of the hall.

There are a number of architectural 'actors' on the exterior: the idiosyncratic bench object that squats in front of the entrance, like a character in Beckett's theatre; the embedded bronze objects in the façade making reference to the history of the hall as a site of political (Fenian) and gender-based (suffragette) struggle; the cryptic references to Resurrection City, the architect Howard Raggett's theological vision of architecture's relationship to meaning; and finally, the yawning arc over the entrance surmounted by the growth of green tiles that lead to the parapet. The interior is a luminous stage space that transforms a space of learning, a theatre and lecture hall, into an expressionist environment similar to Poelzig's Grosse Schauspielhaus (1919) and includes the two vast eyes that illuminate the interior. While both the urban and the interior stage are tied together by the randomized complexities of the Penrose tile pattern, they are utterly different inversions of the same form of representational complexity than Plato's original. Where Plato's example is located within an interior space governed as a closed system, Storey Hall situates its entrance in the public realm open to the random presence of passers-by, and the Hall which is itself a gateway to a luminous interior. The congruence with Plato is the question whether the constraints of conventional judgements of form, order and effect, Plato's shadows, constitute a reality or are inferior version of noumenal truths.

Proposition: Philosophical puppet theatre
The most obvious exploration of this would be the theatrical space of the puppet theatre since the overall space is not only a recreation of conventional theatrical models but also one mediated by the abstractions of the puppets. As the form and movement of the puppets dictate the relationship between them, the puppeteer(s) and the audience, there is the opportunity to look clearly at how reality is represented and engineered.

As for destruction, performance, like behaviour, exists indexically and is destroyed, evaporated, by time and the arc of the narrative. So, in thinking about certain forms of architectural behaviourism, the question is always: When does it stop?

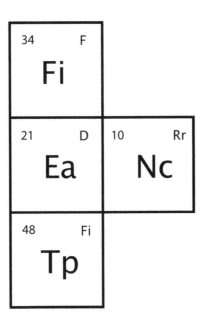

Rebus 21

Destruction

Proposition 21: Earth

The Names (1982), by Don DeLillo, is a story that traces the travails of an American risk analyst in Greece, the Middle East and India. Central to the character's story is an encounter with a death cult that choose victims based on their names and locations. The relationship between the two is simple but also brutal as there seems to be little higher purpose, if that were possible, to the executions. What DeLillo implicitly points to in the text is that the process of naming is the fundamental act of meaning-making and, like the death cult, the process is simultaneously arbitrary and significant. The final episodes of the book describe the moment when the principal characters realize that the death cult's nihilistic destruction of random persons has no other meaning than the antithesis of language as an organizing medium that is desperately needed in a world that is always, already, teetering on chaos.

Paul Carter's *The Road to Botany Bay* (1987) also documents the instrumentalization of naming that forms part of the colonial enterprise of the nineteenth-century exploration. Carter tracks the incessant and unrelenting logic of mapping and territorialization that underpins the western encounter with the Australian continent, and in doing so, appropriates it into a linguistic drama. We must, of course, recognize that Carter's project is explicitly an examination of a western colonial practice, and he is clear on that fact. But he also notes that the self-appointed task of redefining an entire continent according to interests totally incommensurate with the Indigenous inhabitants has produced a narrative of those encounters, for good or bad. Ultimately, the act of naming both confers a form of self-defining history on a location more than it attempts to just create a simple map reference point. As we will see in a later chapter, the map/territory relationship is a constant negotiation between a place and its identifying features, but in considering the use of naming to facilitate this process we will see the power of language to create and to occlude.

At the basis of both *The Names* and *The Road to Botany Bay* lies the implicit use of naming and signification in an inchoate world, one that is approached as an insistent material presence that must be something. For DeLillo's characters, the final descriptive scenes of *The Names* emphasize the inherently visceral and material reality of the world that lies outside of signification, the world that falls through the sieve of the proper noun and remains nameless but still present. Both texts, one fictional and one historical, establish a reality that insists that the world is a terrestrial limit of our experience, a dusty horizon of finitude, but that the process of naming is the moment in which historical time is established and a narrative can commence.

We can see an illustration of this in *The Names* when the main protagonist, Owen Brademas, spends time in Athens, deliberately avoiding an encounter with the Acropolis. He refuses to even look at the site/architecture with the most iconic form of historical persistence, a persistence that seeks to communicate from another time and an alien world view. It is because, for him, it is as incoherent and unknowable as any other historical fragment despite its assumption into the mediated economy of western cultural icons. His estranged partner, an archaeologist, and fellow traveller, also an archaeologist, both struggle with the meaning of the fragments of earthenware her work uncovers. Hers is the classic Hegelian dilemma of encountering evidence of another culture but being unable to attribute meaning to them without understanding the contextual purpose of the objects.

Without knowing whether the object is significant or trivial, it is impossible to understand whether it represents a purposeful investment for the original culture, and whether that investment can be translated into contemporary explanatory discourse. For Brademas, the Acropolis, for all its fame and its role within historical narratives, is equally opaque to him as the material reality of historical work always exceeds the narratives created to explain their significance. So, as *The Names* illustrates, the division between the named and the unnamed evidence of historical intentionality separates what can be said, and what remains silent. And this ineffable silence is doubly entailed when we consider the process of archaeology and the retrieval from the earth of evidence of historical presence – the material is silent until it is 'discovered' and silent until it is placed within an interpretive framework.

So a number of processes are in place here, the need to place meaning on the world through signification/naming; the escape from this net that the majority of the world actually effects; and the uncovering of buried evidence of signification as a retrieval of communication.

How is this architectural?
While archaeology, the retrieval of material from silence, is coupled to the process of naming, it is another thing to go looking for a place, a context or a site in which the creation of architecture can participate. While it is clear that an architectural project inevitably changes the narrative of a location, the challenge is to work in that narrow band where it is uncertain whether the work is silent or whether it speaks. Michael

Heizer's *City* (1972–2020) installation in the Nevada desert is a monumental architectural ensemble that recalls the process of discovery and comprehension that archaeology attempts in its practice. Similar to Rachel Whiteread's *House* (1993), it is solid in both a literal and thematic sense, entirely devoid of an interior. Where Whiteread's structure, however, gave form to the scale and surface of domestic interiors in an urban setting, *City* is without any indexical markers. Perhaps this is a consequence of the fact that it is set in the desert of Nevada, but the closeness to monumental meaningless is enhanced by its emergence from a landscape that is devoid of the markers that Carter recognized in the early 'explorers' in Australia. Their inability to 'see' characteristics that could be named and employed in the overall project of colonization is inversely reproduced in the desire of artists such as Heizer to escape the process of naming. That he would perversely title the work 'City' points directly to the experience of DeLillo's characters in encountering the material of other histories and other narratives.

Proposition: The *Gerry* outpost
Gus Van Sant's 2002 film *Gerry* takes the viewer on a journey with two lost protagonists in the desert of Death Valley. The narrative peters out into the continual recitation of the name 'Gerry' as a means of pushing back the inevitability of the suffocating silence of the landscape. This project would find them a destination for their wanderings.

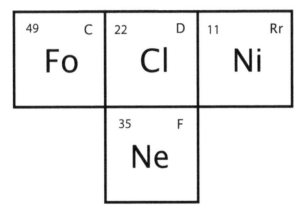

Rebus 22

Destruction

Proposition 22: Clouds

One of the most astute texts on the deep philosophical consequences of modernity is Marshall Berman's *All That Is Solid Melts Into Air* (1982). The title is a quotation from Marx and captures the transient nature of the 'fixed, fast-frozen' beliefs that society has immutable rules on the nature of social relations and the promise of emancipatory freedom. Berman's book is in three parts, the first of which is a consideration of Goethe's *Faust* (1808) as a parable on the consequences of what modernity brings to the philosopher/scientist. The other parts examine aspects of modern literature, Marx and the consequences of Robert Moses's transport infrastructure developments on old New York. Modernity, Berman argues, has created a constant environment of meaningful choice in which the need for change and development both drives innovation and undermines the efficacy of its discoveries. He discusses how the urban planner for New York, Robert Moses, like Faust, chooses to destroy aspects of the world in order to assert the triumph of bourgeois consumption and further imprint this economic model, as if New York required it, onto the growing urban and suburban populace of the city.

Moses's changes in urban form were (are) as permanent as transport infrastructure tends to be, creating use patterns for the city that became absorbed into the particular challenges of urban life, including displacement, marginalization and opportunistic development. Berman's point here is that the consequences of Moses's 'will to power' is that the technical modernization that he brought to urban planning was the antithesis of the palpable philosophical opportunities of modernity. As importantly, the reality of life within urban enclaves is that they are as mutable as the architecture is unchanging.

For New York, and for architects of a particular form of modernity, finding ways for architecture to 'melt into air' is a quite a specific challenge. The very condition of the persistence of materiality means that an architecture that is liquid or gaseous seems impossible. Yet there are a number of ways in which we could consider the challenge of Marx to be fulfilled or, at least, to have been explored.

To do this, we need to think of Goethe again and remember his championing of the English amateur scientist, Luke Howard. Howard wrote a study of cloud forms *On the Modification of Clouds* (1803) in which he set out the first popular nomenclature for cloud formation and classification. Cirriform, cumuliform and stratiform variants were the names given to the topology of effects observable to the casual eye, and from which all other variants were classified. So, for Goethe, the delight he took in Howard's method was in part based on the gesture of giving semantic solidity to effects that were, by definition, entirely fleeting and transient yet were as durable and timeless an experience as any natural phenomena. And even though Goethe did not, presumably, have clouds in mind when writing *Faust*, it illustrates for us the interesting thought that we are constantly encountering the mutable and transient in all scales of human experience. When James Gleick in *Chaos: Making a New Science* (1987) popularized the study of chaos theory and the attempts to give complex mathematical form to seemingly disparate events such as smoke, traffic jams and the stock market, it was another acknowledgement of the ubiquitous challenge to give form to the seemingly formless.

The metaphor of 'the cloud' goes beyond the reality of natural phenomena and their considerable poetic role as a metaphor for formless form. The employment of the idea of a 'cloud' when discussing data sets reminds us that the metaphor is intended to imply both a 'place' in which an unknowable volume of data exists and a state of unknowing since the exact size and characteristics of the cloud are constantly changing.

How is this architectural?
The challenge of forming the formless, if it is not a non sequitur, is a task that requires a careful definition of what constitutes a cloud, what are its material properties and how is it intended to behave. Diller and Scofidio's Blur Building (2002) on Lake Neuchatel in Switzerland was, by most definitions, entirely without any defining requirements of form or programme, the result of which was a structure (building?) that allowed occupation and then deliberately compromised the faculty of vision in determining the scale of the enterprise. It was an eloquent gesture, like the installations/photographs of Berndnaut Smilde, that defy the scale of the rooms within which they are staged. Looking at Smilde's images, there is a clear dialectic between the architectural space that is the setting for the cloud event and the 'cloud' itself. As Smilde has made clear, the event of creation is solely for the photograph and is not a performative piece, allowing us to encounter the mysterious coincidence of events, mutable and immutable, only in the evidence of the image. For Smilde, the architectural setting is the locus delicti, the crime scene, in which the evidence of the cloud needs to be interpreted. The Blur Building similarly has no definitive state, and hence form, yet is effortlessly focused on the questions that architecture always asks of thoughtful observers.

Similar attempts to give form to cloud formations, whether natural phenomena or synthetic, remind us of the data mapping exercises of digital applications that harness topological algorithms to spreadsheet data and spatial boundary definitions. Beloved of urban-scale architectural practices, the mapping and re-mapping of these information sets provides a clear visual analogy to the metricized differences in the spreadsheets in which they are born. Further, as an undertaking of visual palimpsestry, the over-mapping of different data sets allows users to read differential tendencies and predict formal changes across a territory. What is clear from these processes is that the diagrammatic properties of information are crucial in communicating and defining certain causational effects. If you over-map road/car accidents and, for example, intersections with visibility issues and drug/alcohol testing locations, they inevitably reveal certain spatial strategies undertaken by the owners of the information. The imaging of this information through explanatory diagrams arguably guarantees an optimized focus on the most relevant stages of the visualization process: What data do we want to see? How do we compare sets? What is the actionable consequences of the comparison? How do we optimize the formal outcome to ensure a viable half-life?

For most architectural projects, this results in a level of determinacy that gives assurance to the other members of the design team, and, the client(s), that the solution has viability even if it constitutes a non-standard solution. The beauty of the Blur Building is that it guaranteed a form inasmuch as the vapour cloud described a form, but not one that could be determined in advance.

However, arguably, this reliance on the use of data sets to determine optimized formal outcomes does not exhaust the nature of how the translation from information to form may take place. In particular, it removes any viable political narrative that may attach itself to the consequences of those data sets or topological changes. It is only when the data sets themselves are interrogated to display their tendencies do we get the secondary analysis that demonstrates the immediacy of the political. Robert Moses's plans for New York, or any socio-cultural data mapping exercise that works towards a morphological transformation of the data, has real-world consequences that is both the expectation and the, sometimes, fearful outcome.

Gas vs. cloud
Clouds are not, of course, composed just of gases, there are also suspended liquids and solids. A cloud is not solely part of the third state of materials though it may behave in some instances in a similar manner when physical mechanics are applied.

A cloud's formlessness and its visibility depend on the internal forces that suspend and distribute the vapour droplets in relation to each other, and the external forces, temperature and air pressure that deliver the energy that serves to dissipate and disperse the droplets into water again. So the analogy for architecture might be that it turns on the moment in which an invisible gas (data) exists in a state where it is becoming a suspended liquid (potential form) on the way to eventual solidification (architecture).

Turning again to Berman's use of Marx, which is bound to an evolutionary view of modernity as a constant entropic force, it is clear that he is addressing both the minor idea of change but also the more dominant idea that the material for consideration is in a constantly transitive state. Architecture, in this view, is the belated attempt to fix in place tendencies that must always be grasped and ultimately named. Luke Howard's decision to apply a geneology of terms for cloud formations applies also to the evolving expressions of form. In this sense, Reiser and Umamoto's *Atlas of Novel Tectonics* (2006) or François Blanciak's *Siteless: 1001 Building Forms* (2008) looked for alternative genealogies of the processes and precipitates of architectural design, illustrating the complex procedural stages of design development within a context, for Resier and Umamoto, of regulation, politics, buildability, budget and material innovation. Ultimately, processes and their results go through an Adamic process of acquiring referential terms as a shorthand for understanding their place within a periodic table of potentialities.

So, the architectural consequences of this can be imagined if we intersect the definitions of gases: low density, indefinite shape/volume, compressibility and expandability, diffusivity and co-mingling, and pressure, with the emergent geneologies of form that the twenty-first century is currently delivering. The point at which the gas/cloud/data/brief coalesces into a form, even momentarily, is the moment of architecture.

Proposition: The Berman Baths
If Marshall Berman was to conceive of a *res publica* in which the 'construction' of a cleansing space was also the construction of a social form, what would it be?

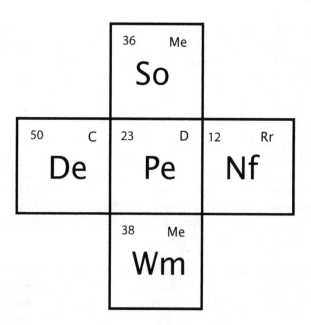

Rebus 23

Destruction

Proposition 23: Perversions

The architectural work of Jean Jacques Lequeu (1757–1826) is almost inexplicable in today's understanding. In many respects, the heterogeneity of the projects, their departure from the strict canon of Neoclassicism and the embrasure of an array of exotic influences demonstrate some of the most diverse intellectual appetites of the French Enlightenment. In addition, the presence of a folio of pornographic and gender indeterminate images side by side with architectural works begs the question: What was Lequeu thinking? Pornography in any published form was strictly censored in late eighteenth-century France, so Lequeu's images, his *Figures Lascives* (published for the first time in 1986), were as personally dangerous as they might have been liberating.

The first definitive study of Lequeu, Emil Kaufmann's *Three Revolutionary Architects, Boullée, Ledoux, and Lequeu* (Kaufmann 1952), concentrates exclusively on Lequeu's eclectic architectural designs that fuse an interest in exotic, non-western elements with a neoclassical organization. These works, Kaufmann argues, tie him to the struggle for an *architecture parlante*, a speaking and meaningful architecture, that Kaufmann saw as a core desire of the Enlightenment. It is Lequeu's idiosyncratic inclusion of a range of visceral and primal obsessions that set him apart from the strict boundaries of what then, and now, constituted architectural taste.

The fusion of architectural form and ideas of transgressive sexuality at the basis of this work are, like that of the Marquis de Sade, core explorations of the French Enlightenment and the tolerances of social values for sexualized forms of transgression. De Sade's interests in the limits of libertinage of course saw him imprisoned a number of times for corruption of public morals, a fate that did not befall Lequeu principally because of his general lack of notoriety in comparison to the Marquis. And yet, in architectural terms, it is difficult to find a body of work that is so explicitly sexual in terms of the overall output. Was Lequeu a pornographer and minor architect, or is there something intrinsic between his design work and his retinue of sexualized images?

Phillipe Duboy's major study of Lequeu identifies him as an enigma while problematically suggesting that Marcel Duchamp had a role in his popularity. Duboy is conducting a reverse critical historiography that connects, respectively, transgressive and restrictive behaviour in Marcel Duchamp and Le Corbusier with Lequeu. While Duboy's study is itself a collection of conjectures and conundrums, he correctly identifies the vitally transgressional nature of his work. The gaze in architecture has been a subject of study and speculation since the critical interest in forms of scopic organization emerged in architecture literature in the late twentieth century. Martin Jay's essay, *The Scopic Regimes of Modernity* (1988), considers the relationship between forms of Cartesian spatial organization that we typically associate with the graphic construction of perspective and the concomitant ambition to trap and hold the subject/object relationship of vision.

In addition, to construct subject matter pictorially is to apportion them a relational value to other content in the image. So for Michel Foucault, famously, Velazquez's *Las Meninas* (1656) is a complex interplay of sight-lines between the figures within the portrait group, the painter who is part of this space and is paradoxically painting himself into the courtly portrait, and the absent (or obscured) principal viewers, the King and Queen of Spain. Foucault, like Jay, is interested in the complex spatial relationship of power and observation that constructed images convey and further, Jay is interested in alternate forms of vision that rely on visual taxonomies and *folies du voir*, or vision that is deliberately indeterminate and unsettling.

Folies du voir, for Jay, are typified by Baroque painting and the complex interrelationship between image and (architectural) setting in the large-scale perspective renderings typical of artists such as Andrea Pozzo. The extraordinary visual effect of these images is intended to convince the viewer of a sublime spatiality beyond the material limits of the church and also of the possibility that the artificiality might extend down into our own space. At the borders of these works, visual cues often illustrate figures that seemingly sit both within the space of the painting and also the space of the church. The overall effect, some centuries later, is one of intoxicating and vertiginous volumes of form in a visual tumult that prevents our eyes from settling on a monocular organization.

Transgression
So does Lequeu's interest in sexuality and the gaze define an especial form of architectural transgression, or is it an (arguably) uncomfortable relationship that exceeds what makes sense for an architectural avant-garde? Lequeu's images are so clearly a-systemic in contrast to Boullée and Ledoux's that we are forced to see equivalence between his architectural and pornographic images and that they are in some measure declarative of his own complex relationship to sexuality and architecture. There is clearly a complex presentation of Lequeu the architect/constructeur as a sexually non-binary figure which is itself an usual and difficult

characteristic to incorporate into an architectural proposition. This goes to the heart of the question of what constitutes an architectural transgression. It is distinct from the form of transgression that is conventionally political or arises from challenges to historical continuity because it is entirely located within the existential questions that Lequeu is singularly asking and facing. What is the difference between myself and my architecture?

Is Lequeu's work an expression of a holistic view of his life or one that entails embellishments and ellipses? This is where the genuinely transgressive characteristics present themselves, the development of a life lived and expressed according to the impulses of the self. In this respect, the encounter with boundaries that blur the difference between architecture and self in Lequeu's work is a challenge to any other architect that seeks to go down this path, or to find out if there are boundaries between work and self.

Perversion
Does the state of perversion exist within architecture? If it is acting as an instrument of transgressive behaviour, is it inherently fostering and directing that behaviour? Surely inasmuch as it is agreed that architecture has some form of directed effect on persons, would not enhanced aspects of sexuality and erotic behaviour be a possibility? The work of Douglas Darden (Schneider 2004) was focused upon, before and following an ultimately terminal diagnosis of leukemia, the question of who he was and how architecture was able to represent aspects of his life. Darden's drawings, like Lequeu, were predominantly orthographic chiaroscuro renderings of imagined projects and attempted to give a fully focused, again like Lequeu, rendering of architecture as an object. Darden explicitly emulated Lequeu's self-portraits as a form of *memento mori* and, while consistently engaged with the relationship of literary mythos to architecture, took the opportunity to understand and respond to Lequeu's lasciviousness.

Our question then is: Can perversion, inasmuch as it might be considered an expression of an attitude towards morality and libertinage as Lequeu and Darden seem to suggest, be represented in architecture? And also, does the gaze towards these forms of expression employ the objectifying precision of perspective or the dissimulated boundaries and narcotic immersion of *folies du voir*? Clearly, in his historical moment, Lequeu adopted the clarity and unrelenting eye of Enlightenment visuality, but is the same flirtation with sensuality relevant now?

Some questions:

> 1. Is it possible to imagine an architecture that exhibits the introspection and candour of Lequeu and Darden?
> 2. How would this architecture express itself as part of a libidinal economy of images?
> 3. Is there a direct correspondence between fetishization of the architectural object and the emergence of modern disciplinary modes of sexuality?
> 4. Is there a place for these questions within an expanded field of identity politics?

How can it be architectural?
When Peter Greenaway conceived and directed *The Draughtsmans' Contract* (1982), the film was intended to explore the conceit that an architect/draughtsman was able to forensically 'see' a location, while also being blind to the true currents of intrigue that surrounded the terms of his engagement. His insistence on libidinous conditions to the contract is ultimately the cause of his death and, it can be argued, Greenaway chose the period of the late eighteenth century to communicate the intimate relationship between the emergent logic of measure and draughtsmanship and the transgressive act of murder. The question for architecture now might be, what would that contract be now?

Finally, if we also consider Alfred Hitchcock's *Rear Window* (1954), the incapacity (a broken leg) of the protagonist who voyeuristically watches his apartment neighbours is pivotal in limiting the character to an impotent observer of the lives of others. The material reality that makes this possible is the modern apartment he inhabits and the relentless transparency of modern architecture. A further question emerges, is transgressive architectural voyeurism about what you can see, or what is hidden?

Proposition: Edith Farnsworth's identity kit
In this project, the emphasis is upon determining and communicating identity as scrupulously and clandestinely as possible. The language of form is, of course, architecture.

7: Measure

In the reconstruction of a theory of architectural design, one of the clearer modalities for discussing what that might *be* should come from the concept of measure of what *is*. Having spent half of this book finding ways to undermine received wisdom on referential and semantically stable ideas of architectural meaning, it is worthwhile saying what it could be, as much as what it might not be. The chapters in this section review different approaches to the idea of measure and its translation into meaningful architectural form. The first chapter starts with the great mediating environment of the modern world: money. It is a commonplace of architectural education and of the dreams of the avant-garde that the prudential organization of effort should not impede either the standards of innovation, teleological and ideological goals of equity and justice or the ability to imagine a material culture that can support the vast level of human labour necessary to emulate the complex architectural forms of other eras and cultures. Money and the parsimonious management of value, it is argued, are the death of the great potential for architectural exploration. However, as we shall see, if we think of monetary value as an economic algorithm capable of complex expressions, it is possible to see that cooperation equates with success.

The second chapter concentrates on a further exploration of the idea of rule-based behaviour. The temptation to compare the architecture and philosophy of Ludwig Wittgenstein can lead to tenuous associations between his propositional structure in the *Tractatus Logico-Philosophicus* and the house designed and constructed for his sister. A better approach, it is argued, is to consider what 'following-a-rule' means in the context of design decision-making. Understanding and exploring what an architectural 'rule' might be can help us to understand how to adhere or break them.

The third chapter again looks at an asymptotic aspect of design, the mutual obligation requirements of a 'contract'. Contracts are core aspects of architectural practice and are designed to protect the interests of the signatories, but what about contracts for more esoteric or unfulfillable aspirations? The emergence of conceptual art practice in the 1960s fundamentally challenged the transactional relationship between artist and patron/viewer. For the very reason that the art market has deeply monetized aesthetic experiences, conceptual art often deliberately questioned the expectations of the 'purchaser' for the specific aspiration that 'art' should be free from this value system. Nevertheless, at its core, the equating of experience with consumption encouraged conceptual art practitioners to create a contractual 'market' in which the purchaser participated in an agreement to receive some form of experience. The idea that you could contract to receive an esoteric and immaterial 'work' both ironically challenged the mainstream art market while acknowledging the efforts of the conceptual artist. How that might function for architecture remains an open question.

Finally, the fourth chapter looks at the abstract concept of 'life', initially borrowing Michel Foucault's writings on the emergence of discourses on the identification and propagation of life through architectural means. To bring this analysis into the present day, the chapter looks at the proposition that digital methodologies of emergence borrow heavily from biological metaphors. The suppressed premise of this type of work, it is argued, is that any morphologically generative system is, because it emulates 'growth', inherently aligned to biological systems. As we will see this is not as straightforward as the analogy promises since biological systems themselves have complexities that the architectural work ignores. Finding a method for measuring the life of an architectural system and proposing a synergistic relationship with the natural world still remains a goal.

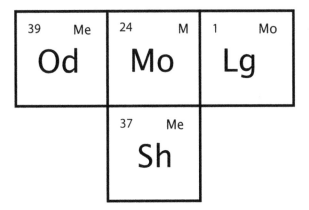

Rebus 24

Measure

Proposition 24: Money

Money and monetization are an important part of the business of construction. It is so clear a statement of the fundamental conditions of architecture that, in many other contexts, money and the cost of architecture is not even mentioned in discussions of architectural theory. Of course, there are opportunity cost (OC) implications in the decision-making process of designing but, for the purposes of much of architectural theory, this is a separate and regrettable incursion of the realpolitik of economic exchange into the world of ideas. Clearly, there are transactional requirements in designing and building of which money is the intermediary condition but, we hopefully ask, 'Could we please just consider how these ideas are developed away from the mundane constraints of budgets and value management?' There is considerable sympathy for this point of view because, in a related sense, it has a formal similarity to the requests for social justice or equality where the cost of that justice is the re-distribution of wealth. Justice shouldn't be at the cost of economic benefit for some and the detriment of others, everyday values tell us, and not all architectural justice problems are best addressed through the lens of monetary value. But within this view, there is, at the very least, a model of transactional relationships that needs to be investigated regarding the relationship of architecture to money.

Money and the behavioural realities of how money is managed impinge directly on a number of aspects of architectural design: perceived and intrinsic value; trust; usury and profit; gambling and speculation; asymmetric market knowledge; microfinance and wealth distribution, and; state intervention. All these areas directly form the context within which the complicated and expensive process of thinking about and building architecture requires. This is true not only for the pragmatics of achieving construction but exists as suppressed premises for architectural theory as well.

Issues of social justice within architecture turn on issues of participation, client identity, access to the decision-making process and tangible outcomes for underrepresented individuals and groups. Generally, these are issues that can and are being addressed as an expression of changing demographic profiles of architecture practitioners, and of societal values. However, these actions are different to more macro issues of finance and the structures of financial interdependence that have a profound effect on whether social values can be meaningfully addressed in the first place. If we are looking for conceptual models that will allow architects to effectively pursue social justice goals, the degree to which the process is entangled with financial management, or divorced from it, is crucial.

Any form of engagement with financial structures requires knowledge of their behaviours and tendencies. Because of the very nature of money as an approximate instrument of value, of course, there are instances where social value does not demonstrate a clear return on investment (ROI). The (invisible hand of the) market is uninterested in value systems which are not directed at the general principle of demonstrating a value proposition that is timely and achievable. All investments, private or institutional (but not necessarily by the state), generally prefer certainty and continuity of behaviour in satellite industries such as architecture and construction.

This doesn't mean that disruptive and innovatory strategies have no opportunity for support from financial agents outside of architecture, it just means that the nature of the value must be articulable in the language of the actions of finance. It does, and this is the real challenge, mean that a monetary value must be designed into the general argument. If an architect is designing social housing for a client group without the financial means to engage design professionals or build the structure, the financing body will need to have other means by which they can identify and monetize the benefit to them. This is a brutal truth of financial institution governance since the long-term viability of the institution is its first priority. While architectural theory, and indeed most speculative architectural projects choose to ignore, or at least bemoan, this state of affairs the forces of finance and the abstract definitions of value it brings need to be understood in order to be directed at projects that might warrant this support.

Financial institutions are no strangers to complex contractual structures for identifying and leveraging growth opportunities and for minimizing risk. The 2008 financial crisis stemmed from 'epistemic' failures, or the lack of overall knowledge, of the synthetic collateralized debt obligations in domestic housing loans in the United States, as well as asymmetric knowledge and behaviour of individuals within financial institutions that allowed the derivatives to be created and sold. While these financial contracts existed entirely independently of the bricks and mortar houses and the income of the persons affected by the leveraging, a better model could involve the creation of financial models in which the risk is indemnified by other, more stable transactions. Financial institutions, or enough of them if properly incentivized, will adapt any investment opportunity to be coherent to the market, provided the risk is properly described and managed. So, the opportunity exists for architecture to articulate investment model(s) that understand the investment strategy of institutions and to find ways to activate them. Ultimately the best models will come from a translated alignment of design value models and monetary value modelling.

How is this architectural?
Game theory tells us that the emulation of behaviour in contested environments (the market) allows for individual decision-making and strategic assessment of future value. If we take this process into the design studio, a game can be constructed in which the outcome is an architectural design and where the design process relies on limits and potentialities that are tested in a market. In this instance, studio participants are the marketplace, competing for investment opportunities in design. They are able to determine physical limits such as site size, building volume, material choice and programme while also creating future value by identifying and monetizing (however imprecise) the prospective value, including triple-bottom-line calculations of social impact and global sustainability. Social value calculators, however simplified, can be used to determine the level of engagement across a broad range of social sectors that might, in the climate of the studio, otherwise be ignored since the value proposition might otherwise be thought to be subjective. Beyond the restrictions of physical limits, the identification of competing theoretical goals, also sufficiently monetized to be coherent within the game scenarios, helps to situate the project in a 'real-world' model of competing interests and values.

Transactional design is the goal of this project. In Georg Simmel's *Philosophy of Money* (1900), he discusses the relationship between value and identification in the engagement with the production of goods, services and experiences. Money is the most ubiquitous intermediary correlate of value, and the most intrinsically banal. But it serves the function, of course, of granularizing the value chain of dependent variables in complex constructions such as architecture. The monetary marketplace game played out in the studio makes these granular decisions visible.

A studio example
The process of exchanging, buying and selling, within the closed economy of the studio indicates the value of OC, ROI, real and perceived value, rational choice, incentivization and margin analysis. Within a studio environment, a scenario can be imagined in which all students commence within a fixed economy – for example, participants 'bid' for a selection of development sites in a closed auction format. All participants have, say, 500K to spend on a parcel of land and construction. The more expensive the land, the less money is available for construction. Construction

costs are fixed at a specific value ($2000/m2). Hence for a 150K spend on land, the student then has 350K to spend on construction which, at $2000/m2 allows for 175 m2 of building fabric. All participants have a set brief of accommodation, in terms of spatial use (not area), that they are required to fulfil.

Participants are also permitted to on-sell portions of their budget, if savings are achieved, either to purchase additional land (at an ad hoc/market values determined by individual transactions between neighbours, gain additional construction budget (at the set rate of $2000/m2) or upgrade the quality of finish (increasing the construction budget for designated items/finishes), etc.

Much like *Monopoly*, the anti-trust board game, specific marketplace interactions (such as passing 'Go'), can allow for a reassessment of the recapitalized value of interim design solutions. Those solutions that the market (the studio student population) deem desirable, via a voting system, gain an increased valuation (through sweat equity) to enhance their overall budget (up to 20 per cent). As an example, this employs simple, fixed and agreed economic values to challenge the participant to optimize the relationship between effort, external value and future potential.

Game theory
A more specific application of game theory can be employed to determine the viability of competitive vs. cooperative scenarios. The competitive scenario can be modelled on the Prisoner's Dilemma and Nash's Equilibrium, while the cooperative scenario can employ Shapley Value calculations to establish the relative advantages of cooperative behaviour. The Prisoner's Dilemma narrates a situation where two isolated prisoners who have (allegedly) committed a crime together are facing the prospect of confession or denial and the consequences of imprisonment. If both deny guilt, they get a minimal sentence (one year), if one admits and the other denies the admitting party gets a maximal sentence (five years) and if both admit they get a medium sentence (two years). Nash's equilibrium number for this equation is for two years since it is the most rational choice for both parties, all things being equal. In architectural terms, we can characterize this in terms of a competitive marketplace in which firms can choose to invest in promotional activities (negative revenue) to attract business (positive revenue) in comparison to an imagined (or real) competitor. If neither do so, the Nash equilibrium is zero since there is no cost for lost business; however, if one commits then the other stands to lose disproportionately. Indeed, this is a reality of competitive marketplaces generally.

A more complex form of behavioural analysis concerns the determination of Shapley Values in cooperative endeavours. Imagine three firms that have the desire to engage with a complex design problem, but with different capacities to progress towards a solution that requires 1000 hours of work. Firm A can commit a maximum of 100 hours, Firm B can commit a maximum of 500 hours and Firm C can commit 1000 hours. Obviously, Firm C can competitively complete the project on its own, but the value of including partners can be calculated. This is the Shapley Value. For this particular example, the calculation of how much cooperative effort is required for the three firms is the following: Firm A needs to undertake 33.3 hours, Firm B needs to undertake 233.3 hours and Firm C needs to undertake 733.3 hours. These hours represent the value of cooperation with a partner that is willing to share load proportionate to capacity. In the event of any dividend, this is also the proportionate credit each firm should enjoy. In practice, cooperation between firms is usually a function of imperfect negotiating skills and imperfect knowledge of the market, but if assessed via game theory some more equitable outcomes are possible given that it contributes to improved knowledge of the context.

How is this architectural?
Conjecturally this model could also be used as a validation for cooperative effort in incorporating theoretical research into the design process. While different participants have differing capacity for this type of design development, there is a cooperative scenario in which these capacities are aggregated for the common good. Ultimately, a value can be determined for cooperative research and a valid argument made for a level of design improvement due to this cooperation.

Employing both competitive and cooperative models in approaching a design problem as complex as architecture encourages the isolation of different design decisions to simplified models that can be successfully, and sequentially, resolved. The question of whether to develop social value infrastructure in tandem with profit-driven commercial outcomes inevitably involves the assessment of behavioural options that, importantly, make money and values within the model (temporarily) equivalent. While there is obviously much more to the design and practice of architecture, the actual implementation of these models in actual practice, it helps to isolate those problems that cannot be solved through simple analysis.

The challenge within architecture is to not only design a totality within an economic environment in which the aggregation of values materially coincide to produce a series of complex entities – but also to demonstrate and visualize the margin analysis of that process. Visualizing potentials and tendencies or at least embedding them within a project as a method of maintaining value is a potential of architecture. For architectural practice within any economy, whether the real-world market economy or the conjectural world of the esteem economy, defining competitive and cooperative options is important.

Investment, whether it is time or money, is an expression of confidence in the shape of future behaviour and value. Investment as a form of approval and support is an inescapable reality of all complex endeavours that require multiple parties for success including those with different value systems. To succeed in this cooperation requires understanding the tools employed to make decisions and to ascribe value.

Proposition: The bank of everybody
Create a scenario in which the translation of values between individuals is assessed through multiple iterations, competitively and cooperatively. Engage in both modalities, including multiple partners to solve design issues and, in so doing, determine the relative advantages of behavioural choice.

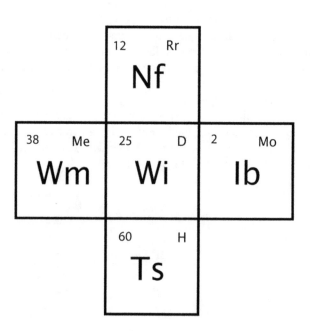

Rebus 25

Measure

Proposition 25: Wittgenstein

Ludwig Wittgenstein's philosophical career is famous within the Anglo-American tradition of certainty and the relationship between logic and epistemology. Wittgenstein's principle achievements, and influence, relate to his perceptive understanding of the logic of sense and reference and in particular the coincidence of our capacity to think and to communicate. For Wittgenstein this was a pursuit of certainty as opposed to a pointless cultivation of ambiguity. Now it is a gross mischaracterization and simplification of the difference between the Anglo-American and Continental philosophy to say that the former prefers precision to ambiguity while the latter enjoys the rich polythemy of multiple associations without seeking definitive answers, but for the purposes of an initial understanding it will serve to show the nature of Wittgenstein's project. So why is certainty important, and why Wittgenstein?

Wittgenstein's early work, the *Tractatus Logico-Philosophicus* (1921), traces a sequence of propositions about the world and the nature of what can, and cannot, be known. But importantly, the process of understanding what can be known is not one of simple discovery, as if there was a 'there' to be discovered, but a clarification of what is already present in the world and is sensible. In the text, Wittgenstein sets forward a series of axioms, commencing from '1.0 The World is all that is the case' to '7.0 Whereof one cannot speak, one must pass over in silence' (1921: n.pag.). Between these axioms, in an increasingly complex set of sub-axiomatic propositions, Wittgenstein sets out a series of logically consistent propositions about how we propositionally 'picture' the world.

Wittgenstein, and logic in philosophy, is interested in the distinction between the patterns of cyclic confusion and repetition that constitutes everyday life, and the nature of clarity and methodological consistency that is the opportunity of human thought and experience. He points out, or infers, that if having logical certainty regarding what we say about the world is important, including difficult questions regarding ethics and aesthetics, then we need to be clear in how we assert certainty. The alternative, a form of relativism in which we are happy to acknowledge diametrically opposed opinions as being equally real and valid, ends up as a form of intellectual nothingness. While the need to acknowledge the existence of differing opinions is often the most politic, or polite, method for ensuring respect and harmony in a debate, it does nothing towards answering the core question of what is legitimately true, or what ought to be the case.

Thinking about architecture, we can consider a design proposal as a proposition regarding a possible 'state of affairs', a material reality which might be brought into existence if constructed. Because any architectural proposal is an exceptionally complex entity involving constructional logic, material performance, behavioural expectations of users, environmental predictions, semiotic effects of form, etc., the ability to distinguish between that which is propositionally stable and that which requires a suspension of disbelief regarding specific aesthetic and ethical attitudes is crucial. For example, all other things being equal, a house made of cheese may not be aesthetically enjoyable to many persons but it would still be a sensical proposition about a possible state of affairs.

In the early, *Tractatus*-based, version of Wittgenstein's thoughts on the relationship between language and the world, the 'state of affairs' description is sometimes referred to as his 'picture theory' of language. The imputation is that we 'see' the world as a complex array of events, facts and perceptions – but we 'stabilize' this experience through the faculty of language to 'correspond' to increasingly more specific propositions about the world. Wittgenstein's 'Picture' theory purports to describe the purpose of language in forming sensical propositional statements regarding the world, as both fixed and dynamic states. As an architect, think of the nested, and consistent, set of drawings (definitions) that we make in creating a building, from overall diagrams to increasingly specific details. The diagrams correspond as accurately as possible with what is encountered. What we cannot (if that is possible) diagram, Wittgenstein is saying, we cannot strictly speaking say that we know.

Wittgenstein's later philosophy, usually considered to be summarized in the *Philosophical Investigations* (1953), criticized this position and famously described the 'meaning as use' argument for language. In this instance, Wittgenstein pointed out that there are many other forms of communicative behaviours that allow us to interact with the world and expect that they will be successfully effective. He mostly points to the interrogative and speculative functions of everyday language: asking questions, proposing outcomes, suggesting alternatives, etc. that happen in *specific* instances. He is not proposing a general theory of language, which on his terms is actually untestable, but rather pointing to the (un)remarkable reality that all we have is language and communication with which to engage with the world. There isn't more language to be learnt, or more general rules to be determined, but we do need to be clear in how we employ language and rule-following to make sense of the world and to effectively engage with it (including architectural design).

While there has been scholarship, within architecture, regarding Wittgenstein and the relationship between his philosophy and architecture, it is fair to say that most commentators have struggled to see an effective relationship. The house (1928) he completed in association with a local Viennese architect Paul Engelmann (who one suspects did most of the documentation), for his sister in the city of Vienna is generally studied to see if it, somehow, reveals aspects of his thinking. While there are a number of interesting aspects of this house that speak to his approach to the process of building and the construction of a meaningful environment, it is not clear what aspects of his philosophy are engaged with. There are, of course, the famous stories about his desire to raise the ceiling of a room a minor amount to suit his sense of proportion, or the design for radiators that tested the limits of engineering tolerances, but these are the characteristics of a fastidious designer and are not, for that reason, particularly 'philosophical'.

The house is devoid of any form of decoration or embellishment, yet it still retains an overall organization and set of spatial volumes that are in keeping with Wittgenstein's personal experience of large bourgeois houses in the upper echelons of Viennese society. In particular, there is an iconic photograph of a female figure standing in front of one of the sets of doors demonstrating the height of the handles in the region of 1500 millimetres above the floor level consistent with where door furniture was placed in luxurious mansions from the nineteenth century. This in itself points to the tension between ergonomic rules, conventions of scale and abstraction. The endorsement of contemporary modernism would, for Wittgenstein, have been consistent with his interest in the 'objectivity' or *Sachlichkeit* of contemporaneous architectural discussion. But is it philosophical?

Nana Last (1998) suggests that the use of paired door sets (a set that opens inwards plus a set that opens outwards) means that the choice of coding, transparent-as-public and translucent-as-private created anomalies in internal elevations. Last argues that these anomalies, along with the reflective properties of the doors, reflect a corresponding ambiguity in meaning consistent with Wittgenstein's later philosophy. As we have seen, Wittgenstein was no less concerned with precision and the (non)sensical nature of propositions in his later work than in his earlier, so ambiguity could never have been a specific aim. Moreover, as one reads personal accounts of his attitude towards tasks, it is the problem (solution) that interests him, not the avoidance that comes with deliberate ambiguity. Last's analysis of the doors is significant in one particular respect though, the fact that rule-based design decisions cannot be uniformly applied across the project.

The problem of 'following a rule' in any interrogative or performative context was, for Wittgenstein, both a recognition of the importance of this type of behaviour (the search for consistency) while acknowledging the arbitrary manner with which we assume others are following the same rule-systems that we recognize. The analysis of this is complex and nuanced and has had the attention of major contemporary philosophical figures such as Saul Kripke, but we can summarize some points worth considering within architectural practice.

How is this architectural?
Much of the communicative media of architecture relies on the agreement (rule-based) regarding the considered markings made to represent a building project. Drawings and models are representations of possible actions towards a construction or a potential state of affairs. The control and application of rule-based communication allow us to set conditions for both the enactment of a material change and also the expectation that the outcome of rule-based activity will meaningfully 'express' the rule(s). This is the contractual test of the construction industry, as well as that of the relationship between the client(s) and end-users and the architect: What rules must be adhered to in order for expectations to match across parties, or more accurately, for different parties to 'picture' the world in a consistent and self-similar fashion. We can imagine an infinite regress where increasingly accurate and granular specifications of an architectural project would finally ensure consistency across all rule conditions – but that might well just be the project itself.

Many rules we employ as everyday conventions of an agreed reality are not tested because they would act as a distraction from the achievement of normal life conditions – philosophers don't wonder what a piece of toast is before eating it. But in the exploration of what constitutes the boundaries between sense and nonsense in establishing rule-based behaviour in speculative 'pictures' of the world in the future, the interrogation of how rule 'worlds' between discrete systems either cohere or differ is crucial. In architecture, the setting of specific rule conditions that emulate consistent conditions enables us to direct our attention more efficiently at instances where we feel the inconsistencies of competing rule systems are more valuable. The purpose of this is to identify different rule ecologies that, through scrutiny, might breed alternate patterns of material engagement with the world. For Wittgenstein, as Last suggests, this would have come in the recognition that the incommensurability of the door puzzle under the existing design rule conditions meant that he had to leave it unsolved. For Wittgenstein, this is the proof of the rule-model and an exposition of the 'fact' that the world delivered tangible evidence of the success and failure of rule systems – obvious to an architect, but perhaps a novel experience for him.

There are many extant attempts to systematize design behaviour according to rule and pattern ecologies, particularly in the application of complex systems and artificial intelligence to seeming 'wicked' problems, but the value does not lie, one can argue, in solving and creating a more extensive rule set. A general theory of architectural design does not address the Wittgenstein/Kripke problem of rule-based behaviour having no external definition, but it does confirm that the more interesting propositions about architecture turn on the discontinuities of interleaving rule-systems. Paradoxically, the counter-factual imagining of alternate rule ecologies and the recognition of their (dis)continuous application tell us more about what architecture might be in the future.

Proposition: Wittgenstein's snakes and Kripke's ladders
Imagine a design game in which participants take turns to apply different rule-based conditions to both the design and the interpretation of an architectural project. Following each mutation of form and light, including the initial distribution of mass, the subsequent player has to propose a linguistic picture of the 'state of affairs' they see. Each iteration becomes a rule-based appearance that they have to further elaborate. Repeat until self-similarity exhausts all options.

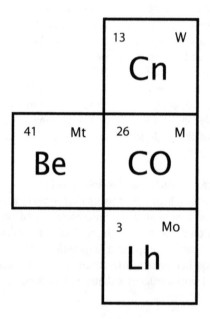

Rebus 26

Measure

Proposition 26: Contractual Obligation

Continuing the question of how form emerges from any number of disparate circumstances, one of the less obvious routes may be via the minutiae of contract relationships between parties within an architectural project. In normal circumstances of course, the contract relationship comes after a briefing process or, later in the timeline, after the creation of a design and documentation package that describes the contract conditions for the construction of a work.

Yet the nature of how this contract is formed, and the conditions attached to the fulfilment of the contract can vary wildly depending on the nuanced expectations of the parties to the contract. It is a reality of contract relations generally that they strive to comprehensively capture the duties, obligations and expectations of people and of material outcomes, yet are always an imperfect rendering of the reality of how actual behaviour and performance plays out. Of course, when a divergence occurs and exceeds tolerable limits, the contract documents become the definition of last resort. Testing the limits of contractual relations can become a path towards a remedy for parties, but it can also expose differing expectations and liabilities.

Contract theory generally poses the equilibrium of contractual equivalence between contracting parties based on the voluntary nature of the agreement. A contract is not formed when parties do not voluntarily assent to the conditions contained in the documents and is different to the type of expectations entailed by laws of tort and fiduciary obligations. Where forms of tort require a general expectation of obligation to unnamed other parties and generally require a civil remedy, and fiduciary obligations similarly ensure that responsibilities of care are fulfilled, contracts are agreements for a benefit by two or more parties usually within specifically defined circumstances.

For architecture, or more specifically for architectural design, the challenge in determining a contractual relationship that adequately captures the expectations of all parties is especially challenging. In essence, all the contract can usually point to in terms of fulfilment of terms is the construction of whatever is described and captured within the documentation. This is obvious of course, but it is also a challenge to the type of contractual relationships that may be imagined and created. If we consider the considerable legal difficulties surrounding the ownership and transfer of rights within the art world, particularly within conceptual art, some sense of the puzzle emerges. The gallery owner, Seth Siegelaub (1973), in the early 1970s created a contract intended to cater for the emergent class of conceptual artists whose work, quite deliberately, chose to problematize the relationship between 'work', 'value' and 'aesthetic content'. Just as Marcel Duchamp's Ready-Mades, some decades earlier, had flirted with the idea that aesthetic merit and financial value are only tenuously connected when intrinsic properties are concerned, so too were the plethora of works by conceptual artists that declared, for example, that all the world was their artwork (Piero Manzoni 1962), or a telepathic message (Robert Barry 1969). In all of these pieces, there is fierce resistance to the standard art-world contract of an aesthetic object created by an artist and sold to a collector as a unique and original expression of that artist's ability. Siegelaub's contract form was a serious attempt to confront the dynamics of an art world that managed to monetize all material relevant to an artist yet excluded them from any fiduciary benefit from subsequent sales of the work. Of course, in the context of the emerging conceptual art movement of the mid 1960s to 1970s, the idea that a contract could be sufficiently robust to ensure equity to both parties was philosophically, and legally, challenging.

Siegelaub's contract model was a form of information asymmetry in which the value proposition for the contract parties rested on their willingness to accept the unknown future value of artworks and/or the reputation of the artist. These types of contracts represent a more tendentious type of contract since there is the expectation that the chances of successful completion of the contract are less than optimal. Contracts in which there is information asymmetry generally devolve into three types: moral hazard, adverse selection and signalling. Moral hazard contracts entail the danger that one or more parties may be incentivized to undertake questionable behaviour to fulfil the contract; adverse selection contracts entail the reality that contracts (such as insurance) usually imply that parties to the contract are more likely to offer diminished information, and; signalling contracts where it is in the interest of parties to deliver optimum information to each other to improve the likelihood of success. In all of these instances, including those developed in a similar fashion to Siegelaub, the measurement of conditions is paramount.

How is this architectural?
For architecture, the contractual obligation of a building rests on several expected relations: the expectation that a design will be produced that aggregates and delivers the potential of the client assets; the contract for documenting a project to the point that successful cost estimates can be determined; the contract for acting for the client as a design creator; the contract for producing a series of experiences that, arguably,

exceed the material definition of the building project. More interestingly, the difference between what can be feasibly identified within a contract and what might be expected but not enumerated or cited is the point at which the most interesting architectural ambitions can be explored.

For artists' contracts like Siegelaub's, there is an expected ROI, a commercial risk that there will be future value following the execution of the deliverables, implying that the imbalance of expectations is balanced by the negotiation of perceived needs in the future. Curiously, since this was one of the philosophical canards that conceptual art was engaged with, it sought to juxtapose definitive conditions with ephemeral content. Were the contract to be tested in court, and there is no evidence that this occurred, but should it have been, competing definitions of what constituted the 'work' in the case of a performance piece might have been difficult to establish. Was the work the artist, the props they may have used, a recording of the event, the purchaser's experience, etc.? Since one of the purposes of conceptual art was to distinguish art practice from the market-driven production of consumable objects in a speculative economy, the fundamental antinomy between proof-of-value and proof-of-existence in conceptual art represents the philosophical tension the practice embodies.

Conceptual artists rely on the manipulation of this relationship; indeed the art world (Dickie) determines the shape and legitimacy of these contract forms. Conceptual art and *arte povera* deliberately ask what the un-economic consequences of behaviour and making may be. It is about nothing else other than finding what cannot be monetized. In this case, if we think about the moral hazard, adverse selection and signalling examples with respect to this work, some interesting issues arise regarding the mutuality of obligations between artist and collector, or artists and viewer. Moral hazard and adverse selection refer to an imbalance of information between the two parties. So in the relationships described, this may mean that either party has information about the subject matter, or the artwork, in question that is imbalanced. There are many potential examples on the artist's side: the work may not be unique, the artist may not believe the work is of value, the artist may not believe it is 'Art' and the artist may not be the originating maker or owner. Conversely, the owner/collector may know the true commercial value of the work; they may not think the work is 'Art'; they may be intending on destroying the work – or any other number of actions. In moral hazard scenarios, one of the parties has information prior to the contract that is not divulged, in adverse selection the information becomes known after the contract is agreed. So what does this mean, and was this anticipated?

In many respects, the clear discontinuity between conceptual work of deliberately little material value, made with little effort, and deliberately hostile to the idea of market fairness, *is* the ethical boundary that is deliberately being explored. Having the opportunity to stare into the eyes of Marina Abramović for a period of time in her *The Artist is Present* (2010) infers the relationship between her and the other participants has an unknown, but real, value. Of course, this is the point.

In architecture, it is possible to imagine a similar situation. The architect may be repeating old design tropes (uniqueness), they may be unconvinced of the design process and outcome (authentic value), or they may be unconvinced of the 'architectural' qualities of a project (fidelity). Similarly, the client may conceal their interest in the architect's 'architectural' abilities (concealment), so they may not be interested in 'architecture' at all (but want a building), and may not wish to contract for 'architecture', as opposed to design, documentation and management services. The fact that it is, sadly, easy to imagine these states of affairs in practice makes the issue of how you contract for 'architecture' even more important to consider.

So, how do you contract to secure 'architecture'? It may be tenuous to rely solely on the experience of conceptual art practice, but it is certain that the limit of rational tolerance that conceptual art explores might have some information for a discipline, architecture, in which the status of the quality of being 'architectural' is deliberately unvalued, or contested. In a different type of asymmetric contract situation, the practice of signalling serves the function of providing the other contracting party with information that will help them participate in the arrangement. Marina Abramović 'signals' that she is an artist who potentially undertakes artistic events, alerting the art market that the potential contract conditions of her performances will bring 'art' into the domain of the commissioning party. Similarly, architects signal their potential contract conditions by participating in activities that are sometimes legally, sometimes culturally, defined as architecture. The cultural reputation of architects, their market identity, is varied in order to contractually distinguish them from alternate choices. The lesson from Marina Abramović is that she is exceptionally efficient, economically, in contracting to produce internationally significant art wherever she is brought to be. Even though the physical cost of 'performing' the work for 736.5 hours was probably exhausting for Abramović, ultimately the ROI for her and the Museum of Modern Art in New York was presumably significant.

This is the point at which we can propose some questions regarding the contracting of 'architecture'. We should consider these questions not at the level of business management, but at the more philosophical level of finding out what 'architecture' is. What is the least costly, or most effective, method for producing the effect of architecture? Is it through sole practice (labour efficiency)? Is it through producing minimal material outcomes (cost efficiency)? Is it by declaring, like Bruce Naumann, that whatever one declares to be one's 'architecture' is the case (recategorization)? The point is that these are live questions and continue to be both debated and, importantly, contracted.

Proposition: The architecture contract game
Contract with another party to provide 'architecture'. Do not assume that this is a building, or a design for a building unless you are willing to point to the material fact(s) of the contractual outcome that satisfies the contract for 'architecture'. Ask yourself whether the tools of representing architecture or the institutional definitions of 'architecture' are necessary and sufficient conditions for the contract to be successfully completed. Importantly, be prepared to wield asymmetric information in your favour.

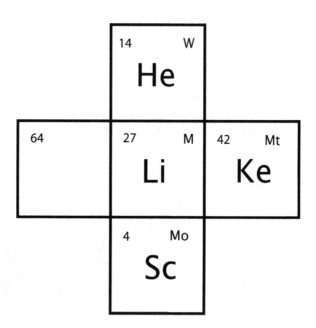

Rebus 27

Measure

Proposition 27: Life

Is life measurable? Certainly, a great deal of the efforts of scientific and rational discourse has been directed at the confirmation of this proposition, and with considerable success. But is life measurable within more constrained definitions that impact on the subject and direction of architectural design? Most architectural theory assumes that there is some level of causation between the activities of design and the tangible outcomes for the users. However, we would like to problematize this situation to determine how architecture does, or alternatively does not, affect life. Also, there persists a confusingly vast number of ways in which this could be pursued. Depending on how we define 'life' and how we determine what counts as supporting or diminishing life experiences, the possibilities seem endless. Obviously more focused measures are necessary and in particular a more focused measurement of how and why the measure of 'life-like' activities on the design side of architecture is valuable.

Conventional architectural design wisdom attributes the process of designing to human activity as, for example, a pattern-making, or collaborative, or scenario testing, or rule-following process. At its most heroic, this is presented as a work of individual genius, or creativity, that is communicated to a receptive and literate audience. More pragmatically, this is then followed by an explanation and analysis that is tested for consistency and viability. Inevitably, part of the testing process has focused on the interaction between the architect and the tools of design. While it is generally assumed that the tools have a benign, or at least supportive, role in allowing the architect to communicate the complex proposition that is architecture, the emergence and evolution of digital technologies have changed this fundamentally.

One of the goals of current digital ecologies is to explore the utility and interoperability of digital tools that permit the levels of formal definition and data acquisition that have been previously unachievable. Much of the discourse that has emerged from this process has had two goals: first, to better emulate the human process of designing, mirroring the organic behaviours of architects by creating enhanced tools to remove the need for repetitive, Cartesian functions (CAD, BIM for example), and second, to explore the capacity of digital modelling to emulate more complex geometries and emulate natural systems that occur in organic examples of morphological growth. That this betrays a bias towards a naturalistic fallacy, the belief that if something appears 'natural' it is inherently benign does not seem to have had an effect on these efforts.

Employing computational algorithms designed to optimize aspects of the architectural design process has placed considerable emphasis upon the role the architect plays in 'improving' a brief through the design and construction of different material realities. The adoption of the language, and some of the processes of morphogenetic development by architectural theorists, has instead tended to emphasize processes that mimic a kind of Darwinian theory of selection and optimization. The suppressed premise in this approach is that not only are the material properties of structures and surfaces demonstrating systemic economic efficiency but there is also the unacknowledged ambition that it will infer different types of human experience and, presumably, existence.

These complex systems, it is argued, allow more nuanced and bespoke solutions to design problems, permitting a broader range of forms to be designed and, potentially, constructed. Further, the process of harnessing the form-finding capacities of complex geometries meant that solutions that hitherto have been characterized as 'expressive' of human will could be freed from the stigma of seeming to be the arbitrary selection of a designer. The idea that certain materials responded to inherent form-types depending on the limit conditions of their physical properties, and that architects are engaged with the craft of material transformation, meant that there seemed to be opportunities for a productive synthesis between morphogenetic and emergent systems and speculative architecture.

'Emergence', as Helen Castle noted (Castle 2004), became a signifying term for a body of work, from Bernard Cache to Greg Lynn to NOX to Achim Menges, Michael Hensel and Michael Weinstock to R&Sie(n), that looked for paradigmatic similarities between form-making ecologies in non-architectural disciplines. Ultimately, and this is the genuine success of the movement, it was looking for an expanded field definition of architectural practice that created new roles for architects outside of the systems of land ownership, labour and capital of current market models. For that very reason, a practice that embraced constant, transitive morphologies seemed more attuned to a resistant politics than corporate models. It also promised the thrill of matching the capacity for complex forms in three-dimensional digital modelling systems with a body of theory, and biological science, that bridged between technical scientific questions and the natural world. Ultimately, the holy grail of matching morphogenetic forms with sustainability seems to be a possible and inevitable outcome.

There were problems however, and the emphasis on matching biological systems of growth to architecture brings up the parallel reality that these systems ruthlessly edit out unnecessary material – which is fine with protozoa, or anything non-sentient, but not so much with people. To understand this, we need to look at the science a bit more closely.

Christina Cogdell's brilliant analysis of this tendency points directly at the eugenics-based process in her *Toward a Living Architecture? Complexism and Biology in Generative Design* (2018) in which she traces the complex relationship between the study of evolutionary biology and computation processes. Initially, the idea is that the genes, phenotypes, DNA and other biological quanta that form part of the science were compared to a kind of 'programme' that played itself out according to the chemical propinquity of the constituent elements. That there was considerable overlapping interest between biologists and early theorists of computation, including Alan Turing no less, meant that ideas of convergence between the disciplines were encouraged. In the exploration of these ideas in architecture, we see two significant strands of development: architecture as a natural biological system 'grown' according to the organic properties of the constituent organic materials, and architecture developed according to metaphors of growth and self-selection matched to ideas about the empathic value of 'natural' emergent geometries.

Going forward to early pioneers of architectural computation such as John Frazer in the 1970s, the search for a language to explain the purpose and value of computational algorithms to an architectural audience brought forward the opportunity to see genuine scientific rewards in the matching of human practices to the sciences of complexity. Early computational study recognized that aspects of architectural design regarding repetitive and complex solutions in the formal typologies of buildings, and the distribution of development in vernacular urbanism could be mathematized and plugged into predictive models. These studies tended to see themselves as complementary to conventional design practice, prior to the mass adoption of digital modelling in the 1990s. It was with the advent and exploitation of applications that could visualize complex point-data sets as well as NURBS surfaces that the relationship between computational geometry and natural systems developed a serious challenge to ideas of design authorship.

Into the current century, the proponents of morphogenetic architecture would claim that the issue of eugenics misses the purpose of their projects, the simple optimization of resources, and has nothing to do with racial policies, but the general issue raised by Cogdell doesn't merely disappear with that caveat. Matching the architectural design process to certain biological metaphors inevitably shifts the responsibility for these consequences to abstract processes and not to specific architects or their clients, but issues of selective promotion and elimination still seem to flirt uncomfortably close to the principal tenets of eugenics.

The paradox for architects working in this field is that the developed relationship between evolutionary biology and computing has brought this ethical question front and centre into the debate on the future of architectural practice. The general encouragement to ensure that scarce resources are employed as efficiently as possible inevitably brings forward a full acknowledgement of the role of preferential choice in determining design priorities. In instances where the structure of decision-making in architectural design makes choice obvious, it is usually the most risk-averse option that tends to be favoured.

By proposing automated and discretionary systems that removed human judgement by presenting optimized 'solutions', it is tempting to see this as an economic tool that efficiently uses scarce resources. However, as Cogdell points out, it is almost impossible to predictively determine whether the growth patterns of microbial protocell forms will be of use for architecture unless heavily 'directed' by infrastructure, including growth media and scaffolding. Conversely, the employment of the ur-metaphor of 'emergent growth systems', when applied to architecture, returns the issue to that of selective breeding and the use of preferential choice as discussed above.

The problem with imagining a future architecture which is involved in the 'emergence' of biological forms of intransitive or transitive morphologies is that the manipulation of collective effects, the (dis)aggregation, swarming and enfolding of relationships is a form of Darwinism at best, and fatally politically agnostic at worst. This at the very moment the politics of affect are allowing vast swathes of the information economy to be cynically manipulated. Paradoxically, almost, it is in the field of praxis politics that the exercise of selective morphogenetic solutions should be explored. How do you aggregate and optimize proximities of resources and information to demonstrate some form of ethical goal?

How is this architectural?
As we have seen, the process of allying biology to architecture is deeply architectural insofar as a great deal of attention has been paid to the formal opportunities it presents. However, it is worth returning to the basic discursive context of this conversation and considering the use of the idea of 'life'. The same complex set of definitions that

Foucault employs in his book *The Will to Knowledge* (1976, 2006), in particular the notions of biopolitics and biopower, seem to have relevance here. Foucault considers the development of disciplinary structures, like architecture, that promote specific forms of behavioural governance to be emblematic of distributed self-regulation and a general symptom of late-capitalist society. For the emergent systems we have been discussing, Foucault's observations indicate the continual presence of ethical questions regarding the process of design and the anticipated effects of that design. Morphogenetic architectural projects, either as actual or metaphorical biological systems, cannot avoid discussions of the anticipated human and environmental outcomes of the design process.

Proposition: Greener/grass/graves – The 'meataphor'
What is the architecture of a project that seeks to grow sentient creatures, or the conditions for life? Can it be entailed into questions of biological determinism, gene theory and the operations of selective hylomorphism? How do we assess and allow biopolitics to reticulate through the metaphors of emergent formal geometries?

8: Site

Continuing the discussion of the constructive basis of architectural theories, this section looks at a series of variants of the idea of 'site'. Consideration of the site of an architectural project can have an effect on the project anywhere from minimal to fundamental of course. And while the relative details of a particular site will always be specific to that 'location', if it is one, there are opportunities for thinking about how architecture might consider what the term site denotes. The first chapter looks at questions of documentation and abstraction contained in the map/territory problem. Can a site ever be divorced from the representative tools employed to identify key features and potential avenues of development and enhancement? Further, is this process always directed towards those elements that preferentially describe a site's approachable reality? If we commence a project with the understanding that the site is, by definition, resistant to any form of architectural intervention, what becomes of the will-to-architecture?

The second chapter looks at two instances of sites that already fulfil this anti-architectural character, the terrain of transport and terrain vague. At first, the motility of vehicles is paramount and defines a landscape as the consequence of this condition. Arguably, it is completely hostile to any conventional expectations of architecture since the commitment to movement at velocity excludes the stabilities of architecture. Similarly, the discarded spaces that are adjacent to these forms of infrastructure are so characterless that they have their own identity: terrain vague. This term has grown to include any form of landscape that has escaped the utilitarian gaze of the market, and whose dereliction is so pronounced that it is trapped as a place in which architecture is undesirable and, possibly, impossible.

The third chapter extends this analysis to consider places of exile. As an extension of the idea of an expanded definition of site, the place that is specifically about exile (*locus solus*) is defined by its physical and psychological distance from a centre. As a design problem, this location is governed by the logistics of its isolation. How do you build there, is access to it abandoned, how is it maintained or left to decay? Since most sites are defined by their proximity to other conditions, the place of architectural exile represents a limit condition of what we consider to be a place.

Similar to the chapter on exile, the fourth chapter looks at the logical limit of possible site conditions. Using a simple form of modal logic, the logically possible but intuitively impossible proposition that you can have an architectural work that has no site and no project is discussed. This is more than a game of semantics, it is argued, because it takes seriously the idea that there are logical possibilities that are a legitimate area of architectural theory.

Finally, the fifth chapter in this section looks at an ultimate idea of site, that of atmospheres. An atmosphere is, by definition, an environmental condition that is mutable and indeterminant in a way that seems to be antithetical to an architectural project. However, if we think creatively about how an atmosphere can be manufactured and managed the question of site changes again. Having looked at limit definitions of a site, the idea of a median state that temporarily balances competing environmental actors completes the question of how sites are considered a generative condition for architecture.

4 Mo	15 W
Sc	**Hy**
43 Mt	28 M
Mtc	**Sa/t**

Rebus 28

Site

Proposition 28: Site Affectivity/Transgressions

A core philosophical question regarding the identity and utility of territories turns on the map/territory problem. At its simplest, the issue rests on the difference between a location and a representation of that location. It is the thinking mapmaker's dilemma of what to choose in determining the factual and diagrammatic content within a map. At what scale does the map lose the ability to convey nuances of the location selected? What are the diagrammatic conventions that should be prioritized, and are they interoperable? As an extension of these basic conventions, we can then think about ways in which the process of mapping can be strategic and imply positional influences on each other. Further, do maps attempt to reproduce authenticity, or produce inauthenticity, to the degree to which their representational identity is obscured by other heuristic ambitions?

The classic description of this problem exists in Jorge Luis Borges's story 'On Exactitude in Science' (1946), which succinctly describes the creation, and consequences, of a 1:1 scale map that envelops a landscape. There are other iterations of this relationship and the degree to which abstraction allows for the map to be smaller than the territory or, alternatively, to exceed the territory through an abundance of information means that the tension between reality and its representations is always contested. For architecture, of course, the approach to documenting, analyzing and extrapolating from a diagrammatic representation is a core activity. It means the selection of what to include or exclude from a representation is constantly open to interrogation since it generally illustrates the core data points of a design problem, presuming it retains the function of a map and not an illustration.

There is, here, the important distinction between diagram and illustration that frames the process of architectural image making. A map, as a working definition, contains only those glyphic marks that indicate a metrical relationship to other information of a similar type. The potential overlay of other strategies for territorializing an area and illustrating other conditions, the palimpsest, can be contrasted with the initial map to determine concordances and dissonances. As further maps are overlaid, the opportunity to recognize propinquities in the emergent work can become clear, or alternatively may become a white noise of information. Geoff Murnaugh (2016) pointed out in his essay '_applyChinaLocationShift' that this manipulation of maps can be engineered to provide as much indeterminacy as certainty. When viewing Google maps of Chinese cities, there is a consistent, off-set shift between the map and the satellite image, making casual investigation sometimes confusing. Anecdotally, this is the consequence of Chinese authorities delicately, but deliberately, confusing the information, but it also shows an opportunity for deliberately misreading the information. Eyal Weizman (2011), in a project that sought to capture this form of ambiguity and politicize it, looked for the locations on the Israeli maps of the very complex border between Israel and the Palestinian territories and created a design project that occupied the thickness of the border line which, at scale, was sufficient to locate a building in the ambiguous zone defined by the cartographic definition of the limit of Israeli territory. Weizman discusses the difference between a border and a frontier, in which he points to the inherent violence in forcibly dividing any territory through the ministrations of governance.

And finally, Gordon Matta Clark's early exercises in winkling out the physical, jurisdictional and intellectual anomalies in tiny fragments of New York real estate, *Fake Estates* (1973) undermined the presumption that cartography has already and exactingly covered even a highly developed location such as New York. Matta Clark searched for, found and purchased tiny parcels of land, usually thin slivers between conventional lots, that the city would auction off. While presumably, the purpose of the auction was to encourage adjacent owners to absorb the land and, thus, consolidate their conventional properties, Matta Clark's intervention allowed him to gesturally make these anomalies visible. For Matta Clark, the anarchic purpose of this was to illuminate these 'territories', employ the language of urban planning and surveying to bring them to life and then celebrate the absurdity of the gesture as a conceptual expression of 'art as intentionality'. A recent revision of these projects carried out by the galleries of Queens Museum of Art and White Columns, sponsored responsive works and tours to these locations, those that still existed since Matta Clark, who died in 1978, had long since relinquished ownership of the land. The divergence between the considerable attention, creative thought and discussion these parcels of land brought about and the immense banality of their reality is profound.

How is this architectural?
Clearly, the definition of a site and the process of filtering appropriate and actionable characteristics are core components of how an architect approaches a site and contextually attuned project. It is fundamental to conventional reality that a project be grounded in some dialogue between the world and itself, and the material tangibility of that location finds some way to express itself through the architect's response. This is not always the case, of course, and there are a myriad number of projects that paradoxically seem to ignore a site but are then subject to the vagaries

it offers. It is here that the map/territory dyad is especially relevant for there are two ways in which the architectural process can develop its map-like or cartographic capabilities: first, it can attempt to faithfully and conventionally document those qualities of the territory in order to achieve a form of synergistic construction of the site; and second, it can deliberately reterritorialize the identity of the location by manipulating the tools with which it is analyzed and the representational means by which this is communicated.

While there is a straightforward argument that the first approach is already flawed in the assumption that *any* intervention is without prejudices and interests, it can be said that conventional expectations mean that the genuine intention is towards giving a full account of the site, however complex and contested. In the second instance, the effort is towards a design strategy that consciously manipulates select aspects of a site for the express purpose of reinforcing architectural or other strategies. This is, in effect, a form of cancellation of those site qualities that do not cohere with the design approach that mandates what counts as visible, can be diagrammed and can then be acted upon.

Proposition: The mapmaker's un-made bed
Another way of approaching the map/territory problem, and its architectural consequences, is to think of a site's affectivity as an expression of its cultural identity. In Michel Houellebecq's *The Map and the Territory* (2010, 2012), he writes of the consequences of tourism as a cartography of 'authenticity'. Rather than identifying morphological information that serves as a form of architectonic ground, there could be two different ways of mapping, and reading, a site. The first could follow the resistant model and identify sites that are impossible for architecture, all for the challenge of finding out how to treat them architecturally; the second could adopt the Houellebecq model and 'picture' authenticity as it is represented within the extant media of a location. Like a form of a hyper-real dictionary, the maps of desire and consumption implicit within tourism, are there to be analyzed.

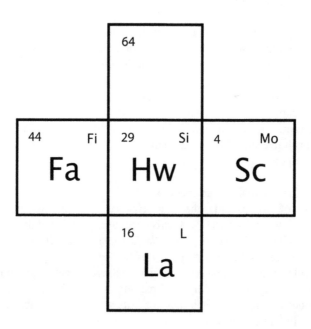

Rebus 29

Site

Proposition 29: Highway

> Soon I discovered that this rock thing was true
> Jerry Lee Lewis was the devil
> Jesus was an architect previous to his career as a prophet
> All of a sudden, I found myself in love with the world
> So there was only one thing that I could do
> Was ding a ding dang my dang a long ling long
> Ding dang a dong bong bing bong
> Ticky ticky thought of a gun
> Every time I try to do it all now baby
> Am I on the run?
> (Ministry, *Jesus Built My Hotrod*, 1992: n.pag.)

The relationship between the highway, or the automotive street, and landscape has a long and complex history. While all overland routes evolved from animal and wheeled traffic, the industrialization of travel through the motor vehicle, and the adoption of the car as a mode of personal transportation, brought a culture of touring and expeditionary adventure that deeply affected late twentieth-century culture. Whether it continues to do so is questionable given the moment of peak oil, and the evolution of engine systems that are based on renewable energy plants, and whether the development of artificial intelligence systems for piloting and navigating vehicles will become a norm.

So the relationship between a car, as a technological expression of identity, and human experience may well be coming to an end, or morphing into some other form of cultural symbiosis. But at the moment it retains an influence on the economics of domesticity as the second-most expensive outlay of most households. And given the diversity of car types and target ownerships, it would seem that the potential for motor culture to continue to influence the architectural form and language of cities, suburbs, townscapes, public spaces and the natural world is unchanged. Because a transport and road system coexists with the means to traverse it, and which conversely inflects architecture, this is a relationship more acknowledged than interrogated.

Dirt realism
Some of the consequences of this symbiotic relationship are that the urban forms of living, working, manufacturing, storing, transporting and growing that make up the synthetic world-form run into the natural landscape that serves as the location

for these activities. This is not new of course. Yet for all the focus on the culture of those forms of infrastructural work, it is the landscapes that are dominated by the service infrastructure that generally receive little attention. Because there exists considerable focused attention on the design of landscapes that serve ceremonial or aesthetic purposes, the urban landscapes that exist in the marginalia of transport territories tend to be considered a negative consequence of the need for utilitarian areas. As Andrew Tolland (2020) notes, Liane Lefaivre appropriates the term 'dirty realism' to suggest places that exist at the margins of urban development: the railyards, highway borders, disused carparks, vacant land and freeway runoffs that are left as an abject consequence of development.

These places are a direct consequence of industrialized transport, as they exist to allow for the safe movement (and sometimes the 'safe' destruction or crash zone) of transport. Our encounters with these spaces are either within the confines of industrial transport, seen through windshields at high speeds, or through fences that prohibit access, but never with any intimacy that might require us to recognize micro-identities or even plans of remediation. This is not the first time these spaces have been considered architecturally. Denise Scott Brown, Robert Venturi and Steve Izenour's *Learning From Las Vegas* (1972) is a pivotal study of déclassé spaces and places in the late-industrial city, and August Endell's *Die Schönheit der grossen Stadt* (1908) reviews the industrial landscape of buildings and spaces, both concerned with the dividend of formless and ad hoc solutions that exist in contrast to the designed spaces of the city.

Car love
Of course, the highly individualized experience of vehicles, the car in particular, is rich with evocations of the experience of driving. The entire automotive industry is deeply involved in the mythologization of cars as aesthetic objects and of driving as an existential experience. The list of cinematic expressions is endless, but we can selectively remember Monte Hellman's *Two Lane Blacktop* (1971), Peter Weir's *The Cars That Ate Paris* (1974), Richard C. Sarafian's *Vanishing Point* (1971), George Miller's *Mad Max (Road Warrior)* (1979), Steven Spielberg's *Duel* (1971), Rob Cohen's *The Fast and the Furious* (2001) and Ridley Scott's *Thelma and Louise* (1991), to name a few. Yet the context within which these narratives operate is, naturally, focused on either the car interior or the landscape of the street and highway. These contexts are devoid of distracting complexity at the scale of the car since their function is to act as a backdrop to the actions and behaviour of the vehicles. When the car stops, in these examples, the protagonists are usually considered to be

(temporarily) disengaged from the safety of the vehicle in a hostile environment that is generally considered featureless. A momentary focused image of struggling plant life or antagonistic fauna (non-urban) or urban decay and vandalism (urban) alerts the viewer to the inherently hostile nature of these contexts.

The absence of any expectation of a benign experience of nature in these contexts is a direct consequence of the velocity of transport. Cars, buses, trucks and rail-cars travel through places at a speed that makes it impossible to give them an identity that makes them a 'place' of any significance. These spaces are nominally divided by boundaries, fences and changes of surface, but effectively there is a continuous 'dirty' landscape of nondescript land with whatever forms of plant life can survive the conditions.

This 'dirty realist' landscape, as Lefaivre says, is the space that has arisen as a consequence of architectural and infrastructure projects that are, at best, desultory in their treatment of surrounding spaces. So the question, once the narratival hostility to these spaces is understood, is how to reframe their properties. In landscape theory, this study has evolved into a consideration of areas considered as 'terrain vague' a term coined by Ignasi de Solà-Morales (1995) in his famous essay of the same name. Similarly, the French theorist of landscape, Gilles Clément, has described the 'unloved' parcels of landscape that have been ignored by the actions and desires of either agriculture, garden design or construction, as a 'third landscape'. These landscapes exert their own autonomous identity, resistant to definition as not-garden, or not-agriculture. For Clément and for de Solà-Morales, there is the recognition that the utilitarian and interventionist strategies of development are directed at cleaning up the 'dirty' in 'dirty realist' landscapes.

How is this architectural?
As de Solà-Morales says, the architectural encounter with *terrain vague* is generally violent, insisting that the landscape be rehabilitated and incorporated into a citizenship of productive identity. From his point of view, like Clément, the last approach one might make to addressing these sites is architectural. It is better to consider the delicacy of what has survived, perhaps thrived and acknowledge its ecological significance outside of the domain of conventional landscape definitions. The process of re-wilding these sites, permitting them to evolve as self-regulated domains means that they enjoy a novel identity free from utilitarian definitions. So how could architecture possibly be beneficial in this circumstance?

It seems perverse to attempt to create further 'dirty' contexts that feed the nihilistic tendency of destructive interventions, yet perhaps there is a material language of form that is attuned to the life cycle and material resilience of the *terrain vague*. Temporary shelters, or ad hoc constructions are the first thoughts, but the risk of fetishizing a form of architectural *arte povera* seems disingenuous. Patrick Barron and Manuela Mariani's edited text, *Terrain Vague: Interstices at the Edge of the Pale* (2014), speculate on possible interventions, but these are largely preservationist. Architecture, in this instance, is defined as monuments, largely forgotten or deliberately temporary. One suggestion by the contributor Jennifer Scapettone stood out however, the vast landfill servicing metropolitan New York, the incredibly named *Fresh Kills Landfill*. This landfill, one of the largest man-made structures, will eventually become a park, but what if it could be harnessed to make something more specifically architectural? Perhaps something more structured, but inherently the consequence of its abject origins?

Perhaps an architectural response could emulate the images of primal occupation created by Superstudio, a cartesian plane of emergence that brackets the *terrain vague* as a phenomenological 'thing in itself'? Superstudio is generally most famous for the Continuous Monument project in which the vast white cuboid structure spanned the globe, but I think it is in the *Dodici Città Ideali Twelve Ideal Cities* (1971) that the opportunity exists to work cooperatively (and architecturally) with the *terrain vague*. These cities, borrowing from Calvino's *Invisible Cities* discussed earlier, are explorations of different city forms, obsessively measured in the manner of Renaissance treatises, but focused on a post-apocalyptic world. Imagining a thirteenth city, perhaps named 'The City of Fresh Kills', that takes the form-making and site-defining impulses of architecture and revivifies this landscape may be a way of thinking this through architecturally.

Proposition: Fresh kills speedway
Imagine a drag-racing track or speed circuit that combines the velocity of high-speed transport and the groundscape of *terrain vague*. Situated in the 'City of Fresh Kills', this facility would grow from the detritus of urbanity and provide a spectacle grounded in an evolving and resistant wild terrain, in a kind of cooperative detente between transport, architecture and the third landscape.

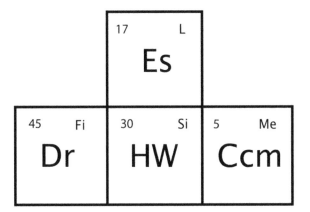

Rebus 30

Site

Proposition 30: High Way

The relationship between empty and isolated places and the process of creating remote architecture is fraught with the tension between the need to escape society and the logistics in bringing construction to the location. You can isolate yourself, but can you endure in the isolation, physically and psychologically? While a truly isolated location is beyond the network of roads, paths and seaways, an important aspect of isolation comes in the consideration of the architecture that (d)evolves in high and far places. The pursuit of loneliness is both a test of existential resolve and the ability to endure separation from human relations, generally with the aim of enhancing self-knowledge (epistemic security) and (possibly) testing the legitimacy of some supra-human order – perhaps asking yourself the question: Is there a God? Without wishing to predetermine theological outcomes we can nevertheless ask the architectural question: Is there an architecture of loneliness?

Loneliness
Loneliness generally is considered a toxic consequence of modern existence, in particular the lack of social cohesion and bonds caused by the intersection of housing availability, employment, cultural marginalization and social isolation. In these instances, there is considerable literature on the role of architecture in alleviating some aspects of these conditions. Architecture is just one factor, but it is a commonplace for responsible housing projects to subscribe to the need for social inclusivity and to search for design outcomes that mitigate the effects of loneliness across a broad spectrum of demographics.

There is a model for the experience of loneliness which is if not a positive life experience then a meaningful one. It is the exile. The rhetoric surrounding the idea of the exile in a 'wilderness', or place of (in)voluntary banishment, rehearses their isolation as an enactment of the individual's proximity to destruction. It relies on the knowledge that the physical and psychological pain the exile suffers is unequivocally their own. Generally too, the place of exile is a location, or state, that is forced on the participant, or found by happenstance. The idea of making an architecture of the exile seems to defeat the purpose of the banishment if it becomes a place of respite. So it is important to distinguish between voluntary and involuntary exile. We will concentrate on the former.

If we think about the architectural colonization of the isolated location, intuitively it requires the diminishment of perceived discomforts and, arguably, the pain of exile by creating those external instruments of shelter and society that demonstrate the end of loneliness. So the architecture of the lonely place is both the instrument for mitigating the discomfort and is also the instrument for extending and perpetuating its experience. For example, the stylites of the early Christian Church would mount a column in a remote location and, through their insistence on occupying the structure and maintaining their relation to God through continual devotion, would spend extreme periods of time at heights up to fifteen meters above ground level. For Simeon Stylites, in the fifth century CE, it would be 37 years before he finally died. It was an act of self-abnegation, exile from conventional society and, presumably, an enhanced spiritual experience. That it was endured for such an impossibly long period of time, Simeon died on top of his column, makes the intense relationship between life and place even more extraordinary. Whether Simeon or any of the other devotees would be considered lonely is another question as the act of dramatically self-removing in a specific location in itself attracted attention. Paradoxically for Simeon, his self-exile made him a popular authority on matters of piety and, arguably, provided social cohesion in the context of his community.

But the architecture of loneliness is another question, and the creation of an architectural construction in a place that ensures and governs the experience of loneliness would seem to be a perverse form of asocial behaviour. The development of this idea can be understood by examining the idea of authenticity of experience, epistemically and ontologically. In the course of everyday life, the sense of how personal autonomy guides our understanding of authentic experience is a crucial aspect of self-determination. It is the demonstration of a self-reflexive understanding of the authenticity of behaviour: know thyself. The challenge architecturally is to create a location, or environments of effects, or constraints, that govern this process.

The column and the clearing
For the Simeon Stylites, it was the column he ascended and occupied, for the hermit it could be the cave in the wilderness, for the writer it could be the cabin in the forest that Aleksander Solzhenitsyn or Theodore Kaczynski occupied. The architectural location is the place where the tools of the lonely are stored in order to manufacture the purpose of their loneliness: gathering, combining, producing and legitimizing the reality of the exile. For Heidegger, this was the *Lichtung*, the clearing, in which a clear (yet bounded) space appears as the pre-condition for self-awareness.

The desert is also, in Heidegger, a *Lichtung* (a clearing) but is by definition a clearing without a boundary since there is no evidence of the consequences of clearing, only of a pre-existing nothingness (desert). But there is also the shift in lens that sees the clearing of the small, the miniature topography of small shifts in the surface, without a prospect of a middle ground. So even in a seemingly, indistinct environment, the opportunity for discerning difference exists. For Simeon Stylites it was the transformation of existence from the horizontal plane to the vertical axis.

Loneliness is then a condition that may be pursued and enhanced or overcome. And in being overcome the exquisite self-knowledge that it might have brought is also diminished. The benefit of social bondedness cancels out the experiment in isolation and endurance.

How is this architectural?
While the terminology we have been considering has alluded to Heidegger, specifically *Lichtung*, we could also include *Ereignis* (event) and *Weltbild* (world-picture) and *Gestell* (framing), as well as his description of the fourfold (earth, sky, divinities and mortals); however, it would be distracting to simply enter into the Heideggerian ecology of language and speak of the architecture (construction) of loneliness simply on those terms. The general trajectory, I would argue, of Heidegger's project and certainly of the many architectural theorists that employ his terminology is towards the repair of the self through an enhanced awareness of one's place in the world (*Dasein*), rather than the trials of denial and separation that are consistent with voluntary exile and loneliness.

We may wish to think about James Turrell's ur-project, the Roden Crater complex (1977–ongoing) and its vast reconfiguration of a crater as a ceremonial space for secular rituals. However beautiful as this construction is, it is more a site of pilgrimage that is ultimately focused on the contemplation of the vastness of the Arizona sky than a place of loneliness and exile. It is, as its press literature states, 'A gateway to observe light, space and time'.

Counter-intuitively, I'd like to suggest thinking about the 1972 project by Rem Koolhaas, Marian Vriesendorp, Elia Zenghelis and Zoe Zenghelis: *Exodus, or the Voluntary Prisoners of Architecture* in which they constructed a narrative regarding the role of urban architecture. The premise is simple; a city (London) is divided into the good and bad halves through the instrument of architecture (a wall). Various characteristics of the megastructure are described, but essentially it emulates the phantasmagorical thinking of Superstudio we have seen previously. So what to think of this project in relation to the challenge of loneliness?

It makes architecture the focus of the social travails of the city. It is the source, and the cure, of the urban malaise of a desire that can only be satisfied through architecture, yet is also a source of frustration due to the impenetrability, physical and philosophical, of construction. On these terms, true exile is the encounter with an architecture that constantly defies accommodation. Michael Heizer's *City* (1972) or Rachel Whiteread's *Ghost* (1990) and *House* (1993) could demonstrate this since they are neither monuments nor tombs, in the strict sense of representing a state of affairs or acting as a mnemonic device. Ultimately perhaps the measure of the success of an architecture of exile and loneliness is the degree to which the challenge of identifying, responding and critically (re)constructing architecture is endemic to the experience. Exile, in this sense, is the compulsion to continually build meaningful structures for the sole purpose of one's own obsessive separation from society. If we think of the diverse collection of work that is gathered under the label 'Outsider Architecture', the work of obsessive and, usually, self-taught constructors we get a sense of the project. Or if we consider the convoluted interiors of Kurt Schwitter's *Merzbau* (1937–48), the constructions of an artist who was in constant exile. From consanguinity with Dada artists he admired from Germany, Norway and the United Kingdom, each time Schwitters responded to exile, indifference and loneliness by creating constructions imprinted with his complicated relationship with the world. The question, and the challenge, is how to bring the lens of architecture to this state of being.

Proposition: Caliban's cabin
In Shakespeare's *The Tempest* (1611), Caliban is the half-human creature that Prospero relies upon and reviles. Having lived on the island prior to the arrival of the banished Prospero and Miranda, Caliban is left at the end of the play with the uncertainty of whether he is to remain in servitude to the Duke in Milan or remain on the Island. Similarly, in Robert Browning's 'Caliban upon Setabos' (1864), Caliban seethes at his creator, Setabos, recognizing that he (Caliban) is as much a beastly product of his world as other life forms and will never be released from this mortality. So how does Caliban make architecture for himself?

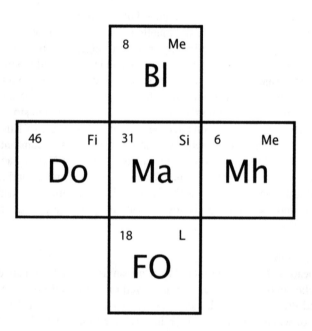

Rebus 31

Site

Proposition 31: Manufactured

What is a site? Is it the true characteristics of a place, or one that is merely filtered by the instruments employed to measure it; or one that is entirely processed in order to support its illogicality (Disneyland); or evolves as a consequence of a work that is imposed upon it? Site conditions are usually the default ground from which all projects emerge since the very purpose of the architectural project is to demonstrate a form of extensionality latent within its location. We have addressed a number of these questions earlier, but the questions regarding the specificity of certain aspects remain to be explored.

What is a hidden site? Or a false site? Or a site that is deliberately imperfectly known? In some respects, it is the incongruities of site knowledge that are more interesting than the orthodox obligation to be consistent with the datum conditions. While it is possible, of course, to produce a work that utterly reconfigures its location and hence erases the complexities of the historic present, and it is obvious that the imposition of any work into a location changes its future identity, what of the site that is hidden and unknowable?

In some respects, this seems to be little more than a false parsing of descriptive language since a 'thing', let alone a complex entity such as a site, cannot be known and unknown simultaneously. Geoff Murnaugh's outstanding *BLDGBLOG* is consistently dedicated to acquiring different intellectual instruments for knowing a location and questioning its constructive tendencies. And while Murnaugh is committed to finding innovative and thematically unorthodox methods for reconsidering what the 'ground' of architecture consists of, we can agree with his general proposition that the symbiotic relationship between site and architecture is, literally, a *Grundfragen* or foundational (grounding) question.

So, conjecturally, we could say there are three plus one site-condition types:

> 1. The first is the null set, site does not matter and is indistinct. The project is paramount.
> 2. The second is the set in which the site is considered fundamental and contiguous with the project to the point where they are indistinct.
> 3. The third is the general truth set in which site and architecture have mutual and perceived relationships. Site defines and responds to the relative material/engineered composition of the project.

Plus one:

> 4. The site does not exist, in a conventional sense and is by ordinary measures ineffective on architectural interventions, it is a false site. Similarly, projects may not exist as a necessary condition, though may be conjectured.

In the first condition, the presumption is that site is *terra nullius* and that the process of forming architecture is, like that of the digital plane in a three-dimensional modelling programme, inconsequential to the self-referential design transformations of the architecture itself. Some will lament this condition as an abrogation of the idea that all places have a *genius loci*, but the fact remains that much work is completed with this level of deliberate ignorance.

In the second condition, the number of sections is vast since it constitutes the norm of practice. The relationship between ground and expression is, as Bernard Cache describes in *Earth Moves* (1995), an intimate topological outcome of latent formal vectors, ones that shape the form of the town of Lausanne. The extension of Cache's argument is that he sees a formal continuity between pre-existent and geological transformations and those of the vernacular civic organization and building traditions that have evolved at the location. Cache's proposition is radical inasmuch as it refuses to differentiate between the formal continuity of context and gesture. All architecture, in this mode of reading, is the involution of propinquities of the latent forces of a site, or alternatively, a confrontation and estoppel of these vectorial forces. The Farnsworth House, by this reading, is both an eruptive 'flowering' of the flatness of its location on the site and a punctum that masks its violent confrontation with the plane of its appearance.

The third site condition is, in many respects, the process of extending the effects of condition two to become condition one. In deleting, cancelling and removing the effect of inter-determinacy between site and architecture particular strategies of dominance and occupation are made apparent and identifiable. The difference is one of rhetorical force and direction. In this state, we see the building's dominance as the final outcome of the process of emplacement on a site that no longer meaningfully exists as a critical counterpart to the architectural project. Stan Allen's (1997) (in)famous essay on field conditions illustrates a form of diagrammatic rendering of the vectorial fields of influence between objects within a field. For Allen, the site and the objects cohere in a tension that ultimately situates the architectural project as the outcome of this figure/ground relationship. The dynamic and temporally fluctuating conditions between project and site mean that the minutiae of a site are meaningless outside of their diagrammatic effects on the disposition of the project.

These three categories form the general class of site strategies that architectural projects work from vacillating between an indifference to the site to an obsessive adherence to the material and historical realities that assume a context is anterior to a project. In all cases, site is the condition that exists beyond the effective control of the project even though the project will come to be contiguous with that first encounter and, naturally, form a future site in and of itself.

The fourth condition, the false or fake site, seems to offer something else. At the outset we can see a few possibilities here with respect to the other conditions, first there is no inherent and necessary relationship between site and project; second, there is the possibility that the project is always, recursively, the site irrespective of the scale at which the project is imagined, and; third, there is never a project possible since there is a site, conceivably, in which no project could occur.

The first three conditions of site and project describe the general organization of theories of architecture and context that drive many descriptions of the challenges of architectural theory. Conjecturally, we can say that site + project = architecture since we are asserting that all of the conditions (1–3, plus 4) describe architectural approaches to the effect of site on the design process. It can be far more complicated when we come to start defining what exactly is inferred by the idea of 'site' or 'architecture', but projects that are either a combination of site and project (most work, including Allen) can be contrasted to those in which site is ignored completely (digital), or conversely, that the site is the project (Cache). The fourth we will consider once we have set out a method of characterizing these variants.

Modal variants
In essence, what we are considering here is a version of the necessity and probability characteristics of modal logic. If we take the view that there are two factors for consideration – site and project, then the general proposition is that site + project = architecture. If we were to translate these states into values, where a factor (either site or project) is present, it is given a value of 1, and where it is absent, it is given a value of 0. In modal logic, there is also the possibility of introducing versions of these which attribute a negative value to one of the factors, i.e. -1, but in this example we will stick to a positive presence (1) or an absence (0).

A simple matrix of these possibilities will give the variants of either (0,0), (1,0), (0,1) or (1,1). In this scenario, the first condition is (1,0), the second is (0,1) and the third is (1,1). The fourth (0,0) could be considered in two ways: trivially to be the absence of both site and project, a null set, but there is also the possibility of remapping these numerical identities back on to our semantic and situational use of the site/project/architecture triad. In this sense, (0,0) can be rephrased as (−1,−1): not-site and not-project.

While this terminology may seem tendentious when we try and think about what a not-site or not-project might be, if we introduce the idea of necessity and possibility then it can become clearer. Remember that we are not trying to define, once and for all, what the relationship between a site, a project and the recognition of architecture actually is, but to offer ways of thinking clearly about the relationship.

Necessity and possibility
Without introducing further notational complexity, there are conditions in modal logic where it is important to understand the relationship between necessity and possibility of actants. Intuitively we know that in our basic equation of site + project = architecture, there will be characteristics where there will be necessary conditions for it to make sense, and most importantly, possible conditions that make it conjecturally interesting. 'Possibility' is a propositional state that architectural theory deals with as a matter of course every time it puts forward a methodology for new work, or for reinterpreting existing states of affairs.

Modal logic considers five states that are linked by conditions: necessity, possibility, analyticity, impossibility and contingency. Most of these are the consequence of determining whether things are necessary or possible, most importantly in our case, for considering propositions in which conditions are not necessarily but possibly true, or for when you consider the variant that things are not possible, but necessary. Modal logic provides a way for considering the negative states of necessity and possibility.

So, returning to our basic equation of site + project = architecture, we can describe some further variants, in particular those referring to the issue of the false or fake site. In the case of the not necessarily but possibly true, we can imagine a scenario in which there are necessary site conditions and possible projects, or not necessary projects and possible sites, etc. It becomes interesting when we have not-possible sites and/or not-possible projects. What does this mean?

How is this architectural?

It is clear that the consideration of things possible and necessary, in the first instance, provides a consistent line of dependencies that describe the various configurations of site, project and architecture that we can imagine. This works not just for the relationship we are considering, but can work for finer-grained analysis of, say, what are necessary and possible conditions in the definition of architecture for example. So here is the point. We want to be able to say that the relationships between criteria are non-trivial and, as a consequence, authentic. But if we think of a scenario in which the not-necessary and/or the not-possible are considered – maybe a fictional site or project, or maybe a fictional conclusion as to what is architecture – we run up against the problem of fictionality generally, that it is not authentic.

Modal logic addresses this question, explicitly, via the consideration of possible worlds in a manner that is actually very familiar to architecture. There is a possible world modal logic demonstrates, in which it is authentically the case that what is considered not possible *is* possible. Criteria of possibility in *our* world do not hold in this possible world, hence the proposition is not necessarily impossible. So, a speculative architectural project that is exotically fictional and flouts any number of 'our world' rules is not insensible, it is authentically consistent with the premises created to describe it. Returning finally to our fourth (0,0) variant, we can see that the situational definition of a not-site or a not-project is an entirely consistent expression of the logically consistent fictionality of architectural speculation.

Proposition: Deep fake estate

Extending our work from Proposition 28, imagine a project that cannot be sited in an our-world location, cannot be defined according to our-world criteria and provides an expression of architecture that is our-world unfamiliar.

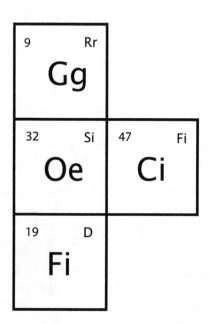

Rebus 32

Site

Proposition 32: Other Ecologies

One of the core directives for architecture studios, and practice also, is the requirement that we understand the mediation of the environment. In general, architecture is always about environmental mediation in some form, but the issues of the relationship between comfort levels, functional expectations and human physiology do not always stretch further than a median expectation of normal limits, and abstract notions of comfort and human performance.

Of course, three separate systems are in play in this relationship: the human physiology (including phenomenological awareness of atmospheres), the building systems and localized meteorology. The interfaces between the three systems are cooperative inasmuch as they each have an ecology of warmth/coolth/moisture transference that regulates the individual experience, but this says no more than we are constantly attempting to mitigate the conflictual relationships between the systems to achieve a constant state and, hence, a conservation of energy generally. We can think of many instances in which the temporary suspension of the idea of comfort and functionality is made in order to impose different temporary objectives – the sauna, the ice bath, the wind tunnel, the lookout and the tomb. In these, the suppression or stimulation of one system in order to enhance the experience of another is calibrated to the senses of the user. In some instances, it is about temperature or physical comfort, in others it is about psychological experience (agoraphobia and claustrophobia), but they are essentially the outlier experiences of the bell curve of social tendencies.

What of an architecture that operated just in those limits? Or one that applied the systemic effects of extreme experience unevenly across the human experience? In normal circumstances, the control of the systems of experience is limited to those of the body and its clothing, and to the system of the enclosure, the architecture.

What of an ecology of extremity that is actively chosen: too hot (desert or volcanic proximities), too cold (polar environments), or too extreme (within a storm) or too isolated (space)? While the median comfort condition is assumed to be the band within which functioning occurs, the adaptation to extreme environments means that there is a need to address both the pragmatics of comfort as well as an expanded notion of what constitutes a tolerable 'atmosphere' of experience.

There is a difference between the measurement of physiological responses to an environment and a sensitivity to its 'atmospheric' qualities that are, naturally, an extension of that physiological experience. Employing a different term that has contemporary currency, these might also be characterized as atmospheres. The difference here, and one that most commentators on the aesthetics of atmospheres generally acknowledge, is that architecture has a special capacity to generate atmospheric conditions in which the heightening of certain qualities can be the conscious outcome of architectural design. As Gernot Böhme says:

> Atmosphere is the prototypical 'between' – phenomenon. Accordingly, it is a difficult thing to grasp in words against the background of European ontology – Japanese philosophers have an easier time of it with expressions such as *ki* or *aidagara*. Atmosphere is something between the subject and the object; therefore, aesthetics of atmosphere must also mediate between the aesthetics of reception and the aesthetics of the product or of production.
> (Böhme 2017: 25)

Böhme tends to overemphasize the 'staging' of atmospheres as the method for bringing certain types of atmosphere to attention. He describes the role of the art-director as wholly focused on building a certain atmosphere that is part of the synaesthetic experience within the space of the theatre and the narrative of the performance. Yet it is clear also that while all circumstances have an 'atmosphere' of some kind, it is just a stand-in term for ontological awareness, specific atmospheric experiences are governed by the management of the incident environmental factors that determine that specificity. It is at this point that it makes sense to return to the idea of tolerance and what is tolerable within an atmospheric experience.

How is this architectural?
Generally speaking, the science of environmental engineering defines certain comfort bands that human physiognomy can function within. There is no need, or attempt, to granularize the nature of this band since it is acknowledged that it is a working assumption and to criticize these assumptions would distract from the other aims of the engineering process. Yet, as architects, it makes sense to speculate on how extreme environments actively require the consideration of the atmospherics of comfort. It does not make sense to never feel cold in an Arctic environment, hot in a desert environment, etc.

This is more than adjusting the thermostat of the heating, ventilation and air conditioning system however, and it is here that the question of atmosphere in Böhme's sense can be considered. In part, it requires an understanding of how atmospherics are currently described, and the way in which these experiences are tied to narratives of placedness and phenomenal engagement in a location. Kathleen Stewart's description of social interactions in her essay 'Atmospheric Attunements' (Stewart 2011) is, like any descriptive narrative, imbued with an attention to the detail of human experience. However for Stewart, unlike a creator of fiction, it is an argument for a different, perhaps radical, way of describing *genius loci* within the discipline of planning and environmental design.

To make this architectural requires both the attention to environmental mediation that is within the technical design remit of architecture and the capacity to narratively describe the expanded atmospheric experience that would ensue. It is a disposition that, unlike many other chapters in this book, does not entail specific formal strategies or diagrammatic analyses. Yet it speaks to an experience of architecture that is far more representative of everyday experience for non-architects.

Proposition: The book of atmospheres
In essence, a project of this kind does not require any specific type of formal or programmatic drivers in order to capture the relationship between atmosphere and architecture, but it is true that an extreme environmental condition can be the setting for expanded experiences. *The Book of Atmospheres* can be both the crucible of the form of attention to atmospheres that extreme conditions create and the narrative of the experience.

9: Fidelity

The idea of fidelity in architecture is linked to the traditional triad of *venustas, firmitas* and *utilitas*. *Firmitas*, which can be translated as being structurally sound and economically efficient, brings to mind also the relationship between modes of measurement in architecture and building, and those in other expressive media. When we consider the role that the diagramming of data plays in parallel disciplines, it is possible to consider whether the translation into a representative media allows there to be a crossover into architecture. The idea of fidelity implies that this diagramming needs to be accurate and that benefit of this precision is that there is clarity in its application and use. Fidelity also promotes the idea that the outcome of this level of accuracy carries the benefit of promoting trust in the systemic application of abstract representations.

The first exploration of the concept of fidelity looks at the supposed relationship between architecture and music. Notwithstanding the popularity of the idea that architecture is 'frozen music', it seems sensible to ask how that relationship might work without compromising both disciplines. Since the principal purpose of music is not to provide an analogy to architecture, or for architecture to be studied solely for its musicality, the question remains of what structural relationships might legitimately exist between the two. The development of avant-garde musical forms that explore the consequences of a graphic manipulation of the score, and of the instructive relationship between composer and performer, allow us to consider how this might be architectural. Ultimately, the proposition tentatively suggests that it requires the management of narratival aims to find a middle position between the disciplines.

Looking more closely at this relationship, the second chapter studies examples of diagrammatic complexity in avant-garde music. By looking at architectural examples that are specifically and deliberately 'tuned' to sound performance, the two sides of the equation between music (or rather sound) and architecture can come together. For both sound pieces and architecture, representational media attempt to stand in as an instructive projection of a future state – the performance is 'played' and the architecture is 'constructed'. Crucially for both, the kinaesthetic process of materially presenting an outcome has an indexical meaning to the viewer/audience, though the duration of the two differs widely. But should it? Could a musical/sound piece outlast an architectural performance? Further, *is* the process of embodiment and emplacement always idiosyncratically specific to that moment given the consistency of the score or drawings? These are not simply questions of relativism but could point to another way of performing architecture.

The final chapter of this section examines the idea of non-Euclidean geometry and in particular the relationship between forms of documentation and their projections into our world. The distinction between orthogonal and cartesian geometry that architecture has relied on and that of non-Euclidean geometry is not simply an expression of an axiomatic anomaly. The behaviour of parallel lines across a curved surface that converge, such as lines of longitude, can usually be ignored in architectural documentation but the fact of the existence of these axioms compels us to think about their applicability to architecture. Again, it is a question of fidelity to an abstract model and an acknowledgement that for every architectural expression that responds to, or proposes, a cartesian site condition, there are a vast number of complex sites that create a different form of governance. Ultimately, it is an issue of topological coherence, the understanding of the role of non-Euclidean topologies (of the mathematics of vectors and surfaces) that nascent digital technologies have enabled us to investigate.

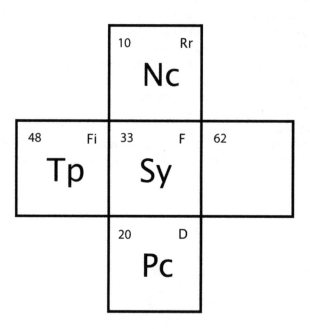

Rebus 33

Fidelity

Proposition 33: Synaesthetic

One of the most overused analogies in architectural theory is the observation that architecture and music demonstrate similar synaesthetic properties. Goethe's popular but inexact observation that 'music is liquid architecture, architecture is frozen music' (Goethe n.d.: n.pag.) has been used to point to the clear aesthetic criteria the disciplines share, but it has been generally used to justify any number of music-based architectural projects that, once saddled with Goethe's quote, are meant to demonstrate their inherent musicality. Goethe is clearly pointing to issues of time and duration in the comparison: architecture endures, music is ephemeral, and both demonstrate complexity. Isomorphically, this stems from the suggestion that the complexities of orchestral or multi-instrument music demonstrate sufficient harmonic consistencies which are, within the context of the composition, similar to the structural symmetries and over-determinations of architecture. Where a grid line may serve as the location for a structural member, a cladding system, a surface pattern and a piece of furniture, so too the sheet music of an orchestral piece, or of a Pro Tools or Ableton file, will align sonic experiences that synchronize complex aural relationships.

Similarly, core terms relevant to both disciplines are shared: rhythm, harmony, structure, pattern, texture/timbre, movement, tempo, duration (Bergson), amplitude, frequency and phase. Indeed in the pedagogy of architecture, the employment of terms familiar from music is often used in acculturating novice architecture students to the spectrum of aesthetic judgements in the discipline. Arguably, music is more universally and instinctively understood than architecture and, by calling on this language, there is a familiarity with the relationships between musical experience and the significant empathetic enjoyment it creates. People like music, people learn to like architecture.

What seems generally unsatisfying in the music and architecture analogy is the general lack of specificity of what precisely counts, and how it effectually works, in the relationship between the 'architectural' in music and the 'musical' in architecture. The general answer seems to be 'everything' since the two disciplines seem to be similarly complex and involve the orchestration of a complex level of aesthetic stimuli. Duration stands out as a particular influence since it requires movement of the figure within the architecture emulating the duration of a musical piece.

Jenefer Robinson (2012) cites the effect of music to create a form of bodily engagement that invites listeners to anticipate and reach fulfilment with the progress of a musical score. The degree to which the combinatorial organization, including aberrant compositional flourishes, etc., is recognized accords with the enjoyment and awareness of the music as a fulfilment of particular vectorial directions of tone, key and pitch. She argues that architecture is the same inasmuch as there are similar expectations of fulfilment, though it is unclear whether the species of attention within architecture is as necessarily developed since selective listening is different from indifferent wandering. It also presumes (and maybe this is alright) that it is possible to attend to different components at different times while ignoring, or being distracted, at others.

Some questions emerge from this: Why would we assume that there is the opportunity to undertake a design project that is generated by the structural characteristics of a single score? What of the opportunity for multiple scores to be concordant with a single architectural work, or vice versa? Does that create a break in the entailment, or does it merely point to some overlap of features which it is the task of language to dwell upon? Since the idea of attribution and causation is fluid, how is it possible that an architectural structure might be sufficiently consistent in its exploration of visual rhythms to evoke the idea of music?

But why can't Chartres Cathedral be compared to a K-pop song, or Arvo Pärt to a McDonald's? What is the 'harmonic' relationship between music and architecture that adequately does justice to both media? The Renaissance concept of *concinnitas* famously articulated by Alberti in *De re aedificatoria* (1443–52) explicitly identifies the correspondences between a study of harmony in music and the idea of proportion in architecture. Principally, the suggestion is that the pragmatic recognition of regular formal and compositional devices was sufficient for the analogy to 'work'. However, as music, and architecture, became increasingly complex and self-referential the insistence on their being an overall structuralist aesthetic schema for both diminished in popularity. Furthermore, the idea that a single score might drive an architectural project seems fanciful. And yet it has.

Moses und Aron
Famously the employment of Arnold Schönberg's unfinished opera *Moses und Aron* (1932) served as a governing motif for Daniel Libeskind's Extension to the Berlin Museum (Jewish Museum) (1999), one of the most famous examples of a clear and intentional relationship between architecture and cognate ideas in philosophy, history

and music. For Libeskind, the project represented the opportunity to memorialize cultural references that demonstrate historical and philosophical moments consistent with the melancholy duty of the museum to remember the exiled and murdered Jewish population of Berlin. Specifically, Schönberg's music and libretto describe a journey of redemption that Libeskind felt was important in the overall thematic orientation of the building. That Libeskind, properly speaking, relied more heavily on the libretto does not diminish the entwined effect of music and narrative, given the aesthetic wholeness of the opera overall.

Considering the brief for the museum project: how to represent the absence of Berlin's Jewish population as a consequence of the war, *Moses und Aron* is certainly an apt model for a work dedicated to the impossibility of representation. Moses, the prophet who returns from exile, receives the help of his brother A(a)ron to communicate the Word of God. The trials of Moses in leading the Jews of Egypt turn on the continual struggle to present an authentic representation of *Yahweh*. It is more than an iconoclastic moment since it is, historically, a moment prior to a developed culture of representation of a sublime and transcendent abstraction, Hegel's sensuous presentation of the idea.

This is the core programmatic issue for Libeskind in the *Between The Lines* (1990) project that became the Jewish Museum. For this reason, the allusion to Schönberg is apt, since the core of his libretto is the struggle for authenticity between the brothers: Moses who is in contact with the transcendent experience of God, and Aron, who must translate this into the language and experiential understanding of the Israelites. For Schönberg, the musical language of twelve-tone, dodecaphonic music offered a form of tonal complexity that communicated both the intense lexical conflict between Moses, Aron and the Israelites and the open-ended question of naming and representation: How do you speak the name of God? For Libeskind, the tension in the narrative was definitive of the architectural programme itself. Arguably, it is more difficult to see a direct correspondence between the score and the architectural project since the narrative is markedly stronger, and it seems that there are very few instances of the direct influence of music, as sound or as score, on architecture – perhaps Iannis Xenakis's Philips Pavilion (1958) for Expo 58 in Brussels is the sole exception. While there is a considerable body of musical works that claim influence from architecture, the converse seems elusive.

Stockhausen
Perhaps part of the issue of influence comes from the differing trajectories of modern architecture and avant-garde music in the second half of the twentieth century, and

of the explosion of vernacular and popular music forms that now dominate music culture. If we consider abstract composers such as Karl-Heinz Stockhausen or Pierre Boulez, the work is clearly exploring the limits of auditory expectation. Listening to any representative sample of their output, the complexity of the auditory soundscapes including the shifts between sonic density and silence, focus and spatiality, mean that any transcription of this work into architecture would be gestural at best.

Karl-Heinz Stockhausen's interest in the development of a sonic experience that explores the limits of what was familiar and tolerable in auditory experience was, to him and those who appreciate his work, nonetheless music. His employment of auditory technology, primitive synthesizers and other technologies that fuse music production and recording inevitably created a fetishization of the synthetic, as opposed to analogue, qualities of music. So, in one sense, Stockhausen's work anticipates the explosion of digital composition that is now part of mainstream music in the twenty-first century. The question remains whether it is any more 'architectural' because of its basis in technology or whether any contemporary composer is any closer to producing work that might be naturally translated into architectural design practice.

How is this architectural?
Given the content that we have been discussing, it would seem difficult to imagine how there could be an obvious and coherent translation between the disciplines or a process where music could provide a design model that could be translated into a creative architectural outcome. By distinguishing between the acoustic qualities of the music under consideration, analogue or digital, or the graphic notational score, we can clarify the problem but it is not clear what might be the most obvious direction. Obviously, performance venues are designed and calibrated to certain musical styles using acoustic engineering, and perhaps that is the limit of the translation. But a design process for architecture that is not specifically constructed in this matter, or is for a brief that is non-musical, seems problematic. As we will see in the next chapter, the idea of 'fidelity' needs some more consideration.

The challenge in Goethe's quote remains unfulfilled. Perhaps the most telling performative aspect he points to is not music or architecture, but the idea that it is 'frozen'. Temporality in both musical performance and in its graphic transcription is the key. The determination of a moment in which translation between the two disciplines is possible may well be the most productive way of analyzing and responding to what is, as Libeskind says, 'between the lines'.

Proposition: UnFrozen – Glass on the beach

What is the libretto (narrative) that would place architecture within music, and conversely, music within architecture? Before the act of design, there must be the intentional selection of a narrative field that determines the qualities of spatial, physical and auditory experience. Choose or create a narrative and determine how one would stage it as an architectural experience that endures, and in which the participants do not perform, they just *are*.

34 F	49 C
Fi	**Fo**
21 D	10 Rr
Ea	**Nc**

Rebus 34

Fidelity

Proposition 34: Fidelity

When I first visited Pisa, I was excited to see not just the Leaning Tower but, more importantly, the Campo dei Miracoli within which Pasolini shot scenes from his *Medea* (1969). Wonderful as that place is, it was also the formal and acoustic precision of the Baptistry building that was a revelation. At a designated moment, an attendant unannounced sang a single tone calibrated to the shape and scale of the interior. The initial tone evolved into a series of overtones and resonances determined by the dome of the interior. The building harnessed the energy of the vocal performance and amplified its characteristics beyond the conventional spectrum of sounds. In contrast, another memory is from the Tate Gallery in London, some rooms from a Jean Tinguely sculpture whose clank/whir/whiz criminally echoed through the white rooms like an intruder. In the first instance, sound was considered part of the musical spectrum and took advantage of the waveform and frequency of familiar sound signatures, whereas Tinguely's work was deliberately intrusive and asymmetric with the expected experience of an acoustic environment.

Acoustic 'tuning' of a space is an immediate relationship since the performance space may well be constructed to function in a similar manner to a resonating chamber of an instrument. Potentially, the fixed nature of this resonance chamber would allow performers to create sounds of specific frequency and duration suitable to have an effect courtesy of the phase of the wave(s) created. Music is composed, of course, of a number of standing waves of a duration particular to a piece. The resonance of the Baptistry in Pisa is achieved by a note played or sung at a particular pitch that matches the distance between the performer and the reflective surface of the interior from which the sound is reflected and amplified.

There is a scalar relationship between the size and shape of the interior of the Baptistry and the wavelength of the sound. The building acts, like any analogue musical instrument, as a physical limit to the general principle of sound reverberation and attenuation. The limit (the architectural interior) also acts as a resonance chamber and, as such, different architectural forms can theoretically be tuned to different chords. There are a number of physical manifestations of this, from work such as Shea Trahan's transcriptions of resonant frequencies as three-dimensional digital models to the Swiss artist Zimoun's sound installation pieces. In the former Trahan, as an architect, is attempting to tune the building form to the morphology of the waveform, whereas the installation pieces of Zimoun employ space as a resonant chamber generally, but do not attempt to coordinate musical harmonic relationships in any form or arguably involve the gallery environment in any way other than the incidental. Zimoun's work encompasses sonic environments that vary from the compounding effect of multiple styrofoam hammers on cardboard boxes to the enveloping rustle of billowing plastic sheeting. They are abstract in form and have little immediate connection to conventional musicology yet are clearly preoccupied with the immersiveness of sound. Because his work is essentially concerned with the aggregated noisescape of multiple, identical sources the sculptural experiences of the installations can be recognized as having a certain mechanical consistency that creates rhythmic pulses as the percussive sounds rise and fall.

Conversely, Trahan proceeds from the measurement of the waveforms via the analysis of cymatic formations that graphically visualize the frequency of different sounds. The translation of these graphical representations into three-dimensional form provides Trahan with material to speculate on an acoustically 'tuned' structure in much the same way as the Baptistery at Pisa functions. His work explicitly attempts to develop architecture from the standpoint of the physics of sound and, as a consequence, produce forms that are tuned to the morphologies of cymatic formations. The limitation to this approach, as is immediately obvious, is the limited number of meaningful formal variants that can be produced. Most are products of a radial geometry, seem to be single-use and lack a critical engagement with the complexities of programme and spatial hierarchies. While the singularity is important and applicable in certain circumstances, the difference between the acoustic drivers of Trahan's project and the complexities of modern music (and architecture) are not necessarily catered for. To look further into this complexity, particularly in contemporary music, it is necessary to investigate the relationship between contemporary sonic composition and the notation that has developed to express it.

Cardew, Xenakis, Ligeti
There is a contrast, clearly, between musical resonances that are additive and purposefully benefit from conventional tonic variations vs. the aberrant soundscapes of found music/sounds, natural world recordings, silence and performative spaces. In the former, there exists a separate graphic language that transcribes the sounds of the instruments into a legible and reproducible form, sheet music, whereas the soundscapes of the latter generally have no graphic translation other than occasional instructive prompts. There is also the expectation that the sounds of music, when it is understood to be part of the general tradition of composition and performance,

can be meaningfully communicated. There will be variations of interpretation by performers, but with a graphic score, there is the expectation that the 'work' can be repeated. John Cage's *4'33"* (1952) is of course the fulcrum between these two conditions since, for the duration of Cage's piece, the only sounds the audience experiences are the incidental noises of the context.

If we presume that incidental soundscapes are deliberately undocumented, and resistant to further development, that leaves us with those musical compositions that seek to interrogate the process of composition and design. A particular example of this is the work of the English composer, Cornelius Cardew, and of subsequent explorers of musical and graphic indeterminacy such as Iannis Xenakis and György Ligeti.

Cardew's most famous work, *Treatise* (1967), is a vast graphic transcription of potential sounds completely divorced from conventional musical notation. It is without melodic lines that conventional scores rely upon, including musical staves and time signatures. Instead, there is a rich graphic tableau of shapes and linear notations that it is the performer's responsibility to respond. *Treatise* is an enormous, 193-page visual exploration of line and shape that suggests relationships between performative behaviour, sounds and the listening experience without dictating exactly what this might be. Looking at the score, as an architect, you are immediately reminded of the relationship between graphic notations such as plans, sections, elevations and their role in indicating possible formal, programmatic and material relationships.

Similarly, the work of Iannis Xenakis and (early) György Ligeti employs complex visual scores that require an interpretive leap between notational strategies and sonic, or musical, outcomes. While both composers have also employed conventional forms of notation for different pieces, Ligeti especially, their experimental work demonstrates a concerted effort to find a mode of transcription that adequately communicates the character of the piece. Xenakis's *Pithoprakta* (1955–56) and Ligeti's *Artikulation* (1958) demonstrate this approach. Both pieces have incredibly complex graphic scores that, like Cardew, suggest approaches to performance based on assorted shape grammars. Because they are interested in the exploration of novel expressions of sound experience and the empowerment of the performer, the scores of these works immediately suggest a form of creative communication that mirrors that of architectural drawing. The score is the transcription of an event and of the experience of participants. Moreover, the graphic style of composition, particularly for Xenakis, an architect, and Cardew, who trained and worked in graphic design, can easily be compared with the autonomous process of sketching and thinking that is part of architectural practice.

How is this architectural?
It is through the comparison of the graphic composition of the works of Cardew, Ligeti and Xenakis with architectural drawing that we can make the most effective transcription between the two disciplines. Of course, the purpose of the musical scores is to create a sonic experience while architectural drawings are indicative of possible material and formal constructions, but the deliberate (mis)reading of both would seem fruitful. What would it be to take Cardew's treatise and propose that it served as a form of architectural notation? Conversely, what would be to take an architectural drawing, perhaps something like Libeskind's *Chamberworks* (1983) drawings, and find sonic equivalents to them? The graphic similarities between the two forms are not coincidental, and surely there is, in Libeskind's work some memory of his training in classical music. The core question that unites the architectural and music works is the understanding that the graphic form is essentially instructional, and requires the fulfilment of musical performance or constructional activity to activate its full potential. In the case of Libeskind, and indeed most speculative architectural imagistic representation, there is also the reflexive condition in which the drawings are *about* drawing (or image making) as a unique architectural activity. To 'draw' is to make notational marks that both represent and suggest some state of affairs, however personal and gestural, and to 'draught' is to conceive the pre-conditions for a future state. The translation from the first to the second, as we know in architecture, captures the intensional forces and the extensional opportunities in drawing/sketching that it is the task of draughtsmanship to stabilize.

Proposition: Treatise town, the Cardew city of musical philosophy
Cornelius Cardew was deeply committed to the development of freedom in the composition and performance of music. Perhaps his musical work was also the diagram of a free architecture? What if Cardew was an urban planner and an architect as well as a composer?

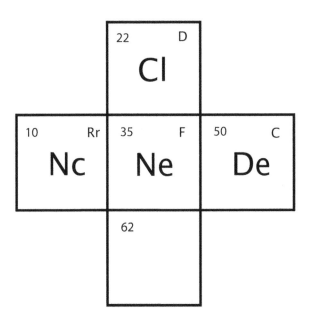

Rebus 35

Fidelity

Proposition 35: Non-Euclidean

One of the assumed premises of architecture and its relationship to the idea of fidelity is that for any descriptive orthographic representation, the space of the appearance of architecture is always within Euclidean geometry. The history of the relationship between conceptual projections of architecture and the means through which it is represented is long and need not be summarized, since the awareness of the presence of the 'tool' of geometry is fundamental to the discipline. In essence, this means that parallel lines are always conceived as having no point of intersection and that the construction of perspective as a graphic approximation of stereoscopic vision is a foundational technical moment for architecture as a design practice even though it is known that these lines do not intersect in orthographic (plan) projections. Sebastiano Serlio's *Tutte l'opere d'architettura, et prospetiva* (1537), like many texts that emerged from the craft tradition of construction, commences with the fundamentals of plane geometry and proceeds to demonstrate how the virtual space of a perspective drawing of a town square or a rustic scene ultimately mirrors the immersive experience of the eye. What is significant, in Serlio's example, is the proposition that geometry orders the world and that there is a reciprocal influence between the order of architecture and the unruliness of nature, particularly in the woodland scene.

The relationship between perspective as a conscious construction of space and its use in architecture was later codified in Erwin Panofsky's *Perspective as Symbolic Form* (1927, 1991). Panofsky argued that forms of spatial representation, particularly in architecture and painting, mirrored the philosophical relationship between individuals and the world. More recently, Alberto Pérez Gómez and Louise Pelletier's meditation on the 'perspective hinge', echoing Panofsky's approach to symbolic form, included the transformations of spatial experience that cubism and proto-modernism implied (Pérez Gómez and Pelletier 1997). Different types of transformational geometric drawing, they argue, denote subtly different approaches to the design process and the significance of work.

Parallel lines are assumed in building, but do they intersect on the plane of the earth if they are excessively long, i.e. meet at a pole, or are parallel and have different lengths because they are following paths that are consistently parallel? In effect, no building is close enough to this scale to meaningfully be affected by this condition; however, there are some projects of geometry, ballistics, that do take the circumference of the earth and its rotation into account (as well as weather effects). The shortest version of this occurs in long-range sniping.

The French mathematician Henri Poincaré is an important modern figure in this regard, particularly for his studies on topology and the mathematics of surfaces of complex curvature. Poincaré took the philosophical position that the fundamental difference between plane geometry, conventional othographics and that of curved surfaces was more than a function of different forms of spatial representation. For him, topology better represented the intellectual relationship between measurement (order) and the world in its complexity. Since all plane geometry representations ceased to function consistently, once they became excessively large, it made sense to refer to the more complex definitions of algebraic geometry. Topology generally is the foundational mathematical language of three-dimensional modelling programmes that are ubiquitous in architectural design and have driven the changes in form-making in the last 30 years. In particular, topology is a form of mathematical representation that prioritizes paths over points and employs splines to describe both lines and surfaces.

The language of mathematical topology gave architectural theory an extended vocabulary for describing the formal properties of work and the techniques by which these forms were produced. Planes became surfaces, edges became vectors, change became differentiation, and paradoxically for such a mathematically exact process, precision became chance. The abruptness with which conventional modernism defined enclosures and the degree to which it could be attributed to binary thought (charactersied as manipulative and simplistic) gave over to the smoothness of differentiated surfaces and the indeterminacy of conventional orientation. Tacitly, it also gave sustenance to the desire for architecture and real-estate value to be uncoupled and that the economic driver for maximizing utility could be put off for more cultivated ends. So the work of Lynn, Gehry, NOX, Hadid, Levente and others represented a new approach to the challenge of accurately employing non-standard geometry and, subsequently, incorporate it into the construction process.

How is this (not) architectural?
Of course, any proposition that commences with the foundational media of drawing and modelling is implicitly entangled with architecture. However, there are a few characteristics of non-Euclidean geometry that may be further explored. There are two main avenues, path-based transformations and the language employed to identify them. Path-based transformations can be employed to emulate simple geometries but

are also capable of significantly more complex geometries without having to revert from a point(s)/vector analogy to algebraic expressions. Importantly, graph theory can be employed to determine the relationships of vertices to edges and the paths between them to determine adjacency characteristics and behavioural propinquities. Graph theory abstracts architectural plans and attributes to them certain behavioural rules. By analyzing how the rules affect the scale and sequence of spaces, predictable behavioural models can be objectively established. Of course, the more complex and idiosyncratic the rules, the more constrained the spatial relationships, but the potential exists for creating a way of sequencing volumes that are not simply intuitive.

For example, Euler's topological problem of the Seven Bridges of Königsberg was originally a challenge to define a route that is unique and obeys certain rules of organization and performance for path-based solutions, much like a solution for a maze. Recent developments in 'space syntax' and the application of graph theory to architecture have attempted to take this path-based behaviour and mathematize wayfinding in building plans. While this is essentially a post-construction analysis of existing buildings, the opportunity exists for employing it as a design tool to quantify intuitive approaches to architectural interiors. The application of graph theory as a tool of analysis in vernacular architecture, which is essentially cell/node based has been established and elaborated by Michael Ostwald (Dawes and Ostwald 2013), transforming the work of spatial syntax, and identifying ways to move into a more three-dimensional experience. There are two ways, possibly more, to take this. The first is to apply the mechanics of graph theory to complex interior volumes that are more than cellular; the second, conjectured by Ostwald, is to distribute this method to the online game community for whom the analysis of game maps is crucial for success in combat scenarios. Understanding, and mathematically describing, how game maps are navigated by elite players can deliver the classic military technology dividend of innovation based on the extreme experience of conflict.

Regarding the legacy of Serlio, Panofsky and Pérez Gómez, we can see that the language of symbolic form has grown to incorporate the developed vocabulary of graph theory but can now include the vernacular language of game-based strategies as well. While this is still indeterminate on the Adamic process of naming topological typologies with any consistency, the incorporation of behavioural descriptors with the sheer abundance of form variations offered by contemporary modelling extends the architectural toolset beyond standard Platonic geometries. Confrontingly, it can be argued that the 'symbolic form' of contemporary architectural space may well be more militarized than we understand.

Possible project: The seven buildings of Königsberg
Using non-standard geometries and the analytical tools of graph theory, design and conjecture how a building might have clarity and opacity when spatially experiencing it for the first time: as an aggressor storming the citadel or a defender protecting democracy.

10: Melancholy

The first question that should be asked, and answered, is: why melancholy? In a book on architectural theory, it seems counter-intuitive to think of the negative aspects of human experience and the potentially disappointing nature of sadness. But melancholy is more than sadness, certainly as far as the chapters covered in this section are concerned. The first reference point for melancholy is Albrecht Dürer's famous engraving of *Melencolia I* (1514), famously analyzed by Erwin Panofsky who recognized the allegorical aspects of the image and the evocation of a 'saturnine' disposition typical of human experience in general, and of creative artists in particular. In this section, I propose a developed version of this analysis that presents the ambition for change and positive development that is, arguably, inherent in the general project of modernism, yet recognizes the limitations and inherent 'tragedy' of failure in modernity's ambition for a reconciliation between desires and outcomes. By looking at some of the expressions of modernity that we encounter in popular culture, we see how the mechanisms for creating, manufacturing and consuming the products of modern culture inevitably create a picture of existential failure (hence melancholy) rather than fulfilment. This position is not new; it is the consequence of many studies in the general field of cultural Marxism and develops ideas we have originally seen in the chapter on Redemptive Objects. Yet, because the experience of modernity is so ubiquitous it is logical to treat it as an inherent aspect of any constructive theory that seeks to engage with the spectrum of contemporary culture.

The first chapter looks at the enduring effects of 'Pop' culture as a field of naturalized content for critically creative practice. If one of the purposes of creative work is to mimetically reproduce recognizable forms and effects of contemporary life, to make it 'relevant' to current audiences, it is important to understand the semantic mechanisms employed to make this connection. The question of how a copy can be considered inherently authentic, one of the core quandaries of postmodernism, is examined in the context of architectural expression. The flurry of abstract representations of historical motifs in architecture in the 1980s and 1990s has largely been forgotten because of the rise of digital culture generally, but the core question of the simulation and simulacra remains. Is it the melancholy acknowledgement of the death of innovation?

The next chapter extends this question to look at the spatialization of mass reproduction and consumption. The phenomenon of the 'consumption environment' that is now ubiquitous across advanced economies paradoxically promotes the deep psychological engagement with commercial objects and commodity fetishism, exalting the Faustian relationship between shopping and life that Victor Gruen unwittingly unleashed. Shopping is more than a simple act of commerce, it is a deep and entrancing simulation of community and reality.

The final melancholic gesture that might link architecture and the world of material exchange is considered in the chapter on working models. Architectural models can always be thought of as simulations of a larger, more complex reality, but they are also a thing in themselves. Arguably, an architectural model, or rather a model made architecturally, is an object that acts as a tool for acting on the world. It is entirely conceivable that this type of model/tool does not act as a representation of another state or scale but is an instrument for making materially 'real' a constellation of ideas. Is this a futile, or melancholic, wish for architecture? Is it possible to make a model of a counter-factual state? The third chapter opens this question and asks how these models might be housed.

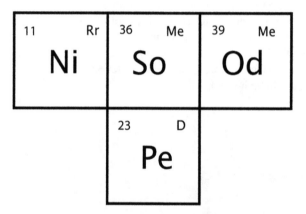

Rebus 36

Melancholy

Proposition 36: Soap

Roland Barthes's *Mythologies* published in 1957 contains a collection of essays on the false-consciousness of mediated images prevalent in French popular culture in the post-war period. France, like much of the western world, was both recovering from the disastrous effects of the war while also participating in a cultural transformation influenced by a resurgent US economy. These changes saw the development of media imagery that celebrated consumerism and a post-war experience tentatively, and temporarily, free from conflict. Capitalism and advertising, of course, had been a major component of French urban life since the nineteenth century, but Barthes's essays revealed the deeply anthropological basis of messaging in mass media culture. For Barthes, there was a fascination with the symbolic value of advertising and popular culture that anticipated Pop Art's appropriation of the symbolic economy of the media of advertising, film, television and magazines.

Contemporaneously, Susan Sontag's essay 'Notes on Camp' in *Against Interpretation* (1966) describes an aspect of everyday aesthetics of popular culture in the 1950s and 1960s. Similar to Barthes, but without the demystifying emphasis, she notes the emergence of 'camp' as a form of sentimental expressiveness that is intrinsic to popular culture. Her book, like that of a number of counter-culture texts such as Jeff Nuttall's magnificent *Bomb Culture* (1968) narrated the experience of dissatisfaction with the dominant cultural values while also recognizing the energy within popular culture as an expression of identity and difference. Barthes, Sontag and Nuttall were all concerned with the effects of popular culture beyond what had been popularized in the discourse around Pop Art. While the material of Pop was concentrated largely on the more transient and modish aspects of everyday life, in architecture, it was also a continuation of the renunciation of historical values, and the employment of historical formal languages, a position intrinsic to modernity. So, for architecture to engage with the Pop culture, questions emerged regarding what specific subject matter counted as Pop architecture.

As is well known, when Robert Venturi designed and publicized the Vanna Venturi House (1964), he was signalling the potential for employing historicist architectural elements with the collagist sensibility and ironic detachment of Pop Art. In doing so, it catalyzed a question that had been present in contemporary literary theory: How do historic cultural works signify their meaning and value in the present tense? The Vanna Venturi house referenced stylistic elements from neo-historical sources such as Edwin Lutyens, the Treasury building at Petra and other anonymous sources. So the work is really focused on the anti-modern inclusion of historic elements rather than whatever might be considered contemporary. It is only later, in the *Learning From Las Vegas* (1972) phase of the practice of Venturi, Scott Brown and Izenour that the question of contemporary influences emerges. This is the moment when the question of how the intersection of popular culture and architecture became a serious subject of analysis and creative expression. Moreover, it is with the development of teaching practices centred on these themes at the University of Pennsylvania, and the incorporation of this into a viable commercial design practice that Venturi and Scott Brown created an architectural practice whose design ethos was premised on the selective retrieval and quotation of architectural elements using, or at least reflecting, contemporary vernacular elements.

This begs the question, what is Pop architecture and can it exist anymore? Is it the quotation of any form of 'referential' elements, contemporary or historical, or does it require that the referents are specifically contemporary? Further, in a world in which architectural culture is more concerned with pressing issues of digital materiality, identity politics and the exploration of alternate modes of (re)presenting reality, do we take the material of history to be simply intellectual white noise? Considering the quaintness of Sontag's evaluation of camp 'affects', or Barthes's analysis of anthropological *mythoi* is the debate between contemporary and historical forms even worth considering?

How does the Pop sensibility of Venturi, etc. translate into an architectural project? How are references from Pop culture to be incorporated into a design process that does not transgress into poor taste or the definition of a moment that is already banal and so specifically misses the mark in terms of symbolic values? Is modernism the safe harbour of taste that followed the efforts at historicism that marked the postmodern efforts of the 1970s and 1980s? How to revive, if possible, any form of cultural referents that are symbolic or participate in a symbolic economy without becoming Camp, in Sontag's terms.

Much of the analysis of the semantic value of images relies on their unconscious adoption by cultural producers, or, in 'some' cases their conscious use by exemplars such as Venturi. In cases where the effect is already superseded, or melancholy, such as Charles Moore's Piazza d'Italia (1978) in New Orleans, or the Mississauga Civic Center (1987) in Ontario by Jones and Kirkland or Michael Graves's Portland Building (1982), there is the sense that the effort to demonstrate a nostalgic connection with some historical sensibility is misguided at best and cynically camp at worst. Critical opinion of the more explicit historical recreations in these examples insists that there is a fundamental incommensurability between the use of architectural languages that were considered obsolete by the middle of the twentieth century and contemporary society.

However, it is also true that the motivations of the New Urbanism movement that promoted the development of towns, such as Poundbury in England and Seaside and Celebration in Florida, had at their core, the belief that positive urban experience did not come from the proliferation of anonymous town centres indistinguishable regarding their place and population. Instead, New Urbanism argued that civic identity required the sense of history, however manufactured, that these projects projected. However these towns reflect a fantasy of an unproblematic world fixed in time and without any sense of the complexity of social relations that exist in broader society. Semantically, the languages of vernacular and historicist form they employ demonstrate the same ironic referentiality of Pop. Ironically, it connects them more to the forms of ideal community usually associated with radical socialist values than to a model for future development – which makes for an unusual sense of cultural dissonance when one remembers that the developer of Celebration was the Disney Corporation.

What is the positive answer to this? Is it to acknowledge, as with Quinlan Terry the unalloyed adoption of a historical language that unselfconsciously emulates/mimics constructional and decorative languages from a previous era, or to re-cast historical referents as an aspect of vernacular critical regionalism? In effect, and oddly, the Terry option seems to have a more problematically challenging set of premises because it has, in effect, a more openly clear agenda and is not compromised by the need to systematize the process of adaptation – how to abstract the elements of previous styles as a practice of constant compromise.

To summarize, the question of historical referents and the developed idea that architecture could perform the semantic function of symbolizing *some* form of historical continuity, occurred at both the level of an individual building's elements and the context within which it was sited. Yet there is a significant difference in the selection of seemingly arbitrary icons of popular culture in the work of Warhol, Rauschenberg, Hamilton and others vs. the use of historical motifs in architecture. This represents a differing level of criticality in approach. Pop Art selected material that was simultaneously ubiquitous and fetishized but could potentially be replaced by alternate selections, whereas practitioners of Pop architecture such as Venturi,

Moore, Graves, Terry and others referenced, however distantly, the idea of an architectural canon.

There is an alternative approach however that acknowledges the critical distance necessary to fuse popular culture and architecture. It turns on the rhetorical force of the 'copy' and the employment of a semantic economy that requires the viewer to understand the value of a simulated physical environment. When the Australian practice Ashton Raggat and Macdougall designed the National Museum of Australia (2001) in Canberra they intentionally 'quoted' the zig-zag pattern of Libeskind's Extension to the Berlin Museum, as well as recreating Le Corbusier's Villa Savoye, except coloured black rather than white. The avowed intention was to thoughtfully reference the relationship between 'Australia' as a political and cultural concept and the legacy of disenfranchisement that indigenous aboriginal communities suffered as a consequence of colonization. The fact that the quotations are unambiguously recognizable (Libeskind was famously displeased) guaranteed the semantic force of the gestures. Similarly, the 'copying' of Zaha Hadid's Wangjing Soho complex in Beijing (2014) by a developer in Chongqing created an unusual scenario in which the copy was finished prior to the original. In both instances, the fidelity of the copy delivered the most effective form of aesthetic dissonance. That this practice, in both cases, relies on the ubiquity and fluidity of digital information tells us that Pop architecture is most effective when it flaunts its disregard for intellectual property boundaries.

In Barthes's essay in *Mythologies* on 'Soap Powders and Detergents', he points to the psychological need for bubbles to signify the process of cleaning although they play no role in the actual chemical process. Similarly, the presence of the 'bubbles' of historical references in architecture performs the same role. Extending the metaphor, towns like Seaside, Celebration and Poundbury are a form of urban 'bubble bath' that is demonstrably historical (and pleasurable, presumably) without impinging on its citizen's forms that are devoid of contemporary luxuries. Similarly, the studiously carefree employment of an architecture that is wholly copied, not as fragments but as legible references, challenges the tacit assumption that creativity is an exercise in originality alone.

Proposition: Control C, Control V: Adobe headquarters
What would the headquarters of the Adobe Inc. organization be like if the full capabilities of its current applications were employed in the design? What 'quotations' could be matched to the representational requirements of a multinational company that exercises the market dominance it currently enjoys?

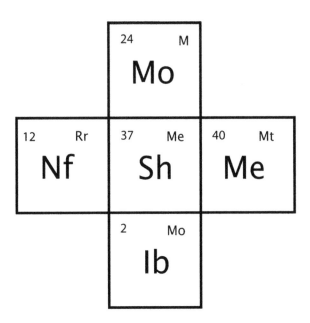

Rebus 37

Melancholy

Proposition 37: Shopping

In her perceptive analysis of the intersection of multinational capitalism and international terrorism within the typology of the shopping mall, Suzi Mirgami (2017) discusses the highly overdetermined and, in her words, militarized organization of shopping. Malls, she argues, are essentially bunkers that are designed to provide a seamless location for the continual flow of transactions, undisturbed by weather, distracting social events or politics. And as she points out, the incidence of a terrorist event at the Westgate Mall in Nairobi, Kenya in 2013, is clear evidence of two antagonistic forces coming into conflict equating the symbolic importance of the shopping mall as a site with the event of dramatic and extreme political agency.

While very few shopping malls are the subject of extreme forms of violence and antagonism, it is certainly true that the current evolutionary form of the shopping environment is a highly disciplined experience in which decades of investigation into retail behaviour coalesce. Shopping malls specifically even more so than traditional 'high-street' retail environments within urban and suburban locations, are heavily overdetermined to optimize the free flow of transactions. As privately owned space, usually by multinational retail giants, they are deliberately designed to minimize incidental distractions that might draw people away from the core behavioural requirement that they continue to transact money for goods and services.

The most comprehensive analysis of the shopping centre, or mall, from an architectural perspective is still *The Harvard Design School Guide to Shopping* (Koolhaas et al. 2001), which contains numerous articles and photo essays analyzing the evolution of the typology and the inviolable relationship between every design decision and the management of capital. The truism that a shopping mall has no exterior is borne out by the iron-clad relationship between car parking and the big-box form, emphasizing the schizophrenic contrast with an interior that demonstrates an overabundance of dramatic yet controlled urban facades.

While this typology is now almost ubiquitous and has its own domains of celebratory expression and critical analysis, it is an architectural phenomenon that has a problematic relationship with academic forms of theoretical analysis. An inherent hostility towards the uncritical celebration of consumption and an indifference to ideas of authentic urban experience and the craft of construction means that, Harvard notwithstanding, there are significant reservations regarding this form of design work. While there have been outlier attempts to engage with aspects of the typology such as SITE's Best Products showrooms in the 1970s, and Jon Jerde's unashamed willingness to fulfil the Gruen model of retail, it is fair to say that few architectural practices celebrate their retail work as much as more-esteemed projects in the cultural sphere. As Jerde's firm continues to claim: 'We are like psychoanalysts, uncovering the dreams of our clients and making them come true', implying that the role of the architect within the development of shopping spaces is as much about the psychological profiling of clients and consumers as much as it is about design discourse. In particular, it is about the suppression of regional and cultural differences in order to maximize the value-management of the retail 'experience'.

Yet there are clear points of resistance to this phenomenon. While the ubiquitousness of retail complexes is recognized, it is also a truism that cycles of economic activity can affect them particularly adversely. Transformations in local spending patterns because of competitor proximity, household wealth, transport logistics or other disruptive events can fatally compromise the effectiveness of shopping malls. The corrosive influence of empty retail space, and the phenomenon of 'dead malls' has created a form of notoriety for the failures of 'shopping'. In the face of the optimism of practitioners such as Jerde, the reality of urban and suburban brownscapes demonstrates the half-life of these models. Since the lifespan of certain mall features is limited to the duration of their popularity, the rapidity with which they come to no longer represent the aspirations of their target user groups means that at the apogee of their seductiveness as wish fulfillments, they are already becoming obsolete.

There is an interesting nexus of behavioural determinism and architectural theory here. At the individual level, it reminds us that the fundamental performative requirements of these complexes are transactional. Shopping as the fundamental transactional relationship is both hedonic (pleasure-giving) and utilitarian (obligatory behaviour). As such, the mechanisms for amplifying the hedonic experience are continuously managed to ensure that the experiences of pleasure and fulfilment are promoted. The fetishizing of the goods for a transaction is accompanied by and reinforced by immersive environmental cues. The question is, can or should architecture participate in this behaviour?

The general principles of hedonic consumption presume that any shopping environment will aim to maximize its effect by ensuring a sufficiently diverse series of consumption experiences. Understanding the dynamics of different user groups and their pliability in relation to hedonic consumption is important within the discipline of marketing, but it is less clear when we question the role of the architectonic environment in relation to this. While a purchasable commodity may have qualities of being necessary and pleasurable – scented soap for example – or all utility (plastic bin bags), or all pleasure (a movie), the question emerges as to whether the spatial qualities of the mall or the detailed design decisions of particular elements (themed and branded retail) are meant to be reinforcing utilitarian or hedonic ends.

How is this architectural?
The fact that the shopping mall is an established typology with a well-drilled interaction between form, effect and function begs the question of whether there is any discretionary space for individual interpretation, or whether there is a point to reinforcing the psychological and market forces that they demonstrate. A proposal that resisted dominant trends would be dooming itself at the point of conception to failure, all other things being equal. The core relationships seem to be between the individual purchaser and their required and desired objects, and the collective experience of the mall space and the (lack of) visibility of social behaviour that is not governed by the mall operators. In essence, it is about the interaction between self-awareness and the awareness of group behaviour.

Inherently, the mechanisms for self-awareness in a shopping environment, like gambling, tend to limit the amount of impulse purchasing and excessive spending. Also inherently this allows shopping to transform from a private to a public space when the sense of autonomy and self-awareness is enhanced. At the simplest level, an internalized public space such as a shopping environment is constantly working to counter this sense of self-awareness. The architecture of public space then is, like an anti-Panopticon, best served when awareness is present and actionable.

So what could a resistant form of this typology be like, and can this resistance be, in any fundamental way, architectural? There are two paths that emphasize the purely and exclusively utilitarian function and eliminate the hedonic experience or focus fully and comprehensively on the hedonic principle. Arguably, this is the point at which the pragmatic purpose of shopping is fully enveloped and pushed aside by the unrelenting promise of hedonistic wonder.

Potential project: Hamilton's pharmacy
While Banksy's Dismaland (2015) is probably the most fully melancholic expression of the cynicism and unimaginative illusion of choice in multinational corporate fun parks, there may be others. Perhaps the current generation's Hunter S. Thompson, Hamilton Morris, can provide the path to altered states of consciousness?

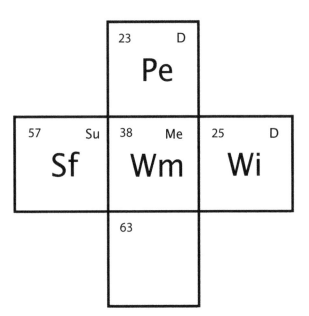

Rebus 38

Melancholy

Proposition 38: Working Models

Historical models of events, battle recreations and cosmological models all share relationships between the strategic positioning of vectors of influence and the temporal moment at which the model is fixed. While a map indicates a terrain of possible movement patterns and the opportunity for both directed, random and other patterns in between, the 'working' model fixes a set of relations as an intransitive reflection of a transitive condition. As models, they are representations of a reality that selects aspects of a state of affairs, without conjecturing the outcomes that will follow. They represent a complex chronemic (or polychronic) reality in which various parts of the model, usually the human figures but also the trajectory of mechanized components such as vehicles or planets, can imaginatively assume different dispositional relationships in the next instance. This is how we can imagine them 'working'. Inspecting the model prompts us to ask: Why this moment? What will follow from here? Usually chronemics refers to an expression of an individual's inherent sense of time, but we can see here that these models activate the viewer's ability to project the complexity and contemporaneity of experience onto the static, atemporal scene they are viewing. But what of architectural models, and in particular of the process of creating architectural models that engage with a temporal, and behavioural, moment?

According to Daniel Libeskind, his *Three Lessons in Architecture: The Machines* (1985) 'do not work in the realm of objects, but in the realm of ideas', which can be taken to mean that they don't work in the sense that they are machines that will perform a function, but they do 'work' at the level of ideas, or thought processes. They are models of a dispositional relationship between a series of concepts that Libeskind felt relevant to the process of making architecture, employing the tradition of the architectural model to make 'real' this conceptual process. Yet they are clearly mechanized and have the capacity to reconfigure themselves if employed. But are they tools that can be activated, and should they be? Without getting into the minutiae of what an 'idea' is, the implication is that the machines don't 'work' in some conventional sense of being a tool that has specific functional outcomes. So, in what ways do architectural models show themselves to be about something other than the miniaturization of a project? And can they work or function in a way that moves from representation to functional outcomes?

If you consider the form of models of historical scenes, dioramas and the types of displays employed by museums to vividly show a historical event, their function is aligned with the narrative(s) they are presenting. What the visitor sees is a model of the battle, or encounter, or narrative moment, that the institution wishes to dramatize. As Umberto Eco describes in *Travels in Hyperreality* (1990), a preoccupation with simulation and the creation of historical fidelity runs deep within late-modern culture. For Eco, the presence of techniques of simulated historical and imagined artefacts in the live entertainment industry of the United States from Las Vegas to Disneyland is proof of an obsession with simulation as an instrument of the (sur)reality of events.

Architectural models share the same preoccupation with this contest of reality. What they do not do, generally, is to attempt to represent an indexical moment in which a certain state of affairs is taking place. And this makes sense since the purpose of the working model is to give a general description of the form and material that the projected work may employ, not purport to show how it will be used in a specific circumstance – like a diorama. It would be perverse, though probably fun, to create a model that showed a client the moment some significant life event of theirs was taking place. In doing this, the project may create a narrative that presumed a knowledge of the client's behaviour that was incorrect and/or inappropriately familiar. It is an odd scene to contemplate, but is this not what the client themselves are privately doing? And is it not valuable to engage an audience with a narrative that describes the intimate relationship between the architectural project and the events it houses, particularly as a proof of concept?

So how does a working model, of ideas rather than objects, function? Libeskind's structures from the Venice Biennale were compelling objects for the very reason that they were engaged with the complex process of thinking about how we meaningfully make architecture, connected to the constellation of interests that a historical imagination can employ. The Reading, Remembering and Writing machines promoted a structuralist approach to architectural meaning inasmuch as the machines had finite operational dimensions. The Reading Machine had a fixed set of gearing ratios, circumference and capacity for storage; the Remembering Machine (as an imagined fragment of a Giulio Camillo's Memory Theatre) had limited movement of the counterweights, crane arms and pulleys; the gears of the Writing Machine, and the permutations of its faces, had similar finite operations as a 'destabilized technology' linking surrealism, mysticism, cartography and a Phaedrus-like suspicion of textual language.

The models are about ideas precisely because they have no representational role, despite the precise and finite nature of their materiality. They are models of the artefacts they engage with, Ramelli's model and Camillo's project, that also activate a cast of other object identities, including Nietzsche's Zarathustra, Kafka's Odradek and Raymond Roussel's Martial Cantarel. As Marco Frascari (1989) identifies in his writings on Scarpa, the compelling chiastic relationship between *logos* and *techne* is a recognition that architecture is principally a structuring of objects and their interrelationship, but also one that constantly considers the lexical opportunities for this relationship. Working models such as the *Three Lessons* specifically promote this lexical richness, particularly when compared to conventional models that are predominantly representational.

So how is it architectural?
In many senses, this is answered by the references that congregate around Libeskind's projects, and the fact that his early work concentrated strongly on the questions of meaningful formal strategies in design practice. Of course, the *Between The Lines* project that came to be known as the Jewish Museum in Berlin is the most familiar work and one that elegantly demonstrated the idea that objects, or the absence thereof, can be organized as components of an architectural programme. With a methodology such as this, the temptation is to focus on a series of interconnected components that effectively have a machinic relationship to each other, reproducing a mechanical series of functions irrespective of whatever symbolic order they may allude to. There are two trajectories that can be catered for, the 'working' model that creates a temporal moment in the lives of its occupants and the didactic model that gathers a series of mechanized relations of its constituent parts.

Proposition: *Locus Solus*: The machine shed
A machine shed is, by everyday definition, an anonymous space in which a collection of mobile machinery is stored for use in other contexts, perhaps agriculture, earthmoving, etc. What of a machine shed that was bespoke to the geometries and needs of certain mobile machinery, including the upkeep, modification and use of the machines as the technology of grain harvesters and D9 bulldozers deserves its own environment. What then if that shed is employed to house the bizarre collection of devices created by Raymond Roussel in his surreal novel *Locus Solus* (1914)?

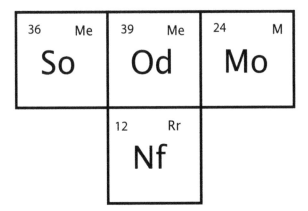

Rebus 39

Melancholy

Proposition 39: Odysseus

Max Horkheimer and Theodor Adorno's *Dialectic of Enlightenment* (1944, 1972) is a book that, famously, attempted to confront the mythologizing tendencies of modern capital, and subsequently succumbed to the same form of culture industry appropriation by well-meaning academics in the last quarter of the twentieth century. By arguing that modern forms of cultural production (art, films, popular music, television, etc.) are complicit with the more brutally coercive aspects of modern industrial capitalism, principally by masking and mythologizing its reality, the inherent class inequities of modern life can be exposed. The clarity and power of this analysis have proven to be foundational in the production of academic analyses of the relationship between coercion and free choice.

In *Dialectic of Enlightenment*, and in particular, a section examining the episode in Homer's *Odyssey* in which Odysseus encounters the Sirens, Horkheimer and Adorno use the narrative to describe the choices possible when confronted by the effects of instrumentalized thinking, the constant urge within modernity to demythologize the experiences of the natural world and to subsume it within a rationalized discourse of production and latent, idealized, value. While there is nothing intrinsically novel in this analysis in terms of the ethics of consumption and the instrumentalization of organic relations, what Horkheimer and Adorno specifically achieve is to demonstrate the relevance of myth to contemporary experience. Yet the question should also be asked, why Odysseus? And why choose one of the great narratives of the western tradition, Homer's *Odyssey*?

As Katie Fleming (2012) astutely explains, the choice of Odysseus represents a number of things to Horkheimer and Adorno. Principally, as exiles in the United States during the Second World War, the narrative of an individual exiled from his homeland and driven by homesickness to return was personally felt, but the use is much deeper and informative than just personal sympathies. The Philhellenic tradition in German scholarship dates from the Enlightenment itself, and there is a profound history of German romantic philosophy, culminating in Nietzsche, adopting and contesting the intellectual tradition of Ancient Greece. When Horkheimer and Adorno employ the myth of the *Illiad*, and in particular the encounter with the Sirens, the subject matter is as much an analogy of the instrumentalization of myth and labour as it is a rejoinder to the deeply tragic German adoption of the most extreme forms of mythologizing of homeland. Counter-intuitively, Odysseus is not a positive, or simplistically noble, hero, but an agent of instrumental force impelled towards conflict in pursuit of his desires. This is the narratival identity of Odysseus, but he also stands in as a representation, to Horkheimer and Adorno, of the force of conflict as an engine of change, and that this force is both violent and cunning. As highly educated and refined intellectuals, their personalities and behaviour were a stark contrast to the aggression and physicality of Odysseus. For them, Odysseus represented a form of enlightened individual whose self-serving rationality suppressed the interests of all around him. In contrast to the bullying, murderous and mythologizing National Socialists, the Nazi party, Horkheimer and Adorno spoke for a disenfranchised and 'homeless' cadre of exiled intellectuals, mostly Jewish. One of the purposes of *Dialectic of Enlightenment* was to confront the attraction to a mythologized association of Greek and German culture 'Kultur', a relation which seemingly sanctioned a chauvinist and barbarous aspiration for dominance. To this end, Horkheimer and Adorno relate a number of scenes in which Odysseus's cunning and instrumental behaviour are mirrored in modern concepts of the self, as the target of their work is not simply the barbarism of the Nazi party, but of modern society itself. As Fleming notes, the episode in which Odysseus orders the execution of the 'faithless' maidservants compresses the force of irascible judgement with the pathos of their death – as the small detail regarding the twitching feet of the executed illuminates. This scene, for Horkheimer and Adorno, is a moment in which the mythological narrative of Odysseus's return is a 'homecoming' that delivers terrible and violent consequences on a servant class that is disobedient to the concept of social order. There is no nobility in these actions, just the exercise of brute power in the interests of the ruling class. A return 'home' in this instance, a return to 'homeliness', entails the suppression of other, dissenting voices.

This reading of Odysseus is compelling as it demonstrates the persistence of myth as an allegorical instrument in the maintenance of power within modern society. As Horkheimer and Adorno further note, the picaresque sequence of episodes in which Odysseus and his crew encounter a series of characters, usually mythological, demonstrate Odysseus's employment of cunning, rationality and his dominance over his crew. The episode in which Odysseus orders his crew to block their ears and tie him to the mast in order to counter the desirous, but fatal, call of the Sirens illustrates the differing experiences of the ruling and ruled classes. However, it would be a mistake to reduce their reading of the *Odyssey* to simple class conflict. Odysseus's experience of the Sirens is the equivalent of an encounter with the most extreme and visceral aesthetic affect, so overwhelming that it drives the listener to destruction. That the crew is forbidden from experiencing this phenomenon, and Odysseus is prevented from organically responding to it, is telling. Odysseus's incapacity turns a potentially narcotic and irrational experience into a dramatic performance, much like the relationship between the audience and the performers within a theatre. For Horkheimer and Adorno, this is a core operation of enlightenment reason, to de-mythologize and suppress the viscerality of bodily experience and transform it into a commodified entertainment.

At this point, we can consider a contemporary of Horkheimer and Adorno, Walter Benjamin, and consider his (in)famous early study (1923) of German tragic theatre from the seventeenth century, translated and published as *The Origin of German Tragic Drama* (1923, 1998), but conventionally known as the *Trauerspiel*. Benjamin, as an idiosyncratic but brilliant savant of the cultural expression of modernity, took as his *Habilitationschrift* (equivalent to our Ph.D.) the study of a genre of drama that was prevalent within courtly circles in the Germanic principalities of the seventeenth century. These dramas were (in)famous for their pessimistic perspective on the intrigues of royal courts and the coincidence of violent mortality played out on the stage. At the same time, the mechanics of theatre design and the creation of various illusionistic devices for expressing the presence of a transformational process, or the intercession of a mythical figure, meant that, in essence, technology was being put in the service of melancholy.

Because the principal audience for these dramas was the local monarch of the Principality or Kingdom, the dramas were focused on the trials of reconciling a uniquely pessimistic Lutheran world-view with the role of the regent as the focus of the politically lethal intrigues of court. Benjamin argued that these plays were substantively different from the dramatic tradition that emphasized, in the Aristotelian tradition, the experience of emotional and intellectual catharsis but instead dramatized the reality of violent confrontation without redemption. For Benjamin, this spoke directly to the *realpolitik* experience of societal change and the conflicts of power. In addition, making direct reference to the allegorical tradition of the visual arts, this theatre form communicated the complex manner in which visual examples, Dürer's *Melancolia I* (1514) is a key example, presented the evidence of a world without resolution, or eschatological salvation.

In Klibensky, Saxl and Warburg's analysis of *Melancolia I*, they point out that the figure is characterized by her inability to employ the tools of creative, rational endeavour that surround her. The melancholy is both the consequence of inner disquiet and external frustration. Dürer's image is the first major syncretic portrayal of the intersection of geometry, melancholy and Saturn, fusing human capacity, infirmity and cosmological influences in the same allegorical image.

As Michael Osman (2005) astutely notes, Benjamin recognized that the communicative method of the *Trauerspiel*, as an aesthetic whole, was to fuse the drama of the play with the mechanics of the theatre. The creation of mechanical devices to simulate weather effects, the intercession of mythical figures, rapid changes of scenery, along with the single-point perspectival focus on the regent-as-audience meant that modern technology was drawn into the service of allegorical tales.

When we remember Horkheimer and Adorno's analysis of the encounter with the Sirens, and Ulysses's employment of devices for distancing himself and the crew from the overwhelming experience of their aural and visual entrapment, we can see that the mechanics of simulation both present and prevent the possibility of a transformative experience. Significantly, in both the narrative of the *Odyssey* and those of the seventeenth-century dramatists of the *Trauerspiel* plays, the violent drama of modern life is presented as an experience without enlightenment. Tying Horkheimer and Adorno's *Dialectic of Enlightenment* to Benjamin's *Trauerspiel* study, however temporary and tenuously, allows us to think about the role that architectural space and the staging of effects plays in dramatizing the experience of modernity.

How is this architectural?
The scene of destruction that the *Trauerspiel* text describes emulates the problem of *mythos*, the suspension of disbelief and the role of speculative reason for architectural production. The analysis of the travails of myth in the face of enlightenment reason, as Horkheimer and Adorno present it, mean that the rationalizing tendencies of modern architectural culture seem destined to eradicate, or suppress, creating architectural works that, contrarily, wish to illustrate *mythos*, however melancholy. But what does this mean, to architecturally address *mythos*? And what are the consequences of the brief analysis of *Dialectic of Enlightenment* and the *Trauerspiel* texts for this question?

There are many ways to explore this, but the coincidence of the two texts and the particular example of baroque theatre mechanics that Benjamin alludes to (and Osman describes) can encourage us to think of the relationship between architecture and the mechanics of illusory devices. Whether this is though the mechanical means of dynamic componentry such as Jean Nouvel's Institute du Monde Arabe (1980) or the work of Shin Takamatsu. Both of these examples, though divided by a gulf of cultural contexts, share an engagement with the melancholy consequences of technology. While Nouvel's project ostensibly attempted to emulate the complex patterns of Islamic decorative surfaces via an array of mechanized occuli, the inevitable obsolescence of this device presents an equally doomed attempt at a rapprochement between the western and Islamic worlds. Shin Takamatsu's entire oeuvre, arguably, interrogates the compelling presence of technology, without needing to create mechanized devices. His work defies any simple characterization of instrumental relations between human experience and instrumental technology. Much like the complex interdependence of technology and sexuality outlined in the analysis of Duchamp's *Large Glass* in Project 1, Takamatsu's work provides a stage for this melancholy encounter.

Proposition: The Theatre of Odysseus
If Le Corbusier could casually declare that a house was a '*machine-à-habiter*', then what is the role of Odysseus as the '*l'homme universelle*'. Further, on the model of Baroque theatre, what is the narrative that places this figure at the centre of the byzantine politics of a contemporary kingdom, the corporate behemoths such as Facebook, Amazon and Tesla that determine our everyday lives? So Odysseus, as an Ur-form of rationality lives and dies within a theatrical space. The royal court is a setting/site and a limit of the actions of the agencies of corporate kingdoms.

11: Metamorphosis

The core question of metamorphosis is change: how things change, why they do so and what, if anything, it means. Architecture is deeply invested in this condition because the contest between permanent forms and their relative resistance to entropy is fundamental to the discipline's ideas of permanence. But of course, buildings endure whereas the people that dreamt of them, constructed them, lived within them all age and die. The febrile transcience and finitude of our existence contrasts, of course, with that of the world. The idea of metamorphosis covered in these chapters addresses the specifically human encounter with this problem. What does it mean for humans to change and, considering architecture, what does it mean for humans to be considered part of the process of evolution within architecture? We generally assume that as our social structures and behavioural interests evolve, our architecture follows and responds after the fact. What, though, of the idea that the human body might be considered part of the architecture? The use of statuary in architectural settings is more than just a decorative device or a convenient practice of representation; it is a proposition that architecture and the human form have a deep existential kinship.

In the first chapter of this section, we consider the idea of bodily change as a function of the fundamental temporality of human experience, but one that can be exaggerated and, sometimes horrifically, re-presented as a parallel form of evolution. Whether it is the stories of Kafka or the sculpture of Bernini, there is a consistent deep insecurity regarding the stability of the human form which these works demonstrate. If part of the broad remit of humanism is an understanding of what it means to be human, or more broadly to be part of the Anthropocene, what does it mean to think about an architecture in which the body and the building are fused?

The relentless cataloguing of bodily form that the human sciences have been undertaking has resulted in increasing complexities in the boundaries between animal and human, in particular regarding the idea of sentience and agency. In these circumstances, the general proposition that architecture responds to and shapes the human condition is further complicated. What then is a bestiary? Are we part of an expanded definition of animality that is concerned with other entities, organic and synthetic, that have a call on architecture. The second chapter of this section considers this question.

Developing this condition further, it is worth investigating the provision of architectural locations and discursive formations that serve to house this process of cataloguing. The developed relationship between architecture and organizational systems is familiar when we are solely discussing human behaviour, but what of an expanded set of creatures that includes both human and non-human members? Do we continue to create zoos as prisons for animals, or as idealized environments, or do we rethink the question altogether?

Finally, in examining extended definitions of human-ness, what of our complex encounter with technology and body transformation? Architecture has participated deeply in devising analogies between buildings as mediating conditions for human experience, from didactic instruments for information exchange to phenomenological vessels for mediating sensual experience. The ubiquitousness of machined environments, from deceptively simple tools to highly orchestrated prosthetic devices, should always make us ask what the liminal condition between humanity and technology might be.

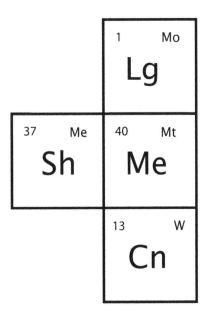

Rebus 40

Metamorphosis

Proposition 40: Metamorphosis

In nova fert animus mutatas dicere formas corpora.
('My mind is bent to tell of bodies changed into new forms.')
(Ovid, *Metamorphoses*, 8 CE)

One Morning, as Gregor Samsa was waking from anxious dreams, he discovered that in bed he had been changed into a monstrous verminous bug.
(Franz Kafka, *The Metamorphosis*, 1915)

The extraordinary and horrific changes that Gregor Samsa undergoes in Kafka's novella, *The Metamorphosis* (1915), describe an event that is inscrutable in its cause, but horrendously real in the effects it has on him and his family. There is a considerable body of literary study that attributes Kafka's narrative to observations regarding Kafka's own sense of discomfort with his personal relationships with his family and others in his personal life, but what is so notable regarding this story is the manner in which it is devoid of the slightest indication of some transcendent meaning in Gregor's suffering. Distinct from other stories such as *The Trial* (1925) and *The Castle* (1926) in which external environmental strife drives the narrative for the principal protagonist, the story of Gregor Samsa is internalized to the room, his bedroom, in which the initial transformation takes place.

In Kafka's other works, the role of architecture is similarly significant, though employed in a different modality. In *The Trial* and *The Castle*, the labyrinthine spatial environments of the Justice Department and the Castle itself are a core element of the narrative. In particular, the relationship between 'K', the main protagonist, and the physical boundary of the titular castle is a constant source of frustration. The narrative exists as a consequence of this exclusion, one in which architecture represents the morphological expression of deterrence and denial.

What distinguishes *The Metamorphosis* is the way in which the act of corporeal transformation that overcomes Samsa is not of his doing, nor does it result in a change that is intended to benefit him. Instead, the transitive nature of his change ultimately destroys him and he is, sadly, unable to reconcile himself to the nature of this transformation. The grotesque transformation he undergoes has an impact on his parents and sister, causing acute social embarrassment and compromising the health of those to whom he owes a debt of familial obligation. As his bedroom has become his *de facto* prison, we might speculate that once the room becomes littered with refuse (like those areas of an uncleaned house in which cockroaches might be infested), the reader experiences an understandable *Schadenfreude* experience of repulsion and fascination towards Gregor's plight.

The model for this form of transformation is Ovid's *Metamorphoses* (8 CE) which recounts a catalogue of origin myths and the power of transitive experiences in the lives of the characters and beings it narrates. Often following a dramatic and threatening event, a character is transformed into another state in order to distance themselves from the current world: Daphne is transformed into a laurel tree rather than be assaulted by Apollo; Pentheus is torn apart by his mother in a Bacchanalian frenzy; Arachne's transformation into a spider by the jealous Athena; Daedalus and Icarus assuming wings in order to escape Minos. In the nature of myths, these stories narrate a series of fundamental tensions between absolute behavioural standards and the idiosyncratic and hubristic actions of Gods and mortals. As philosophy, they express these tensions as personal traits, for good and bad.

Architecturally, and the example of Daedalus and Icarus is a good place to commence, the behaviour of the actors is fashioned by their engagement with the physical landscape in general and architecture in particular. Daedalus, having designed the labyrinth for Minos, is imprisoned on the island of Crete to prevent the knowledge of the structure from being released to potential adversaries. The ill-fated escape from the island by transforming their bodies by fashioning wax and feathers into wings initiates the idea that change carries the potential for liberation or destruction. Liberation, but sorrow, for Daedalus as he escapes, is mindful of the advice of the Gods and achieves an apotheosis, and destruction for Icarus, who ignores the advice, expresses the hubristic desire to fly higher towards the sun and fatally falls to earth when his wings melt. In a number of instances, the use of an architectural setting is intended to diagram the topographical relationships between opposing forces of behaviour and ethical/moral values. Ovid's House of Fama (fame/reputation/rumour) in particular shows this:

> There is a place at the centre of the World, between the zones of earth, sea, and sky, at the boundary of the three worlds. From here, whatever exists is seen, however far away, and every voice reaches listening ears. Rumour lives there, choosing a house for herself on a high mountain summit, adding innumerable entrances, a thousand

openings, and no doors to bar the threshold. It is open night and day: and is all of sounding bronze. All rustles with noise, echoes voices, and repeats what is heard. There is no peace within: no silence anywhere. Yet there is no clamour, only the subdued murmur of voices, like the waves of the sea, if you hear them far off, or like the sound of distant thunder when Jupiter makes the dark clouds rumble.

Crowds fill the hallways: a fickle populace comes and goes, and, mingling truth randomly with fiction, a thousand rumours wander, and confused words circulate. Of these, some fill idle ears with chatter, others carry tales, and the author adds something new to what is heard. Here is Credulity: here is rash Error, empty Delight, and alarming Fear, sudden Sedition, and Murmurings of doubtful origin. Rumour herself sees everything that happens in the heavens, throughout the ocean, and on land, and inquires about everything on earth.
(Ovid, *Metamorphoses*, Book XII, 8 CE: n.pag.)

Taken in the context of Ovid's general concentration on the transitive state of matter and material being, the House of Fama is solid and intransigent inasmuch as the inevitability of crafting a reputation, as a human activity, could be thought to be so. However, for Ovid the point is that these reputations are as febrile and insubstantial as sound within an echo chamber. So, in this first instance, architecture is the hollow vessel within which insubstantial things might be held. In this instance, architecture has no role in accommodating a metamorphosis from one state into another.

Considering architecture in a different fashion, throughout Ovid's text, the transformation of figures into other states is predominantly the transformation of living beings into statues. Turning to stone is a moment of death for many, but also the preservation of certain characteristics of the mythic figure. For example, when Anaxarete is turned to stone following Iphis's suicide her transformation from living flesh to stone, as punishment by Aphrodite, the moment of final mortality depicts and summarizes the judgement of her character. For Ovid, stone means both the transformation into a superior architectural form while also meaning death for living beings. It is tempting to make the association that marble, or stone, equates to death. It is the opposite of the story of Pygmalion in which his statue of Galatea, so beautiful and moving to the sculptor, is brought to life as a reward for Pygmalion's ardour.

However, when we think through this, the exercise of control in both instances is crucial, as is the lack of agency of the sculpted being. The most famous evocations of Ovid's transformations, Bernini's sculptures in the Villa Borghese in Rome, clearly present the figures both literally and vicariously as objects of desire. In particular, the clearly transgressive and violent nature of the encounter between Apollo and Daphne, and Pluto and Proserpina, tells us that transformation can be a state of extreme emotional stress. That these two sculpture groupings are intended to be viewed in the round, rather than in a specific architectural setting arguably does not diminish their importance for our discussion. When we consider Bernini's more overtly situated architectural sculptures, the *Ecstasy of St Teresa* (1647–52) or the *Fountain of the Four Rivers* (1651), the principles of transformation and transitive states continue. Bernini is following a long tradition of situated statuary that has its roots in the presence of divine figures within architectural settings, most famously in classical Greece. There is a long, detailed and complex history of the study of this relationship, but for our purposes, it is important to remember that the principal tension between architectural and figural expression is the license that figures have to demonstrate the presence of transitive morphological states. Figures exist, and are represented, within an indexical moment that is calibrated to communicate the most important symbolic relationships between the figural actors. When the statuary of the pediment of the Parthenon break from the plane of the pediment, they are activating, amongst many other narratival functions, the interest in change that Ovid would later codify in his *Metamorphoses*.

How is this architectural?
So we have two different modalities between architecture and metamorphosis, either as the scene in which transformation takes place, as the setting for and crucible of that change, or as the particularly corporeal transformation and evolution of the figure *into* stone/architecture, problematizing the intransitive fixity of architecture by introducing figuration that, usually, shares the same materiality.

Regarding the first modality, this leads us back to a fundamental tension in the employment of architectural settings in literature: the degree to which they are either causative or reactive to a protagonist's actions, to their state of mind and of their future behaviour. The bedroom of Gregor Samsa morphs from being a place of individual dwelling and comfort to a prison that his new body instinctively inhabits as an insect would. It is a source of horror that the Samsa family apartment has had, from within, undergone a transformation into a place that is carceral, secretive, shameful and, in the course of the narrative, becomes covered in filth that is un-human. The difference between this condition and that of Ovid is that the reader is uncertain about the degree to which this architectural transformation is a metaphor for other states, and indeed the impression that Gregor's plight is random, unfathomable and irreversible persists.

Regarding the second modality, the body-becoming-architectural is a subject that has clearly been suppressed as a consequence of modernity. The emphasis on abstraction and the championing of non-figural forms of painting and sculpture has suppressed the attention to the specifics of the body, and entirely emptied the question from architectural practice. While in recent years, there has been a renewed interest in the status of bodies, particularly through the study of gender and difference, it tends to occur in the first modality, above, in which certain spaces are defined as inscribing forms of subjectivity or have been historically or culturally associated with particular gendered practices.

One of the reasons for this suppression of a discourse of the body-architecture dyad in modern architectural practice has been the lazy theoretical alignment of figural sculpture with right-wing politics, for example as a legacy of the Nazi party's interest in idealized racial figures in the (in)famous House of German Art exhibition in 1937. As an expression of particularly chauvinistic and lethal racial policies, the question of figuration has largely been avoided for fear of reviving the association of figural sculpture with totalitarian politics. Received wisdom, such as the political discussion that questioned the figural additions to Maya Lin's Vietnam War Memorial (1982), or indeed the hostility to historical figural sculptures of colonial or racially chauvinist figures, is that figuration *necessarily* entails the celebration of these historical moments. In this congruence of politics and representation, the simplistic analogy is that figural sculpture is exclusive and privileged whereas abstraction is ambiguous and, as a consequence, inclusive. Despite the conscious attempts within Art Deco to stylize the relationship, the fact that Art Deco generally has been consigned to a minor role in the progress of modernity speaks (silent) volumes about the avoidance of the issue.

At the beginning of the twenty-first century, the alternative, tentatively and ironically expressed by architects such as Greg Lynn or Mark Foster Gage, is to incorporate cartoon-like figures into architecture which bear no resemblance to a human figure, whether historically constructed or contemporary. Using these forms, one presumes, means that the obligation to engage with the deep neurological experience of recognizing human-like qualities in other objects – the sense of ontic identity, physical vigour and emotional presence – is avoided. The less convincing your portrayal of a human figure, the less of an obligation for it to be judged as credible within the figural tradition. Not even the powerful examples of the work of the English sculptors, Henry Moore or Antony Gormley, or the Italian Alberto Giacometti, have been sufficient to provide a model for thinking through the architecture/figural sculpture relationship. The most abject example of this was surely Michael Graves's ludicrous use of the seven 'dwarfs' as simulated caryatids on the Disney Corporation Headquarters (1990) which served little purpose other than to deter subsequent architects from asking whether a critique of modernist abstraction could incorporate statuary of any kind.

However, this does not inevitably involve, as discussed in Proposition 17, a reversion to the flat ontology in which it is sufficient to create zoomorphic forms that bear *some* resemblance, however monstrous, to the human body. The question still needs to be asked whether architecture can incorporate sculptural forms that attempt to engage with the core aesthetic encounter that figural works entail. Can we imagine an architecture in which figural sculpture is intrinsic to the body of the building? Not simply as a blank box in which the sculptural work is housed, but as part of the complex symbolic and didactic language of representation intrinsic to the fabric of the work? How, for example, could the work of Patricia Piccinini become part of an architectural language of form?

The comparison of Kafka and Ovid that initiated this question, how does architecture engage with bodily transformation and the deep consequences of body politics that this entails, remains an open opportunity. Discovering and elaborating the relationship between the material geometries of architecture and the visceral and corporeal reality of the human body remains a challenge.

Proposition: The uncanny valley headquarters
Imagine if Pixar (despite its incorporation into the Disney behemoth) trained their considerable representational resources on creating architecture. And imagine if they took seriously the challenge of human configuration in all its diversity and complexity. Clearly, the opportunity exists for the company, should it choose to do so, to become the most avant-garde of architectural practices. How would they design?

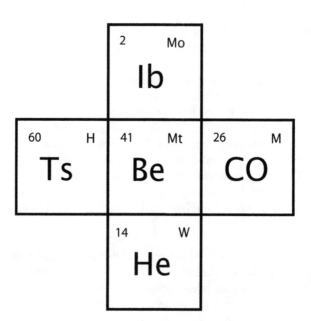

Rebus 41

Metamorphosis

Proposition 41: Bestiary

Continuing the discussion of identity and the complexities in considering the subject of architecture that we discussed in 'Metamorphosis', a related set of propositions can evolve around the intellectual trope of the Bestiary. A bestiary is, of course, the term for a compendium of beasts that is usually described in pre-scientific terms regarding the 'marvellous' aspects of the 'natural' world. There are two ways in which we can address this: either as an expression of the imperative to create categories, the Foucauldian discursive formations that create abstract definitions of properties, or as a form of becoming-human (or becoming-animal) that defines those aspects of the human condition that are employed to distinguish a 'presentable' human experience from the brute, visceral and corporeal realities of existence. In both instances, the definition of what constitutes a 'human' is a contested set of properties and behaviours.

A bestiary is, by current definitions, a pre- (and post-)human catalogue. In Michel Foucault's *The Order of Things* (1987), the domains of representation in language, or in the discursive contexts that 'things' occupy, the relationship between a name and a series of entailed functions and capacities is constantly tested. In some instances it is lost only to be 'recreated' through the process of interpretation..

In all, representation and its vicissitudes are the core mode of bringing-to-appearance. And by representation, it is understood that all forms of similitude are flawed by the mechanical process of transcription and description. Foucault uses the famous extract from Jorge Luis Borges's story referencing a Chinese Encyclopaedia ('Celestial Emporium of Benevolent Knowledge', in 'The Analytical Language of John Wilkins', 1942). While it is clear, in this instance, that 'Chinese' in Borges's mind denotes complex, foreign and unknowable, the list must be read in its entirety to fully see its counter-intuitive qualities:

1. Those that belong to the Emperor
2. Embalmed ones
3. Those that are trained
4. Suckling pigs
5. Mermaids
6. Fabulous ones
7. Stray dogs
8. Those included in the present classification

9. Those that tremble as if they were mad
  10. Innumerable ones
  11. Those drawn with a very fine camel hair brush
  12. Others
  13. Those that have just broken a flower vase
  14. Those that are from a long way off look like flies.
(Jorge Luis Borges, 'The Analytical Language of John Wilkins', 1942)

Borges's short piece is essentially a series of academic and scholarly veils that present the reality of John Wilkins as a historical figure, and also as an extended fictional simulation of academic scholarship. Foucault found the list fascinating as, incidentally, it described his own encounters with shifting meanings between words and things. Wilkins's interest in a 'natural' language in which all names inherently and unambiguously meant the thing they referred to, and Borges's attempted revival of him, was meant to point to the impossibility of that very project. Foucault, in his works, continually encountered the discontinuity between proposed structures of knowledge, and the actual behaviour of persons within them and, in particular, the difficulty in representing knowledge. For example, while the Periodic Table of elements represents certain qualities of singular chemical elements, as we noted in the introduction, its form as a table is only ever a representation or diagram of the complex interdependency of all chemical elements.

For these reasons, we can ask what role architecture has in presenting an 'Order of Things' within its general role in emplacing objects and behaviours. To briefly note a similar shift in the domain of representation that Foucault describes in the late enlightenment, in the discursive formations of 'Life', the idea of function in architecture becomes consistent with the modern epistemic realization that life can (ideally) be cultivated via technical apparatuses: a pineapple can be grown in a greenhouse, a reformed citizen from a panopticon, an enlightened *philosophe* from a phalanstery. For architecture, the idea that a function or programme could be designed in order to effect certain characteristics in users has become part of the profession's *raison d'etre*.

So, a bestiary is essentially a periodic table of life forms. The term, in its conventional sense, is associated with medieval encyclopaediae that document real and imaginary creatures without distinguishing, deliberately or otherwise, whether their 'reality' is important. Griffins sit adjacent to giraffes allowing for a shared form of fictional and situational equivalence. An architectural bestiary, moving beyond a conventional

Zoological Garden, would demonstrate the ambition to situate various life forms in proximity to environments.

The other modality of bestiary that is worth reviewing is the bestiary of the becoming-human and the becoming-animal. These suggestions are sketched out in Gilles Deleuze and Felix Guattari's *Thousand Plateaus: Capitalism and Schizophrenia* (1980, 1987) in which conventional properties of the human condition, how we define ourselves socially, are challenged for their inherently oppressive and instrumental effect on the self. Deleuze and Guattari's book is a wild and freewheeling challenge to all forms of received knowledge and has been famously influential in encouraging critical thinking within architecture through notions of nomadology and the virtual. It also reminds readers of the fact that the human body produces waste and is constantly convolved with the reality of a body's trajectory towards decomposition. Philosophically this serves the purpose, for Deleuze and Guattari, of reminding us that the thinking, feeling and acting subject is a deeply and inescapably corporeal animal.

Ultimately, the challenge that Deleuze and Guattari pose is the question of what constitutes 'person-hood' and how do we construct a sense of self that includes the sense-of-self of other sentient beings in our presence. That we share self-awareness with human and non-human life forms means, for them, that an authentic sense of being with others would include our own presence within any categorial organization. So the list of categories at the beginning of this chapter begins to make more sense since they share, by implication, a shared sentience that is distinct from conventional scientific (or legal) definitions and is ultimately for us to unravel.

How is this architectural?
We can begin to explore this question by considering five types of bestiary. As the purpose of looking at the idea of a bestiary is to interrogate the nature of the subjects it creates, then the degree or manner in which architecture inscribes, supports or excludes different forms of subjectivity directly correlates to the modality of the bestiary and its defining conditions. It also includes the suggestion that an architectural bestiary describes the heterogeneity of examples that are collected under the idea of non-standard typologies. The bestiary types are:

> 1. A bestiary in which the pre- and post-rational manifest a Dionysian tableau.
> 2. A bestiary in which political difference is reverse-engineered.

3. A bestiary in which the status of human and non-human (animal) is questioned.
4. A bestiary in which sentient and non-sentient life exists.
5. A bestiary in which artificial intelligence treats all organic processes as economic models.

Bestiary 1
In this example, the architectural example would explicitly address the heterogeneity of forms and objects in an architectural canon, the purpose of which is to find the fictional world within which mutable forms can exist together. If you can imagine Sir John Soane's House designed by Bruce Goff, or Francesco Borromini's version of the Barcelona Pavilion, then the incommensurability of the design ethos and the integrity of the iconic example is the point of the exercise. Whatever compromises of form and content occur, the value of the exercise is its inherent monstrosity, and that it is incoherent (and most magical) until it is explained.

Bestiary 2
In the reverse politics of this bestiary, the governing assumption is that the effects of architecture can be calibrated to specific world-views and to the production of different forms of the human subject. If we extrapolate the proposition that architecture is a social condenser, then the application of its effects creates increasingly fine-grained and idiosyncratic ontological experiences that cater to an increasingly atomized series of life views. Counter-intuitively, architecture contributes to political (dis)agreement because of the *reductio ad absurdum* of considering the idea that there is a 'personal' architecture for all life experiences. Consequently, the trajectory of all efforts is disagreement and incommensurability across architectural experiences. Architecture, in this sense, is the bestiary in which a diversity of examples means that subjectivity is unceasingly unstable.

Bestiary 3
In this modality, the question of humanity and animality is present. How do we cohabit with other sentient beings in a manner that is different from a master/slave relationship? The tension between a system that is inherently directed at the benefit and use-value of human social interactions does not necessarily map onto human/becoming-human relations. Further, how do we devise an architecture that is directed towards the unmaking of humanity towards some form of animality? We may see this as an exercise in ethical consanguinity between humanity and the extended

sentient world, but it is a challenge, and perhaps an emerging ethical necessity, to determine how to create an effective architectural response to these conditions.

Bestiary 4
This modality employs the speculations of object-oriented ontology to wonder about the life of things. Objects stabilize our relationship with the world as they affirm our place in it on a daily basis and provide a method for checking the complexity of that relationship. While it may be impossible to surveil the ontic reality of things in the world that are separate from us *as* objects, we can exercise our imaginations in seeing the potential, emergent dispositions that they have for each other. It sounds fanciful, but how does the crockery in our kitchens, or the books on our shelves, or the furniture in our bedrooms consider their relations? Inherently, of course, we cannot know this without anthropomorphizing them, but we can speculate on the effects of their hylomorphic propinquities. Arguably, the collective intention of Surrealism and many subsequent forms of non-abstract artworks is to be directed at the empathic range of this condition.

Bestiary 5
This form of bestiary steps outside the issue of sentience and acknowledges the philosophical problem of zombies, robots and their relation to artificial intelligence models. What are entities that demonstrate every aspect of sentient behaviour, every nuance of feeling, emotion, engagement and motivation yet are recognizably not 'alive' or are the product of learnt behaviour? A philosophical 'zombie' is an intellectual exercise in which all of the external indicators of another sentient being is present before us (these are not the animal zombies of fiction), yet we are aware that they are not 'alive' in a meaningful sense. Similarly, the question of sentience in artificial machines, such as anthropomorphic robots, challenges us to consider them to be receptive to the effects of architecture. How do we 'house' these entities?

Proposition: Anthropocene post office
The post office has been, historically, the organizational nexus for gathering and distributing information between people. It is the model for the distribution network for information prior to telephony and digital messaging given its role in providing a specific location for gathering, organizing and communicating with others. It is also an opportunity to consider the different bestiary forms outlined above and affirm a specific material reality, an architecture, in which these relations might be explored.

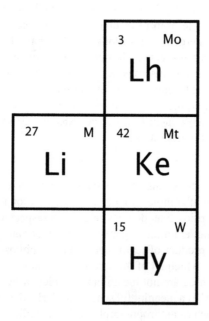

Rebus 42

Metamorphosis

Proposition 42: Kennels

One of the great challenges that emerged from discussions of the concept of the Anthropocene as a distinct temporal phase of the earth's transformation is the realignment of design issues to include species other than humans. There are complex arguments for the different levels of agency that this involves, and the complex attendant ethical issues of inter-subjectivity between species, but in essence, the challenge is to make something that demonstrates an understanding of this moment. Unsurprisingly, it does not mean more zoos, at least not as traditionally configured.

One thing an approach such as this does not constitute, and this point needs to be carefully made, is the anthropomorphic fallacy that certain species share motivational behaviours similar to humans. In particular, the culture of 'domestication' of certain animals, birds and reptiles does not infer that there is a consistent and shared intersubjectivity in which the domesticated creature is understood by the 'owner' or behaves in a fashion that emulates human behaviour. The attribution of emotional responses to some creatures by humans does not entail the reality of them possessing or exhibiting those emotions or motivations.

Revealingly, there is also considerable documentation of *fabulae* in which the border between human and animal identity has been crossed to the point where the core existential issue is whether this constitutes just an anomaly of the human condition or some type of transgression. When the character of John Merrick screams 'I am not an animal, I'm a human being!', in David Lynch's *The Elephant Man* (1980), he is voicing the uneasy relationship between the concept of human and non-human at the heart of all fictional stories of transformation, in this case a man who 'appears' to be an amalgam of human and animal characteristics. Additionally, of course, there are numerous folkloric stories that navigate between human and animal interactions in which the consciousness and expressive intelligence of animals is paramount.

Singer's utilitarianism
Peter Singer, the Australian ethicist, has written extensively on the nature of humanity's relationship towards the diverse volume of species with which we come into consistent contact. Pets, livestock and urban creatures all have a symbiotic relationship with human society, mostly opportunistic, but they are also conscious creatures with whom we share the planet. Singer's *Animal Liberation* (1975) was a landmark text in considering the nature of human treatment of non-human animals.

In this book, and in Singer's approach to ethics generally, he argues that animals have a degree of sentience that make their behaviour consistent with an emotional life in which ensuring the greatest good is the best outcome, and the minimizing of the suffering of animals should be at the forefront of this. Because Singer's argument is essentially a version of the 'greatest good' argument for the altruistic support of others around us, he suggests that the consistent considerate treatment of animals results in the greatest general avoidance of unnecessary cruelty.

The effects of the Anthropocene, naturally, have brought this relationship into question. The rate at which human activity has caused extinction of species is well-documented and sufficiently troubling in the context of climate change, for us to consider how other species in our immediate circle of agency might be assisted rather than be simply the collateral damage of economic and industrial systems that do not include this criterion in their performance indicators.

Singer's utilitarianism, though not without issues, points to the idea of equivalence between species and the adoption of practices to minimize harm to non-human animals. So there are two scales to this question, that of individual behaviour and the choices involved in, for example, choosing to personally limit one's diet exclusively to plant-based products or to recognizing the large-scale effects of Anthropocene behaviour on entire ecosystems. Individual choice vs. a mass strategy is a constant challenge within architectural practice as the disjunction between bespoke and typological solutions is a constant challenge within architecture, just as it is in ethics.

Generally, in practice, utilitarianism of this sort is distributed across 'stakeholders' and 'user groups' etc., but the greater challenge is to expand it across scenarios in which the long-term beneficiaries are non-human, in this case – of engaging with a post-Anthropocene world that recognizes the mutuality of animal experience. An alternative ethical framework is called the 'capability approach' in which support and care are afforded according to a person's capabilities for fulfilling a full and meaningful existence – the implication being that those without means to do so deserve the care of those who have greater capabilities and opportunities. In essence, it is an activist approach as it focuses on actions that should be initiated, rather than a rights-based view that does not necessarily require action.

How is this architectural?
Given the current inevitability of the imposition of boundary conditions on animal species, for their and our protection, the nature of that boundary and the

mutuality of distancing mean that we can think of the border as either a 'right' to safety and protection and/or an instrument for achieving happiness and enhancing capacity. Modern zoos that distinguish their role as being conservation rather than entertainment focused are premised on the task of species protection and education rather than spectacle. In reality, that commercial requirement is never far from the surface and does not address the reality that the 'exhibits' could quite happily exist in their natural habitat rather than the architectural construct of the zoo.

The Swiss biologist, Heini Hediger, took seriously the idea of death within zoos, particularly the structural problems associated with the close proximity of habitation of species and particularly of the architectural and management environment of zoo exhibits. Practically speaking, Hediger argues in *Man and Animal in the Zoo* (1963), that one of the greatest threats statistically to animals within a zoo is building and enclosure design. While Hediger promoted a frank discussion of how zoos produce death and also rely on the death of other animals for food, his general position was utilitarian. While the term does not come from Hediger, the concept of biopolitics in which the consciousness of mutual reliance between humans and other animals is at the forefront of his criticism of the traditional zoo.

But if zoos remain problematic in terms of their compromised functioning, it might be more effective to consider structures that are based in the domestic realm. Kennels are domesticated artefacts, like suburban post boxes, that miniaturize the place of the animal in the domain of the house. The kennel is a miniaturized domesticity imposed on the dog as a pack animal. It is a shelter but is also a gesture of domestic tidiness of which the animal is the most unruly disturber. And while there are instances in which persons commit to a form of shared habitation for domestic pets, sometimes with significant consequences for psychological and sanitary health, the challenge is to find a form of habitation that understands and acknowledges biopolitics and the fetishization of animal identity as 'brethren'. The personal zoos of persons such as Michael Jackson and Joseph Schreibvogel (the 'Tiger King'), to name two famous contemporary examples, are extreme examples of the personalization of a domestic relationship of kinship.

Creating an architectural response that understands and develops these characteristics, whether at an institutional or domestic level should understand, at the very least, that the structuring of capability for both human and non-human animals should be paramount. While one solution is to forgo the creation of zoos and even of domestic pets, but if that level of transformative behaviour is unlikely, then the 'housing' of non-human animals should start with the principle of 'do no harm', then the question is how to enhance and support their capabilities. It is at this point that one of the great challenges of human and non-human society emerges: how do we know what they want?

Proposition: The do-little do-much zoo
How to make an enclosure, or suburb, that modulates the corridor of movement between animals and humans. What are their patterns, how do they observe us? How do they engage with other species, including humans, how do they disengage?

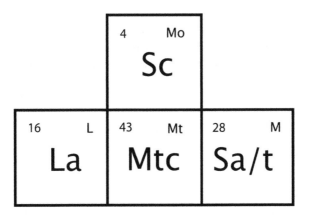

Rebus 43

Metamorphosis

Proposition 43: Mechanization Takes Command

In *Mechanization Takes Command: A Contribution to Anonymous History* (1948), Siegfried Giedion outlines a history of the immersive and totalizing influence of mechanistic system organization, scientific management and the abstraction of technology in its relations with the organic world. More specifically, he looks at the history of patents from the nineteenth to the early twentieth century to explain the incursion of modern design into everyday life. The book is fascinating, not for the final summary that advocates for an 'equipoise' between humanity and machine technology, but for the profoundly problematic evolution of a relationship between modern industrial products and human experience. When Marshall Berman (1982) discusses Marx on the market economy, he reminds us that the emergence of a vast field of objects and practices available for purchase is a truly unique experience in history, and that the bourgeois interior was more than a simulation of the display of aristocratic power that interior decoration had largely functioned to demonstrate. Bourgeois market consumption depended on hunger for self-recognition that the modern individual would embrace in the objects they purchased and displayed.

Of course, Sigfried Giedion is best known for the landmark text S*pace, Time and Architecture: The Growth of a New Tradition* (1941) which documented the transformations in the design of modern spaces and modern formal languages in architecture. His analysis of the way in which the rhetorical focus on 'space' allowed conversations across a number of creative disciplines permitted him to see consistencies in the spatial organization of Cubism, De Stijl, the Bauhaus and in the work of the major figures of early architectural modernism, particularly Walter Gropius and Ludwig Mies van der Rohe.

Giedion's history of technology and the development of industrial design believes it is agnostic on the role of market consumption and that the question of whether mass industrialization, production and consumption were natural outcomes of a scientific and rational world-view is moot. However, when we look at the history, as Giedion does, of the industrialization of comfort and posture in chair design, or the process of organizing, slaughtering and 'processing' livestock, there is the sense that our relationship to technology is far more problematic than at first glance.

If we focus on one aspect of that history, the mechanization of bathing, the intersection of health, morality, sensuality and mechanical system design, a great deal is revealed. It should also be said that another choice of focus, the mechanization of livestock processing, is similarly revealing and shadows the industrialization of slave labour and genocide within the Holocaust.

For Giedion, there is a clear line of development from the identification of simple human behaviours to the identification that these can be assisted through the intervention of a mechanical device that efficiently emulates aspects of the behaviour. The kneading of bread dough, the dividing of the dough into consistent loaf-sized portions, a process of baking that is consistently applied and timed, the slicing of bread to facilitate even slices and optimum use – all these phases in the creation of bread are now subject to the management of a mechanized process that is separated from the skills of individual bakers.

In this example, the transformation of a process that had formerly been controlled by the skills and facilities of individuals has now been tied to processes of manufacture that, importantly, diminish the need for judgement by the baker and increase the possibility of economies of scale and time. The mechanized process produces a sufficiently similar product to the hand-crafted item within tolerable limits and, most importantly, gives the authority for the quality of the product to a relatively much smaller group of manufacturers rather than individual bakers and customers.

Prosthetics
Consistently, through Giedion's book, he reviews the emergence of mechanical devices that transform human action into devices and apparatuses that exist as prosthetic extensions of human capacity. He also reviews the evolution of simple items such as chairs and records the transformation of pieces of furniture into specialized devices. Transportation chairs, the bath and vacuum cleaners are discussed as expressions of the competing interests in providing forms of comfort and cleanliness through the development of technical solutions that owe nothing to ideas of taste and fashion.

But what is clear as a subtext of Giedion's survey is that the development of domestic technology fundamentally alters the idea of 'homeliness'. For Giedion, the lessons of *Mechanization Takes Command* is that the Taylorized solutions to tasks, from the industrial to the personal are consistent with the development of an abstract and disembodied occupation of the modern interior. In the final chapter, 'Man in Equipoise', a vision of future architecture as an elaborate command and control centre is imagined. Or in the alternative, he also recognizes that much of modern architecture's obsession with abstraction and industrial design is suppressing the idea that the modern interior should demonstrate an abundance of these devices. Should there be more or less mechanical prosthetics, ultimately becomes the final question for him, and moreover, the degree to which the human condition is deficient and requires extensional devices is left as an open condition.

Ultimately, the clockwork and mechanical universe of Giedion was elided by the interest in the technologies of building construction, facilities management and stable-state environmental standards that were first articulated in Reyner Banham's *Architecture of the Well-Tempered Environment* (1969). Banham recognizes in the late 1960s that the tendency of architecture was increasingly towards management systems rather than the creation of form-based modern typologies. The shift from object to process is a crucial characteristic of the continuing negotiation of the consequences of modernity. As Mary Lobsinger (2016) notes, the development of a form of architectural history that evolves from the study of objects (including architecture) in their context to one that tracks the evolution of certain behavioural tendencies is emblematic of the inherent fluidity of modern experience. Giedion's history of the 'anonymous' developments of prosthetic behavioural devices is a more appropriate model than his, and others, focus on stylistic changes.

How is this architectural?
The cultivation of systems is now clearly established within both architectural practice and the academy, despite the obvious and ongoing emphasis upon singular built outcomes. The challenge in understanding how a generalized system, for example telecommunications, becomes a device (phone or laptop) and how that change infers behavioural preferences within architecture is clear. While this does not preclude any of the varied formal strategies that continue to be proffered as novel formal developments, the interlacing of form and performance is a continual test of whether the solution displays some optimized state.

An interesting, and counter-intuitive, development of this may be two-fold, either a return to the mechanical as a visible manifestation of changes in phenomenal experience, or a rejection outright of any form of environmentally mediating role for architecture.

Proposition: The well-tempered prosthetic
It is possible to imagine an architectural project that assumes no form of environmental or behavioural assistance to the user. It is impossible to remotely heat or cool, impossible to clean, impossible to inhabit within conventional domestic models of habitation, impossible to work within and impossible to keep secure. Yet it is also an extension of the gestures of living, an elaborate device for addressing these issues.

12: Fiction

In this section, we turn to the question of fiction as a convention of abstract, imaginative communication testing the boundaries of what can be considered real and viable vs. that which deliberately sets itself outside of everyday experience. Further, we look at the role of fiction in determining the ground for asserting the difference between what can be objectively proven vs. that which requires certain suspensions of disbelief. Architecture, at the stage of conception and planning, is deeply enmeshed in the development of speculative conditions that change the circumstances of the world. The task of this section is to understand some of the operations of fiction in relation to architecture and further, to communicate the value of this new condition to our present.

The first chapter looks at the historical anomaly of the ruin as both a materially vivid condition, and one that entails sensitivities to the ambiguous temporality of the ruined structure. The propensity for any risk-based enterprise to undergo catastrophic failure can be compared to the fundamental temporal proposition of architecture that will ultimately approach a state of ruin. For this reason, in projecting the life of a building into the future, much like Joseph Gandy's rendering of John Soane's Bank of England (1830), the tension between the present and the imagined future is tantalizing.

Exploring this temporal distance further, the second chapter looks at the relationship between literary evocations of future states and their representation in images. Literature in most forms, but especially fiction concerned with the evocation of unknown or temporally dislocated future states, asks us to understand the logic of how this place came to exist, and the dominant state of affairs it represents. Any fiction that speculates on how life is to be lived, either as an extension of contemporary tendencies or as a wholly new phenomenon, calls on its architecture to demonstrate the material qualities of this condition.

Expanding on this condition, fiction also asks us to consider counter-factual conditions for logical consistency and their equilibrium with the rationalities of the present. Looking at Immanuel Kant's overdetermined attack on the mysticism of dreams, it reveals that for every determinate position that asserts its dominance, there is a kind of equal and opposite effect, a doppelgänger, that exists as a fictional possibility. Within this logic of phenomenon and noumenon, despite the prohibition against shallow mysticism, our culture of imagination continues to explore the question of the fictional double. And in contemporary society, arguably, it is the filmic world where this continual experiment continues to blossom. The fourth chapter looks at the simple, but profound force of space and time in cinema as an apex in the employment of emotional and predictive behaviour. Cinema employs complex narrative structures to introduce, release and examine the myriad possible modalities with which architecture might be put at the service of a rich ontological experience.

Finally, we look more deeply into the instrumentality of the genre category of puzzle-based fictions, ones that propose clear structural relationships between the environmental forces, particularly architecture, that govern the evolution of the plot to present an entailed state of affairs. The puzzle film or fiction, like that of the detective story, requires the audience to understand the implacable force of environment in the resolution of antinomous forces. In these circumstances, it is clear that an expanded definition of architecture can come to incorporate the design of these fictional proposals. Architecture is always about form, but it is the understanding of how form shapes meaningful narratives that we see its enhanced capacity for demonstrating profoundly speculative outcomes.

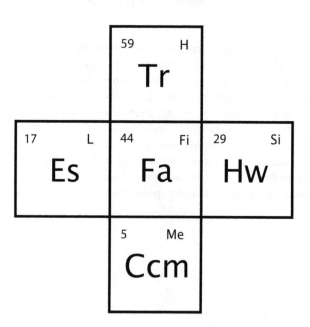

Rebus 44

Fiction

Proposition 44: Future Archaeology

> 'You maniacs! You blew it up! God damn you,
> God damn you all to Hell!'
> (Charlton Heston as Captain Taylor in *Planet of the Apes*, 1968)

The idea of archaeology and the encounter with the fabric of history is a strong theme within architectural design. The presence of fragments of previous buildings/objects asserts a continuous presence in the design process. The literary concept of the palimpsest, a text that has had erasures and overwriting but still retains the outline of the previous glyphs, has been used as an analogy for the process of overbuilding and adaptive reuse of existing fragments in contemporary schemes. In Rome, there is a building at the corner of Via del Ponte Rotto and Via Luigi Petroselli, close to the Tempio di Portuno and the Foro Boario, which is essentially an amalgamation of classical and medieval fragments fused to create a form of architectural expression. Further along Via Luigi Petroselli, San Nicola in Carcere is a similar exercise in the persistence of the fragments of the past, this time incorporating temple fragments transformed into a church. Are they works of architecture? Is there a singular design sensibility governing all aspects of the building, externally and internally? Of course, the answer is that there isn't, and as Robert Venturi speculated in *Complexity and Contradiction in Architecture* (1967), there is a legitimate aesthetic and heuristic purpose to considering this a mode of architectural practice. In itself, these are just two of hundreds of buildings around Rome which are the product of this accretional development, but they demonstrate that the integrity of a design need not come solely from its visual consistency.

In architectural design, there is a subset of design approaches that acknowledge the antinomy between the constructive projection of a building design that asserts its immediate relevance, and the knowledge that it has already extinguished its criticality once built. Trivially this is the case with all buildings, and architects naturally attempt to future-proof their designs to ensure that their effectiveness and relevance have the longest possible half-life. In fact, it can be argued that the entire project of architectural history, as taught in architecture schools around the world, is intended to simultaneously preserve and promote exemplars of architecture, while also pushing back against the argument that they are no longer intellectually relevant.

However, the inevitability of work becoming obsolete, or *déclassé*, means that the spectre of irrelevance is always present. The suppressed premise is that this is a design consideration that is, at best, ignored or, at worst, glumly acknowledged as an inevitable consequence of the onward march of time and taste. However, there are projects that acknowledge this reality and explore the temporal uncertainty of their moment, projecting a future that includes the immanent reality that they will either be irrelevant and consequently form part of the greater banality of the urban environment, or will degrade to the point where the material coherence they originally expressed is compromised to the point of ruin. Intuitively, even Hitler's instruction to Albert Speer to create a version of his *Die Ruinenwerttheorie* ('Theory of Ruin Value', 1936) in creating the model for the new Berlin expressed the romantic notion that the inevitability of death and destruction circumscribed the ambitions of the Third Reich.

Interestingly, Ruin Theory also exists within the domain of Actuarial Risk Theory, the probability of bankruptcy and insolvency that fundamentally governs the conduct of commercial insurance operations. But where ruin is a condition that is acknowledged in insurance risk and requires a balance between assets and potential liabilities to be regulated, the concept of ruin in architecture is mostly ignored or like Speer, more esoterically imagined and embraced. For both, it constitutes an engagement with risk.

If we consider the practice of architecture to be more than the single vector of production through to construction and occupation, the understanding that the moment of design might also entail the creation of risk, or ruin, makes the embrasure of ruin (or ruin-like conditions) a part of how design might be imagined.

Ruin
When the taste for ruins dictated the construction of 'ancient' structures such as the follies of William Kent's eighteenth-century landscapes in England, or the artificial landscape of the Parc des Buttes-Chaumont in Paris (1864–67), the practice of 'ruination' constituted an active embrace of a temporality that was effectively trebled since it expressed the contemporary moment in which it was designed and the concurrent taste for the antique, the time from which the ruin was semantically chosen as a synecdochal representation, and, importantly but less obviously, the degree of ruination that the work had undergone. This 'ruination index' allowed for the simultaneous calibration of the work's recognizability as a version of an antique or gothic model and of its purposelessness as a functioning structure. The

more ruined it was, the less recognizable and hence less semantically effective it was as a representation of a historical past. Yet the more complete (or less ruinous) the building was, the less effective it was as an evocation of the mortality of architecture.

This tension continues through to contemporary evocations of materiality, particularly in the romantic and charismatic writings of persons such as Juhani Pallasmaa, who is himself evoking a nostalgia for material experience in the work of Gaston Bachelard. For Pallasmaa (2016), a clear distinction is made between the componentry of architecture and the unfashioned material with which buildings are constructed. The empirical visual and physical sensation of stone, in Pallasmaa's view, is a fundamental experience, ontologically prior to our understanding of its use as a keystone or column. Pallasmaa argues that the weathering of materials, and the changes they express, constitutes their core indexical identity. They undergo a process of change that communicates their strength, frailty, chemical complexity, etc., all of which are considered poetically significant, and through doing so, allow us to see architecture as a thoughtfully managed process of bringing this material experience for presence. Arguably too, as an enhanced demonstration of modern abstraction, it can also lapse into the banality of the superficiality of 'mood boards'.

We can contrast this with the argument Marco Frascari describes in the famous 'Tell-the-Tale Detail' (1983) essay mentioned previously, where the primal experience is that of the detail, the 'logos of techne' which communicates the transformation of matter (building materials) from one state to another. For Frascari, and by extension for Carlo Scarpa from whom this argument is derived, the communicative power of the detail is in its ability to allow us to see this transformation. Details 'communicate', in drawn and constructed form, by showing the expression of the techniques of manufacturing and conjoining. Inevitably these details evolve from the physical properties of the material employed, but essentially they communicate the design intelligence employed to construct them.

While Frascari, in this essay, has nothing to say about the idea of ruin, the buildings in Rome described earlier are clear examples of the employment of fragmentary signifiers opportunistically incorporated into contemporary needs. As details, they communicate the persistent vitality of these archaeological fragments and engage us in a debate as to whether their ad hoc use is meaningful. Luigi Moretti's famous Casa 'Il Girasole' (1955), also in Rome, inserts a fragment of a stone human leg into the architrave of one of the ground floor windows in what is otherwise an elegant modern building. What is the point of this, what does Moretti risk in creating this stylistic anomaly? Is Moretti's detail a fragment of an actual archaeological ruin (it isn't) or is it the expression of a collagist sensibility that demonstrates the same approach to design as that of Kent and the picturesque movement?

So an architecture which engages with the idea of ruin inevitably engages with perceptions of risk, the risk that the quotations are only internally coherent within a limited circle of understanding and that the 'logos' is incomprehensible to outsiders. It is also a method for projecting forward an archaeological practice that is also architectural, creating propositions for future persons to treat architecture as a conundrum of temporal referents. For architectural theory, different from that of actuarial insurance, risk is always a positive value that is projected forward. When Charlton Heston's character in *The Planet of the Apes* (1968) falls to his knees and we see the ruined Statue of Liberty at the end of the narrative, it fundamentally realigns the context of the story's actions. The presence of a ruined fragment of his (our) past creates a vacuum in understanding what events lead to the ruin and a realization that his present is (imaginatively) our future.

Proposition: Moretti's leg
If we substitute Captain Taylor from *The Planet of the Apes* with a fictional Captain George Hegel, we can activate the potential for the ruin to be historiographically significant. Hegel's philosophy of history considers the evidence of the past to demonstrate characteristics of purposiveness that is sensible within current domains of thinking. The tradition of the graphic 'reconstruction' considered philosophically and fictionally can allow us to generate any number of counter-factual, but coherent, versions of architecture. When we look at the engaged human leg trapped in the window frame of Luigi Moretti's Casa 'Il Girasole', we can wonder how to reconstruct its critical purpose.

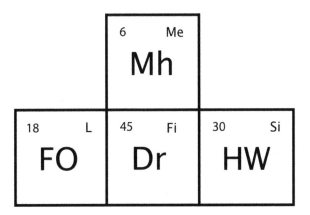

Rebus 45

Fiction

Proposition 45: Dreams

One of the most rigorous academic analyses of the complex literary and philosophical issues within science fiction literature is Frederic Jameson's *Archaeologies of the Future* (2005). As one of the leading figures in cultural Marxism, Jameson is mostly known for his trenchant and influential discussion of postmodernity, specifically in literature but extending into cultural studies generally. By viewing cultural production of all forms as complex examples of the political and economic ideologies that give culture its context, Jameson's version of cultural Marxism flirts with the obvious and the incisive.

Science fiction, as a genre, is inextricably tied to the development of modernity and, at its most general level, constitutes attempts to navigate the conflicts and opportunities that contemporary technology might bring in the future, for good or bad. While there are a number of sub-categories within the genre, depending on the interests of the author or artist, cultural theorists such as Jameson consider it to be a distinct organic expression that simultaneously expresses desire and repulsion. Importantly, in both literary and visual forms, the speculation that times to come will be significant, and sometimes terrifying, allows writers and visual artists to extrapolate on tensions in contemporary society. By presenting worlds that their audience will recognize as hauntingly familiar, however strange, the extrapolation of core tensions in contemporary society is made visible.

When, for example, China Miéville in his novels, such as *The City & The City* (2009) or *Perdido Street Station* (2000), or the artist Mike Winkelmann (known as 'Beeple') create visions of hallucinatory presents, they invoke a context in which these literary and visual worlds present a reality, a 'nowness'. This nowness, in all its ambiguity, is recognizable as being structured by causal forces, however mysterious the origin of their political and technological intentions. As Jameson argues, these visions of conflictual states of utopian hope and pessimistic despair provide a meta-commentary on contemporary conceptions of risk. The sense of attraction and repulsion to these visions, their *Schadenfreude*, is likened to the conciliatory role of dreams in moderating conflicts that occur within our waking lives. Whether this is legitimately the case, or whether the literary and visual output of science fiction represents this process at a level beyond the individual, there is clearly a role, demonstrated by the popularity of the genre, for visualizing the fictional consequences of contemporary obsessions. Crucially, this process is a core characteristic of the speculative imaginings of many contemporary architectural projects, particularly within the intellectual climate of those schools of architecture that have normalized and championed these outcomes.

For Jameson, the principle frame for understanding the conflicts and obsessions of visionary fictional settings is the question of their political machinations, and ultimately their utopian promise. Questions of political power, personal identity, gender, bio-politics, environmental engagement and technological instrumentalism are structurally foregrounded in the narratives since it is their circumstances that are most clearly novel. Genre sagas such as the *Star Wars* franchise are most interesting, arguably, for the coherence and conflicts of their worlds more than the narrative arcs of the characters.

How is this architectural?
The most immediate method for looking at the science fiction genre through an architectural lens is to distinguish between text-based and visual forms. In the case of text-based material, such as Miéville or any of the authors of visionary environments, the exact form of the worlds, its architecture, is left to the reader's imagination. Cover art or the occasional illustration can stand in as reference points, but the principle engagement is with the reader's grasp of fictionality, or transfictionality in the case of worlds that incorporate recognizable urban and architectural elements in a fictional narrative. The reader supplies sufficient granular 'feeling' for the location, depending on the text, to make sense of the narrative itself. Transfictionality melds the real with the unreal, grounding the peculiarities of the narrative in a world that has undergone transformation but allowing the reader to 'inhabit' recognizable urban and architectural settings.

In contrast, visual depictions of imagined worlds that have a significant architectural component lend themselves to immediate analysis and extrapolation. If we look at the work of the visual artist Daniel Docui for example, his concept art for game spaces entails significant architectural and urban form, often combined with gargantuan technical infrastructure. In Docui's work, generally speaking, the moment of the image occurs in a temporality after the failure of the infrastructure to retain its integrity. Engineering behemoths have collapsed and idealistic urban planning has been reduced to *ad hoc* occupation alluding to a post-technological, post-apocalyptic scenario. His images are, as mentioned previously, a mode of futurist archaeology that exists in a direct lineage from the *Carceri* images of Piranesi in the eighteenth century.

The challenge of these images, for an architect, is not necessarily to emulate their graphic style or subject matter but to reverse engineer the world to discover what technological and social organizations might have created these vast projects in the first instance. While most of these images come from a position that appeals to a target audience who might only have a vague interest in their origins, as architects we will inevitably ask more rigorous questions. In the same manner that we might interrogate an architectural project that illustrates a visionary circumstance, and critique it for the motivating ideas that the architect drew on, we can scrutinize the images of Beeple, Docui and many of the game-focused concept artists for traces of possible architecture.

A final note is worth making regarding the purpose of the concept-art images we've been discussing. In their standalone context, their meaning and purpose are only known in a limited fashion. In their first iteration, they are intended to either be illustrative of a more comprehensive text-based narrative, as discussed earlier, or as visual prompts to game designers whose task is to create the three-dimensional worlds that the games spaces occupy. It is a structural reality that the complexity of form, animation, texture and lighting of these concept images is rarely achieved by the game environments themselves since the level of detail required in the modelling and performance phase of game creation precludes this level of detail.

Yet as Moore's Law delivers increasingly sophisticated hardware and software developments for personal computing, the gap between concept art and gameplay is decreasing. Arguably this means that the binary in game design between ludic functionality (task-based 'play') and narrative depth is similarly being reduced. The worlds are richer in detail and the challenges of increasingly complex narratives that are more 'logically' tied to the player's actions are similarly increased. For architecture this poses an interesting, parallel opportunity for testing the intuitive aesthetic occupation and social behaviourism of designed structures and spaces.

Possible project: Reverse engineering, reverse architecture
From an image selected from the vast online Creative Commons resources available, model an architectural work. Invest it with functionality, purpose and a sufficient narrative to explore and present the purpose of its existence. Take, for example, China Miéville's, *The City & The City* (2009). Look at the twin cities of Besźel and Ul Qoma, and from the near-identical form that they share construct a fragment of the third, imaginary city, Orciny.

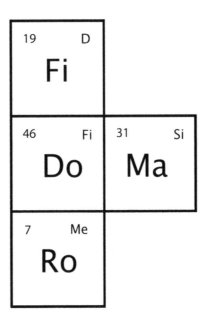

Rebus 46

Fiction

Proposition 46: Doppelgänger

The idea of the double in fiction is an important, but niche, concept that refers to the question of our singular presence and the possibility that an alternate version of the self exists in our own space and time. In José Saramago's novel, *The Double* (2002) (reinterpreted and filmed as Denis Villeneuve's *Enemy*, 2013), the main character discovers the existence of a double version of himself, an actor in a movie he watches. Like many fictional circumstances, the tension between reality and the events of the narrative continually contests the causal consequences of actions and reactions. The idea that an exact replica of oneself is in the world creates the uncomfortable sensation that the possibility of meeting the 'other' might entail the most horrific form of existential dread.

Suffice it to say the impossibility, or unlikelihood, of the premise drives the narrative in both book and film. It creates a scenario in which suspension of disbelief is balanced by the seeming normality and banality of the contextual circumstances. While this is true of most fictional works, the idea that a double can exist in a parallel world that is matched to our own creates a rich series of potential moments when the two realities impossibly meet. It is the question of how we understand the presence of the fantastic and the rhetorical language we choose to describe it. It is in this scenario that I would like to discuss a different form of double and relate a story about the relationship between the Swedish mathematician Emanuel Swedenborg and the German philosopher Immanuel Kant during the late eighteenth century.

Swedenborg, a generation before Kant, was originally a highly respected mathematician, but during his life came to believe that a series of dreams he was experiencing were of such a vivid and compelling nature, that he had to share the experience. These were originally collected in his *Drömboken*, or *Journal of Dreams* (posthumously published in 1850). He wrote voluminously on the mystical interpretation of the Old Testament and the Torah and, in the mystical tradition, rhapsodized on the depths of meaning that lay behind the text of these works in *Arcana Coelestia* (1749). Kant, on reading Swedenborg, focused on two things. First, he looked at the idea of a metaphysical world that lay behind empirical experience which he dismissed as frivolous and unknowable, and secondly, at the rhetorical force with which Swedenborg used language to communicate the sensate immediacy of the mystical experience.

Kant dismisses the purported knowledge of places that are beyond the apprehension of empirical experience. In his refutation of Emanual Swedenborg's *Arcana Coelestia*, and subsequent insistence on the presence of an afterlife he mocks the idea that a spirit may occupy a space in any format, or that it could be co-present with our material reality. So, while Swedenborg's intellectual trajectory took him from science to mysticism, Kant rectifies the impulse to see Divine agency in all experience and for there to be a preservation of 'the unknown' in human affairs. Kant wrote an anonymous refutation of Swedenborg, *Dreams of a Spirit Seer* (1766), in which he poked fun at the idea of Swedenborg's project, and at the ghosts and other apparitions Swedenborg 'saw' – either as dreams or as putative real experiences. But why would Kant take the time to do this?

One of the challenges presented by Swedenborg's text, and mystical affirmations of other-worldly deities, is that the burden of proof rests on the rhetorical skill of the writer. Further, Kant was interested in the fundamental aspects of epistemology: extensionality in space and time. For him the problem was that mystical writing professed to give the same spatio-temporal qualities to metaphysical (ghostly) entities as it did to human experience. For Kant, this meant that the denial of non-human entities was a pre-requisite for a credible discussion of the phenomenal world (that which we individually experience) and the noumenal world (those things that theoretically exist and are strictly non-knowable to human experience). Noumena, it should be stressed, are not imaginary in any sense but are theoretically real and form part of Kant's larger *Critique of Pure Reason* (1781).

And yet the spectre of mysticism and the rhetorical sustenance of its reality continued to occupy Kant. He recognized that discussion of things spiritual (including the 'soul'), whether from orthodox religion or other experiences, had a meaningful effect in everyday conversation. While this did not mean that metaphysical entities existed in reality or in the eighteenth-century mind, it did mean that the effect of rhetorical discussion made sense as a presentation of the speaker's reality. Moreover, the degree to which the dreamer's reality rhetorically aligned with the listener or reader (or viewer in the modern world) afforded a coherence and reality, however temporary, to their visions.

The dream has the double effect of spatializing a series of experiences that have a complex purpose for the dreamer, but which also negates the experience of reality as there is no necessary and idiosyncratically relevant meaning in the place(s) of the world. Where every dream has, for an individual, some vestige of purpose, not all aspects of the world, arguably, carry that same degree of reflexivity. Every dream space or location is disposable and exhibits purposiveness only for so long as the dream narrative needs to be sustained. This is the scenario for *The Double* (Saramago 2002), as it is for all fiction.

Causality in dreams is the question that Descartes posed when deciding on the proof of an external reality that was subject to sensate experience. If we are not dreaming, or an evil daemon is not affecting our mind, how do we have certainty that the external world exists and that the causality of logical operations is possible? Do you design something that is encountered and that is already situated in some historicized state of affairs? This is the premise of Christopher Nolan's *Inception* (2010) and drives the complexity of the narrative. Further, in dreams there is usually a place inasmuch as there is 'placedness', and there is the impression of physics, inasmuch as there are trajectories of things and the presence of motion such as vestibular sensations (vertigo). The abyss that Swedenborg writes of is, for him, an allegorical finitude which describes a final endpoint of existence, but also a deeply physiological experience.

How is this architectural?
Dreams have locations, or at the very least have aspects of the extensionality of space and time, often for the purpose of allowing the consistency of these things to be compromised. How extraordinary to create a project that makes the substance of a dream, its site and its construction, persistent and controllable - that it might be returned to and scrutinized for the consistency of its effect, and whether it continues to demonstrate the same level of wonder that it presented in the first instance. Francesco Colonna's *Hypnerotomachia Polyphili* (1499) is, of course, the great narration of a picaresque journey through a dream, latterly revisted by Alberto Pérez-Gómez in his *Polyphilo, or The Dark Forest Revisited* (1992). Like *Inception* the layers of causality that are suggested within the events of the story mimic the temporary construction of a space/time experience that troubled Kant some centuries before.

A number of sub-questions emerge, from the principal question as to what 'the architecture in/of dreams' consists of?

> 1. Is it the creation of forms/spaces that are illustrative of a dream? (Surrealism.)
> 2. Is it the development of a narrative that includes specific discontinuous events that do not fulfil a greater narrative of reality? (*Hypnerotomachia Poliphili*.)

3. Is it the narrativization of spaces that would otherwise be normal and unproblematic? (The monstering of the normal in *The Double*.)
4. Is it the assumption and re-framing of architecture that re-programmes behaviour and in so doing creates an architectural dream narrative? (The stacking of causalities within *Inception*.)

Proposition: The nap of reason – Kant's cabin
While the description of the overall site of a dream can be achieved through the most fantastic of architectural projects, it is a reality that the events that occur within a dream and the consequences that are foreshadowed in their causal universe can differ wildly. The challenge is to show that the dream exhibits, in its full expression, a chain of events and locations that speak of human experience.

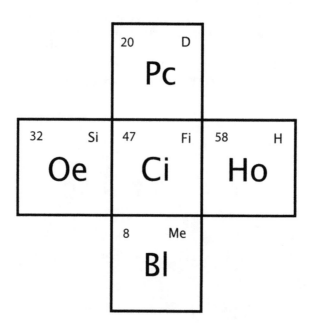

Rebus 47

Fiction

Proposition 47: Cinema

> The buildings in movies, on the other hand, have been designed to fulfill one precise and exclusive role in a film, and in a particular scene. This is the only architecture that is truly functional, both psychologically and emotionally.
> (Juan Antonio Ramirez, 'Ten Lessons [or Commandments] About Architecture in the Cinema', 1992)

The proposition that there are significant thematic similarities between cinema and architecture is one that has many enthusiastic adherents. Quite apart from the trainspotting pleasure of listing films that document the use of significant (or interesting) architecture, and work that speculates on the futurology of social relations within utopian and dystopian settings, the intersection of narrative and scene within film studies seems to provide a chimerical opportunity for architects to imagine how film and architecture might productively combine.

As an academic exercise, films such as Ridley Scott's *Blade Runner* (1982) and Fritz Lang's *Metropolis* (1927) have famously been (over)analyzed to see evidence of dystopian urban architectural experience, arguing that the complexities of the characters' behaviour are supported and enhanced by the phenomenological *qualia* of the set design. There is a minor industry in creating lists of films that architects should see, though the reasons why this must be the case is never made fully clear by the list-makers (though we will look at it below). Similarly, these lists also serve as introductions for the non-professional audience to the idea that architecture has a clear role in creating locations that can not only be imagined but also realized. Clearly, one of the major, and intractable, points of difference between cinema and architecture is the need for architectural work to endure and functionally 'perform' for longer than the instant it might be caught on camera. So, in many senses, the relationship between cinema and architecture is married to the idea of how the moments of cinema, those shots which present an architectural environment as an established presence, might be translated into an actual, and enduring, presence in the world outside of cinema. The fundamental complexity of cinema, that it presents the *mise-en-scène* of a world as performatively real, offers the tantalizing possibility that the circumstances in which cinema's narrative reality exists might be transferred into everyday life.

Cinema and cinema theory constantly question the presentation, perception and manipulation (ambiguity) of reality. The constant anxiety at the lack of reality in the cinematic presentation of the world governs the need for theory. Inversely, the constant material reality of architecture anchors/chains it to forms of reality that have no ambiguity, and potentially no narratival complexity.

On narrative
The link between narrative and outcomes in cinema, as a methodological examination of possible behaviours within defined circumstances, matches the modern expectation within architecture that the effects of architectural work can be imagined, trialled and tested. When we see certain actions within a narrative responsively defined by the architecture it inhabits, it reminds architects that their work forms the settings for a wide array of behaviours. When the protagonists in *Die Hard* (1988) fight their way through an innocuous and generic Los Angeles office building, ultimately causing its destruction, the entire arc of the plot only makes sense in the context of the characters surpassing that banality and weaponizing the building to their situational advantage.

But film is just light on a screen, without a tangible and materially persistent reality. And a narrative, usually, ends with some form of rapprochement between characters and environment, even if it is their destruction. As viewers of the narrative, we understand that the effects of the location have had consequences that are tangible and coherent – the desert is unforgiving, the city never sleeps, the suburban facade masks domestic complexities, for example. While this is often an ambition of architecture, to engineer specific experiential and existential outcomes, it rarely can guarantee the level of narratival specificity of cinema.

Cinema functions to educate the viewer on the consequences of environments, including architectural environments, and the role they play as an index of personal and social identity. That this lesson is temporal and evaporates as the cinematic experience ends, does not diminish the didactic consequences of how we see the world generally, or architecture specifically. Every instance of the cinematic experience, arguably, entails temporary subjectivities inscribed by the experience of movement and time within a narrative. And while these experiences are inherently mutable and unstable, they clearly are also effective in creating an aesthetic (and ontological) effect no less persistent than that of any other experience – with the enhanced entailments of the narratival arc with which they are enmeshed.

Movement and time

Surprisingly, there has been little developed engagement with the theories of cinema within architecture, other than to construct the lists mentioned before or to suggest generally that cinema 'constructs' spaces that might be considered architectural or employ architecture for effect. Looking at one theoretical version, among many, the two books on cinema by Gilles Deleuze *Cinema 1: The Movement Image* (1989) and *Cinema 2: The Time Image* (1989) provide a unique opportunity to understand the possibilities of an architecture/cinema nexus. In particular, Deleuze's first book, *Cinema 1*, provides a familiar discussion of the role of visual representation in avant-garde art practice in the nineteenth century, culminating in the organic development of cinema as a unique, and distinct, form of expression in the twentieth century. Deleuze identifies three aspects of cinema craft that define its mode of appearance: the frame, the shot and montage.

There are considerable complexities within these categories; in fact, Deleuze, and subsequent commentators, consider this to be more a taxonomy of effects rather than a unified theory, but even a short summary will show the potential for thinking about architecture. The frame is the space of the image that is directed at objects (including architecture) capturing their existence in time and through motion (real or implied). It also acknowledges the omission of content external to the frame that is implied by the particular selection. In viewing a film-still, the argument goes, you see the implied relationship between actors and their environment, much as conventional image analysis in painting is constructed. In cinema, the effect of movement and time allows the director to imply consequences and developmental relationships between the subject matter in order to advance the narrative – similar to theatre.

Reviewing the aspects of the 'shot' Deleuze points to the fixity, or motion, of the camera as a seeing 'eye' which implies a form of vicarious subjectivity between the viewer and the scene. Changes in camera behaviour allow the viewer to inhabit different subjectivities sequentially within the narrative. Finally, montage, or editing, is the accretional process of juxtaposing movement and time events in relation to each other, implying a third state created through the process of that juxtaposition: You see the hand, then you see the gun, and through interpolation you understand the relationship between the two. So far there is nothing novel in this presentation, but in Deleuze's exploration of the unique complexities of subjectivity, and the fusion between vision and auditory experience, he recognizes that cinema demonstrates a unique opportunity to think about the nature of experience. Ultimately the suggestion is that it has evolved as a philosophical instrument specifically to address how we encounter the world and narrate our relationship with it.

How is this architectural?
Architectural theory, when it does address cinema, usually concentrates on the act of vision, that the cinematic eye is employed to present certain spaces and spatial relations between characters/things/environments. The temptation is to consider the architect and the film director to be equally engaged with the production of a reality that is theirs to control. Usually, this aspiration comes from the side of architecture, hoping that their work could be lifted from the banality of everyday reality and be as lusciously and phenomenologically viewed as the lens allows; and for the people who occupy the spaces, the hope is that their lives will be imbued with a drama and notoriety as a result of the architecture that surrounds them.

As the epigram from Juan Antonio Ramirez at the head of this chapter suggests, there is some argument for suggesting that cinema has already addressed the issues of modern complexity and inter-subjectivity that architecture has been struggling to articulate. The economy with which the scenographic designs of cinema, both artificial and real, are utilized to precisely communicate and support a narrative seem to fulfil the promise of what a meaningful architecture might be. There is no false contest between contemporary architectural practice and its social and technological *Zeitgeist* (whatever that may be) because a cinematic process will construct whatever 'world' is necessary and employ whatever forms of causality can be understood, in service of its narrative goals.

Of course, architecture has significant other obligations to fulfil other than a narrative of functional effectiveness that exists in the tightly delimited context of a cinematic work. It has to do many other things simultaneously and has to connect to a vast array of instrumentalities that expect significant structures to give form to. So, the questions are: Is there an architecture that can be made from an analysis of film? Do the structuralist aspects of film theory, including character development, framing devices and narrative analysis, match onto design methodologies within architecture?

Clearly, the question of developed *subjectivities* in cinema, and their encounters with the world, matches architecture's interest in client and stakeholder behaviour. Cinema, to whatever degree it attempts to match reality, provides evidence of a depth of experience that is relevant to an architecture that is engaged with its occupants. Phenomenologically, the attention to the complex *fullness* of the world that cinema provides, including the temporality of moving through space and encountering material richness also matches architecture's specific argument that it is the discipline, *par excellence*, that provides this experiential fullness.

The strongest relationship, however, is the concentration on a specific *narrative* that cinema offers to theories of architectural engagement. Using the techniques of cinema to present specific subjectivities creates a method for explaining how architecture can manage its meaningfulness to affected parties. This is not limited simply to the *post hoc* (outcome) phenomenological experience but should include the process of design as a *propter hoc* (causation) series of events. Intuitively, this already occurs when the issue of design methodology is raised, but often it is left as a series of 'self-evident' developments without a meaningful context. A full narration of the development and effectiveness of architecture should/could start from its embeddness in narrative conventions of story-telling. The fascination with film depictions of architecture is a direct result of the effectiveness with which it enhances the material and spatial qualities of the architectural work and explains its relevance to the complex arc of subjectivities within the narrative. We see how the select aspects of an architectural design are a visual synecdoche for the architectural work overall, and how its specificity coheres with the complex (usually) human scene it supports.

So why the lists of 'architectural' films? Because they are evidence of architectural intentionality, to make architecture is to create an effect. Cinema is a critical vehicle through which the world works out its relationship to many things, love, hope, ethics, justice and also the role of the environment in contributing to the situational complexity of these narratological exercises.

Proposition: Outside the frame
Choose a film and develop the architectural consequences of, at least, one *mise-en-scène*. Acknowledging the deep material and craft reality of architecture, construct the consequences of the scenographic and narratival role it plays.

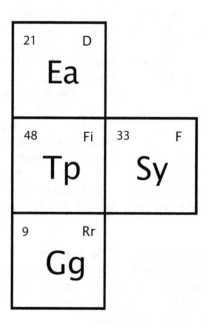

Rebus 48

Fiction

Proposition 48: The Puzzle

Arguably one of the most fascinating narrative conventions within cinema is the puzzle film, or more formally the non-linear narrative. Examples of this type of film are those in which the process of uncovering the narrative is structurally tied to the causal chain of volitional action within the story arc(s). Puzzle films, such as Guiseppe Tornatore's *Una pura formalità* (1994), Bryan Singer's *The Usual Suspects* (1995), M. Night Shyamalan's *The Sixth Sense* (1999), Christopher Nolan's *Memento* (2000) and *Inception* (2010), or Martin Scorsese's *Shutter Island* (2010) juggle the situational coherence of character's behaviour with the sequential uncovering of clues relevant to the character's motivations and the context within which they are acting. As we saw in the discussion of the doppelgänger in Proposition 46, the invocation of dream states, particularly because they invoke unstable forms of causation, creates the structural circumstances for unpacking the mysterious procession of events.

Generally, these films rely on a moment in which the complex intersection of behaviours and events transforms from a series of seemingly incoherent and disconnected episodes into a logical sequence that explains some, or all, of the previously unfathomable states of affairs. The non-linear genre requires the audience to carry a series of developing plot-lines or visual clues that create an evidential proof that illuminates more significant aspects than had previously been realized. As a version of Aristotelian catharsis, the result is a complex film in which a fundamental aspect of its attraction is the contest between appearance and reality in character behaviour and environmental effects.

Puzzle films broadly fall under the category of *fabula/syuzhet* cinema, terms from Russian formalist film theory that respectively refer to story (*fabula*) and plot (*syuzhet*). A plot requires a story, but the formation of the plot, the sequential manner in which information is conveyed to the audience is determined by the type of narrative conventions the author or director believes best engages the narrative storylines and the audience's expectations. Clearly, as a contrast, a simple linear storyline will follow a sequential process in which everything occurs consecutively without interruptions of time or location. In these examples, temporal shifts such as flashbacks or location shifts are generally not used, usually in order to maintain focus on the sequential experiences of the principal characters. In puzzle films, in contrast, aspects of the characters and their motivations, as well as developed knowledge of an environment are held back until the final stages of the film. As a consequence, audience belief regarding the characters and their environments is fundamentally challenged at the end of the last act. Detective stories – though not strictly puzzle films, we will see are entirely based on this genre.

Our principal concern at this stage is to consider the idea that the puzzle film has structural characteristics that can be transferred from a textual account to a diagrammatic representation. Since puzzle films, indeed all films, demonstrate idiosyncratically granular differences the opportunity to compare diagrammatic analyses of these narratives should reveal consistencies between them. Particularly since puzzle films rely on a series of causal revelations.

There are a number of digital applications that have evolved to both support the creation of narratives (Final Draft, Studio Binder), as well as analyze functional aspects of previous forms of cinema (Story Curves) all of which are governed by the visualization of data sets. In the case of Final Draft, in addition to being the text-based environment within which the script is written, the application also assists in creating and organizing the peripheral assets of the script in order to facilitate logistical issues regarding scenes, locations, actors, props, etc. Studio Binder is more visually based and incorporates the organizational requirements that are part of the business of film-making. Story Curves, conversely, is an analytic tool that allows for the visualization of the temporal complexities of a narrative and the interaction and location of characters to be seen in a single, scalable graph – much like an orchestral score. Significantly, none of the programmes presumes that there are standardized solutions that would diminish the need for creative input in the creation of narratives; however, it is clear that with increasingly sophisticated data sets and the development of more finely grained models of story-telling this might be on the horizon. Story Curves, in particular, by revealing consistent visual tropes in the creation of complex narratives advance the ability to unpack the dizzying twists of puzzle cinema.

How is this architectural?
While we can see that the complex cinematic forms of non-linear narratives clearly establish the relationship between location and behaviour to advance their narratives and that the emergence of complex software applications has facilitated this type of story-telling, it is not entirely clear how this might affect either the analysis or the creation of architecture. There are some hints, in particular the characteristics of hypostatized subjectivity that cinema demonstrates, and architecture aspires to,

as outlined in the previous chapter, but what of the idea of narratival complexity itself?

When we think of the use of architecture, or more specifically, of a certain urbanity such as we see in any establishing shot of a city that kinematically zooms in on the location of principal protagonists, we understand the contextual role of the city in establishing boundary conditions for the characters and events. As a visual motif, this is as ubiquitous as any narrative convention. For this reason, when more complex forms of urban story-telling, whether fictional or documentary, emerge that speaks entirely to the question of urbanity and its representation other issues emerge. Works such as Thom Anderson's *Los Angeles Plays Itself* (2003) or Patrick Keiller's *London* (1994) and *Robinson in Space* (1997) interrogate the complex relationship between diegetic reality and non-diegetic narratival and ficto-historical dialogue that transforms the respective cities, Los Angeles and London, into puzzles themselves.

When it comes to specific architectural works the narratival couplet of *fabula/syuzhet*, story vs. plot, tells us something about the potential for exploring puzzles as a model for experiencing architecture, since the question of how one best comes to understand and experience an architectural work is far from clear. When Pierre Chenal films an unnamed woman moving through the Villa Savoye (1929) in *L'architecture d'aujourd hui* (1930) or Jean-Luc Godard follows Brigitte Bardot through the Casa Malaparte (1937) in *Mepris* (1963) the presentation of the architecture is more than incidental to the narrative. Moreover, it dramatizes a movement-type for enacting the phenomenal experience of the work, telling a story about the way that architecture becomes the ground through which the puzzle of the narrative unfolds. Architecture, in this instance, is structurally tied to the expression of the plot as an instrument of its effectiveness. While neither of these films is specifically within the puzzle genre, we can imagine other cinematic treatments, Dario Argento's *Suspiria* (1977) for example, in which the unfolding of the narrative-puzzle is isomorphically tied to the spatial and formal qualities of its architectural context.

When thinking of how we communicate architecture why does it always have to be thought of in terms of a constant diegetic reality in which all of the states of affairs visualized must have specific and causal importance for the architecture? What of the appearance of non-diegetic effects, narration (memory), event (sound), movement (spatial indeterminacy)? Isn't a more interesting architecture one that adopts these characteristics of communication and meaningfulness activated by a parallel discipline – rather than painting or photography?

Film theory rarely foregrounds the relationship between *mise-en-scène*, the construction of the environment within which the narrative of a film is constructed, played out, shot, edited and viewed, and the act of designing. In the main the core relationship is that forged between the director (and perhaps the writer) and the production designer who gives shape to the image of placedness that embeds the film in 'a' world it is the task of the narrative to explain and navigate. Reviewing discussions of film theory, the core interpretive relationship is between the viewer and the characters, their travails within a world, rather than the construction of a world that has an implied life outside of the film. Surely this is an opportunity for architecture?

Proposition: The puzzle of structure
How can architects take the tools of film and narrative design and turn them towards the subject matter of architecture? What is the time and movement image that architecture explores that is unique to the discipline? And ultimately, what are the stories that need to be told, or solved, through architecture?

13: Crime

One of the more infamous pronouncements on the status of architecture within contemporary society was Bernard Tschumi's suggestion, compiled in *Architecture and Disjunction* (1994), that architecture required a criminal act to be really appreciated. As a statement, it introduced his general theory regarding the role of urban spaces as the scenes of contemporary life in their most politically focused forms. Criminality, as a transgressive act, was ultimately also a political act, however nihilistic, that affirmed a relationship to the overall body politic. Thinking about criminality in relation to architectural theory is not necessarily a natural, or intuitive, attitude for most architectural theories. Perhaps it exists as a judgement, after the fact, of the virtues or otherwise of a scheme that has fallen foul of societal attitudes such as Pruitt-Igoe, but it is rarely considered as an actual progenitor of architectural thinking and designing.

But of course, the core tenet of an architectural avant-garde is usually its stance towards a status quo that it considers insufficiently attuned to the opportunities currently available in society. Transgression of any number of core values within design orthodoxy ensures the members of the avant-garde group the notoriety of flirting with the potential destruction of established orders. There is nothing new here, but what is generally missing from this discourse is a more developed analysis of architecture, transgression and crime. Looking at various instances of theoretical and methodological criminality, it will be argued, can tell us more about where the boundary conditions for criminality actually sit. As we will see this can extend from transgressions of taste all the way to modes of criminality that seriously address the formative roles that architecture plays in fostering and enhancing crime.

The first chapter looks at the easiest and perhaps most acceptable form of transgression in architectural design, the promulgation of forgeries. It is usually possible to conceal forgery in architecture through either an appeal to historical quotation or as an expression of a dominant typological *Zeitgeist*, but what of acts of copying that deliberately redefine the creative act of design? What of the difference between autographic and allographic forms of creativity? Is it possible to conceive of architecture as a 'performance' of certain types of quotations? Is there any harm in this?

Extending the question of criminality, we can look further at the role of detection. Using the analogy of the narrative analysis opened up in the previous chapters, interrogating architecture for its transgressions and its crimes can follow the path of crime and detection. Most importantly, the question of consciousness of guilt can be put to those architects who seek to transgress accepted boundaries. Is the transgression a crime that they are aware of, do they admit guilt?

Ultimately, there are structural differences between the vicarious criminal offences of individual architects and the institutional operations and culpability of organizations. If we shift the level of responsibility to that of collective governing agencies then the architect can (or should) see the complexity of how the effects of architecture contribute, or resist, criminal operations. Understanding what Eyal Weizman calls the 'political plasticity' of architecture allows us to see where responsibility lies. But what guilt does architecture carry in these situations? How is architecture to be punished for its role in the chain of negative outcomes it has a role in shaping. The fourth chapter, on Punishment, looks at the evolution of architecture as a disciplinary practice to an emancipatory one.

Finally, one of the greatest taboos, cannibalism, is considered as a condition of architecture. If a design is not directed solely at the concerns of the Anthropocene, how does architecture consume us, and conversely how does it absorb us? What is that condition of annihilation that architecture both flirts with and desperately attempts to avoid?

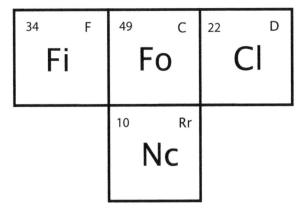

Rebus 49

Crime

Proposition 49: Forgeries

One of the less discussed aspects of modernity, and one of the consequences of restricting the formal idiosyncrasies of architectural languages, is the self-similarity of many projects. As we saw when looking at Soap in a previous chapter, the issue of originality vs. forgery is appreciably different within architecture than, most obviously, in the art world. Since forgery, as a legal concept, is tied to the volitional copying of work and misrepresenting its provenance, the issue rests on forms of attribution and intrinsic vs. extrinsic value. Within the financial economy of the world of fine art, the tension between these two conditions has a long and complex history but is essentially premised on the idea that the value of an art object is represented by its exchange value in the marketplace.

How is a forgery different from a copy? Is it just the incentive to deceive, and profit? Contemporary art accreditation processes defer to forensic detection of provenance and material evidence before they make a case based on aesthetic merit. The purpose of this form of analysis, of course, is that it is scientific and can demonstrate inviolable evidence regarding the age and forms of material that have been used, and in particular the historical knowledge of what materials were available at which particular times.

However, studying a forgery to pinpoint the characteristics that differentiate it from an original also only serves to focus upon a difficult proof: that those elements particular to the original are demonstrably superior to the copy – a difficult task. While it is possible to prove that the original work was completed with the materials at hand in the day, does that mean that subsequent copies are necessarily inferior if using modern materials?

And while there is considerable manipulation of an artwork's relative status within these high-value environments, the core discontinuity is between the material value of its components (oil, canvas, marble, bronze, etc.) and the exchange value of the work itself. Arthur Danto's famous institutional definition of 'art', that it is whatever the 'Artworld' chooses to define as art (everything from more conventional craft-based definitions to performance, ephemera, transient and conceptual works) further complicates the question of value vs. originality. The Artworld acts as an ecology that moves collectively to promote those artefacts (if they can be called that) which enjoy status within a system of value and exchange that is communally agreed upon, yet is notoriously mutable and dependent on systems of patronage. In such a nuanced and financially valuable system of course the question of forgery goes to the heart of financial value, but not necessarily to that of aesthetic experience.

Interestingly, Casement (2020) identifies the role that signatures and signs of authoring carry in determining the legal status of forgeries as it is easier, in one sense, to prosecute a fraudulent practice when it involves the idiosyncratic employment of a signature rather than a work overall. If you were to 'produce' a Picasso-like painting that was indistinguishable from his general oeuvre in terms of painterly skill but lacked the signature, would it be valued the same as one that is unquestionably his? The attribution expert will argue that this form of emulation is impossible as the finite body of work produced by 'Picasso' is not an 'open set' and does not allow for extra evidence of his output.

A copy may well be similar in all material instances to its original model, particularly if the issue of individual authorship is absent or downplayed, and of course, any item that is manufactured as a multiple will challenge the idea of authenticity and intellectual property. The market for reproductions of furniture items and other items in which design authorship is valued again creates an intersecting Venn state between original items of designated good 'taste' and those that are reproduced to satisfy a market that exceeds the available number of items.

Digital issues
Philosophically, a forgery can (theoretically) be entirely consistent with its original source, or as near as discernable outside of the scientific proof described above. Digital art, for example, is premised on an ecology of production, storage and representation that is unable to structurally restrict copying, if we consider copying to be a form of forgery. It is for this reason that recent adventures in creating 'artworks' as non-fungible tokens (NFT) have attempted to explore the price sensitivity of purchasers towards these 'artworks' that arguably have no intrinsic value other than their fame or imputed desirability. Precisely because they are not legitimized by the 'Artworld' of dealers, galleries and academic institutions, they have a temporary desirability for a cohort of purchasers who have a parallel interest in the disruptive effects of digital technology. Purchasing a 'meme' for example, by definition a semantic gesture of limited value, almost guarantees that the purchase price will ultimately be superseded by a lesser valuation once the notoriety of the meme expires. The entire process, fascinating as it is as an economic event, is a form of hyper-game-theory economics in which the ability to ride the up-swing of value is of as much social value as the

financial cost of the items in question. That this phenomenon came from the same societal pool as those interested in cryptocurrency is no coincidence, though there is no *necessary* entailment between either NFTs and cryptocurrency since it is entirely possible to purchase NFTs with conventional currency.

Because the emergence of the NFT market is clearly concerned with issues of authenticity and originality (since they are non-fungible), their relationship to blockchain technology is fundamental. Potentially this is the point at which the very issue of forgery becomes moot once all items of value have been designated an irreplaceable identity within the blockchain universe. However, this is a state that is yet to come.

Back in the material world, ultimately, for a work to be considered a forgery there must be a clear volitional intention to deceive and for the viewer to deliberately be mistaken in their estimation of a work's qualities. The considerable industry that has developed around issues of intellectual property is a testament to the tension with which issues of originality, value and reward are managed in creative and acquisitional disciplines.

Value is not taste

Importantly, and incidentally, the status of art is not consistent with questions of taste, which is managed in an entirely different set of social systems, more wide-ranging than the 'Artworld' though they share a Venn space inasmuch as a demonstration of familiarity with the aesthetic challenges of the artworld is often, socially, thought to demonstrate a level of socially esteemed (or ridiculed) degree of taste. Terry Eagleton's *The Ideology of the Aesthetic* (1988) provocatively locates 'taste' within the development of a middle class that seeks to differentiate itself from labouring classes and esteem activities that are, intrinsically, separate from the productive cycles of capital. His argument is convincing and complex, particularly since the relationship between the management of authenticity within expressive mediums has continued to evolve in parallel with changes in marketplace capitalism. Ultimately, Eagleton arrives at the simple truth that aesthetic experience is not the same as taste, though it has been the complex and relentless business of bourgeois capitalism to conflate the two and to exercise social power through the management of access to 'culture'. The genius of forgery, in this respect, is to opportunistically vitiate the institutional (Artworld) control over access to authentically 'tasteful' experiences. The crime of art forgery is largely exercised against institutions and individuals with sufficient disposable income to bear the consequences of their place within this system. Ironically the photocopier and the personal computer have done more to liberate the 'royal kingdom' of aesthetic experience from the owners of the intellectual property of authentic aesthetic expression than any storming of cultural barricades.

While this is true, one can argue, at a general level of institutional critique, the individual encounter with forgeries, in contrast, is uniquely challenging. Is a forgery inferior for being a forgery, or is the knowledge of the existence of a forgery (though currently indistinguishable) the moment in which you recognize the need for more training in the experience of understanding the work? The so-called undetectable forgery is actually a challenge to the viewer's skills more than a deception played upon them. We know that this is, in fact, a commonplace occurrence when we think of the ubiquitous visibility of works of art via digital reproduction. We wonder, as Walter Benjamin and Jean Baudrillard did, whether the process of mechanical reproduction robbed us of some intrinsic, alchemical experience of revelation; or more troublingly, whether we would have recognized it when we saw it.

How is this architectural?
When we see an example of 'historical revival' architecture is it in any way diminished, or does it require us to think of forgeries? Once we recognize that Greek temples do not sprout in Nashville, Tennessee or Gothic cathedrals in Melbourne or Mumbai are we compelled to discover the source of this anomaly? Is it the subtlety of forgery to conceal this requirement, or rather to encourage deeper scrutiny? To answer this, I think there is value in considering the approach to 'denotation', 'exemplification' and 'suggestion' in the analysis of architecture by the American philosopher Nelson Goodman, but also significant commentators such as Maurice Lagueux (1998) and Remei Capdevila Werning (2014).

Without going into the depth necessary to adequately describe all of Goodman's subtlety of thinking on issues of how architecture and meaning coincide, we can make a few preparatory statements before considering the idea of how authenticity, or 'forgery', might be considered in architecture. Goodman identifies that art generally has a role in representing states of affairs and that this process involves issues of how it denotes and/or exemplifies certain characteristics, bearing in mind that denoting and exemplifying are linked, but distinct, concepts. So, for example, the 'Greek' temple in Nashville denotes a number of properties but may not be an exemplar of them.

In architecture, the question of autographic and allographic production is important. Autographic works are singular items that, by definition, if copied are, in our terms, potentially 'forged'. Allographic works, in contrast, have a system of representation such as musical scores or architectural drawings that can conceivably have multiple iterations. It is then possible to imagine scenarios in which a building might be considered unique (autographic) rather than typological (allographic). At an even more finely grained level, there are components of an autographic building, any standardized item or solution, that are clearly allographic – doors, lighting, panel systems, etc.

Intrinsically, the practice of architecture already understands this and is sufficiently skilled to be able to make discriminatory judgements as to when standardized componentry or standardized design configurations are sufficient to allow the project to continue without compromising those autographic elements that denote an idiosyncratic design approach. Of course, as part of the broad approach to architecture, there is considerable variability in this approach, and also a tacit recognition of how noteworthy projects manage to balance this challenge. Arguably, in cases of exceptional works that are recognized as being as entirely about the vision of the architect, they approach the level of a 'sample' in Goodman's terms, something in which *all* non-trivial aspects of its qualities denote, for example, Tadao Ando. A Tadao Ando building is an exemplar of its Tadao Ando-like qualities.

But what of copying/quoting, and of forgery? Maurice Lagueux (1998) develops Goodman's distinction by referring to examples in which the deliberate employment of a denotative element that is 'false', his example is the use of *trompe-l'oeil* spatial effects, 'suggests' a quality without it actually being present. They manifest an 'intention' but are unable to denote and exemplify a quality since it is not present. Paradoxically, they most effectively denote the philosophical 'problem' of employing quotations, or 'suggestions', as a practice in architectural design *in itself*. They effectively denote the reality of formal continuity by creating instances of that quotation/suggestion behaviour. This is the form of recursive thinking that, ultimately, be-devilled the pastiche forms of quotation used in the more banal versions of postmodernism, as we saw in the chapter on Soap. However, it doesn't then disqualify the process of quotation. On the contrary, it articulates the reality that many architectural works deliberately 'quote' aspects of other works as a fundamental expression of the continuity of architectural culture.

This also makes the idea of forgery in architectural design increasingly interesting. If forgery is the volitional deception of the viewer then perhaps the responsibility for uncovering that deception falls to the viewer because of their lack of critical facilities. It also, as outlined above, acknowledges the reality of more complex fungible assets within digital architectural culture and the concomitant freedom to employ them in a variety of circumstances that skirt with the issues of taste and class identified by Eagleton.

Proposition: The half-tone Nelson
This project should concentrate on the profound and complex history of a secret and idiosyncratic library of architectural forgeries. The stair of the Villa Mairea, the doors of Santa Maria Church de Canaveses, the oculi of the Brion Vega Tomb, whatever can be found can be remade and, ideally, hidden.

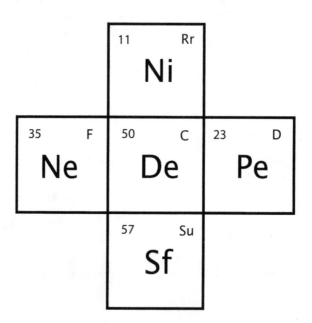

Rebus 50

Crime

Proposition 50: Detectives

Is architecture a criminal act? Bernard Tschumi (1994) made the case that in order to practice architecture it may be necessary to commit a murder. It is an inflammatory and disturbing suggestion, but of course is moderated by the realization that the metaphor describes a behavioural limit rather than an actual command. Tschumi, in his *Advertisements for Architecture* (1994), is concerned with an approach to architectural theory that first takes seriously the idea that architecture forms a specific type of knowledge and that, second, this knowledge is defined by its mutability. In one sense this seems to be an unsatisfactory form of definition since the very thing that a theory of architecture might pursue is the identification of core qualities that remain constant irrespective of context. For Tschumi, as it was for the generation of architectural theorists affected by the re-valuation of values associated with the social changes of 1968, direct *realpolitik* action required direct means. If those means involved protest and, potentially, violence then the ends justified the means. While Tschumi is careful to define the limits at which the idea of violence can be incorporated into the practice of architectural design and critical thinking, the flirtation with transgressive conditions is a constant element of his approach to theory.

Violence in architecture, it turns out, is the recognition that certain spatial practices involve the acting out of subversive actions, using buildings in idiosyncratic and perverse ways for outcomes never intended by the original designers. Similarly, the employment of design decisions that subvert modernist design methodologies of self-similarity literally crashes into orthodox forms and causes a form of aesthetic and ideological dissonance. To create forms that deliberately question conventional ideas of firmness, commodity and delight create a space for an intellectual avant-garde that connects ideas of intuitive expressionism with a critique of institutional aesthetic (but not political) values. Within this careful and deliberate carnage of intentions in the 1990s, deconstruction flowered. Some 40 years on from the rise of practices such as Coop Himmelb(l)au, Zaha Hadid, early Gehry, Gunther Domenig and Tschumi himself, the palimpsest of deconstruction reminds us that, prior to the evolution of environmental and digital design ecologies, the 'vicissitudes of theory' (Frampton 1982, 2007) was the principal preoccupation of the avant-garde.

So how do we judge these self-consciously aggressive acts? In comparison to the discussion of forgeries in architecture, and the role that architects play as forgers, copyists and volitional criminals in design, the alter ego of this behaviour could be the detective. There is a serious role to be played under the general banner of 'detection' and the concept of justice, and we will look at this in the next chapter, but for now, it is possible to speculate on the attitude of detection that architects play in the process of considering and executing a design process. But for the analogy to be meaningful, the crossover of responsibilities from criminal detection to creative practice should be more narrowly defined.

Consciousness of guilt
Consciousness of crime involves the evidence of behaviour that is directed at mitigating potential guilt towards a criminal, or unacceptable, act. Taking the analysis of Wittgenstein regarding pain behaviour and self-knowledge, the question is whether we 'learn' that we had intentionality as opposed to acting in an intentional manner, and whether others can infer *that* intentionality from observing our behaviour. Criminality is a process of detection and inference of the actions of others. So what is a crime in architecture? Or what is a moment of transgression if it is not something that is learnt, or self-observed, but is acted out and then *a fortiori*, implies an intentionality towards transgression in design.

Perhaps the role of the detective, like that of Wittgenstein's discussion of pain, is expressed in the architect who first attempts to discover what Tschumi's *crime* of architecture might be? If we distinguish between intention and behaviour, what an architect might think in contrast to what was actually done, then architecture is divided between intention and act.

Further, and arguably, intention is the state of mind in which the state of thinking about architecture escapes culpability, as intentions are always hidden behind the complex evidence of the material reality of architecture. No architect ever intentionally, it is said, creates a project whose purpose is to harm users, but do they ever wish to suggest certain forms of discomfort? Is this Tschumi's criminal act?

Intention and evidence
Evidence of intention, including a consciousness of guilt, is a fundamental aspect of criminality and judgement within the legal profession. So can we choose to create an architecture that is innocent of its effects since there is no proven evidence of intention? While it is going to be interesting to push this idea further, we have arrived at a point where the court of public opinion judges architecture, as opposed to discussions within the professional culture of architectural theory. The lay person asks of architecture,

how could this be done, why would they create such disharmony, or sterility, or chaos? But they only see the act and not the intention. Put simply, public opinion, like popular expectations of how justice systems work, considers thoughts and beliefs to be outside of the purview of prosecution: 'You can't prove what I was thinking' protects the architect from the judgment of history because historically, the design decisions of one era cannot be judged by the standards of future scrutiny.

Perhaps too the crime is to continue to consider that there *is* a practice that needs to be theorized, for the context for adjudicating a crime requires the production of a law, a criminal, a victim and a process of adjudication and punishment. If we are thinking about committing crimes within architecture are we considering actual negligence or the more abstract culture of transgressive thinking? For architecture, this is the point at which the analogy becomes clearer, and make it distinct from the rule of tort and the obligation of the architect to make design decisions that do not, allegedly, harm future users. In a scenario in which the 'laws' of architectural theory are sufficiently loosened, the possibility of corrective investigation becomes moot – or is only ever the province of a historical detective searching for evidence of lost relevance – asking the question: When did history end?

How is this architectural?
The detective story requires us to see that 'certain disagreeable realities of the world exist' and that the consequences of their existence are to place us in mortal, or virtual, danger. If there is no crime in architecture, then there is no need for detection, evidence, motive, proof, judgment and punishment. But if there *is* a 'crime' in architectural thinking what does that mean for how we undertake architectural practice that purports to be consciously guilty of intentionality?

'So contrary to our initial presupposition, what makes sense is that I can know what someone else intends, but not what I myself intend' (Větrovský 2018: 602). He makes this point regarding the difference between knowing what others have done (perceiving intentionality) vs. knowing what oneself has done. His point, in the context of legal jurisprudence, is to point out that war criminals do not 'discover' their intentions once they are pointed out to them. It does not make sense to have an intention but to not know what it is or be conscious of it. The corollary, in architecture, is that our criminality is intrinsic rather than consciously chosen, or recognized.

So are architects criminals or detectives? In this sense, the narrative of this entire book is an architectural version of Powell's *The Anarchist Cookbook* (1971), though probably quite amateurish and ineffective in comparison to the actual manual for extreme civil disobedience. But the question remains of how and why we might choose to criminalize aspects of architectural thinking, or how we might choose to detect and prosecute aspects of the same material. If the dominant paradigm in architecture is 'do no harm', then Tschumi's challenge is to find out where 'harm' is most effectively necessary in architectural design and thinking.

Possible project: True detective
The narrative of Nic Pizzolatto, the writer and creator of the television series *True Detective* (2014–19), references the fiction of Thomas Ligotti. Ligotti's fiction is considered to be relentlessly bleak in its assessment of the human condition, and the employment of Ligotti's world-view is considered to be consistent with the reality confronting the 'detective', as an archetype. In the face of the brutality of human behaviour, concepts of justice and redemption are considered to be a folly. There are two projects in this state of affairs: the detection of crime in architecture, and the detection of crime in architectural theory, both of which work out of the Tschumi Detective Agency.

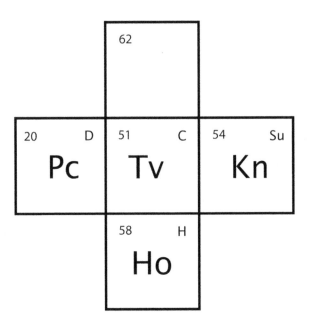

Rebus 51

Crime

Proposition 51: TV Eye

Much discussion of the role architecture plays in the governance of behaviour centres on the presumption that it is possible to coercively manage social relations through material boundaries. In fact, architecture's relevance within a contemporary discourse on its effectiveness within the construction industry generally commences from the understanding that architecture will, in the first instance, satisfy the complex requirements of the brief and the stakeholder's wishes at the most pragmatic level, then will additionally function as a type of environmental petri dish for positive social behaviour. Architecture, when thoughtfully constructed, is both a pragmatic service to create limits to behaviour and a context where, hopefully, beneficial behaviour is fostered. There is considerable statistical evidence that connects the quality of the urban environment, and in particular the decision chains of architectural and urban design, to outcomes that are intended to promote particular social behaviours, and combat those which are considered to have negative effects. Jane Jacobs's *The Death and Life of Great American Cities* (1961) is the progenitor of those books on architecture that argued that the role of the architect was/is to positively understand the social formations of the communities it serves. It is a matter of record that Jacobs was right in her attitude towards urban planning, and the preservation of the architectural and urban fabrics of communities. Jacobs's legacy was to update the relationship between architecture and politics to include a more complex, and inclusive, definition of social identity. In the context of our discussion of 'crime', her narrative pitched forces of economic and spatial power vs. the disenfranchised.

As Eyal Weizman (2012) puts it, architecture has the capacity to be 'politically plastic' in its use, acting as both a context from which actions are analyzed as well as an instrument for the management (militarization in Weizman's terms) of behaviour. Of course, the social engineering aspect is well-recognized so long as we recognize it is unnecessary to discuss the politics of operating a child-care centre in the same breath as the Berlin Wall or the US/Mexico border. But the idea of political plasticity makes sense. In Weizman's analysis and in his subsequent work in describing the architectural agency within the contested landscape of Israel, Palestine and the Occupied Territories, 'political plasticity' perfectly describes the lethal capacity of architecture to be evidence of territorial transgression and the site for forensic analysis. By extension, if we speculate on the 'plastic' aspect of 'political plasticity', the idea that architecture acts as both a mould and as a casting of current political norms of social behaviour is interesting. It reminds us of the 'empirico-transcendental doublet' that Foucault (1994) speaks of when discussing the effects of the modern episteme on the human subject. For Foucault, and by extension for Weizman, the modern self is both the result and the agent of political discourse. It is the plasticity of the mould and the casting that allows architecture to represent shifting forms of political meaning and to enact mutable and multiple types of social behaviours. For Weizman, and his Forensic Architecture project, the capacity for architecture to be read as the outcome of forms of conflict, either as built structure or as damaged or ruined structures, allows architects to be especially attuned to determining the strategic forces at play.

Ultimately this analysis rests on issues of visibility and 'seeing': 'seeing behaviour' that is subject to a disciplinary gaze, being 'seen' by a structure of observation and 'seeing' the results of both controlled vision and transgressive resistance. Weizman's practice is usually directed at specific instances of extreme and catastrophic violence such as the ongoing Israel/Palestine conflict, the 2020 explosion in the harbour of Beirut as well as numerous contested sites and incidents around the world. Beyond this mode of investigation, at quieter but more comprehensively dispersed levels, there is also the recognition and understanding of how ubiquitous forms of surveillance participate in a mutual relationship of control and evasion. This organized surveillance ecosystem, particularly as it is implemented in London, creates the information for a topology of safety and criminality. To be is to be seen.

TV eye
Current forensic-based televised crime focuses consistently on the presence of CCTV information and the employment of visuality (or occlusion) in the public demesne. Seeing criminality aids in the identification and prevention of criminal behaviour, yet it treats only the symptom of the social and ethical choices that lead to individual criminality. So how does architecture fit into this rubric? At the most intellectually banal level of analysis, it is simple to say that architecture can contribute to the political plasticity of crime prevention or propagation through the visual transparency of public behaviour, making spaces that permit or prevent secret behaviour to occur. Most discussion that links architectural practice to the issue of crime as an undesirable social activity usually concentrates on either crimes against property, or crimes committed opportunistically because of the proximity of vulnerable groups to individuals or groups whose *raison d'etre* are criminal activities such as illicit substance commerce, criminalized sexual activity or threats of physical violence.

Contemporary fascination with criminality turns largely on the vicarious enjoyment of making decisions that are manifestly antagonistic to society and to standards of humane behaviour. And because individual decision-making is largely hidden by our thought processes, criminality is ultimately a philosophical problem as much as it is societal. How can we judge whether criminal behaviour is consciously entertained by an individual, or is the outcome of their environment? This explains, in part, the entertainment value of criminality, and narratives in which behavioural choice is considered to be either intrinsic or environmental. The outcome of the criminalizing environment, and the tests of strength between antagonists ultimately, in a narrative, is usually resolved through a visible resolution of consequences.

This is to be distinguished from Weizman's analysis that charts the operations of state actors to reinforce behavioural compliance on large segments of a population as part of an overall strategy of division and suppression. So, two groups of power are involved, the state and its effective instrument, the police force, and the loosely assembled aggregations of criminality, gangs and gang-like individuals who see a commercial benefit in responding opportunistically to structural urban characteristics of the built environment. But the issues of criminality also rest on individual choice, no matter how constrained that choice is by circumstance and need.

Desert
In philosophy, the concept of 'desert', referring to something that is deserved, reflects the difference between deserving and being entitled, usually to a benefit of some kind. When we couple the idea of political plasticity and the twin notions of casting and moulding with 'desert', then we arrive at the idea that perhaps the morphology of urban locations creates a scenario where criminality is a predictably 'deserved' outcome. Rather than pretending that the consequences of design are arbitrary, but hopefully benign or positive, 'desert' may also be a punishment. It is easy to imagine situations in which an individual may be deserving of some prize but may not be entitled to it as a consequence of some other contextual factor. On the obverse, the suggestion that a criminal act is the responsibility of the criminal actor underpins the legal system and reinforces the notion of personal responsibility. The complexity for architecture, as a practice, is that there also seems to be a body of knowledge that asserts that certain urban forms or, speculatively, architectural languages may be a precursor to crime. This idea, the temporality principle, made famous by the story and subsequent movie *The Minority Report* by Philip K. Dick (1956) and Steven Spielberg (2002), asks whether a prediction of a predisposition to criminality asserts its inevitability.

In the movie version, the preponderance of surveillance and tracking technologies allows the 'Precrime' unit to predict future criminality and pre-emptively apply justice to the predicted criminal. While this model of justice seems, at a utilitarian level, to be efficient and preservative, the issue for architecture (as it is for the book and movie) turns on whether the targets of the prediction 'deserve' their assessment and its consequences. There is an argument that the form of urban spaces and the technologies for surveillance transforms them into sites of criminality – either through the over-reach of the state, or the enhanced visibility of individuals who become defined as (pre-crime) criminals because of their visibility. Conversely, the enhanced level of data and the specificity with which it can be applied already creates a state guilty of excessive and disproportionate punishment. This is Weizman's charge against the lethal levels of state-sponsored violence that occurs within conflict zones.

How is this architectural?
Much of this turns on what commentators think are the core activities of architectural design and what share architects have in the credit or responsibility for activities within it. If we think that a positive urban or architectural solution can exist because the populace, collectively and individually, 'deserve' the consequences of that design proposal, do we syllogistically accept that they 'deserve' the consequences of urban criminality should that turn out to be the effect of the design? When economic circumstances created the phenomenon of 'dead' malls, was that the responsibility of the architect who originally designed the mall, or of the, say, adjacent complex that caused its demise?

Instinctively, we might think that criminality or malfeasance has nothing to do with architectural design, other than for it to be the unwitting backdrop to unfortunate events. Is the issue of crime and architecture one that analyzes the effects of architecture and the manner in which it forms the context for the promulgation of crime, or is it a situation that is ubiquitous within the built environment and just has to be accepted as an unfortunate reality? The notion of 'desert', what persons deserve as a consequence of their precondition prior to an evaluation of consequences is important here. We believe we are entitled to good architecture, but is it what we deserve? And rather than thinking that this represents a stalemate condition in which the designer is doomed to the vagaries of subsequent events, perhaps what architecture is really good at is punishment.

Potential project: The revolution will not be televised
What is the city that Gil Scott-Heron envisaged? Where do lives matter for him, and the others that wish to live safely and with the hope that the city itself is not trying

to destroy them? If the reciprocal struggle between control and resistance is the principle subtext of modern urbanity, the imbalance between the creators of visual culpability and the subjects can be balanced by those spaces that are unmoulded, or whose plasticity is so ductile that it can never ossify into a final form. Design a distributed system that is formless cannot be moulded and is sufficiently un-architectural to be invisible.

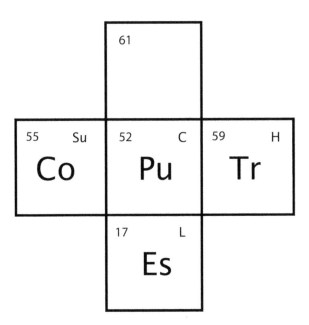

Rebus 52

Crime

Proposition 52: Punishment

In the 1980s, one of the legacies of the adoption of critical theory in architectural practice was the considerable influence of Michel Foucault's analyses of disciplinary structures in the emergence of modern society, as we discussed in the previous chapter. The Modern Episteme, according to Foucault (1973), entailed the development of various forms of surveillance and control that demonstrated relations of disciplinary power. The emergence of definitions of the modern subject in the domains of medicine, jurisprudence, botany and mental health had the coeval effect of creating institutional forms that mirrored the management of these knowledge forms, or discourses. The healthy subject, the just subject, the living subject and the mentally capable subject were subject to analysis for their functional capabilities. As a consequence of these categorial definitions, the recognition of aberrant behavioural types had the twin effect of identifying these instances for exclusion from society, and for a series of remedial operations designed to rectify their (in)capacities. For Foucault this explained the emergence of the modern clinic, for both medical and psychological reasons, the creation of prison typologies that distinguished between the different forms of criminality, and the general recognition that structures such as greenhouses could be employed to alter an environment and propagate life forms – all of which provide a parallel discourse on the 'utilitas' of modern social organizations.

For a building to 'function' in the sense we currently understand within architectural theory, it requires the presumption that architecture materially governs the life experiences of users and reiteratively normalizes certain behavioural patterns: a school creates school children, an office creates office workers, a hospital creates medical staff and patients, and controversially a prison creates prisoners/criminals, etc. These patterns simultaneously allow modern forms of economic and scientific activities to take place, while also inscribing certain identities, expectations and philosophical outlooks on the people therein.

But of course, we are (or believe we are) more than the sum of social definitions we occupy, however these Venn diagrams of environmental experiences may intersect, or how complex they may be. For architecture, there is a conflict between the pragmatic, centripetal-like recognition that much design work relies on abstract definitions of client needs and behaviours. This presumes that people behave in roughly similar ways and that generic solutions are sufficient. Contrast that with the equal and opposite aspiration to create a bespoke solution for targeted stakeholders catering to particular user groups, or certain focused ideas. In prison architecture, there are two unique and opposed client groups, the commissioning governments that are aiming to efficiently provide shelter to a structurally antagonistic inmate group while broadcasting the political message that prison is punishment, and the inmate groups who have the expectation of some form of disciplinary experience, some measure of protection and who yet are involuntary residents who would, usually, wish to stop being engaged with the architecture. So the design of prisons deliberately emphasizes generic solutions for the precise reason that there is little appetite for individual accommodation. This is the punishment, along with the reality of living in a hostile society with few individual freedoms. The so-called positive outcome is the proposition that the architecture supports a process of behavioural reform. So, as we can see, and as research has shown, the history of carceral architecture is caught in the punishment/reform dyad, attempting to serve the wishes of the commissioning parties and, usually, attempting to limit the negative effects on the prison populace.

This state of affairs could be inimical to any architectural project if it was assumed that all typological architectural formations equally shared the power to coercively control users, or uniformly applied coercive pressures – that a school worked in the same fundamental way as a prison. However, we are aware that the many subtle differences in the application of these typologies implies that the network of power relations exists principally as a meta-analysis of the project hovering some distance above day-to-day operations. The influence of Foucault and others in defining the discussion on these questions is central to any understanding, given the consistency of his approach to the question across fields.

Design vs. behaviour
If we look at outlier examples of prisons, particularly those in which the exercise of power is minimized, some interesting issues emerge. In maximum security institutions, there is a confirmed relationship between instances of violence and self-harm and excessive structural limitations of prisoner behaviour. In contrast, contemporary Scandinavian prisons are currently being modelled on an enhanced trust relationship which ignores the need to project the image of abstract and unrelenting punishment. In this system, the assumption is that prison is the denial of time, not the denial of humanity. An outlier example, differently conceived, is the ad hoc self-management of the prison community in San Pedro Prison in La Paz, Bolivia. In San Pedro, prisoners operate a system of governance that mirrors life outside the prison, including social groups, extra-judiciary justice and arbitrary punishment. Essentially it is an arrangement of convenience in which prison governance is unable to exercise

control at anything other than the macro level of basic imprisonment. Humanity, in this instance, is whatever can be eked out from a Hobbesian system of survival, and the individual capacity to mitigate discomfort within the facility.

A famous historical experiment regarding the question of real and assumed behaviour in a carceral environment is the Stanford Prison experiment. A short version of the 'experiment' can be related. Two groups of university students at the prestigious Stanford University in 1971 participated in an 'experiment' in which they assumed the roles of prisoners or guards. Left to their own devices and with questionable supervision, the experiment got out of hand and incidents of brutalization and insurrection escalated, including arbitrary solitary confinement, hunger strikes and physical beatings. As a short version of the manifold genre of prison narratives it reminds us of the accounts of Boethius, Dostoevsky, Malamud, Gramsci, Solzhenitsyn and even Albert Speer. These relay the dehumanizing effects of the architectural context, one acutely attuned to the deadening life cycle of the prisoner.

From this, we can see the negative connotations of criminality and the creation of behavioural norms that transgress the positive definitions of social identity. While there are certainly attempts to change, or to reclassify, the nature of punishment in a carceral environment, it is clear that it is beyond the capacity of architecture to effectively create, or cause, since usually a definition of criminal behaviour in an individual is the outcome of volitional behaviours that are judged to transgress social norms. It is agreed that a number of countries, the United States in particular, have significant issues in managing a process of mass incarceration that is ineffective in preventing recidivism, costly, prone to self-perpetuation by private operators and with larger societal effects because of the inequitable experience of incarceration by peoples of colour.

Usually architecture is incidental to this problem, apart from the clear investment in prisons and their infrastructure, and the most particular requirements of capital, return on investment. And yet we continue to have the suspicion that, like the children in Plato's cave, there are environmental drivers that shape particular ontologies. Developing this idea further and proposing a contrarian outcome we can ask: how do we create a phenomenal experience that supports, or creates, transgressive behaviour? Or alternatively, how do we find a way to invert, or divert, the relationship of punitive effects from architecture to individual?

The simplest solution is to radically diminish the complex interrelationship of judicial oversight, incarceration and private enterprise. In so doing, the need for an architecture of imprisonment diminishes, at least in theory. Naive as this option may sound, it has its adherents. The arguments for forms of technological monitoring of offenders in the parole and probation cycles of incarceration are based on wishful thinking regarding surveillance equipment and forms of remotely delivered punishment – ankle monitors that administer electric shocks when an algorithm detects criminal behaviour. The faith in technology papers over issues of human rights and the potential for innovative avoidance strategies, but these exist nonetheless (Bagaric et al. 2018). While this sounds a lot like the pre-crime scenario we examined in the previous chapter, the ultimate issue for architecture might be to consider two things: what to do with the empty real-estate of prison architecture, and how, more philosophically to punish architecture for its part in effectively assisting in the phenomenon of prisons and incarceration?

Perhaps the most emblematic example of this issue is the former concentration camp at Auschwitz. Questions regarding the preservation of the notorious death camp have been politically fraught since its liberation by the Red Army in 1945. Because Auschwitz has the reputation as one of the most notorious and lethal carceral environments, its new function as a *memento mori* for the deaths of its prisoners and the effects of the Nazi extermination policies of the Second World War means that its preservation is deemed necessary. Arguably, there is considerable opinion on this matter, the current 'use' of Auschwitz as a museum-like experience serves as a complex warning regarding the racial policies of the Nazi state, but what are the politics of rebuilding, refurbishing and maintaining a death camp? It is a reality that the existing buildings and infrastructure are in decay and the tension between wishing the evidence of the site to begone from the earth is tempered by the need for tangible memorials so that the lessons are not forgotten. Various design strategies have been proposed, one in particular mentioned by Robert Jan van Pelt and Deborah Dwork in the authoritative *Auschwitz, 1270 to the Present* (1997) in which the grid of remaining hut foundations in the Birkenau section is crossed by a single, uncompromising concrete path, hollowed out where the huts themselves had been. The path enters and departs via a break in the external fence line to de-emphasize any sense of ceremony. Similarly, Eric Kahn and Russel Thomsen's *Perimeter Stacks* (2015) project proposes a stockade of logs harvested from around the world that form an impenetrable barrier around the same area, preventing entry.

For both projects, the core architectural issue is that the events of the site cannot be represented in a fashion that would adequately communicate the reality of its horrors. The projects seek to punish the design by quarantining it from exploration and removing any vestige of romantic engagement with the ruins.

In this respect, if we ask the converse question: What is the punishment of architecture rather than the architecture of punishment? The answer might be in adopting a far more lethal attitude towards those instrumental building forms that have been employed to facilitate gross forms of human barbarity. We can restrict these examples to just the type of building programmes discussed here, but what of other forms of inverse punishment? Can we find a way, other than simply adopting the proposition that architecture is completely autonomous and structurally disengaged from its use-form, to empty it of all programmatic effectiveness?

Potential project: The prison-house of rationalists + the building without qualities
There are two project types here, one that looks specifically at the de-institutionalizing and forgetting of architecture, and one that removes any form of programmatic determinism. The first project might ask us to re-purpose the prison or camp of our choice? How does it cease to function and, ultimately be forgotten? The second project asks us to create an architecture without coercive qualities, that is all affect without effect.

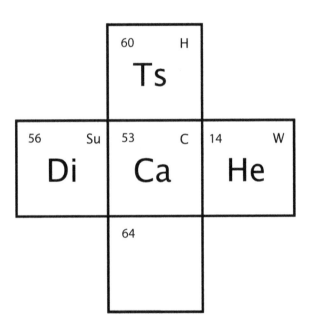

Rebus 53

Crime

Proposition 53: Cannibalism

> I shall now therefore humbly propose my own thoughts, which I hope will not be liable to the least objection.
> (Jonathan Swift, *A Modest Proposal*, 1729)

So commences the core argument of Swift's fiendish proposal to consume children. He proposes that the antidote to population growth and poverty is the sanctioning of a brutal form of infanticide. It is also, let it be said, clearly a satirical commentary on the state of poverty and social relations within Ireland under the rule of the English in the eighteenth century, and of the mathematization of social problems. The revulsion it happily provoked, when published, stems from the blithe acceptance that cannibalism is a reasonable, and rational, approach to the dilemma of modern governance.

Anthropophagy, the consumption of human flesh, has horrified society for a considerable time, and while reputedly practised in certain social groupings historically, it is now considered one of the most taboo of behaviours. Incidents of organized and opportunistic cannibalism are well documented in accounts of famine and of military brutality in the twentieth century, particularly in Ukraine and in the Pacific theatre of the Second World War. While these crimes seem distant now, the practice still haunts the imagination, particularly within fictional representations of criminal depravity. From Shakespeare's *Titus Andronicus* (1588–93) to Cormac McCarthy's novel *The Road* (2006), the literary exploration of the consequences of a cannibalism links the final breakdown of social order to the consumption of human flesh, voluntary or otherwise.

Cannibalism is another expression of the metamorphosis of the agent into another state, this time via the transgression of the most horrific of boundaries. In terms of the exploration of crime in architecture, it is arguably the final state of abjection. In the sphere of contemporary performance art abjection, in particular the abjection of the human body, is a core concern of practitioners and theorists. Though performance art as a recognized practice predates it, Julia Kristeva's *Powers of Horror: An Essay on Abjection* (1982) is considered a pivotal exploration of the transactional relationship between representation, desire and the challenge to look at the psycho-analytic drivers of aesthetic engagement.

Picking up on Kristeva's position, and contextualizing it within debates about postmodernism in the 1980s and 1990s, Hal Foster (1996) points out the tensions in practice and theory regarding the employment of deliberately transgressive subject matter and methodologies in art practice, and the fetishization of abject and excremental material as a confrontation with value. Both positions were adopted to place artists in an oppositional and critical relationship towards commercialism and the art market generally. Vito Acconci's *Seed Bed* (1972) and *Artist's Shit* (1961) could be considered representative of these positions. However, behind these practices and their intentionally pyrrhic outcomes, there are larger questions articulated by Kristeva and others regarding the desire to find other aspects of human subjectivity that can exist outside of the conventional forms of representation that, arguably, we have all absorbed as normal. The 'Real', for Kristeva and those influenced by the psychoanalysis of Jacques Lacan, is that state of the world that may be glimpsed only when we recognize the horror of our protean desires. The world we encounter, or more accurately the representations we concoct to occlude the brutality of existence, is always shadowed and vivified by the Id of the 'Real'.

In these circumstances, cannibalism could metaphorically be considered to govern the practice as a whole, since both desire, destruction and the transgressing of fundamental taboos have driven this engagement, though only metaphorically. Vito Acconci, and many other practitioners of performance art would, at times, subject their body to extremes of sensation and performance, but they generally stayed (just) within legal boundaries of behaviour.

How is this architectural?
In architecture it is almost impossible to imagine a circumstance in which the limit of behavioural norms could be transgressed in such a way. As much as the destruction of works of architecture might constitute a form of abjection of intention, famously like the 'Anarchitecture' of Gordon Matta-Clark, it is difficult to imagine a constructive practice that could produce the effects of performance art. Though imaginatively one could consider what the context might be for the staging of these demonstrations, the construction of the performance between artist and audience, usually these locations are secondary to the acts therein.

Alternatively, cannibalizing architecture might involve the consumption and reuse of components of architecture for a new building. Because to cannibalize also implies the transgression of social taboos regarding the consumption of human flesh, so it might be for architecture. But there is clearly a distinction between buildings and bodies though the temptation is to treat this as an opportunistic analogy. If anything is clear regarding the discourse surrounding cannibalism, transgression and abjection, it is that it involves a concept of (in)tolerable limits of behaviour. Adaptive reuse does not horrify anyone.

Adrian Stokes, the English architectural theorist, famously compared the experience of seeing and emotively responding to the carving and modelling of architectural facades with the sensation of a character expressing themselves on a stage. A person experiencing a building, for Stokes it was Renaissance and later buildings in Florence and Venice, was like the meeting of two animate and conscious beings. His own writing would emphasize this experience, speaking of his impressions of a building rather than any attempt at objective description. Stokes' method was a more personal version of the philosopher Susan K. Langer's evocation of the role of 'feeling' as the primary ontological encounter with the world. Langer (1953) wrote incisively about architecture and the role of 'feeling' in aesthetic experience, without the obfuscation and self-referential jargon of Heidegger. For her, feeling was a pre-linguistic encounter with the fullness of the world.

So what of cannibalism? If we align the exceptional levels of heightened feeling: fear, disgust, repulsion, attraction, guilt, hunger, desire, etc., associated with the act of transgression in cannibalism (and some performance art) we have the beginnings of a linguistic palette of action. While these extremes of emotion are far beyond what Langer envisaged, or Stokes experienced, they express an emotional limit consistent with the status of how the sensations of human experience have been theorized in recent years, including Kristeva. To consider the components of architectural experience to be an encounter with the Real, architecture is then a 'world' crafted to communicate the spectrum of emotions, including those at the limit of tolerance. The primal temple constructed from the flesh, skin and bones of sacrificed animals, the sublime terror of Piranesi's *Carceri d'invenzione* drawings as interpreted by Manfredo Tafuri, and the *Unheimlich* house of horror imagined by Anthony Vidler and presented by Tobe Hooper – all of these draw on the emotional ambivalence we feel for an architecture created to consume us. Importantly, these are representations of states of affairs that we feel prior to the question of whether they are referentially clear, i.e. we feel it before we recognize it.

Of course, the principal human experience described here is vision and the associated visceral responses that come from an encounter with visually disturbing material. Ascribing meaning to these encounters is initially problematic, particularly when describing inexact sensations such as feelings. The fundamental aesthetic problem defined by Richard Wollheim in *Arts and its Object* (1971) of 'seeing in and seeing as' drew attention to the distinction between what we literally visually encounter, 'seeing in', vs. what we recognize things to be, 'seeing as' (1971: n.pag.). Resemblance and representation are not the same things.

We will look more fully at this in one of the following chapters, Hope, but for now, given the discussion on feeling and the limits of visual tolerance, it is worthwhile considering how architecture can resemble, and represent, in this context. The physical 'realness' of performance art means that there is no representational gap, it *is* what happens. The behaviour of the artists is immediate and does not represent some other action, such as is the case with theatre. For architecture conceived at the extremes of visceral experience, it too must look to invoke the same level of aesthetic intensity and, in the case we are employing cannibalism, not only to horrify, to repulse, but also to be desirous.

Potential project: Chthonic clinic
What of a project that was intended to heal and harm in equal measure? Given this breaks the social contract between architecture and society, to produce environments that do not transgress the mutuality of respect between architect and audience, how are we to imagine otherwise? Perhaps a bespoke location in which architecture *is* the performance, one constructed at the limit of aesthetic tolerance?

14: Surface

To round out our development of propositions about architecture that have attempted to avoid the trap of promoting one formal methodology over another, this section looks at the question of surface. There is considerable literature that covers the debate between complex morphologies and thin veneers in architecture, all variations on the duck and decorated shed binary, but if the first encounter with architecture is arguably visual we can consider what it is that we see, when we see. This section starts with two fundamental modalities of how the surface appears and how it is transformed within digital culture. The Semperian encouragement to understand a surface as the result of the transformational geometry of a line (a thread) that is woven to become a surface (a carpet) can be transposed into the fundamental digital grammar of point, line, plane and form. The first chapter, on the topological study of knots as expressions of mathematical conditions, looks at the way we employ them to activate one of the fundamental propositions about modes of seeing set out by Heinrich Wölfflin. The evolution and parallel development of modes of seeing in painting and architecture that he proposes has an uncanny parallel in digital modes of defining and representing complex geometries within architecture. A knot, then, is the fundamental expression of the tectonics of jointing and binding of forms.

Extending this consideration, the coincidence of collage and digital surfaces is examined in the next chapter. The thinness with which real and apparent depth in surfaces is created through the use of collaged forms is now a ubiquitous issue for architecture, irrespective of the complexity of its geometry. In both analogue and digital instances of collage, this has consequences for how the abrupt encounter between different instances of pictorial fragments affects meaning in architectural surfaces. The discreteness of each of these instances, their monad-like character, is a confirmation that continuity is achieved across the surface of the image-plane – without collapsing the semantic individuation and discontinuity that collage presents. In architecture, the question of whether architecture is form or surface bears directly on this relationship.

Staying with surfaces, but with more levity than German critical theory usually provides, there are also the programmatic veneers of event spaces. These take their form from the spontaneous or even camouflaged character of their operations. The nightclub or discotheque is a case in which the successful expression of its purpose, hedonistic pleasure, is a direct function of its ability to stage a spectacle that removes the occupants from everyday markers of life. Much like the casino or the shopping mall, the suspension of critical expectations is the *raison d'etre* of the typology and the architecture of these spaces is always about the economy of surfaces. In particular, for the discotheque, as a space premised on the uncertainties of after-hours behaviour, the question is asked whether this constitutes a 'minor-architecture'.

Finally, we look at the condition of *sfumato* and, to an extent tenebrism, respectively characterized (though diminished in meaning) as 'smokiness' and 'sheen'. *Sfumato* is a term that has emerged from art theory to address certain painterly qualities of surfaces, ones that mask the indexical gestures of the painter's hand. This smoothness, it can be argued, is a phenomenal quality also of modern architectural expression and the machined qualities of contemporary construction. It is the obverse of the types of material tangibility promoted by theorists such as David Leatherbarrow, promoting the fungibility of materials such as glass, aluminium, steel and plastics, rather than the phenomenal specificity of timber, earth-based construction and (certain forms of) concrete, ceramics and masonry. Surfaces, we conclude, are not only the carriers of meaning in a strictly pictorial sense, they are also the plane of appearance of architecture, emerging from incoherence into critical 'light'.

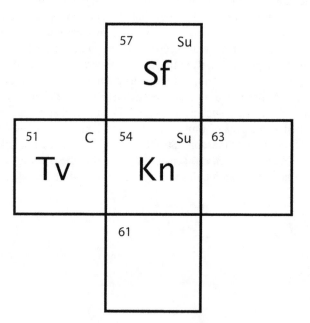

Rebus 54

Surface

Proposition 54: Knots

Gottfried Semper's *Four Elements of Architecture* (1851) contains, of course, four categories of form and place making: hearth, roof, enclosure and mound. For Semper, the principle of enclosure most specific to his study of *Grundfragen* (fundamental questions) on architecture was the proposition that all wall-forms (enclosure) evolved from a woven surface whether it was timber or textile, the hearth is the progenitor of the tile or masonry, the roof is the most basic primal covering, and, other wall-forms that were based on physical mass were essentially extensions of the mound condition. Architecture, for Semper, divides between the open and closed form-types. Furthermore, for Semper, these transformations are fundamentally anchored in vernacular craft practices but emerge in more sophisticated forms as self-consciousness of design as western architecture evolves. Arguably, the idea of the wall-as-woven-surface continues to be tacitly followed in contemporary transformations of modernity, just as ideas on mass form were grounded in ideas first broached in the mannerist period. For Semper, and for those who have looked again at his categories as an alternate, trans-historical reading of architectural theory, these categories serve as a useful meta-definition of architectural forms. The applicability of vernacular craft to contemporary industrialized processes, the argument goes, is an attempt to ground contemporary technology in an a-historical and a-political narrative.

As Wes Jones notes, in his essay 'Can tectonics grasp smoothness' (2014), Semper's ideas are essentially a distinction between an assemblage of parts or a smooth and consistent mass from which volumes are sculpturally removed. The assemblage methodology involves the bringing together of parts into a type of performative or compositional unity, a construction of an aesthetic experience in which the part is a constitutive element of a systemic whole. Aesthetically, the open-form type requires the viewer to 'constructively' recognize the compositional unity of a work made up of recognizably discrete parts. In contrast, in the manner of Michelangelo's approach to sculpture, the closed-form type comes from a process that entails the uncovering of the sculptural form from within a block of inert substance. For figural works, for example, this entails the understanding of when 'life' becomes apparent in what had hitherto been an uncommunicative mass.

Heinrich Wölfflin, a generation after Semper, extends the analysis of formal and textural qualities in art, speculating on a general theory of visual arts, particularly painting, sculpture and architecture. His *Principles of Art History* (1915) was specifically targeted at the transition from Mannerism to Baroque in the sixteenth and seventeenth centuries, but the analysis is remarkably apposite when considered in relation to Semper and to recent attempts to characterize contemporary developments in digital architecture.

Wölfflin's analysis contains five principle points:

1. Linear to painterly – from drawing to surface.
2. Plane to recession – the plasticity of the surface becomes apparent.
3. Closed tectonic to open a-tectonic form.
4. Multiplicity to unity.
5. Absolute clarity to relative clarity.

Wölfflin takes the issue of open and closed forms and suggests that the transition from the first to the second characteristics is part of the analysis of a work that is internal to the work (avoiding issues of context and historical continuity, points 3–5). For Jones, and other theorists of the digital, the use of Semper and Wölfflin allows them to situate contemporary work in a discursive context that acknowledges the cosmetic similarities between the work of Bernini and Gehry, or Borromini and Lynn. As Jones points out, there are limitations here, but the temptation to renew the interest in form and surface from the intellectual lineage of German critical history is strong.

If we develop Wölfflin's first two points with respect to architecture, and in particular Semper's ideas on vernacular essentialism, then a few interesting propositions emerge that immediately change the idea that some form of 'primitivism' or essentialism is sufficient for thinking about the constitution of surface. Classic German critical historiography ties the development of formal and design practices to an historical narrative that is, at times, immutable in terms of archetypes of formal solutions, or developmental as an expression of the immanence of modernity and modes of adaptation. In this respect, Semper's ideas on fundamental building practices ask the reader to connect the pre-modern and pre-critical world to our current modern, critical circumstance – but does it matter? Is it important if Kengo Kuma's adaptation of the vernacular Japanese craft tradition is linked to a general theory such as Semper's? And is it important to see the development of the line to a surface in Wölfflin's critical analysis as a progenitor of later theories of digital form-making in architecture?

The first point, the transformation of the appreciation of the line to the surface describes the development of a drawing practice in which the line describes the limits of the architectural component, whether it is a panel, a brick, a beam or the infinitely thin painterly line between colours. How a line intertwines with itself to become a surface presumes that it already possesses a thickness, yet the spline that describes the complex attitude of the line is essentially the mathematical expression of this physical reality – much in the manner in which the solution to a labyrinth expresses the form of its path. Taking the Semper model, the elaboration of the line into a complex continuity that returns on itself and forms into knots is the pathway to the structured aggregation of knots that create macrame or knitting – surfaces. We will look at knots below, but it is worth commenting first on the relationship among lines, surfaces and topological study as a precursor to a contemporary 'architecture' of topological forms premised on the mathematics of topology.

How does the line of a drawing, or digital model, translate into the complexities of a surface? In the first instance, it is through the tracing of a line (infinitely thin) into a series of patterns that describe the forms of complexity that a labyrinth may produce. It is the distinction between a surface as a field of coordinates and one that is defined by the bezier splines within a Non-Uniform Rational Basis Spline (NURBS) surface. The transformation from a single vector to a surface of continuous differentiation calls both the analysis of Wölfflin and the discipline of mathematical topology into play. While architecture generally frames its critical meaning within the tradition of the expressive arts, there is a clear intersection between the definitions of complex surfaces in mathematical topology and the employment of these forms in architecture. The question is, what does it mean? In a study conducted by a group of scientists and a visual artist (Anderson et al. 2015), Alessio Corti, a mathematician, shared sketch diagrams that helped define their interest in topology within the mathematical sciences. The use of drawings to test the efficacy of mathematical definitions drew a link between the abstract reasoning of mathematics and the visual proof of a topological solution. For architecture, one of the possible meanings (or uses) becomes clear: linking the study of craft activity of knot-making to fundamental architectural practices provides a subsequent link to the study of knots-as-architecture or topology-as-architecture.

Knots
Knot theory, as a component of the study of topology, is an interesting and bracketed subset of this process. Simply put a knot is a continuous line that can be manipulated to create a complex formal outcome without breaking the continuity of the line.

A circle is the simplest form of this, which then develops into increasingly complex patterns typified by the knot patterns of Celtic, Islamic and Medieval design. Inherently, the study of topology within the mathematical world is intended to make formal complexity clearer not for the purpose of understanding tiling patterns but for the far more complex mathematics of defining knot paths (Neuwirth 1979). In contrast, the parallel study of emergent systems in architecture that is modelled on biological evolution, while similarly focused on issues of efficient solutions, opportunistically recognize that the recursive nature of knot-forms can be matched to self-organizing systems that occur in the natural world. A knot-system, in this way of thinking, is an efficient method for taking a line and creating a surface, and consequently a three-dimensional knot-form.

How does a knot become a form: textiles that are woven but also those that are continuously knotted to create a form of constriction (and loosening) of the joint. A macramé work is essentially a surface of knots that imparts structure via the mechanical and material properties of the yarn employed. As sailors and fishermen learnt many millennia ago, the combined properties of a yarn's tensile strength and the distributed forces in knots make for effective tools for fishing and sailing. The question for architecture, and it is at this point that study of topology is relevant, is when the pattern of knot-forms assumes a three-dimensional, spatial properties and becomes a (potentially) inhabitable structure rather than a decorative surface.

How is this architectural?
As mentioned, recursive forms that are similar to the extensionality of knot-forms constitute the basis of discussions regarding complex and generative systems in architecture. As Christina Cogdell (2018) narrates in her experience of taking classes on complex form-making at the Architectural Association in 2011, the assumptions regarding what constituted a 'system' and how that became architecture are problematic. As we have seen earlier, in the discussion of 'Life', the semantic drift from pattern making of forms to architecture brings with it a number of issues and, it can be said, some knotty problems. As Cogdell points out, there is considerable investment in the intellectual convergence of parametric software within architectural form-making (including that which makes knot topology a possible architecture), and on narratives on the intelligence of complex systems. This is where attention to Semper and Wölfflin makes sense. It may be possible to devise forms of architecture that share the same mathematical genealogy as topology and knot theory, but is it necessary?

While complexity and the discussion of emergent systems currently enjoy considerable popularity in some of the more urban centres of architectural education, there is an argument that the process of cultivating versions of this methodology produces little more than a series of pavilions, since there is a fundamental misunderstanding of the relationship between surface and structure. The core issue in translating various metaphorical applications of biology, mathematics and non-Euclidean geometry into architecture is the degree to which the metaphorical interface applies to the broad spectrum of architectural practice. The same can be said of most parallel disciplines to architecture, but it is particularly crucial in the case of those disciplines whose languages of form and plasticity are employed in current digital manufacturing. While Semper's work has the value of reminding us of the craft-based nature of creating dwellings, he did not limit architecture to a single form category.

Strings and paths
So, is there a purpose to knot-theory in architecture? Clearly, any enhanced understanding of the efficient distribution of forces across a surface has a value. The work of Frei Otto in devising the soft-computational models for the tensile structures in Munich (1972) is an originary demonstration of this, and the promise of non-standard geometries continues to offer an alternative to the modernist world of rectilinear solutions. The most compelling use, in my view, is not the knot-form itself as a potential material geometry but the continuity of pathways that knot theory addresses. One of the principle tasks within knot definition is the determination whether paths can be traced so that a single strand can be un-knotted. Definitions of different classes of knots, within knot theory, rest partly on the continuity of a form within 'three-space' and its homotopological similarity with others of the same class. The mathematics is complex but the application to architecture is simple. The path of the thread constitutes a programmatic path within architecture and the knot, like the labyrinth, is a model for devising complex, rational programmatic outcomes.

Proposition: The Knotness Monster
Conceive of a project in which the programme of a building, and the pathways didactically chosen to direct users, is based on knot theory. How many knot forms can be used to identify substantively different path behaviour? How can architecture bind the users into a perpetual repetition of experiences? And should it?

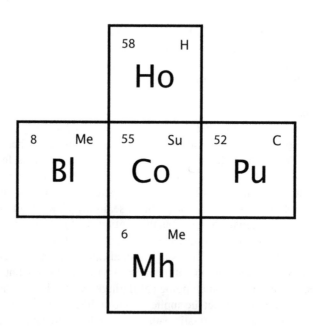

Rebus 55

Surface

Proposition 55: Collage

Colin Rowe and Fred Koetter's seminal discussion of the vagaries of utopian thinking in urban planning, *Collage City* (1979), situates the failure of modernist planning as a rational and technical system, whose visibility always insists on the primacy of the revelation of the system – that the city, or townscape, looks like the outcome of rational processes. The history of utopian thinking, in their estimation, is a negotiation between an idealized state such as the *Città ideale* (1480s) of Piero della Francesca, or seamlessly rational endeavours such as Le Corbusier's *Ville Radiuese* (1924), both of which are problematic because of the a-temporality of the model they propose. They go further and identify futurist thinking regarding utopia as a type of reverse historicism in which the outcomes of the future have already come to pass, like some great historical event outside of the agency of individual cultures. For overtly technical futurists, like Archigram and Superstudio, it can be argued that their images propose a new form of post-historical innocence in which the reconciliation between humanity and the post-apocalyptic is untroubled by issues of political and economic necessity. Significantly, and this will prove to be crucial, the discussion of *Collage City* is concentrated at the level of an historiographical overview and carries the issues of being marginally applicable in any urban analysis, but unspecific to any one in particular. However, the sentiment it expressed, a frustration with modernist social engineering through architecture, was significantly influential.

As a model for urban analysis, and ultimately, urban design, the lessons of Rowe and Koetter have been successfully integrated into the lineage of modern urban design that has contested the relationship between tradition and modernism since the advent of the Garden City movement. Indeed, *Collage City* became a gateway theorem in the 1980s for introducing revisions to urban analysis in the United States that were emerging in Continental Europe and which ultimately introduced the postmodern attitude towards historicist urban forms. Rowe, as a promoter of the urban theories of the Krier Brothers and ultimately the New Urbanism of Elizabeth Plater-Zyberk and others, sought a way to understand the purpose of critical history in the late twentieth century and to find a way to allow historicism to re-enter contemporary architectural discussion without attaching it to retrograde ideological positions.

Scuola Metafisica
Rowe and Koetter's analyses engage directly with the question of utopia and ideology that was first broached by Manfredo Tafuri's *Architecture and Utopia: Design and*

Capitalist Development (1973). Tafuri, and the critical theory that emerged from the Italian architectural scene in the 1960s and 1970s, particularly that of Aldo Rossi, was a model for the continuation of the European avant-garde into the American academy. As a contrast to the specifically new-world writings of Robert Venturi and Denise Scott Brown, the influence of the Italian school directed English-language architectural theory back to the core issues of modernity – how does architecture effectively change the world? Tafuri's quite complex message was premised on the rigorous exploration of critical historiography, measuring the consequences of architecture through the extrapolation of its trajectories of intention with respect to an indexical moment. What, for example, did the languages of abstraction employed by Le Corbusier imply as a general theory of cultural production for a contest between bourgeois luxury and the apparent freedoms of capitalism? For Tafuri, understanding architecture was a far more rigorous question, for both the architect(s) in question and the community in which a work is located, than a mere description of its capacities. Tafuri considered Aldo Rossi's work, for example, to be 'an alphabet of forms that reject all facile signification' (Tafuri 1987: 273) essentially arguing that in the face of mass commodification of the formal language of architectural modernism, the only coherent stance was to negatively deny any form of linguistic 'meaning'. This entailment of language, or ideas of signification, came to be extremely influential within the American context, particularly for Peter Eisenman. In addition, the requirement to read all forms of architecture as imperfect expressions of utopian aspirations framed Rowe's attitude towards understanding what a city might become.

For Rowe and Koetter, their unique contribution was to overtly introduce the idea that a collagist sensibility was primarily at work, since the practice of collage, like that of Synthetic Cubism, opportunistically situated elements of different eras, different formal design orthodoxies, different use-patterns and, ultimately, different metropolitan aspirations within the task of urban architecture. Borrowing Tafuri's references to bricolage, Rowe and Koetter's combination of old and new world theory was to reconcile two forms of urban work, both of which interrogate the context of the modern city and its relation to historical fabric. This was, as Alioscia Mozzato (2019) has identified, the unification of the city as both the 'theatre of prophecy' and the 'theatre of memory'.

Tafuri and Rossi
What are these theatres? And how does their meaning involve issues of collage? Because Tafuri's work was an exceptionally focused study of the ideological context

of early modernity, undistracted by issues of formalism and taste, and serious in its consideration of the emancipatory aims of modernity, the ironic reflections of Venturi and Scott Brown were considered 'infantile phantasmagoria'. For Tafuri, there was no critical dimension to Pop Art as he took the view that it had surrendered to the status-quo of consumer capitalism and served as a form of zombie avant-garde appearing to be critical but in fact reinforcing the division between classes and the perpetuation of a pyrrhic individualism. In this context, Rowe and Koetter were left with the question of how the complexity of the city should be considered.

The two theatre types, 'prophecy and memory', constitute the dialectical contest between urban architecture that can be considered to project a form of future optimism, tempered by the recognition that the city is also the place in which we recognize the meaningful continuity of the past. They are considered theatres because they carry with them the expected suspension of disbelief and imaginative engagement of theatre in a continual 'play' in which architecture performs the role of urban actors. What we might, in other circumstances, consider to be the vivacity of urban life: the intersection of forms of living, commerce, entertainment and politics is considered a form of theatre in Rowe and Koetter's view. In essence, they are extending a view of Rossi that Tafuri promoted.

In the context of the rich and vivid architectural history of Italian cities, Rossi's contemporary architecture created those 'alphabet of forms', simple Platonic geometries that are typologically architectural, without becoming quotations of other works. For Rossi, this was the essence of his 'analogous city', in which architectural forms shared a family resemblance with all other works of design. If you think of the universe of Alessi products, and indeed understand their ideas on domestic objects as 'actors' within the 'stage' of the home, Rossi's city is a greater version of this surreal landscape. Importantly, the role of architecture and of the single building was to distinguish itself as the critical/theatrical event within the general cast of conventional and anonymous building.

Collage and Bricolage
Ultimately for Rowe and Koetter, the technique of creating an architecture that referenced the history of the discipline (much like Rowe's equivalence of Palladio and Le Corbusier's villa designs) meant that they looked to work that was based on some form of historical sensibility, even to the extent of quoting historical fragments. In this respect, they were assimilating the novel, and decidedly un-Tafuri-like, position that Venturi had outlined in *Complexity and Contradiction in Architecture*

(1966) years earlier. What Tafuri latterly considered to be a shallow acceptance of the commercialization of taste had actually expressed a highly refined disposition towards the inevitability of mediated culture. Reconsidering this question some 40 years later, many of the original diagnoses of the complexity of the modern city remain, though the constant transformation of urban culture and the ubiquitousness of digital information and communication mean that something of the unique nature of urban experience in the 1980s is now lost to us.

What remains is the challenge of thinking through the technique of collage as a meta-strategy for urban architecture. We should remember that collage, as a technique, is a uniquely modern phenomenon and that it emerged as a response to the technological capacities of contemporary media and publishing. Moreover, if we are thinking about how to read the complexity of cities and of modern architectural practice, collage refers to the practice of looking at representations of cities and of architecture, through drawings. So Rowe and Koetter's approach is uniquely defined by the drawing and compositional practice of collage, and how it applies to urban design and architecture in plan and elevation. So, how to update the process of collagist design in the age of digital reproduction?

How is this architectural?
If we consider the cross-fertilization of the original expression of a critical collagist practice in the Dada work of Hannah Hoch, Raoul Hausmann, John Heartfield, and Max Ernst, with the techniques of the current day, particularly the digital techniques of Photoshop, there are some comments that can be made. One of the particular characteristics of collage is that the selected image for incorporation is a coherent particularity, deliberately dislocated from its original source. Brought together with other material, the composite image is a new reality, edited to bring forward both its surreal totality and the dissonant adjacencies of the parts. Collage as an architectural practice can then be thought to involve a similar fusion of particularities.

All of this is about the surface of the city, its presentation as a mise-en-scene of activities that are largely mysterious, though discernable. The city is a collage of architectural narratives. The two theatres, prophecy and memory, are populated by the particularities of unique architectural expressions, while buildings themselves are the composite amalgam of detailed particularities merged together. This is as true of Michelangelo's Porta Pia (1565) as it is of Ashton Raggatt Macdougall's National Museum of Australia (2001).

Further, interrogating the characteristics of collage, we can look at the parallel phenomena of pareidolia and apophenia. Pareidolia is the recognition of objects in abstract organizations of pattern, for example seeing a man in the moon, and apophenia is the association of disparate information to wrongly infer meaningful connections. Collage is the classic opportunity to discern these phenomena in an architectural context, recognizing potential other semantic meanings of architectural design and of the context of architecture within an urban context. The contemporary convergence of digital photography and digital collage has enabled artists such as Nicolas Moulin, Matthias Jung, Anastasia Savinova, Filip Dujardin and Victor Enrich to create fictional architectural creations that present an uncanny version of architectural realities. Their 'buildings' depict architectural states that defy any of the conventional barriers to creating a reality based on the complex physical, programmatic and financial requirements that govern everyday architecture. Yet their visions are not trivial, quite the contrary they are incredibly compelling as they demonstrate the potential for architecture to continue to be a project for manufacturing complex versions of reality.

Proposition: The photographer's palace
Explore the intersection of photography, reality and architecture through the medium of collage. However, as architecture, it is important to continue into the space of the image and reverse-engineer the characteristics to find the full three-dimensional, programmatic and political identity of the project. Employing pareidolia and apophenia as techniques for (mis)reading the images, find the architecture that is inherent and implied in the process.

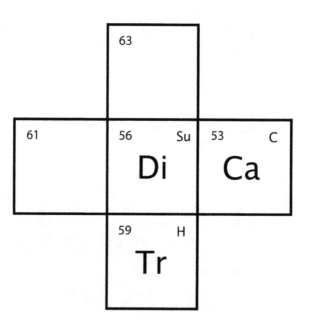

Rebus 56

Surface

Proposition 56: Discotheque

The usual focus of architectural theory is on the instrumental relationships between form and human activity. These activities can be anything from the perceived relationship between a plan and the program of behaviour that it is mooted to occur as a consequence, the activity of designing architectural form itself as a considered analogue approach, the instrumental techniques for creating architectural form with tools that extend the range and precision of analogue means, and finally the further specificity (innately assumed within analogue processes) of being able to load up interlaced options onto an overall form (design development).

Most of the chapters within this book have sought to add complexity to this process by interposing questions as to what constitutes evidence of a design approach and at what juncture is it important to look to tangential information to create alternate solutions. What is challenging in this approach, I hope, is the assumption that the search for non-normative solutions that have incidental or partial effectiveness is that it expands the domain of architectural thinking. Perhaps.

One of the pathways for considering this is concerned with the interrogation of programmatic typologies that do not fit within standard or agreed practice. It would be quite in order for a book on architectural theory to examine houses and hospitals and high-rise offices in acknowledgement of their primacy in architectural practice, but the value in this is also the problem. Standardized typologies tend to gravitate towards self-similar solutions and consequently reinforce generalizable solutions. This is not a problem in ordinary circumstances, but if we have the ambition to grow what we think we know about architecture then alternate paths are necessary, and one of these is alternate typologies.

The discotheque is an unusual typological form because, in the main, it is an interior with quite special qualities that specifically augment the sonic and visual ambitions for the space(s). It is not unusual for nightclubs generally to be addressed in architectural theory, but their relationship to fleeting trends within music and night-time entertainment norms mean that it is difficult to definitively give the history of the nightclub in a way that is similar to conventional projects. In Deleuzean parlance, it is a minor architecture since it is produced as a prosthetic to these conventional projects and acts as a permanent expression of the impermanence of its purpose. The de-territorialization of the discotheque type in relation to more permanent and conventionally discussed work affords it the power of being the antithesis of stability and to being a continual reproof of the stability of material meaning.

The impermanence itself has granular qualities that are equally instructive. The selective use of reflective materials and of darkness signal its consistency with the urban locations they usually occupy. The depthlessness of the city at night, lit by artificial means, is transferred into the club interior, whether as a small enclave or as a massive event space. The light is intended to selectively illuminate and to hide within a controlled environment. Music performs a similar function, either as a completely immersive event that culminates in the bacchanalian expression of dancing, or as a soundtrack to the possibility of sociability. Interior fixtures and furnishing act as stage sets for the expression of the drama of group and individual dynamics, exaggerated to allow for display of group-bonding and sexualized behaviour. As Carlini and Sanchez (2018) point out, club typologies vary but the mechanisms for promoting the expression of altered and heightened social identities is consistent.

So how is this architectural?
There are a number of challenges here. The first is the challenge of impermanence and recognizing that there is no ur-nightclub typology that will remain consistent through varying expressions of contemporary culture. While some club forms deliberately target specific sub-cultures and attempt to encapsulate the totality of that culture, their role is an expression of nostalgia and a specific indifference to contemporary trends. Second, the focus upon an interior or event space does not immediately suggest an engagement with the language of urban form. Indeed, many clubs define their experience by the discontinuity between the public form and interior spaces. Third, the equivalent effects of surface (im)materiality, darkness, performance spaces and alcohol and drug consumption tend to diminish the specific effectiveness of architectural design as a governing aesthetic experience.

In this respect, the architectural dividends are paradoxically quite radical. Consider a design experience in which the thematic function of the building is to hide the interior, and for that interior to contain depths that are deliberately complex and idiosyncratic. The opportunity, spatially, for performance spaces for social display and the construction of view lines across these complexities sits adjacent to the idea of a space for dancing and the performance of music. But then by contrast, the opportunity exists to invert these spaces and externalize them onto the surface of a building and for the building to be a visible honeycomb of sensate complexity.

Consider the Palazzo Zuccari (1590) in Rome or the Palazzo della Civiltà Italiana (1943) in EUR, undergoing the transformation of the monumental into the visceral.

Finally, the construction of narratives of the night, the picaresque encounter of persons under the cover of darkness and the clear distinction between the city of work and rest, and the city of nocturnal entertainment. The persons met, the encounters shared, the stories told and the senses pushed to the limit of their capacity. When you think of the favourite moment in a club, night club or disco scene, the sublimity of the experience is paramount. The consequence of minor architecture such as this, like minor literature, is to construct a sublimity of experience using the less heroic and dominant formal languages and to create a moment that may never be repeated.

Proposition: The rhythm of the night
Choose a building unsuited to the behavioural and aesthetic extremes of club land and transform it into the best night of your life. Not the safest, nor the most comfortable, but the best nonetheless.

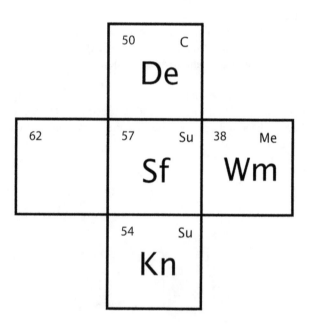

Rebus 57

Surface

Proposition 57: *Sfumato*

One of the defining characteristics of the painting of Leonardo da Vinci is his employment of *sfumato* techniques. *Sfumato* translates as 'smokiness', implying the definition of a form is achieved through the gradation of tone, rather than the articulation of an outline. It is a core aspect of his work that *sfumato* evolved from being a description of a process to a characteristic in and of itself. In Leonardo's work, considerable effort is made to conceal the presence of the indexical brush stroke, creating smooth contours of colour and revealing the three dimensionality of forms through changes in tone and shadow. Painting, as Leonardo recognized, is a representational medium deeply tied to vision and the degrees of visual acuity the eye can discern in what is fundamentally a synthetic simulation of real-world experiences. The contest between the vision and the technique of the painter, and the work created and experienced means that there is a high degree of self-consciousness in the painterly process. The question of how to artificially represent the phenomenal sensation of sight is at the core of his (Leonardo's) technique. For this reason, *sfumato* is more than a novel characteristic or some *trompe l'oeil* effect, but a genuine attempt to balance real and apparent visual definition within a painting.

The contrast with architecture, when it is drawn rather than painted, is the discrimination between the drawing as a diagram and the picture as a representation of an experience. In a diagram, the precision or otherwise of a line does not usually compromise the information in the diagram, unless the line thickness itself indicates specific values. A three-dimensional rendering, when it attempts to represent some form of an architectural project's 'reality', is thus more similar to painting and shares many of the issues regarding fidelity to vision and to the world. Further, as Tanazaki famously reminds us in *In Praise of Shadows* (1977), the emergence of form from darkness, the patina of material weathering on a surface and the sense of indeterminacy that exists in the half light of dusk are fundamental aspects of aesthetic experience.

While Leonardo was not principally concerned with the representation of buildings, we are. The issue of atmospherics in architectural representation is generally less discussed than diagrams, principally since the purpose of a diagram is to interpose itself between the design and a constructed reality. Pictorial representation, as an end in itself, is usually left to persons interested in some form of 'hyper-realism'. In architecture, this is rarely pursued, since the time-cost in making realistic images is not economical in the design process. Further, the creation of realistic imagery tends to constrain a design team to an inviolable version of the design, when somewhat less specificity helps manage attention and expectations of clients and stakeholders.

The issue of *sfumato* or 'smokiness' in architecture is aligned to the idea that forms emerge from a darkness into light. It follows from this that the representation of architecture through pictorial means would borrow meaningfully from that tradition, in particular in the evolution of imagery associated with, for example, the eighteenth century 'revolutionary' architect Etienne Louis Boullée. Paula Young Lee (1998) provides a virtuoso analysis of the pair of images Boullée produced for the Bibliotheque du Roi, from the façade that presents a darkened doorway to the interior, to the monumental barrel-vaulted space emulating Raphael's *School of Athens* (1511), which itself vanishes to a perspective point of an indistinct darkened doorway. Lee's analysis reminds us that the road to modernity in visionary architectural imagery is shadowed by the Neoplatonist obsession with mystical origins of light from darkness. So while the images of Boullée are generally discussed as revolutionary for formal reasons related to the scale of the projects, and the employment of a monumental neo-classical language, the question of visual fidelity and the manner in which precision is married to ambiguity seems to thus include a form of visual and theoretical 'smokiness'.

Sfumato, as smoke, implies an indistinct context from which something emerges, typically the figures of Leonardo emerge from a context in which the emotional engagement of the viewer is intended to oscillate between empathy and observation. On a gradient of emotions and the depth of empathetic attention, *sfumato* communicates the seemingly indeterminate wonder at the smooth inevitability of the scene. The obverse of smokiness, emergence from darkness, is 'tenebrism', the overexposure of light to the point at which form cannot be viewed directly. Tenebrism, or sheen, describes a surface that is reflective and distinct from the darkness that incrementally surrounds it. The work of Caravaggio, as well as Spanish painters such as Goya and Zurbarán, is typically associated with this approach. As a painterly technique that was associated with the same Neoplatonist world-view, the distinction of tenebrism is that it employs, like *sfumato*, the dramaturgical quality of implying narratival complexities beyond the image.

How is this architectural?
The contest between darkness and light within architecture, when not considered a metaphysical quest such as Le Corbusier's Manicheanism or a phenomenological

event like Tanizaki's, is most critically tied to existing means of visibility, and visual immersivity, within digital environments. Digital environments, as architectural creations, have the capacity to deliver increasing levels of visual 'reality' that hitherto was unavailable to conventional architectural communication. The ever present quest for unceasing player engagement in the game industry has driven considerable technological developments in the software available for creating photo-realistic environments. Immersivity in these digital environments depends on texture and atmosphere and the absence of visual cues of the synthetic nature of the creation process (excessive repetition of forms, surface triangulation, over-simplified mesh creation, mis-matched material tiling, depthless textures). While the process for delivering a seamless immersive game environment is still in its infancy, it is now a matter of when rather than if this will be the case. For architecture, this means that the successful use of these environments will enable a design process that can proceed from the diagram to a reality far more atmospherically rich than previous renderings. It also means that the design process can now control any number of material complexities and environmental subtleties dependent on the skill of the architect. Creating a design that is formally simple such as Tadao Ando's Azuma House (1976) but is nonetheless designed to be phenomenologically rich is now a clear capability of contemporary digital technology.

Further, if we (re-)fold in the associations with metaphysical contests between darkness and light, and the subtleties and 'emotional' range imagined by Tanizaki, and also commentators such as Juhani Pallasmaa, it is clear that the nuances of intentionality and immersive engagement that Leonardo directed towards painting can now be facilitated within the architectural design process. Both *sfumato* and tenebrism are activated towards the creation of a viscerally experienced architecture that emulates the textural visual narratives of film. Potentially, the inter-relationship between architecture and cinema can evolve from structural organization of program and the determinants of behavioural typologies, as outlined earlier in 'Cinema' and 'The Puzzle', to one that fully shares the intimate textuality of materials and environments.

Proposition: The smoke-house
What does a smoke-house do as a form of extreme environment? Is it to prepare food, to act as a psychotropic environment, to be a place of leisure? Is it like an alchemical alembic that distils and delivers refined states of experience? How do we consider the emergence of form from darkness and indeterminacy, and the transformation of murky indistinctness to clarity and the sheen of presence?

15: Hope

The final section, on Hope, is intended to draw to a conclusion the process of analysis and speculation of the preceding chapters. At the same time, there are ideas on architectural theory inherent within the three concluding chapters that speak to ambitions beyond the scope of this book. For this reason, the final section is an end to the form of this book, but also a platform for other arrangements of ideas. Nevertheless, this is an acknowledgement that the final chapters are intended to bring the array of categories to an acceptable conclusion on the terms of the book's methodological structure. Or at least that is the hope.

So hope, as a human emotion, is generally characterized as some sort of projection onto current circumstances. It can be completely rational and premised on as much information as is available, or it can come from totally unsupported wishes, untethered to pragmatic standards of what is possible let alone likely.

The first chapter of this section deals with one of the few academic texts that specifically ties hope to cultural production. Ernest Bloch's *The Principle of Hope* (1959, 1986) takes a broad view of culture across different media and times and divines a single animating force, in his view, that remains constant. Bloch calls this *Vor-Schein*, anticipatory illumination, alluding to our deep appetite for revelatory experiences in the world. Bloch was, perhaps, the last of the German-language theorists to construct a universal theory of cultural production, and as such there's a kind of mad brilliance in the ambition to attempt this, and understand the utopian impulses in culture. For our purposes, it mirrors the small ambition of this book to look broadly at non-standard categories of architectural theory.

In the second chapter, '*Tractatus*', the argument returns to one of the core themes of this book, the distinction between real and non-real referents in imagining architecture. Examining again Wittgenstein's *Tractatus Logico-Philosophicus* (1921), we are reminded that propositions can and should be self-evident once their conditions of appearance are understood, and also that it is possible for a proposition to contain elements that have sense, but not necessarily referents, in our world. Essentially, all of the propositions in this book should ideally no longer need explanation once their conditions of emergence are seen, and that this understanding has the capacity for speculative fictional characteristics.

Finally, the last chapter is an encouragement to undertake this form of critical speculation. Trust, like hope, is a behavioural characteristic of any creator, including architects of course, and is a ubiquitous expectation in a functioning society. The difference between human–human trust and human–system trust is an important encouragement for us to continue developing systems that are grounded in an ethics of mutual existence.

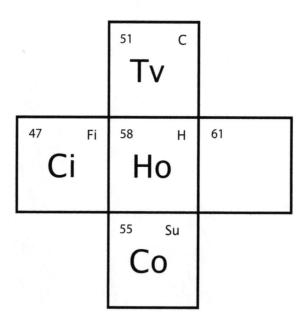

Rebus 58

Hope

Proposition 58: Hope

Hope, we generally think, is a simple human expression of optimism. That when considering what is unknown there may be an outcome, or a revelation, that confirms our best expectations rather than our worst fears. Whether the drivers of hope are the consequence of managing every unknown to the best of our abilities, or the final recognition of the role of chance and luck in human ambitions, the presence of hope, and sometimes hopelessness, is constant. Hope, while idiosyncratic is still tied to rational behaviour since it is the direction of agency at a specific state of affairs that, through effort, might have the chance to change the probability of an outcome, or of the expectation that there are residual dividends even if the final outcome is not wholly achieved.

Hope, as an abstract human value, also drives the economic condition between consistent metrics where an opportunity presents itself and the unknown conditions that may well compromise and vitiate a project. At some level, hope is the engine of any architectural project as it 'somehow' drives the array of assumptions of cause and effect that the project will set into place. In many respects, the suppression of hope is the professional obligation of architecture in order to responsibly marshal scarce material means. At the level of speculation, hope has a freer and more present value, since the various suspensions of disbelief in the project are guaranteed by the sincerity of the agency of hope: 'I hope this is the case'. But hope is also a form of individual commitment to politics since it is a performative command. We can ask the question: Can you produce an architectural speculation and *not* hope it has agency, or effect, or sense? In this respect, hope is distinguishable from optimism, as it is a personal, felt disposition rather than an objective assessment.

Ernst Bloch's *The Principle of Hope* (1959, 1986) identifies a series of stages of affect and agency that fall within the general term 'hope'. Analyzing this emotive state of affairs provides an underlying structure, or topology, of hope as a temporal activity with formal outcomes that can be managed structurally and ultimately expressed architecturally. Bloch's three-volume opus is a forbiddingly dense survey of the tendencies towards material change in the world, surveying historical examples from philosophy, literature, the fine arts, religion, psychoanalysis and, importantly for us, architecture. As a representative figure of cultural Marxism that grew from the Frankfurt School, Bloch's wish was to provide an analysis and endorsement of society's evolution into a utopian state, for Bloch this was (tragically) the Soviet

Union under Stalin. Though naïve in considering that this state may be achievable, the constant presentation of 'hope-like' tendencies makes for compelling reading.

Bloch's term for the main tendency in the emergence of hope in its various expressions was *Vor-schein*, usually translated as 'anticipatory illumination' (Bloch, Zipes 1988). This term captures the immanent ideological character Bloch focused on in his survey, particularly the relationship between religiosity and ideology. For Bloch, the purpose of all significant cultural expression was to create a vision of one of the gentlest, but most ubiquitous, human emotions. The 'anticipatory illumination' was intended to capture the commitment to transcendent values inherent in speculative expressions, much like the commitment to faith that constitutes a core element in religious belief. The hope is that it is possible there will be a benevolent and reconciled future for society, the chimaera of utopia.

For Bloch, the purpose of any cultural expression was that it was directed towards some end, even if the ultimate direction of that end was unclear, or perhaps unbeknownst to the creator. Specifically, Bloch wished to argue for the inevitability of the resolution of conflict towards an eschatological end. As may be obvious, Bloch's academic process was systemic in the fashion of the grand narrative analyses of German scholarship, and in particular, he saw a form of eschatological inevitability in tracking the evolution of the concept of hope. The 'not-yet-conscious' individual works of culture turn into 'objective possibilities' for the transformation of society as a whole and this transformation is collectively and inevitably directed towards a positive state.

How is this architectural?
Considering these aspects of Bloch's work, we can ask some structural questions: How does hope translate into an architectural project that is not negatively instrumental and seeks to govern 'anticipatory illumination' to ends that have potentially negative effects. For all the good intentions of architects, as designers of experiences and moulders of environments, can we be confident (should we care) that the outcome is on the whole beneficial? Perhaps the effect is only partial and that is sufficient. Perhaps some parts of the original aspiration are impossible or mutually exclusive. Can it provide a model for, as yet, unrealized desires? A valid criticism of Bloch's approach is that the project is an attempt to create a series of meta-typologies of hope-like instances, it emphasizes similarities, however distant, where perhaps it is the idiosyncratic differences that are the more relevant or actionable aspects of a work. In architecture, we recognize the value of typological study since the attainment

of developing reproducible models is part of the objective obligations of formal practice, the making of form. How is hope demonstrated through formal practice? There is an intrinsic speculation that causation is an outcome of form-making. It is not indifferent to the quantitative and qualitative outcome of the form-making, but is this condition a minor quality of the process overall? What is it to make something that is 'hopeless' in a philosophical sense (hopeless and helpless) – is this more philosophically rational?

Theodor Adorno's *Negative Dialectics* (1966, 1973) addresses this situation, particularly the question of whether coherent systems that are constantly, and benignly, optimizing themselves is a realistic assessment of the experience of the world. While the general thrust of this book is on the question of the subject matter of philosophy, the attendant emphasis on the questioning of systems is fundamental. It is one thing to say that 'our rewards are in heaven' and another to have to endure the incommensurabilities of everyday life when systemic directions, or prejudices, are structurally directed against you. For Adorno, rather than rush to divine a pseudo-positive outcome in the collective efforts of society, the more mature intellectual stance should be in opposition to normative states of affairs. This seems, on the surface, to be an unnecessarily cynical and dispiriting position to take, yet it rewards us with the authenticity of recognizing false hopes when they, or rather the marketplace of ideas, present themselves to us.

In my view, though not explicitly argued by him, Bloch anticipated this criticism. Reading *The Principle of Hope*, you are struck by the continual emphasis upon the idea of 'the dream', in particular the suggestion that most expressive, creative works inveigle the audience or reader to share the dream state of the creator. The question of whether a dream is a false hope or an example of the pointlessness of sustained effort is anticipated, in my view, in the sheer abundance of examples Bloch asks us to consider. For him, and perhaps for us, the critical investment in the ambitions of a dream precisely allows us to divest the 'real' world of its power. In many respects, this is the programme of this book, to encourage the experimental trialling of new states of affairs that the architectural studio permits and encourages.

Proposition: The hopeless and the hopeful
Two mutually entangled iterations come to mind:

The Hopeless: This could be tested and explored as a purposive nugatory example: What is a hopeless architectural project? What conditions can never be met? How are trivial and statistically slim chances of success created? Can we make a set of conditions about no-hope that asymptotically describe hope?

The Hopeful: Articulate your hopes, as hopes are not facts – and demonstrate how, individually and collectively, they entail formal and experiential conditions that need to be met. The core requirement is that, at the end of the process, you clearly understand what your hopes actually are, and their conditions for successful expression.

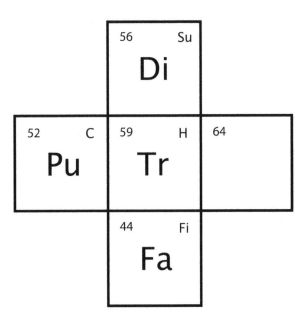

Rebus 59

Hope

Proposition 59: *Tractatus*

In an earlier chapter, Project 25, we discussed the relationship between the Viennese philosopher Ludwig Wittgenstein and the early developments of modernism. We mentioned the development of Wittgenstein's own interest in architecture, including the obsessive level of engineered craftsmanship of the house in Vienna for his sister. Of course, the goal when you have a major philosopher of the twentieth century who is interested in architecture is to interrogate the mutual influences in both directions, presuming this exists. Analyzing the Stonborough-Wittgenstein house with respect to Wittgenstein's work is one mode of understanding how architecture might be philosophical, as is the inverse question that maybe his philosophical work is in some fashion 'architectural'.

While we covered some of the complex aspects of the difference between statements of fact and statements of value earlier, the general structural issue of how Wittgenstein's earliest philosophical work, the *Tractatus Logico-Philosophicus* (1921), approaches its core goals, the discussion of how reality is apparent to us and what we can reasonably communicate regarding it needs further development. More importantly, perhaps, there is a lesson in this approach regarding the limits of theory, and the general definition of how 'theory' works in architecture.

As mentioned previously, the work commences with the first proposition: '1.0 The world is all that is the case'. It ends with the proposition: 'Thereof we cannot speak, we must pass over in silence' (1921: n.pag.). Just prior to the last proposition, Wittgenstein states, and I paraphrase, that if you have understood what I have said, then you need to cast away the preceding propositions, much as you would a ladder after climbing it. By this, he means that if the arguments make sense to you, then there is no need for a recipe for describing them since there is no propositional explanation outside of language. You don't need the phrase 'the sky is blue' in order for you to look outside.

Is this anti-intellectual?
Simply put, the general intention of the *Tractatus* is to describe what is characterized as the 'Picture Theory of Language'. In essence, this means that language, as people employ it, is used to create propositions regarding the world that report what is apparent to them. These propositions can take any number of forms, language, mathematics, images and formulae, but they are intended to be sensible and coherent. One of the difficulties in logic is in accounting for false propositions, 'The unicorn is

here', for example, when it is known that one of the components of the proposition is non-existent. Wittgenstein's achievement, in the *Tractatus*, is to show that we may make propositions that have a sense (we can imagine a unicorn being here) without having to have a stable referent (that the unicorn is real-in-our-world).

So imagine an image that is fictional insofar as it shows a world that does not exist, an architectural drawing for example. It is sensible because we understand many of the pictorial conventions and component elements of the work, but we are not troubled unnecessarily by the overall lack of a referent – it is not an image of a real place that we can check for veracity. In fact, much of the pleasure of these images is in discerning what does not have a referent.

It is necessary, at this juncture, to clarify a few extant misunderstandings regarding Wittgenstein that have come from the camp of architectural theory. Nana Last has written that, in the first instance, the culmination of the *Tractatus* created a 'subject' that 'has to move beyond what the philosophy of the *Tractatus* has defined as thinkable', which is somehow characterized as a 'transgression'. Similarly, she has speculated that the desire to publish the *Tractatus* alongside a later, and equally important, text by Wittgenstein, the *Philosophical Investigations* (1953) means that he was interested in 'space' in some inscrutable fashion. The change in Wittgenstein's thinking from a practice in propositional statements that were logically formed and sensible (made sense) to one in which communication was situationally more fluid is more subtle, and probably more challenging than Last recognized. Ultimately Last wishes to make the claim that the construction of the Stonborough-Wittgenstein house was a pivotal step in Wittgenstein's philosophical development and that his work was fundamentally spatial in the following sense. For Last, the propositions of the *Tractatus* were meant to be cumulative and result in a state that was vertical (presumably because of the ladder metaphor) whereas the propositions of the *Investigations* were horizontal because they acknowledged that statements of reality vs. fictionality, sense and reference, occur within open-ended rule-based systems.

What Wittgenstein was not doing, is discussing a 'subject' that needed to be spatialized through the practice of making architecture.

But there is something that can be retained from this discussion. It is the idea that the *Tractatus* was produced as a work *sub specie aeternitatis*, as a discussion of the universal values of logic in propositional contexts. In architecture, taking this cue, it is the recognition that the propositional ecologies that architectural works create similarly demonstrate universal truths within the boundaries of their own epistemological horizons. For this reason, the architectural drawing that you imagined previously, perhaps now populated with a unicorn, is true and real in the 'unicorn-in-architecture' world it references.

Proposition: The Augean Unicorn Stables
Create an architectural project that combines elements of fictionality but is complemented by a clear hierarchical series of propositions that assert the referential stability of the parts. Moreover, make these fictional elements not functional elements that it is the task of conventional architecture to accommodate, but an architecture of fictional details.

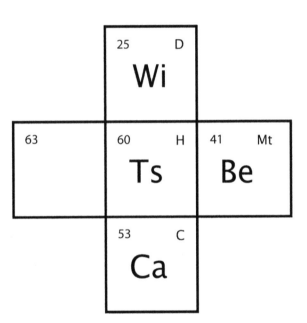

Rebus 60

Hope

Proposition 60: Trust

The final proposition for this book is centred on the idea of the mutuality of obligation and the behavioural implications of trust. While generally we are all able to understand the actions of trust, and the necessity of various levels of trust within the architectural profession for it to function, the way in which trust works at the level of speculative ideas is less clear. Generally, we think of trust as a behavioural expectation between persons as an extension of personal, familial and social identity. This is the general model that has allowed kinship within groups to be extended to anonymous and potentially hostile outsiders, usually in the mutual assurance of shared interests.

Trust itself is not a monolithic category and there are a number of fine-grained definitions of trust and trust contexts that are relevant across not only human relations, but also human–system relations. Human–system relations are originally applied in governance and institutional forms, but are increasingly focused on mediated interactions with technology. Importantly for architecture, while many of our actions and expressions are measurable and can be confirmed by personal interaction, the legacy issue for any architectural project is the trust context it creates. If you consider the legacy effect of architecture once proposed and, in extremity once constructed, it generally requires a series of trust behaviours to occur. Usually, in discussion of professional practice, this comes under the category of legal liabilities defined by the rule of Tort. If an architect, or practice, makes design decisions that are injurious to a party in the future, the architect potentially remains liable for that decision even though the injured party was not involved in the original design decision-making. The basis of this is the reasonable expectation that public environments may not be altered to make them potentially harmful to users within boundaries of acceptable behaviour. Architecture, then, is a system within which persons place their trust in personal safety.

Human–human and human–systems trust are marked by different modes of testing and compliance. In particular, human–systems trust requires the satisfaction of criteria for it to function. Predictive systems such as blockchain networks and the development of artificial intelligence (AI) insinuate another characteristic of the constellation of trust systems that are typical of social relations and the development of increasingly autonomous systems. The clear reality is that human–systems trust relationships are necessary in order to ensure continuity of systems organizations, from the simplest relationships such as traffic lights to AI-based interrogative exchanges that emulate human behaviour.

In this context, human–systems trust is developing from a relationship defined by the visibility of a system which is demonstrably tool-based, to one in which questions of value developed by artificial neural networks emulate human–human behaviour yet have no visible (or obvious) identifiers. Any system that predictively engages with human preferences inherently questions our relationship to more 'primitive' human–tool interactions. It is not a huge leap of imagination to consider the nature of our interactivity with tools becoming more responsive as they record, remember and predictively suggest certain operations they have 'learnt' through prior use. The transition from interactions that are pragmatically responsive (automatic opening and closing, for example) to ones that are more intuitively attuned (emotion-based or predictive) is a predictable development of these systems.

We can imagine the evolution of this interactive technology as it evolves and proliferates throughout our domestic, work and recreational environments. In fact, we can say with confidence that this will be the case, since the evolution of trust (which is active agreement) and confidence (passive agreement) are premised on similar levels of ontic comfort, but differ only in levels of familiarity. The general principle of blockchain technology is to disaggregate specific trust agreement across a broad network of users, preventing manipulation and falsification of information. In this respect, trust does not remain as an active requirement, but is replaced by confidence. If we return to human–human trust systems in which the potential for jeopardy is significantly higher, the obvious model to adopt is a distributed, and externalized version of trust such as that employed within marketplaces such as Ebay or Etsy. In this kind of marketplace, personal reputation and feedback is a crucial management component when interactions rely on the honesty of both parties in a transaction spanning different legal and commercial domains. The risk vs. reward commitment is similar to the explosion of social media communities based on a mediated, performative identity that is ultimately transactional.

These communities, like blockchain technology, are fundamentally polycentrist in their organization despite the efforts to 'game' and manage the attractiveness of identities. Significantly, even within architecture, there is a similar expression of a disaggregated trust community: Archdaily. Exercising minimal editorial control, Archdaily is a kind of polycentrist aggregator of 'good' architecture that presents a bewildering volume of work that is totally reliant on tacit assumptions of what type of work can be on the site, and how it is presented. A potential positive effect of this, in contrast to complaints about the uniformity of approach and the emphasis on certain visual styles, is that it constitutes a shared trust environment not only for architects but also for clients. If procurement is one of the greatest challenges for architectural practice, the potential value in creating a shared trust environment that has demonstrated effectiveness in other locations can go some way to explaining, and demonstrating, procurement agreements in other locations. Perhaps, if the complaint sometimes is that clients and stakeholders cannot envision outcomes, the solution to less engagement with architecture is the creation of a 'trust' environment that permits entry to stakeholders and longevity of the association.

How is this architectural?
But what of trust that concerns the interactions of persons committed to exploring the boundary conditions of architecture? Part of this will involve the complex use of communicative media as outlined above, but it will also encourage the exploration of the limits of what is tenable. Trust, in an architectural sense, requires not only a recognition of the potential reality, or surreality, of a project that may be tested for its coherence and its relationship to current discourses on architecture but also the context within which forms of trust may occur. This is the role of the studio and, hopefully, of this book.

The process of forming, testing and communicating ideas is entirely dependent on the intellectual space that the architectural studio creates. In this space, there is the expectation that sufficient tolerance is extended to any idea that can, with time and effort, be transformed into a sophisticated and intellectually viable proposition. There are a series of limits that are either externally or internally imposed, but it is generally the case that the purpose of speculative architectural projects is to interrogate what those limits are, and why they exist. In many cases what is being trialled for future deployment are the sets of propositional boundaries implied by the project. These boundaries are both virtual, in the sense of being propositional, and physical inasmuch as they require communicative strategies that can narrate the project's potential.

In these cases, trust requires vulnerability (sometimes mutual, or at least cognisant of uneven jeopardy) and the mutuality of obligation within speculation. The failure of a trust contract can vary from thin consequences (disappointment, irritation) to thick consequences (betrayal, psychological jeopardy). The corollary of trust is distrust, but what is the point at which we *should* distrust a human–human or human–system relationship? In an architectural scenario, arguably we should distrust a situation when there is an absence of the *argument* for trust or an absence of the complexity of theory and the need for the semantic assertion of the granular factors that validate a project. So, the proposition that there should be a mindless encouragement to architects to 'Build, don't talk' is a 'distrust' situation. This is not the same as expressing frustration at a lack of attention to active responsibilities, or preferencing conservative consideration over ambition. 'Talk and Build', should be the motto.

So, trust in architecture, in the view of this book, is the mutual assurance that every non-standard solution has the obligation to explain what circumstances will establish confidence in that solution. Unusually, this confidence need not be solely directed at a median standard of agreement, nor should we assume that confidence needs to have a 100 per cent agreement. It is enough to demonstrate the possibility of confidence that there are trustful aspects to a proposition that seeks to express all those complexities that architecture, as a practice, creates.

Proposition: Trust yourself.

Afterword

Constant Gardening

It can be argued that any architectural treatise that can be used as a model for further development needs clear directions. Clear directions in both form-making and theoretical context and discussion. Hopefully, there has been enough consistency and clarity within the previous set of propositions to understand context and then develop meaningful form. The varied content of this book could have been organized in any number of ways, so a decision had to be made whether the organization was encyclopaedic, random, from private to public or some other model. The ambition was to overlay a structure that borrowed from the complexities of a board game, referenced the organization of the Periodic Table of the elements and suggested further, alternate morphologies.

This was the ambition since the intention, at the outset, was to throw a net over a series of correlated ideas that outlined a landscape of concepts and opportunities. In some respects, the methodology of the book is as important as the content since by considering the minutiae of an idea and then positioning it in relation to others, it is possible to describe some of the over-determined aspects of how form and theory coincide in architecture. By using the mechanical constraints of the chess board as an artificial Cartesian landscape, coupled with the simple topological device of the Knight's Tour, it has been possible to generate a series of propinquitous relationships between concepts that ideally will serve as a further intuition pump for architectural ideas. To be clear though, this was not an arbitrary decision. Employing an organizational strategy that was an expression of exponential relationships mapped onto a playing domain ($2 \times 2 \times 2 \times 2 \times 2 \times 2$ or 2^6), camouflaged the overly 'mathematical' relationship of ideas. The mechanical adjacencies in the initial figure in The Knight's Tale Rebus (Rebus 1) are meant to act as intuition prompts to consider other categories that might influence the central proposition. The individual rebus figures that pre-figured each proposition are intended to illustrate this relationship.

Of course, particularly in the North American context, the use of a grid of squares, the nine-square problem, is well established as an introductory design challenge. The grid of 64 squares in the Knight's Tale Rebus is designed to emulate this process but on a significantly enhanced scale, with complex permutations and the opportunity to transition from a flat plane to a three-dimensional expression. To look at this three dimensionality and its evolution over time, we can consider a further mathematical organization that, as a tool of convenience, allows us to build on the 64 square pattern.

As architects we should, by now, be completely comfortable with the use of algorithms as models of behaviour, but we should always be open to the pliability of other strategies. These could be factorial, or even polynomial, algorithmic expressions and it is worth considering the developed model, pictured, that could be constructed using a combination of the planar organization of the Cartesian chequerboard with a vertical linking system such as a Lindenmayer System. The point is, if understood correctly and employed judiciously, systemic organization always carries the potential for richness and growth.

So the final, plus one, proposition is to create three planes that respectively signify inception, emergence and expression. Whether it works as a morphological representation of idea, form and reception ideation remains to be tested, but the point is that inevitably everything we characterize as non-standard, intuitive and randomized is, ultimately, systematically cultivated (like a rare orchid) for its qualities.

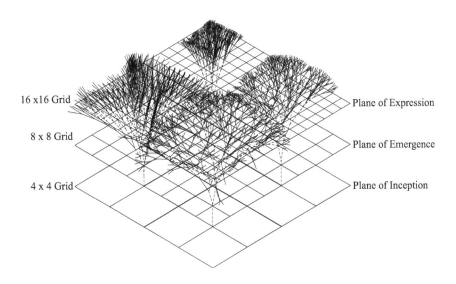

The Architect's Dream – L System

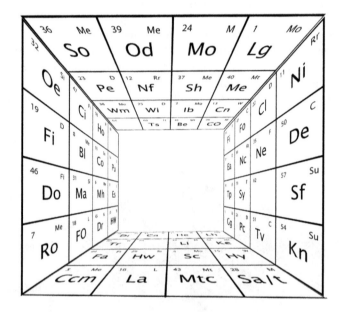

The Architect's Dream – After Serlio

Bibliography

Generally
While the bibliography contains citations for the texts referenced in the body of the book, there were/are many other non-fiction and fiction texts that have been addressed, however partially, in the current volume. These include, but are not limited to the personal selection below:

Books
Alpers, Svetlana (1983), *The Art of Describing: Dutch Art in the Seventeenth Century*, Chicago: The University of Chicago Press.
Bataille, Georges ([1928] 2001), *Story of the Eye (trans. J. Neugroschal)*, New York: Penguin Modern Classics, Urizen Books.
Carter, Paul (1987), *The Road to Botany Bay: An Exploration of Landscape and History, NED – new ed.*, Minnesota: University of Minnesota Press.
Danielewski, Mark Z. (2000), *House of Leaves*, London: Doubleday.
Derrida, Jacques ([1978] 1987), *The Truth in Painting*, 2nd ed., Chicago: The University of Chicago Press.
Eco, Umberto (1980), *The Name of the Rose*, Milan: Bompiani.
Foster, Hal (1996), *The Return of the Real: The Avant-Garde at the End of the Century*, Cambridge: The MIT Press.
Glaeser, Edward (2008), *Triumph of the City*, London: Pan Macmillan.
Hesse, Hermann ([1943] 1949), *The Glass Bead Game (trans. M. Savill)*, New York: Henry Holt & Co.
Hick, John (1985), *Evil and the God of Love*, London: Palgrave Macmillan.
Levi-Strauss, Claude ([1955] 1961), *Tristes Tropiques*, New York: Criterion Books.
Massumi, Brian (2002), *Parables for the Virtual: Movement, Affect, Sensation*, Durham and London: Duke University Press.
Murnaugh, Geoff (2009), *The BLDGBLOG Book*, San Francisco: Chronicle Books.
Nash, Roderick (1973), *Wilderness and the American Mind*, London: Yale University Press.
Nussbaum, Martha (1986), *The Fragility of Goodness, revised edition*, Chicago: The University of Chicago Press.
Vidler, Anthony (2000), *Warped Space: Art, Architecture, and Anxiety in Modern Culture*, Cambridge: MIT Press.
Visser, Margaret (1991), *The Rituals of Dinner*, London: Penguin Books.

Films
Garland, Alex [dir.] (2015), *Ex Machina*, Film4 and DNA Films.
German, Aleksi [dir.] (2013), *Hard to be a God*, Lenfilm Studio and Sever Studio.
Ho, Bong Joon [dir.] (2019), *Parasite*, Barunson E&A.
Lowery, David [dir.] (2017), *A Ghost Story*, Sailor Bear and Zero Trans Fat Productions.
Meirelles, Fernando and Lund, Katia [dirs] (2003), *City of God*, O2 Films.

Nicoll, Andrew [dir.] (1997), *Gattaca*, Columbia Pictures.
Tarkovsky, Andrei [dir.] (1979), *Stalker*, Mosfilm.
Tsukamoto, Shinya [dir.] (1989), *Tetsuo, The Iron Man*, Tsukamoto Shinya.

Introduction: The Knight's Tour
Berkman, Natalie (2020), 'Italo Calvino's Oulipian Clinamen', *MLN*, 135:1, pp. 255–80.
Hollis, Edward (2009), *The Secret Lives of Building, From the Ruins of the Parthenon to the Vegas Strip in Thirteen Stories*, London: Portobello Press Ltd.
Mitchell, Peta (2004), 'Constructing the architext: Georges Perec's *Life: A User's Manual*', *Mosaic: A Journal for the Interdisciplinary Study of Literature*, 37:1, pp. 1–16.

Proposition 1: The Large Glass
Ramírez, Juan Antonio (1998), 'Precision painting (bachelors even)', in *Duchamp, Love and Death, Even* (trans. A. R. Tulloch), California: Reaktion Books.

Proposition 2: Inside the Box
Perec, Georges ([1978] 2009), *Life: A User's Manual* (trans. D. Bellos), Paris: David R. Gondine.

Proposition 3: Life's Harvest
Canetti, Elias (1979), *Earwitness, Fifty Characters*, New York: Seabury Press.
Faccini, Dominic, Bataille, Georges, Leiris, Michel, Einstein, Carl and Griaule, Marcel (1992), 'Critical dictionary', *October*, 60, pp. 25–31.
Frazer, James Georges (2002), *The Golden Bough*, Abridged ed., Dover: DuPage County.
Kafka, Franz (1996), *Amerika* (trans. W. Muir and E. Muir), New York: Schocken.
Malinowski, Bronislaw (2014), *Argonauts of the Western Pacific*, London: Routledge.
Roussel, Raymond (2011), *Impressions of Africa* (trans. M. Polizzotti), Funks Grove: Dalkey Archive Press.
Taylor, William (2004), *The Vital Landscape*, New York: Taylor and Francis.
Warburg, Aby (2009), 'The absorption of the expressive values of the past', *Art in Translation*, 1:2, pp. 273–83 (*Aby Warburg's Mnemosyne Atlas*), https://warburg.library.cornell.edu/.

Proposition 4: Site Cycle
Bataille, Georges ([1928] 2001), *Story of the Eye* (trans. J. Neugroschal), New York: Penguin Modern Classics, Urizen Books.
Ebenstein, Joanna (2012), 'Ode to an anatomical Venus', *Women's Studies Quarterly*, 40:3&4, pp. 346–52.
Schama, Simon (1995), *Landscape and Memory*, Taylorsville: Vintage Edition.
Singer, Thomas (2004), 'In the manner of Duchamp, 1942–47: The years of the "Mirrorical Return"', *The Art Bulletin*, 86:2, pp. 346–69.

Proposition 5: Calvino's City of Memory
Calle, Sophie ([1980] 2014), *Suite Vénitienne*, New York: Siglio Press.
Calvino, Italo (1978), *The Castle of Crossed Destinies* (trans. W. Weaver), London: Picador.
Calvino, Italo (1974), *Invisible Cities* (trans. W. Weaver), London: Picador.
Eco, Umberto (2002), *Art and Beauty in the Middle Ages*, New Haven: Yale University Press.
Lean, David (1955), *Summertime*, USA: United Artists.
Perec, Georges ([1978] 2009), *Life: A User's Manual* (trans. D. Bellos), Paris: David R. Gondine.
Roeg, Nicholas (1973), *Don't Look Now*, UK: Casey Productions, Eldorado Films.
Rossi, Aldo (1982), *Architecture of the City*, London: MIT Press.

Proposition 6: The Machine of History
Libeskind, Daniel (1985), *Three Lessons in Architecture*, 'Progetto Venezia' (Dir. A. Rossi), Venice: Venice Biennale.
Libeskind, Daniel (1992), *Countersign*, New York: Rizzoli.
Yates, Frances (2001), *The Art of Memory*, London: Routledge and Kegan Paul.

Proposition 7: Redemptive Objects
Eagleton, Terry (1988), *The Ideology of the Aesthetic*, New York: Blackwell.
Lavin, Sylvia (2011), 'Architecture in extremis', *Log*, 22, pp. 51–61.
Loeckx, André and Heynen, Hilde (2020), 'Meaning and effect: Revisiting semiotics in architecture', in S. Loosen, R. Heynickx and H. Heynen (eds), *The Figure of Knowledge: Conditioning Architectural Theory, 1960s–1990s*, Leuven: Leuven University Press, pp. 31–62.
Markus, Gyorgy (2001), 'Walter Benjamin or: The commodity as Phantasmagoria', *New German Critique*, 83, pp. 3–42.
Marx, Karl (1991), *Capital*, vol. 1 (trans. B. Fowkes), London: Penguin Modern Classics.
Pool, Robert (1990), 'Fetishism deconstructed', *Etnofoor*, 3:1, pp. 114–27.

Proposition 8: Borges's Library
Bloch, William Goldbloom (2008), *The Unimaginable Mathematics of Borges' Library of Babel*, Oxford: Oxford University Press.
Lewandowski, Joseph D. (1999), 'Unpacking: Walter Benjamin and his library', *Libraries & Culture*, 34:2, pp. 151–57.
Tuckey, Curtis (2010), 'The imaginative mathematics of Bloch's *Unimaginable Mathematics of Borges's Library of Babel*', *Variaciones Borges*, 30, pp. 217–31.

Proposition 9: Glass and *Glas*
Broadfoot, Keith (2002), 'Perspective yet again: Damisch with Lacan', *Oxford Art Journal*, 25:1, pp. 73–94.
Blau, Eve (2007), 'Transparency and the irreconcilable contradictions of modernity', *PRAXIS: Journal of Writing Building*, 9, pp. 50–59.

Crary, Jonathan (1988), 'Techniques of the observer', *October*, 45, pp. 3–35.
Derrida, Jacques (1986), *Glas* (trans. J. P. Leavy Jr. and R. Rand), Nebraska: University of Nebraska Press.
Missac, Pierre (1996), *Walter Benjamin's Passages* (trans. S. W. Nicholson), London: MIT Press.
Vidler, Anthony (2005), 'Nothing to do with architecture', *Grey Room*, 21, pp. 112–27.

Proposition 10: *No* City
Brott, Simone (2012), 'Modernity's opiate, or, the crisis of iconic architecture', *Log*, 26, pp. 49–59.
Collins, Christine Caseman (2006), *Camillo Sitte: The Birth of Modern City Planning: With a Translation of the 1889 Austrian Edition of his City Planning According to Artistic Principles* (trans. C. C. Collins and G. R. Collins), Mineola: Dover Publications.
Dayer, Carolina (2016), 'A magic-real gap in architecture', *bfo—Journal*, 2, pp. 59–68.
Eisenscmidt, Alexander (2014), 'Metropolitan architecture: Karl Scheffler and Alfred Messel's search for a new urbanity', *Grey Room*, 56, pp. 90–115.
Endell, August (2014), 'The beauty of the metropolis', *Grey Room*, 56, Summer, pp. 116–38 (trans. Z. Ç. Alexander).
Köhler, Daniel (2017), 'Large city architecture: The mereological mode of the quantified city', *International Journal of Parallel, Emergent and Distributed Systems*, 32:1, pp. 163–72.
Neu, Jerome (1975), 'Levi-Strauss on Shamanism', *Man*, 10:2, pp. 285–92.
Sabatino, Michelangelo (2010), 'Remoteness and presentness: The primitive in modernist architecture', *Perspecta*, 43, pp. 139–89.

Proposition 11: *No* Interior
Aureli, Pier Vittorio and Giudici, Maria Shéhérazade (2016), 'Familiar horror: Toward a critique of domestic space', *Log*, 38, pp. 105–29.
Benjamin, Walter (2002), 'Paris, capital of then nineteenth century', in H. Eiland and M. W. Jennings (eds), *Walter Benjamin, Selected Writings, Volume 3, 1935–1938* (trans. Jephcott et al.), Cambridge, London: The Belknap Press.
Eagleton, Terry (1988), *The Ideology of the Aesthetic*, London: Blackwell.
Markell, Patchen (2011), 'Arendt's work: On the architecture of "the human condition"', *College Literature*, 38:1, pp. 15–44.
Papapetros, Spyros (2012), 'Movements of the soul: Traversing animism, fetishism, and the uncanny', *Discourse*, 34:2&3, pp. 185–208.

Proposition 12: *No* Form
Cache, Bernard (1995), *Earth Moves*, London: MIT Press.
Elsner, Jas (2006), 'From empirical evidence to the big picture: Some reflections on Riegl's concept of *Kunstwollen*', *Critical Inquiry*, 32:4, pp. 741–66.
Lambert, Léopold (2012), 'Abject matter: The barricade and the tunnel', *Log*, 25, pp. 93–99.

Olin, Margaret (1989), 'Forms of respect: Alois Riegl's concept of attentiveness', *The Art Bulletin*, 71:2, pp. 285–99.

Proposition 13: Conflict

Bevan, Robert (2016), *The Destruction of Memory: Architecture at War*, second expanded ed. London: Reaktion.

Herscher, Andrew (2008), 'Warchitectural theory', *Journal of Architectural Education*, 61:3, pp. 35–43.

Herscher, Andrew (2014), 'In ruins: Architecture, memory, countermemory', *Journal of the Society of Architectural Historians*, 73:4, pp. 464–69.

Margry, Peter Jan and Sánchez-Carretero, Cristina (eds) (2011), *Grassroots Memorials: The Politics of Memorializing Traumatic Death*, 1st ed., New York: Berghahn Books.

Proposition 14: Healing

Anidjar, Gil (2019), 'On the political history of destruction', *ReOrient*, 4:2, pp. 144–65.

Ristic, Mirjana ([1978] 2014), '"Sniper Alley": The politics of urban violence in the Besieged Sarajevo', *Built Environment*, 40:3, pp. 342–56.

Weizman, Eyal (2012), 'Archaeology of the present: Organized crime through the study of urban built environments', *Journal of International Affairs*, 66:1, pp. 163–68.

Woods, Lebbeus (1997), *Radical Reconstruction*, New York: Princeton Architectural Press.

Proposition 15: Hygiene

Bolton, Matthew, Froese, Stephen and Jeffrey, Alex (2013), 'This space is occupied!: The politics of occupy Wall Street's expeditionary architecture and de-gentrifying urbanism', in E. Welty, M. Bolton, M. Nayak and C. Malone (eds), *Occupying Political Science*, New York: Palgrave Macmillan.

Rice, Louis (2013), 'Occupied space', *Architectural Design*, 83, pp. 70–75.

Tschumi, Bernard (1994), *Architecture and Disjunction*, London: MIT Press.

Proposition 16: Language

Alexander, Christopher, Ishikawa, Sara, Silverstein, Murray, Jacobson, Max, Fiksdahl, Ingrid and Shlomo, Angel (1977), *A Pattern Language: Towns, Building, Construction*, Oxford: Oxford University Press.

Austin, John L. ([1962] 1975), *How To Do Things with Words*, Oxford: Oxford University Press.

Chu, Karl (2004), 'Metaphysics of genetic architecture and computation', *Perspecta*, 35, pp. 74–97.

Frascari, Marco (1983), 'The Tell-the-Tale Detail', in J. N. Deely and M. D. Lenhart (eds), *Semiotics 1981*, Boston: Springer.

Patin, Thomas (1993), 'From deep structure to an architecture in suspense: Peter Eisenman, structuralism, and deconstruction', *Journal of Architectural Education*, 47:2, pp. 88–100.

Proposition 17: Ecological Symbiosis
Boysen, Benjamin (2018), 'The embarrassment of being human: A critique of new materialism and object-oriented ontology', *Orbis Litterarum*, 73:3, pp. 225–42.
DeLanda, Manual (n.d.), 'Deleuze and the open-ended becoming of the world', https://www.cddc.vt.edu/host/delanda/pages/becoming.htm.
Gage, Mark Foster (2015), 'Killing simplicity: Object-oriented philosophy in architecture', *Log*, 33, pp. 95–106.
Gannon, Todd, Harman, Graham, Ruy, David and Wiscombe, Tom (2015), 'The object turn: A conversation', *Log*, 33, pp. 73–94.
Matherne, Samantha (2014), 'Kant's expressive theory of music', *The Journal of Aesthetics and Art Criticism*, 72:2, pp. 129–45.
Harman, Graham (2020), 'What is object-oriented architecture', in J. Bedford (ed.), *Is There an Object-Oriented*, London: Bloomsbury.
Zahavi, Dan (2016), 'The end of what? Phenomenology vs. speculative realism', *International Journal of Philosophical Studies*, 24:3, pp. 289–309.

Proposition 18: Flat Out
Gontarski, S. E. (1980) 'Beckett's voice crying in the wilderness, from "Kilcool" to "Not I"', *The Papers of the Bibliographical Society of America*, 74:1, pp. 27–47.
Libeskind, Daniel (1990), 'Between the lines: Extension to the Berlin Museum, with the Jewish Museum', in *Assemblage*, no. 12, London: MIT Press, pp. 18–57.
Venturi, Robert, Scott Brown, Denise and Izenour, Steven (1972), *Learning From Las Vegas*, London: MIT Press.

Proposition 19: Fire
Harris, Anne (2015), 'Pyromena: Fire's doing', in J. J. Cohen and L. Duckert (eds), *Elemental Ecocriticism: Thinking with Earth, Air, Water, and Fire*, Minnesota: University of Minnesota Press, pp. 27–54.
Hegarty, Paul (2008), 'On fire: The city's accursed share', *Log*, 11, pp. 49–62.
Kant, Immanuel ([1790] 1987), *Critique of Judgement* (trans. W. S. Pluhar), Indianapolis, Cambridge: Hackett Publishing.
Zografos, Stamatis (2019), 'Architecture and fire', in *Architecture and Fire: A Psychoanalytic Approach to Conservation*, London: UCL Press, pp. 88–123.

Proposition 20: Plato's Cave
ARM Architecture, Ashton, Steve, Engberg, Juliana, Mackenzie, Andrew, McBride-Stephens, Lily, McDougall, Ian, Raggatt, Howard and Starkey, Lisa (2015), *Mongrel Rapture* (eds M. Raggatt and M. Ward), Melbourne: URO Publications.
Plato (375 BCE), *Republic*, Available at Project Gutenberg: https://www.gutenberg.org/files/1497/1497-h/1497-h.htm. Accessed 20 July 2020.
Plato (360 BCE), *Sophist*, Available at Project Gutenberg: https://www.gutenberg.org/files/1735/1735-h/1735-h.htm. Accessed 23 July 2020.

Proposition 21: Earth
Carter, Paul (1987), *The Road to Botany Bay: An Exploration of Landscape and History*, NED – new ed., Minnesota: University of Minnesota Press.
DeLillo, Don (1989), *The Names*, Taylorsville: Vintage.
Morris, Matthew J. (1989), 'Murdering words: Language in action in Don DeLillo's *The Names*', *Contemporary Literature*, 30:1, pp. 113–27.
Taylor, Ken (1992), 'A symbolic Australian landscape: Images in writing and painting', *Landscape Journal*, 11:2, pp. 127–43.
Van Sant, Gus [Dir.] (2002), *Gerry*, USA: Epsilon Motion Pictures, My Cactus, Tango Films.

Proposition 22: Clouds
Berman, Marshall (1982), *All That is Solid Melts Into Air: The Experience of Modernity*, London: Verso.
Blanciak, Francois (2008), *SITELESS: 1001 Building Forms*, London: MIT Press.
Di Palma, Vittoria (2006), 'Blurs, blots and clouds: Architecture and the dissolution of the surface', *AA Files*, 54, pp. 24–35.
Gleick, James (1987), *Chaos, Making a New Science*, New York: Viking Books.
Helen, Evans and Heiko, Hansen (2014), 'On the modification of man-made clouds: The factory cloud', *Leonardo*, 47:1, pp. 72–73.
Reiser, Jesse and Umamoto, Nanako (2006), *Atlas of Novel Tectonics*, Princeton: Princeton Architectural Press.
Slater, A. W. (1972), 'Luke Howard, F.R.S. (1772–1864) and his relations with Goethe', *Notes and Records of the Royal Society of London*, 27:1, pp. 119–40.

Proposition 23: Perversions
Greenway, Peter (1982), *The Draughtsman's Contract*, UK: British Film Institute (BFI), Channel Four Television.
Hitchcock, Alfred [Dir.] (1954), *Rear Window*, USA: Alfred J. Hitchcock Productions.
Jay, Martin (1988), 'The scopic regimes of modernity', in H. Foster (ed.), *Vision and Visuality*, Seattle: DIA Art Foundation, Bay Press, pp. 3–28.
Kaufmann, Emil (1952), 'Three revolutionary architects, Boullée, Ledoux, and Lequeu', *Transactions of the American Philosophical Society*, 42:3, pp. 431–564.
Miklitsch, Robert (1996), 'The commodity-body-sign: Toward a general economy of "Commodity Fetishism"', *Cultural Critique*, 33, pp. 5–40.
Schneider, Peter (2004), 'Douglas Darden's "Sex Shop": An immodest proposal', *Journal of Architectural Education*, 58:2, pp. 9–13.

Proposition 24: Money
Jones, Wes (2010), 'Architecture games', *Log*, 19, pp. 29–35.
Kulkarni, Ankur A. (2017), 'Games and teams with shared constraints', *Philosophical Transactions: Mathematical, Physical and Engineering Sciences*, 375:2100, pp. 1–15.

Lawson, Julie, Pawson, Hal, Troy, Laurence, van der Nouwelant, Ryan and Hamilton, Carrie (2018), *Social housing as infrastructure: An investment pathway*, AHURI Final Report 306, Melbourne: Australian Housing and Urban Research Institute Limited.

Simmel, Georg ([1900] 2004), *The Philosophy of Money* (ed. D. Frisby, trans. T. Bottomore and D. Frisby, first draft by Kathe Mengelberg), London: Routledge.

Proposition 25: Wittgenstein

Cacciari, Massimo (1993), *Architecture and Nihilism: On the Philosophy of Modern Architecture*, New Haven: Yale University Press.

Kremer, Michael (2000), 'Wilson on Kripke's Wittgenstein', *Philosophy and Phenomenological Research*, 60:3, pp. 571–84.

Kripke, Saul (1982), *Wittgenstein on Rules and Private Language: An Elementary Exposition*, Cambridge: Harvard University Press.

Last, Nana (1998), 'Transgressions and inhabitations: Wittgensteinian spatial practices between architecture and philosophy', *Assemblage*, 35, pp. 37–47.

Lombardo, Patrizia (2003), *Cities, Words and Images*, London: Palgrave Macmillan UK. Language, Discourse, Society.

Pook, David Olson (1994), 'Working on oneself: Wittgenstein's architecture, ethics and aesthetics', *Symplokē*, 2:1, pp. 48–82.

Wittgenstein, Ludwig (1968), *Philosophical Investigations* (trans. G. E. M. Anscombe), New York: MacMillan Publishing Co.

Wittgenstein, Ludwig (2001), *Tractatus Logico-Philosophicus* (trans. D. F. Pears and B. F. McGuinness), London: Routledge.

Proposition 26: Contractual Obligation

Buchloh, Benjamin H. D. (1990), 'Conceptual art 1962–1969: From the aesthetic of administration to the critique of institutions', *October*, 55, pp. 105–43.

De Donder, Philippe and Hindriks, Jean (2009), 'Adverse selection, moral hazard and propitious selection', *Journal of Risk and Uncertainty*, 38:1, pp. 73–86.

Dickie, George (1975), 'What is anti-art?', *The Journal of Aesthetics and Art Criticism*, 33:4, pp. 419–21.

Samuelson, Larry (2016), 'Game theory in economics and beyond', *The Journal of Economic Perspectives*, 30:4, pp. 107–30.

Siegelaub, Seth (1973), 'The artist's reserved rights transfer and sale agreement', *Leonardo*, 6:4, pp. 347–50.

Small, Irene V. (2009), 'Believing in art: The votive structures of conceptual art', *RES: Anthropology and Aesthetics*, 55/56, pp. 294–307.

Proposition 27: Life

Castle, Helen (2004), 'Emergence in architecture', *AA Files*, 50, pp. 50–61.

Chu, Karl (2004), 'Metaphysics of genetic architecture and computation', *Perspecta*, 35, pp. 74–97.

Cogdell, Christina (2018), 'Morphogenesis and evolutionary computation', in *Toward a Living Architecture?: Complexism and Biology in Generative Design*, Minneapolis, London: University of Minnesota Press, pp. 103–42.
Foucault, Michel ([1978] 2006), *The Will to Knowledge* (trans. R. Hurley), New York: Penguin.
Frichot, Hélène (2011), 'Drawing, thinking, doing: From diagram work to the superfold', *Access: Contemnporary Issues in Education*, 30:1, pp. 1–10.
Frichot, Hélène (2013), 'Deleuze and the story of the superfold', in H. Frichot and S. Loo (eds), *Deleuze and Architecture*, Edinburgh: Edinburgh University Press, pp. 79–95.
Hensel, Michael, Menges, Achim and Weinstock, Michael ([2004–06] 2013), 'Morphogenesis and emergence', in M. Carpo (ed.), *The Digital Turn in Architecture 1992–2012*, New York: John Wiley & Sons Ltd.
Weinstock, Michael (2010), *The Architecture of Emergence: The Evolution of Form in Nature and Civilisation*, Chichester: Wiley.

Proposition 28: Site Affectivity/Transgressions
Houellebecq, Michel ([2010] 2012), *The Map and the Territory* (trans. G. Bowd), Taylorsville: Vintage.
Morrey, Douglas (2013), 'Work and leisure', in *Michel Houellebecq: Humanity and Its Aftermath*, Liverpool: Liverpool University Press, pp. 65–113.
Murnaugh, Geoff (2016), *_applyChinaLocationShift/*, 1 March, https://www.bldgblog.com/2016/03/_applychinalocationshift/
Weizman, Eyal and Herscher, Andrew (2011), 'Conversation: Architecture, violence, evidence', *Future Anterior: Journal of Historic Preservation, History, Theory, and Criticism*, 8:1, pp. 111–23.
Weizman, Eyal (2007), *Hollow Land*, London: Verso.

Proposition 29: Highway
Barron, Patrick and Mariani, Manuela (2014), *Terrain Vague: Interstices at the Edge of the Pale*, 1st ed. (eds M. Mariani and P. Barron), New York: Routledge.
Bratton, Denise and Clément, Gilles (2008), 'An interview with Gilles Clément', *Log*, 12, pp. 81–90.
Buck, Holly Jean (2015), 'On the possibilities of a charming anthropocene', *Annals of the Association of American Geographers*, 105:2, pp. 369–77.
Gandy, Matthew (2013), 'Marginalia: Aesthetics, ecology, and urban wastelands', *Annals of the Association of American Geographers*, 103:6, pp. 1301–16.
Harrison, Ariane Lourie (2013), *Architectural Theories of the Environment: Posthuman Territory* (ed. A. L. Harrison), New York: Routledge.
Landry, Olivia (2018), 'Accelerating performance: From car travel to car crash', in *Movement and Performance in Berlin School Cinema*, Bloomington: Indiana University Press, pp. 108–56.
Toland, Andrew (2020), 'Dirtying the real: Liane Lefaivre and the architectural stalemate with emerging realities', in S. Loosen, R. Heynickx and H. Heynen (eds), *The Figure of*

Knowledge: Conditioning Architectural Theory, 1960s–1990s, Leuven: Leuven University Press, pp. 181–94.
Tzonis, Alexander and Lefaivre, Liane (2016). 'Dirty realism: Making the stone stony', in *Times of Creative Destruction: Shaping Buildings and Cities in the late C20th (1990)*, 1st ed., London: Routledge.

Proposition 30: High Way
Battin, Justin Michael and Duarte, German A. (2018), *We Need to Talk about Heidegger*, Frankfurt A.M.: Peter Lang GmbH, Internationaler Verlag Der Wissenschaften.
Joronen, Mikko (2013), 'Heidegger, event and the ontological politics of the site', *Transactions of the Institute of British Geographers*, 38, pp. 627–38, https//:doi.org/10.1111/j.1475-5661.2012.00550.x.
Stang, Charles M. (2010), 'Digging holes and building pillars: Simeon Stylites and the "Geometry" of ascetic practice', *The Harvard Theological Review*, 103:4, pp. 447–70.
Turrell, James (n.d.) *Roden Crater*, https://rodencrater.com/. Accessed 17 November 2020.

Proposition 31: Manufactured
Allen, Stan (1999), *Points + Lines: Diagrams and Projects for the City*, New York: Princeton Architectural.
Gissen, David (2008), 'Architecture's geographic turns', *Log*, 12, pp. 59–67.
McEwan, Cameron (2020), 'The field as a critical project', *Building Material*, 23, pp. 149–72.

Proposition 32: Other Ecologies
Böhme, Gernot (2018), *The Aesthetics of Atmospheres*, London: Routledge.
Gandy, Matthew (2017), 'Urban atmospheres', *Cultural Geographies*, 24:3, pp. 353–74.
Stalder, Laurent and Denton, Jill (2010), 'Air, light, and air-conditioning', *Grey Room*, 40, pp. 84–99.
Stewart, Kathleen (2011), 'Atmospheric attunements', *Environment and Planning D: Society and Space*, 29:3, pp. 445–53.
Trigg, Dylan (2012), *The Memory of Place: A Phenomenology of the Uncanny*, Athens: Ohio University Press.

Proposition 33: Synaesthetic
D'Orazio, Dario, Fratoni, Giulia, Rossi, E. and Garai, Massimo (2020), 'Understanding the acoustics of St. John's Baptistery in Pisa through a virtual approach', *Journal of Building Performance Simulation*, 13:3, pp. 320–33.
Jencks, Charles (2013), 'Architecture becomes music', *The Architectural Review*, 233:1395, p. 91.
Libeskind, Daniel (1990), 'Between the lines: Extension to the Berlin Museum, with the Jewish Museum', *Assemblage*, 12, pp. 19–57.
Robinson, Jenefer (2012), 'On being moved by architecture', *The Journal of Aesthetics and Art Criticism*, 70:4, pp. 337–53.
Wheatley, John (2007), 'The sound of architecture', *Tempo*, 61:242, pp. 11–19.

Young, James E. (2000), 'Daniel Libeskind's Jewish Museum in Berlin: The uncanny arts of memorial architecture', *Jewish Social Studies*, 6:2, pp. 1–23.

Proposition 34: Fidelity

Hall, David (n.d.), 'Cornelius Cardew's *Treatise*', http://davidhall.io/treatise-score-graphic-notation/; https://www.youtube.com/watch?v=Rp_O6QPz7pQ.

Pujadas, Magda Polo (2018), 'Philosophy of music: Wittgenstein and Cardew', *Revista Portuguesa De Filosofia*, 74:4, pp. 1425–36.

Shea Trahan's work can be accessed at: https://www.sheatrahan.com/project-1.

Xenakis, Iannis (1971), *Formalized Music: Thought and Mathematics in Composition* (trans. C. Butchers, G. W. Hopkins and Mr and Mrs J. Challifour), Bloomington, London: Indiana University Press.

Zimoun's work can be accessed at: https://www.zimoun.net/.

Proposition 35: Non-Euclidean

Barczik, Günter, Lordick, Daniel and Labs, Oliver (2011), 'Algebraic expansions: Broadening the scope of architectural design through algebraic surfaces', in C. Gengnagel, A. Kilian, N. Palz and F. Scheurer (eds), *Computational Design Modelling*, Berlin, Heidelberg: Springer.

Chiappone-Piriou, Emmanuelle (2020), 'Uncertainty and poetic inhabitation: Or how to articulate chance', *Contour Journal*, 5, pp. 1–14.

Dawes, Michael J. and Ostwald, Michael J. (2013), 'Applications of graph theory in architectural analysis: Past, present and future research', in *Graph Theory: New Research*, pp. 1–36.

De Bruyn, Eric (2006), 'Topological pathways of post-minimalism', *Grey Room*, 25, pp. 32–63.

Panofsky, Erwin ([1927] 1997), *Perspective as Symbolic Form* (trans. C. S. Wood), Princeton: Princeton Architectural Press.

Perez-Gomez, Alberto (1982), 'Architecture as drawing', *JAE*, 36:2, pp. 2–7.

Pérez Gómez, Alberto and Pelletier, Louise (1997), *Architectural Representation and the Perspective Hinge*, Cambridge: MIT Press.

Shields, Rob (2012), 'Cultural topology: The seven bridges of Königsburg, 1736', *Theory, Culture & Society*, 29:4&5, pp. 43–57.

Proposition 36: Soap

Abrons, Ellie (2017), 'For real', *Log*, 41, pp. 67–73.

Barthes, Roland ([1957] 1972), *Mythologies* (trans. A. Lavers), New York: Paladin.

Sontag, Susan (1978), *Against Interpretation: And Other Essays*, New York: Octagon.

Sudjic, Deyan (2001), 'Australia looks back in allegory at its inglorious past', *The Guardian*, 4 March 2001.

Proposition 37: Shopping

The work of The Jerde Partnership Inc. can be accessed at: jerde.com.

Alba, Joseph W. and Williams, Elanor F. (2013), 'Pleasure principles: A review of research on hedonic consumption', *Journal of Consumer Psychology*, 23:1, pp. 2–18.

Chung, C. J. et al. (eds) (2001), *Harvard Design School Guide to Shopping*, Köln: Taschen; Cambridge: Harvard Design School.

Mirgani, Suzi (2017), *Target Markets – International Terrorism Meets Global Capitalism in the Mall*, Bielefeld: transcript.

Proposition 38: Working Models

Bunschoten, Raoul (1985), 'Wor(l)ds of Daniel Libeskind, Daniel Libeskind: *Theatrum Mundi/Three Lessons in Architecture*', *AA Files*, 10, pp. 79–88.

Daniel Libeskind's *3 Lessons in Architecture* can be accessed at: https://libeskind.com/work/cranbrook-machines/.

Eco, Umberto ([1973] 1990), *Travels in Hyperreality* (trans. W. Weaver), New York: Mariner.

Frascari, Marco (1985), 'Carlo Scarpa in Magna Graecia: The Abatellis Palace in Palermo', *AA Files*, 9, pp. 3–9.

Frascari, Marco (1989), 'A heroic and admirable machine: The theater of the architecture of Carlo Scarpa, Architetto Veneto', *Poetics Today*, 10:1, pp. 103–26.

Proposition 39: Odysseus

Benjamin, Walter ([1928] 1998), *The Origin of German Tragic Drama (Ursprung des deutsche Trauerspiel)* (trans. J. Osborne), London: Verso.

Fleming, Katie (2012), 'Odysseus and enlightenment: Horkheimer and Adorno's *Dialektik Der Aufklärung*', *International Journal of the Classical Tradition*, 19:2, pp. 107–28.

Klibinsky, Raymond, Panofsky, Erwin and Saxl, Fritz (2019), *Saturn and Melancholy, Studies in the History of Natural Philosophy, Religion and Art*, Montreal: McGill Queen's University Press.

Morowitz, Laura (2018), 'Waking from the dream: The Arcades Project, Copia, and the American Consumer', *Cultural Critique*, 101, pp. 1–36.

Osman, Michael (2005), 'Benjamin's Baroque', *Thresholds*, 28, pp. 119–49.

Spurr, David (2012), *Architecture and Modern Literature*, Ann Arbor: University of Michigan Press.

Proposition 40: Metamorphosis

Barolsky, Paul (2005), 'Ovid, Bernini, and the art of petrification', *Arion: A Journal of Humanities and the Classics*, 13:2, pp. 149–62.

Kelly, Peter (2014), 'Voices within Ovid's House of "Fama"', *Mnemosyne*, 67:1, pp. 65–92.

Singley, Paulette (2015), 'Fear of figures', *Log*, 35, pp. 69–79.

Wilkins, Ann Thomas (2000), 'Bernini and Ovid: Expanding the concept of metamorphosis', *International Journal of the Classical Tradition*, 6:3, pp. 383–408.

Proposition 41: Bestiary

Borges, Jorge Luis ([1942] 1964), 'The analytical language of John Wilkins', in *Other Inquisitions 1937–1952* (trans. R. L. C. Simms), Austin: University of Texas Press.

Bruns, Gerald L. (2007), 'Becoming-animal (some simple ways)', *New Literary History*, 38:4, pp. 703–20.

Deleuze, Gilles and Guattari, Félix ([1980] 1987), *Thousand Plateaus, Capitalism and Schizophrenia* (trans. B. Massumi), London: Bloomsbury.

Foucault, Michel (1970), *The Order of Things: An Archaeology of the Human Sciences (Les Mots et les choses)* (trans. unknown), London: Routledge.

Proposition 42: Kennels

Chrulew, Matthew (2013), 'Preventing and giving death at the zoo: Heini Hediger's *Death Due to Behaviour*', in J. Johnston and F. Probyn-Rapsey (eds), *Animal Death*, Sydney: Sydney University Press, pp. 221–38.

Holtore, Cornelius (2013), 'The zoo as a realm of memory', *Anthropological Journal of European Cultures*, 22:1, pp. 98–114.

Pendakis, Andrew (2020), 'Suburbs', in C. Howe and A. Pandian (eds), *Anthropocene Unseen: A Lexicon*, Santa Barbara: Punctum Books, pp. 447–51.

Thornburg, Ann Marie (2020), 'Dog', in C. Howe and A. Pandian (eds), *Anthropocene Unseen: A Lexicon*, Santa Barbara: Punctum Books, pp. 111–15.

Proposition 43: Mechanization takes command

Banham, Reyner (1969), *The Architecture of the Well-Tempered Environment*, London: Architectural Press.

Giedion, Siegfried (1967), *Space, Time and Architecture: The Growth of a New Tradition*, 5th ed., Rev. and Enl. ed., Cambridge: Harvard University Press.

Giedion, Siegfried (1969), *Mechanization Takes Command: A Contribution to Anonymous History*, New York: Norton.

Lobsinger, Mary Louise (2016), 'Architectural history: The turn from culture to media', *Journal of the Society of Architectural Historians*, 75:2, pp. 135–39.

Tallack, Douglas (1994), 'Siegfried Giedion, modernism and American material culture', *Journal of American Studies*, 28:2, pp. 149–67.

Proposition 44: Future Archaeology

Fischer, Ole W. (2011), 'Afterimage: A comparative rereading of postmodernism', *Log*, 21, pp. 107–18.

Harrison, Rodney (2016), 'Archaeologies of emergent presents and futures', *Historical Archaeology*, 50:3, pp. 165–80.

Huyssen, Andreas (2006), 'Nostalgia for ruins', *Grey Room*, 23, pp. 6–21.

Pallasmaa, Juhani (2016), 'Matter, hapticity and time material imagination and the voice of matter', *Building Material*, 20, pp. 171–89.

Proposition 45: Dreams

Jameson, Fredric (2005), *Archaeologies of the Future, The Desire Called Utopia and Other Science Fictions*, London, New York: Verso.

Jorgensen, Darren (2017), 'Anti-Utopianism and Fredric Jameson's archaeologies of the future', in *Colloquy: Text Theory Critique*, vol. 14, Monash: Monash University Press.

Milner, Andrew (2014), *Locating Science Fiction*, Liverpool: Liverpool University Press.
Pike, David (2016), 'Commuting to another world: Spaces of transport and transport maps in urban fantasy', in *Popular Fiction and Spatiality*, New York: Palgrave Macmillan US, pp. 141–56.
Wegner, Phillip E. (2007), 'Jameson's modernisms; or, the desire called Utopia', *Diacritics*, 37:4, pp. 3–20.

Proposition 46: Doppelgänger
Kant, Immanuel (2009), *Dreams of a Spirit-Seer*, illustrated by those of Metaphysics, Charleston: Bibliobazaar.
Nolan, Christopher [Dir.] (2010), *Inception*, Burbank:Warner Bros.
Pérez-Gómez, Alberto (1992), *Polyphilo or the Dark Forest Revisited, An Erotic Epiphany of Architecture*, London: MIT Press.
Rukgaber, Matthew (2018), 'Immaterial spirits and the reform of first philosophy: The compatibility of Kant's pre-critical metaphysics with the arguments in *Dreams of a Spirit-Seer*', *Journal of the History of Ideas*, 79:3, pp. 363–83.
Saramago, José (2004), *The Double* (trans. M. J. Costa), New York: Penguin.
Stroud, Scott R. (2016), 'Style and spirit in *Dreams of a Spirit-Seer*: Swedenborg and the origin of Kant's critical rhetoric', *CR: The New Centennial Review*, 16:3, pp. 1–32.
Villeneuve, Denis [Dir.] (2013), *Enemy*, Toronto: Pathé, Entertainment One, Rhombus Media.

Proposition 47: Cinema
Ramirez, Juan Antonio (1992), 'Ten lessons (or commandments) about architecture in the cinema', *Design Book Review*, 24, pp. 9–12.
Bensmaïa, Réda (2005), 'On the "Spiritual Automaton", space and time in modern cinema according to Gilles Deleuze', in I. Buchanan and G. Lambert (eds), *Deleuze and Space*, Edinburgh: Edinburgh University Press, pp. 144–58.
Brott, Simone (2013), 'Toward a theory of the architectural subject', in H. Frichot and S. Loo (eds), *Deleuze and Architecture*, Edinburgh: Edinburgh University Press, pp. 151–67.
Deamer, David (2016), *Deleuze's Cinema Books: Three Introductions to the Taxonomy of Images*, Edinburgh: Edinburgh University Press.
Deleuze, Gilles (1986), *Cinema 1: The Movement-Image* (trans. H. Tomlinson and B. Habberjam), Minnesota: University of Minnesota Press.
Deleuze, Gilles (1989), *Cinema 2: The Time-Image* (trans. H. Tomlinson and R. Galeta), Minnesota: University of Minnesota Press.
Grosz, Elizabeth (2003), 'Deleuze, theory, and space', *Log*, 1, pp. 77–86.
Pallasmaa, Juhani (2011), *The Embodied Image: Imagination and Imagery in Architecture*, Chichester: John Wiley & Sons.
Lang, Fritz [Dir.] (1927), *Metropolis*, Germany: Universum Film (UFA).
McTiernan, John [Dir.] (1988), *Die Hard*, Los Angeles: Twentieth Century Fox, Gordon Company, Silver Pictures.
Nikolov, Nik (2008), 'Cinemarchitecture: Explorations into the scopic regime of architecture', *Journal of Architectural Education*, 62:1, pp. 41–45.

Tobe, Renee (2017), *Film, Architecture and Spatial Imagination*, Milton Park, Abingdon, Oxon, New York: Routledge.
Scott, Ridley [Dir.] (1982), *Bladerunner*, Los Angeles: The Ladd Company, Shaw Brothers, Warner Bros.

Proposition 48: The Puzzle
Alber, Jan (2017), 'Introduction: The ideological ramifications of narrative strategies', *Storyworlds: A Journal of Narrative Studies*, 9:1&2, pp. 3–25.
Anderson, Thom [Dir.] (2003), *Los Angeles Plays Itself*, Thom Andersen Productions, Los Angeles, United States.
Argento, Dario [Dir.] (1977), *Suspiria*, Rome: Seda Spettacoli.
Buckland, Warren (2014), *Hollywood Puzzle Films*, London: Routledge.
Cavell, Stanley (2004), *Cities of Words: Pedagogical Letters on a Register of the Moral Life*, Cambridge: Harvard University Press.
Chenal, Pierre (1930), *L'architecture d'aujourd'hui*, Review *Architecture d'aujourd'hui*, Paris, France.
Godard, Jean Luc [Dir.] (1963), *Mepris*, Rome, France: Rome Paris Films, Les Films Concordia, Compagnia Cinematographica Champion.
Hanson, Christopher (2018), 'Case studies', in *Game Time: Understanding Temporality in Video Games*, Bloomington: Indiana University Press, pp. 156–89.
Hegglund, Jon (2013), 'Patrick Keiller's ambient narratives: Screen ecologies of the built environment', *Interdisciplinary Studies in Literature and Environment*, 20:2, pp. 274–95.
Keiller, Patrick (1994), *London*, London: Koninck Studios, BFI Production.
Keiller, Patrick (1997), *Robinson in Space*, London: Koninck Studios, British Broadcasting Corporation (BBC).
Kim, Nam, Bach, Benjamin, Im, Hyejin, Schriber, Sasha, Gross, Markus and Pfister, Hanspeter (2017), 'Visualizing nonlinear narratives with story curves', *IEEE Transactions on Visualization and Computer Graphics*, 24:1, pp. 595–604.
Night Shyamalan, M. [Dir.] (1999), *The Sixth Sense*, Los Angeles: Hollywood Pictures, Spyglass Entertainment, The Kennedy/Marshall Company,
Nolan, Christopher [Dir.] (2000), *Memento*, Los Angeles: Newmarket Capital Group, Team Todd, I Remember Productions.
Nolan, Christopher [Dir.] (2010), *Inception*, Los Angeles: Warner Bros, Legendary Entertainment, Syncopy.
Panek, Elliot (2006), 'The poet and the detective: Defining the psychological puzzle film', *Film Criticism*, 31:1&2, pp. 62–88.
Polanski, Roman [Dir.] (1994), *Una pura formalità*, Paris: Cecchi Gori Group Tiger Cinematografica, DD Productions, Film Par Film.
Riche, Nathalie Henry, Hurter, Christophe, Diakopoulos, Nicholas and Carpendale, Sheelagh (eds) (2018), *Data-Driven Storytelling*, Natick: AK Peters, CRC Press.
Scorsese, Martin [Dir.] (2010), *Shutter Island*, Los Angeles: Paramount Pictures, Phoenix Pictures, Sikelia Productions.

Schöning, Pascal (2006), *Manifesto for a Cinematic Architecture*, London: Architectural Association Publications.
Singer, Brian [Dir.] (1995), *The Usual Suspects*, Los Angeles: Polygram Filmed Entertainment, Spelling Films International, Blue Parrot.

Proposition 49: Forgeries
Casement, William (2020), 'Is it a forgery? Ask a semanticist', *The Journal of Aesthetic Education*, 54:1, pp. 51–68.
Eagleton, Terry (1988), 'The ideology of the aesthetic', *Poetics Today*, 9:2, pp. 327–38.
Esquíroz, Josean Ruiz (2018), 'Un/dressing Mies', *Log*, 43, pp. 9–15.
Irvin, Sherri (2007), 'Forgery and the corruption of aesthetic understanding', *Canadian Journal of Philosophy*, 37:2, pp. 283–304.
Lagueux, Maurice (1998), 'Nelson Goodman and architecture', *Assemblage*, 35, pp. 19–35.
Werning, Remei Capdevila (2014), *Goodman for Architects*, vol. 10, London: Routledge.

Proposition 50: Detectives
Bloch, Ernst, Mueller, Roswitha and Thaman, Stephen (1980), 'A philosophical view of the detective novel', *Discourse*, 2, pp. 32–52.
Kulper, Perry (2020), 'A (drawn) practice(d) construction: Relational structuring, chased', in M. Butcher and M. O'Shea (eds), *Expanding Fields of Architectural Discourse and Practice: Curated Works from the P.E.A.R. Journal*, London: UCL Press, pp. 192–213.
Nealon, Jeffrey T. (1996), 'Work of the detective, work of the writer: Paul Auster's *City Of Glass*', *Modern Fiction Studies*, 42:1, pp. 91–110.
Větrovský, Jaroslav (2018), 'Mens Rea, intentionality and Wittgenstein's philosophy of psychology', in M. Bergsmo and E. J. Buis (eds), *Philosophical Foundations of International Criminal Law: Correlating Thinkers*, Brussels: Torkel Opsahl Academic EPublisher.

Proposition 51: TV Eye
Bell, David (2011), 'The irritation of architecture', *Journal of Architectural Education*, 64:2, pp. 113–26.
Brantingham, Patricia (2011), 'Crime and place: Rapidly evolving research methods in the 21st century', *Cityscape*, 13:3, pp. 199–203.
Cooper, Mark Garrett (2003), 'The contradictions of *Minority Report*', *Film Criticism*, 28:2, pp. 24–41.
Denison, Edward (2014), 'Crime against architecture', *AA Files*, 68, pp. 61–68.
Dick, Phillip K. (2013), *The Minority Report (Collected Stories of Phillip K. Dick)*, Burton: Subterranean Press.
Rondeau, Mary Beth, Brantingham, Patricia L. and Brantingham, Paul J. (2005), 'The value of environmental criminology for the design professions of architecture, urban design, landscape architecture, and planning', *Journal of Architectural and Planning Research*, 22:4, pp. 294–304.
Spielberg, Steven [Dir.] (2002), *Minority Report*, Los Angeles: Twentieth Century Fox, Dreamworks Pictures, Cruise/Wagner Productions.

Weizman, Eyal (2012), 'Archaeology of the present: Organized crime through the study of urban built environments', *Journal of International Affairs*, 66:1, pp. 163–68.

Proposition 52: Punishment

Bagaric, Mirko, Hunter, Dan and Wolf, Gabrielle (2018), 'Technological incarceration and the end of the prison crisis', *The Journal of Criminal Law and Criminology*, 108:1, pp. 73–135.

Bonds, Anne (2013), 'Economic development, racialization, and privilege: Yes in my backyard prison politics and the reinvention of Madras, Oregon', *Annals of the Association of American Geographers*, 103:6, pp. 1389–405.

Dwork, Deborah and Van Pelt, Robert Jan (1997), *Auschwitz, 1270 to the Present*, London: Norton.

Eisen, Lauren-Brooke (2018), 'The prison industrial complex', in *Inside Private Prisons: An American Dilemma in the Age of Mass Incarceration*, New York: Columbia University Press, pp. 68–78.

Hays, K. Michael (2016), 'Architecture's appearance and the practices of imagination', *Log*, 37, pp. 204–13.

Hirst, Paul (1993), 'Foucault and architecture', *AA Files*, 26, pp. 52–60.

Kindynis, Theo (2014), 'Ripping up the map: Criminology and cartography reconsidered', *The British Journal of Criminology*, 54:2, pp. 222–43.

Moran, Dominique and Jewkes, Yvonne (2015), 'Linking the carceral and the punitive state: A review of research on prison architecture, design, technology and the lived experience of carceral space/Associer Les États Carcéral Et Punitif: Vers Une Recherche Sur L'architecture Carcérale, Conception Et Techniques D'aménagement De La Prison Et Le Vécu De L'espace Carcéral', *Annales De Géographie*, 124:702&703, pp. 163–84.

Thomsen, Russell (2015), 'The future of Auschwitz', *Perspecta*, 48, pp. 38–45.

Young, Rusty (2018), 'A law unto themselves: San Pedro Prison in La Paz, Bolivia', *Power and Justice: The Architectural Review*, 108:1452, June, https://www.architectural-review.com/essays/a-law-unto-themselves-san-pedro-prison-in-la-paz-bolivia.

Proposition 53: Cannibalism

Deamer, Peggy (1987), 'Adrian stokes and critical vision', *Assemblage*, 2, pp. 119–33.

Foster, Hal (1996), 'Obscene, abject, traumatic', *October*, 78, pp. 107–24.

King, C. Richard (2000), 'The (mis)uses of cannibalism in contemporary cultural critique', *Diacritics*, 30:1, pp. 106–23.

Kristeva, Julia (1982), *Powers of Horror, An Essay on Abjection*, New York: Columbia University Press.

Langer, Susan K. (1953), *Feeling and Form, A Theory of Art*, New York: Scribner and Sons.

Lavin, Sylvia (2011), 'Architecture in extremis', *Log*, 22, pp. 51–61.

Lester, David, White, John and Giordano, Brandi (2015), 'Cannibalism', *Omega: Journal of Death and Dying*, 70:4, pp. 428–35.

Ptacek, Melissa (2006), 'Sacrificing sacrifice', *Theory and Society*, 35:5&6, pp. 587–600.

Schiller, Britt-Marie (2020), 'Fantasies of cannibalism in the art of Louise Bourgeois', *American Imago*, 77:2, pp. 365–93.

Wollheim, Richard (2015), 'Seeing-as, seeing-in, and pictorial representation', in *Art and its Objects, Cambridge Philosophy Classics*, Cambridge: Cambridge University Press, pp. 137–51.

Proposition 54: Knots
Anderson, Gemma, Corti, Alessio and Buck, Dorothy (2015), 'Drawing in mathematics: From inverse vision to the liberation of form', *Leonardo*, 48:5, pp. 439–38.
Cogdell, Christina (2018), 'Self-organizing and emergent architecture', in *Toward a Living Architecture?: Complexism and Biology in Generative Design*, Minnesota: University of Minnesota Press, pp. 27–68.
Neuwirth, Lee (1979), 'The theory of knots', *Scientific American*, 240:6, pp. 110–25.
Jones, Wes (2014), 'Can tectonics grasp smoothness?', *Log*, 30, pp. 29–42.
Podro, Michael (1984), *The Critical Historians of Art*, New Haven: Yale University Press.
Semper, Gottfried ([1851] 1989), *The Four Elements of Architecture and Other Writings* (trans. H. F. Mallgrave and W. Herrmann), New York: Cambridge University Press.
Wölfflin, Heinrich ([1929] 1932), *Principles of Art History. The Problem of the Development of Style in Later Art* (trans. M. D. Hottinger), New York: Dover Publications.

Proposition 55: Collage
Aitchison, Mathew (2011), 'Who's afraid of Ivor De Wolfe?', *AA Files*, 62, pp. 34–39.
Endell, August (2014), 'The beauty of the metropolis', *Grey Room*, 56, Summer, pp 116–38 (trans. Z. Ç. Alexander).
Ockman, Joan (1998), 'Form without Utopia: Contextualizing Colin Rowe', *Journal of the Society of Architectural Historians*, 57:4, pp. 448–56.
Mozzato, Alioscia (2019), 'Colin Rowe and Aldo Rossi. Utopia as metaphor of a new city analogous to the existing one', in *Politics*, vol. 5, Bucharest: Ion Mincu University Press.
Tafuri, Manfredo (1976), *Architecture and Utopia: Design and Capitalist Development* (trans. B. L. La Penta), London: MIT Press.
Tafuri, Manfredo (1987), *The Sphere and the Labyrinth, Avant-Gardes and Architecture from Piranesi to the 1970s* (trans. P. d'Acierno and Robert Connolly), London: MIT Press.

Proposition 56: Discotheque
Carlini, Claudia M. and Sanchez, Zila M. (2018), 'Typology of nightclubs in São Paulo, Brazil: Alcohol and illegal drug consumption, sexual behavior and violence in the venues', *Substance Use & Misuse*, 53:11, pp. 1801–10.
Hebdige, Dick (1979), *Subculture, The Meaning of Style*, London: Routledge.
Munuera, Ivan L. (2017), 'An organism of hedonistic pleasures: The Palladium', *Log*, 41, pp. 102–12.
Reingle, Jennifer, Thombs, Dennis L., Weiler, Robert and Dodd, Virginia J. (2009), 'An exploratory study of bar and nightclub expectancies', *Journal of American College Health*, 57:6, pp. 629–38.

Tarr, Bronwyn, Launay, Jacques and Dunbar, Robin (2016), 'Silent disco: Dancing in synchrony leads to elevated pain thresholds and social closeness', *Evolution and Human Behavior: Official Journal of the Human Behavior and Evolution Society*, 37:5, pp. 343–49.

Proposition 57: Sfumato
Crary, Jonathan (1990), *Techniques of the Observer: On Vision and Modernity in the Nineteenth Century*, Southampton: October Books; London: MIT Press.
Lee, Paula Young (1998), 'Standing on the shoulders of giants: Boullée's "Atlas" Facade for the Bibliothèque Du Roi', *Journal of the Society of Architectural Historians*, 57:4, pp. 404–31.
Nagel, Alexander (1993), 'Leonardo and *Sfumato*', *RES: Anthropology and Aesthetics*, 24, pp. 7–20.
Nelson, Cami (2009), 'From *sfumato* to transarchitectures and "Osmose": Leonardo Da Vinci's virtual reality', *Leonardo*, 42:3, pp. 259–305.
Prendeville, Brendan (2013), 'A heartfelt gesture: Separation and feeling, darkness and illusion in Caravaggio', *Oxford Art Journal*, 36:2, pp. 185–206.

Proposition 58: Hope
Adorno, Theodor ([1966] 1973), *Negative Dialectics* (trans. E. B. Ashton), New York: Seabury Press.
Bloch, Ernst (1988), *The Utopian Function of Art and Literature* (trans. J. Zipes and F. Mecklenberg), London: MIT Press.
Bloch, Ernst (1995), *The Principle of Hope*, 3 vol. (trans. N. Plaice, S. Plaice and P. Knight), Cambridge: MIT Press.
Coleman, Nathaniel (2013), 'Building in empty spaces: Is architecture a "Degenerate Utopia"?', *The Journal of Architecture*, 18:2, pp. 135–66.
Harvey, David and Harvey, David W. (2000), *Spaces of Hope (California Studies in Critical Human Geography)*, Berkeley: University of California.

Proposition 59: Tractatus
Coeckelbergh, Mark and Funk, Michael (2018), 'Wittgenstein as a philosopher of technology: Tool use, forms of life, technique, and a transcendental argument', *Human Studies*, 41, pp. 165–91.
Jones, Wes (2010), 'Architecture games', *Log*, 19, pp. 29–35.
Karatani, Kojin (1995), *Architecture as Metaphor, Language, Number, Money* (trans. S. Kohso), Cambridge: MIT Press.
Last, Nana (1998), 'Transgressions and inhabitations: Wittgensteinian spatial practices between architecture and philosophy', *Assemblage*, 35, pp. 37–47.
Wittgenstein, Ludwig (1922), *Tractatus Logico-Philosophicus* (trans. C. K. Ogden), Trench, Trubner, London: Kegan Paul.

Proposition 60: Trust
De Filippi, Primavera, Mannan, Morshed and Reijers, Wessel (2020), 'Blockchain as a confidence machine: The problem of trust & challenges of governance', *Technology in Society*, 62, pp. 1–14.

Giddens, Anthony (1990), *The Consequences of Modernity*, New York: Wiley.
Madhavan, P. and Wiegmann, D. A. (2007), 'Similarities and differences between human–human and human–automation trust: An integrative review', *Theoretical Issues in Ergonomics Science*, 8:4, pp. 277–301.
Sumpf, P. (2019), 'Toward an "Architecture of Trust"', in *System Trust*, Wiesbaden: Springer VS.
Zacharias, Greg L. (2019), 'Tenets of trust', in *Autonomous Horizons: The Way Forward*, Montgomery: Air University Press, pp. 77–116.

Index

A

Abramović, Marina
The Artist is Present 150
Acconci, Vito
Artist's Shit 303
Seed Bed 303
Adorno, Theodor 59, 218–21
Dialectic of Enlightenment 218–21
Negative Dialectics 333
Alberti, Leon Battista 15, 87
De re aedificatoria 87, 188
Alessi 51, 317
Alexander, Christopher
A Pattern Language 92
Allen, Stan
Field Conditions 176–77
Anderson, Thom
Los Angeles Plays Itself 273
Ando, Tadao 282, 327
Azuma House 327
Anthropocene 223, 237, 239–40, 276
Archdaily 341
Argento, Dario
Suspiria (1977) 273
Aristotle 47, 98
Ashton Raggatt McDougall
Storey Hall 115–16
Aufhebung 53
Auschwitz 299
Austin, J. L. 92

B

Bachelard, Gaston 110, 253
The Psychoanalysis of Fire 110
Banham, Reyner
Architecture of the Well-Tempered Environment 246
Banksy
Dismaland 212

Barron, Patrick and Mariani, Manuela
Terrain Vague: Interstices at the Edge of the Pale 168
Barry, Robert 148
Barthes, Roland
Mythologies 205–06, 208
Bataille, Georges 24–25, 28
Critical Dictionary 24–25
Story of the Eye 28
Baudrillard, Jean 34, 281
Please Follow Me 34
Beckett, Samuel
Not I 101–03
Benjamin, Walter 220–21, 281
The Origin of German Tragic Drama (Trauerspeil) 220–21
Bentham, Jeremy 23
Berkeley, Bishop 20
Berman, Marshall 122, 125, 244
All That is Solid Melts Into Air 122
Bernini, Gianlorenzo 223, 229, 310
Ecstasy of St Teresa 229
Fountain of the Four Rivers 229
Bevan, Robert
The Destruction of Memory: Architecture at War 77
Blanciak, François
Siteless: 1001 Building Forms 125
Bloch, Ernst
The Principle of Hope 328, 331–33
Bloch, William Goldbloom 47–49
Böhme, Gernot
The Aesthetics of Atmospheres 182
Borges, Jorge Luis 32, 47–49, 161, 233–34
The Library of Babel 32, 47–49
On Exactitude in Science 161
The Analytical Language of John Wilkins 233–34
Borromini, Francesco 236, 310
Boulez, Pierre 190
Boullée, Etienne Louis 47, 128, 326

Brott, Simone 59
Browning, Robert
   Caliban on Setebos 173
Buonarotti, Michelangelo 309
   Porta Pia 318

C

Cache, Bernard 154
   Earth Moves 176–77
Cage, John
   4'33" 195
Calle, Sophie
   Suite Vénitienne 34
Calvino, Italo
   Invisible Cities 34–36, 168
   The Castle of Crossed Destinies 35–36
Camillo, Giulio 39–40, 215–16
Canetti, Elias 26
Caravaggio, Michelangelo Merisi da 326
Cardew, Cornelius
   Treatise 194–96
Carlini, Claudia and Sanchez, Zila 322
Carter, Paul
   The Road to Botany Bay 118, 120
Casement, William
   Is It a Forgery? Ask a Semanticist 279
Castle, Helen 154
Chenal, Pierre
   L'architecture d'aujourd hui (1930) 273
chess 3, 5, 346
Chomsky, Noam 91
clinamen 9
Clément, Gilles 167
Cogdell, Christina 312
   Toward a Living Architecture? Complexism and Biology in Generative Design 155–56
Cohen, Rob
   The Fast and the Furious (2001) 166

Cole, Thomas
   The Architect's Dream 2
   Titan's Goblet 2
Colonna, Francesco
   Hypnerotomachia Polyphili 70, 262
commodity fetishism 32, 43–45, 62–63, 203, 212
Coop Himmelb(l)au 109, 285
   Blazing Wing 109
Cornell, Joseph 18
Corti, Alessio 311
Cowper-Powys, John 51
Crary, Jonathan 53

D

Danto, Arthur
   Artworld 278–80
Darden, Douglas 129
   Dasein 41, 172
DeLanda, Manual 98
Deleuze, Gilles 321
   Cinema 1: *The Movement Image*, *Cinema* 2: *The Time Image* 267
   Thousand Plateaus: Capitalism and Schizophrenia 235
DeLillo, Don
   The Names 104, 118
Derrida, Jacques
   Glas 50, 55, 59
Deutsche Werkbund 44
Dick, Philip K.
   The Minority Report (1956) 292
Diller and Scofidio
   Blur Building 123–24
Disneyland 175, 215
   Celebration 207–08
Docui, Daniel 257
Domenig, Günther 285

Duboy, Philippe 127
  Lequeu: An Architectural Enigma (1986) 127–30
Duchamp, Marcel 13–16, 19–21, 28–29, 103, 127, 148, 222
  The Bride Stripped Bare by Her Bachelors, Even (The Large Glass) (1915–23) 13–16, 222
  Boîte-en-Valise (1935–41) 19–21, 103
Dujardin, Filip 319
Dürer, Albrecht 13, 25, 202, 220
  Melancholia I (1514) 25, 220
Dwork, Debórah and van Pelt, Robert Jan
  Auschwitz, 1270 to the Present 299

E

Eagleton, Terry
  Ideology of the Aesthetic (1988) 43, 63, 280
Eco, Umberto 35
  The Name of the Rose (1980) 48
  Travels in Hyperreality (1990) 215
Eisenman, Peter 55, 87, 91–92, 316
  Fin d'Ou T Hou S (1983) 101
Endell, August 58
  Die Schönheit der grossen Stadt (1908) 166
Engelmann, Paul 143
Enrich, Victor 319
Ernst, Max 318
Euler, Leonhard
  Seven Bridges of Königsberg 200

F

Fabula 49, 271, 273
Financial Crisis 84, 135
Fleming, Katie 212, 219
Foster, Hal 302
Foucault, Michel 128, 132, 157, 233–34, 291, 296–97
  The Order of Things (1987) 233
  The Will to Knowledge (1976, 2006) 157

Frampton, Kenneth 54
Francesca, Piero della
  Città ideale 315
Frascari, Marco 90, 93–94, 216, 253
Frazer, James George
  The Golden Bough (1890, 2002) 23, 59
Frazer, John 155

G

Gage, Mark Foster 97–99, 230
Gehry, Frank 24, 59, 199, 285, 310
Geist 41
Genet, Jean 55
Giedion, Siegfried
  Mechanization Takes Command: A Contribution to Anonymous History (1948) 244–46
  Space Time and Architecture: The Growth of a New Tradition (1941) 244
Glaeser, Edward 6
Gleick, James
  Chaos: Making a New Science (1987) 123
Godard, Jean-Luc
  Mepris (1963) 273
Goethe, Johann Wolfgang von 122–23, 187, 190
  Faust 122
Goodman, Nelson 281–82
Goya, Francisco 326
Graves, Michael 208
  Disney Corporation Headquarters (1990) 231
  Portland Building (1982) 206
Great Mosque in Aleppo 74
Gropius, Walter 62, 244
grundfragen 8, 11, 175, 309
Guattari, Felix
  Thousand Plateaus: Capitalism and Schizophrenia 235
Guggenheim 59

H

Hadid, Zaha 68, 199, 208, 285
Harman, Graham 88, 97–99
Harvard GSD
   Harvard Design School Guide to Shopping (2001) 212
Hausmann, Raoul 318
Heartfield, John 318
Hediger, Heini
   Man and Animal in the Zoo (1963) 241
Hegel, G. W. F. 53–55
   Aufhebung 53
Heidegger, Martin 41, 60, 99, 171–72, 304
Heizer, Michael
   City (1972–2020) 120–21
Hellman, Monte
   Two Lane Blacktop (1971) 166
Henderson, Nigel 60
Hensel, Michael 154
Herscher, Andrew 75–77
Hill, Jonathan
   Immaterial Architecture (2006) 8
Hitchcock, Alfred
   Rear Window (1954) 130
Höch, Hannah 318
Hollis, Edward
   The Secret Lives of Buildings (2009) 2
Hooper, Tobe 304
Horkheimer, Max
   Dialectic of Enlightenment (1941, 1972) 218–21
Houellebecq, Michel
   The Map and the Territory (2010, 2012) 163
Howard, Luke
   On the Modification of Clouds (1832) 104, 122–25
Hypnerotomachia Polyphili (1499) 70, 262

J

Jacobs, Jane
   The Death and Life of Great American Cities (1961) 290
Jameson, Frederic 99
   Archaeologies of the Future (2005) 256–57
Jay, Martin
   The Scopic Regimes of Modernity (1988) 128
Jerde, Jon 211
Johnson, Philip 53
Jones, Wes
   Can Tectonics Grasp Smoothness (2014) 309–10
Jones and Kirkland
   Mississauga Civic Center (1987) 206
Joyce, James 29
Jung, Matthias 319
Junger, Ernst 60

K

Kafka, Franz 25, 216, 223, 231
   Amerika (1929) 23
   The Castle 226
   The Metamorphosis 226
   The Trial 226
Kahn, Eric and Thomsen, Russel
   Perimeter Stacks (2015) 299
Kant, Immanuel 97, 98, 99, 107–10, 248, 260–63
   Critique of Pure Reason 261
   Dreams of a Spirit Seer 261
   The Critique of Judgement 98, 107
Kapoor, Anish 75
Kaufmann, Emil
   Three Revolutionary Architects, Boullée, Ledoux, and Lequeu 127
Keiller, Patrick
   London 273
   Robinson in Space 273

khora 55
Kiesler Frederick 60
Klibensky, Raymond, Saxl Fritz, Warburg, Aby 220
Rowe, Colin and Koetter, Fred
   Collage City 315–18
Koolhaas, Rem 68, 172, 210
Koolhaas, R., Vriesendorp, M., Zenghelis, E., Zenghelis, Z.
   Exodus, or the Voluntary Prisoners of Architecture 172
Krell, David 102
Kripke, Saul 144–45
Kristeva, Julia
   Powers of Horror: An Essay on Abjection 302–04
Kuma, Kengo 310

L

Lagueux, Maurice 281–82
Lang, Fritz
   Metropolis 265
Langer, Susan K. 304
Last, Nana 143–45, 337
Lavin, Sylvia 44
Lean, David
   Summertime 34
Leatherbarrow, David 307
Le Corbusier 44, 62, 127, 208, 222, 315–17, 326
   Vers Une Architecture 66
   Ville Radiuese 315
Lee, Paula Young 326
Lefaivre, Liane 166–67
Lequeu, Jean-Jacques 105, 127–30
Lévi-Strauss, Claude 59
Libeskind, Daniel 31, 39–41, 102, 188–90, 196, 208, 214–16
   3 Lessons in Architecture: The Machines 31, 39–41, 214–16
   Chamberworks 196

   Extension to the Berlin Museum (Jewish Museum) 41, 102, 188, 208
Lichtung 171–172
Ligeti, György
   Artikulation 194–96
Ligotti, Thomas 288
Lin, Maya
   Vietnam War Memorial 230
Lindenmayer System 345
Lobsinger, Mary
   Architectural History: The Turn from Culture to Media 246
loneliness 170–73
Loos, Adolf 44
Loudon, Charles 23
Lynn, Greg 67, 87, 154, 199, 230, 310
   Animate Form 66

M

magic realism 59–60
Malinowski, Bronislaw 23
Manzoni, Piero 148
Marx, Karl 43, 122, 125, 244
Marxism 24, 55, 202, 256, 331
Matta-Clark, Gordon 109, 303
   Fake Estates 162
McCarthy, Cormac
   The Road 302
Mendeleev, Dmitri 3
Menges, Achim 154
Mies van der Rohe, Ludwig 18, 50, 53, 80, 244
   Barcelona Pavilion 18
Miéville, China 256–57
   Perdido Street Station 256
   The City and The City 256, 258
Miller, George
   Mad Max (Road Warrior) 166
Mirgami, Suzi
   Target Markets – International Terrorism Meets Global Capi\talism in the Mall 210

Missac, Pierre 53
Modal logic 158, 177–79
Money 131–33, 134–39
Monopoly (game) 137
Moore, Charles
   Piazza d'Italia 206–08
Moore, Henry 231
Moore's Law (Gordon Moore) 258
Moretti, Luigi
   Casa 'Il Girasole' 253–54
Morris, Hamilton 212
Morris, William 44
Moses, Robert 122, 124
Moss, Eric Owen 67
Moulin, Nicolas 319
Mozzato, Alioscia 316
Murnaugh, Geoff 58, 161, 175
   _applyChinaLocationShift 161

N

Neoplatonism 326
Neuwirth, Lee 312
New Urbanism 207, 315
NFT (Non Fungible Tokens) 279–80
Nietzsche, Friedrich 41, 216, 218
Nolan, Christopher
   Inception 262, 271
   Memento 271
Nouvel, Jean 222
NOX
   Lars Spuybroek 154, 199
Nuttall, Jeff
   Bomb Culture 205

O

Object Oriented Ontology (OOO) 87–88, 96–99, 237
Objet-type 44, 62
Occupy Movement 72, 84–86
Odysseus 218–22

Office for Metropolitan Architecture
   SMLXL 66, 68
Omarska Memorial 75–77
Osman, Michael
   Benjamin's Baroque 221
Ostwald, Michael 200
Otto, Frei 313
OuLiPo 8, 34
Ovid 40, 226–30
   Metamorphoses 40, 226–30

P

Palladio, Andrea 101, 317
   Villa Malcontenta 101
Panofsky, Erwin
   Melencolia I 202
   Perspective as Symbolic Form 198–200
Paolozzi, Eduardo 60
Pasolini, Pier Paolo
   Medea 193
Perec, Georges 8–9, 21, 34
   Life: A User's Manual 8–9, 21
Pérez-Gómez, Alberto 198, 200
   Polyphilo, or The Dark Forest Revisted 262
Perrault, Charles 23
Plasticity 276, 290–94, 310, 313
Piccinini, Patricia 231
Piranesi, Giambattista
   Carceri d'invenzione 257, 304
Pizzolatto, Nic
   True Detective 288
Plato 47, 104, 113–16, 298
Poelzig, Hans
   Grosse Schauspielhaus 116
Poincaré, Henri 199

R

Ramirez, Juan Antonio 13, 268
   Ten Lessons (or Commandments) About Architecture in the Cinema 265

Raphael 47, 326
Rebus 4–5, 344
Reflectivity 50, 53–56, 58, 66
Reichstag 74–75
Reiser and Umamoto
   Atlas of Novel Tectonics 125
Riegl, Alois 51, 66, 99
   Kunstwollen 51, 66, 68–69
   Stilfragen 51, 66, 68
Robinson, Jenefer
   On Being Moved by Architecture 188
Roeg, Nicolas
   Don't Look Now 34
Rossi, Aldo 36, 316–17
Roussel, Raymond 23, 25
   Impressions of Africa 23
   Locus Solus 216
Rowe, Colin and Koetter, Fred
   Collage City 315–18
R&Sie(n) 154
Ruskin, John 44

S

Saigon 74–75
Sarafian, Richard C.
   Vanishing Point 166
Saramago, Jose
   The Double 260–62
Savinova, Anastasia 319
Scapettone, Jennifer
   Fresh Kills Landfill 168
Schadenfreude 227, 256
Schama, Simon 29
Scheffler, Karl 58
Schönberg, Arnold
   Moses und Aron 188–89
Schrödinger, Erwin 19–20
Schwitters, Kurt
   Merzbau 173
Scorsese, Martin
   Shutter Island 271

Scott, Ridley
   Blade Runner 265
   Thelma and Louise 166
Scott-Heron, Gil 293
Semper, Gottfried 306, 309–13
   Four Elements of Architecture 309
Serlio, Sebastiano 87, 198, 200
   Sette Libri dell'Architettura 87
   Tutte l'opere d'architettura et prospetiva 198
sfumato 54–55, 307, 325–27
Shakespeare, William
   The Tempest 173
   Titus Andronicus 302
Shyamalan, M. Night
   The Sixth Sense 271
Siegelaub, Seth 148
Singer, Bryan
   The Usual Suspects 271
Singer, Peter
   Animal Liberation 239–40
SITE 21
Smilde, Berndnaut 123
Smithson, Alison and Peter 60
de Solà-Morales, Ignasi 167
Sontag, Susan
   Against Interpretation 205–06
Speer, Albert 252, 298
   Die Ruinenwerttheorie (Theory of Ruin Value) 252
Spielberg, Steven
   Duel 166
   The Minority Report 292
Stanford Prison Experiment 298
Stewart, Kathleen
   Atmospheric Attunements 183
Stockhausen, Karlheinz 189–90
Stokes, Adrian 304
Stylites, Simeon 171–72
Superstudio 315
   Continuous Monument 168
   Dodici Città Ideali (Twelve Ideal Cities) 172

Swedenborg, Emanuel
   Arcana Coelestia 260–61
   Drömboken, or Journal of Dreams 260–62
Swift, Jonathan
   A Modest Proposal 302
Syuzhet 271, 273

T

Tafuri, Manfredo 304
   Architecture and Utopia: Design and Capitalist Development 315–18
Takamatsu, Shin 99, 101, 222
   The Killing Moon 101
Tanazaki, Jun'ichirō
   In Praise of Shadows 325
Tange, Kenzō
Hiroshima National Peace Memorial Hall 78
Tarkovsky, Andrei 109
   The Sacrifice 109
Taylor, William 23
Terry, Quinlan 207–08
Thompson, Hunter S. 212
Tolland, Andrew 166
Tornatore, Guiseppe
   Una pura formalità 271
Trahan, Shea 193
Tschumi, Bernard 86, 275, 285–88
   Advertisements for Architecture 285–88
   Architecture and Disjunction 86, 275
   Architecture and Transgression 86
Turrell, James
   Roden Crater 172
Twin Towers 74

U

Ushida Findlay 67, 101
   Soft and Hairy House 101

V

van Pelt, Robert Jan and Dwork, Deborah
   Auschwitz, 1270 to the Present 299

Van Sant, Gus
   Gerry 120
Velázquez, Diego
   Las Meninas 128
Venturi, Robert 205–06, 207
   Complexity and Contradiction in Architecture 67, 251, 317
Vanna Venturi House 205
Venturi and Scott Brown 39, 67, 103, 207, 316, 317
   Learning From Las Vegas 103, 166, 206
Vidler, Anthony 55, 304
Villeneuve, Denis
   Enemy 260
Vinci, Leonardo da 325–27

W

Warburg, Aby 13, 24–25, 43, 220
   Mnemosyne Atlas 24–25
Weinstock, Michael 154
Weir, Peter
   The Cars That Ate Paris 166
Weizman, Eyal 82, 162, 276, 290–93
Werning, Remei Capdevila 281
Whiteread, Rachel
   Ghost 173
   House 173
Wines, James 21
Winkelmann, Mike 256
   Beeple 256, 258
Wittgenstein, Ludwig 87, 131, 141–145, 286, 328, 336–37
   Philosophical Investigations 142, 337
   Tractatus Logico-Philosophicus 87, 131, 141, 328, 337
Wölfflin, Heinrich
   Principles of Art History 309–10
Wollheim, Richard
   Art and its Object 304
Woods, Lebbeus 71–72, 80–82
   Radical Reconstruction 80
   Terra Nova DMZ 80

X

Xenakis, Iannis 189, 194–96
　Philips Pavilion 189
　Pithoprakta 195

Y

Yates, Frances 39–40

Z

Zimoun 193–94
Zurbarán, Francisco de 326